183

D1421394

Psychopathology in the
Mentally Retarded

Psychopathology in the Mentally Retarded

Edited by

Johnny L. Matson, Ph.D.
Department of Learning and Development
Northern Illinois University
DeKalb, Illinois

Rowland P. Barrett, Ph.D.
Department of Psychiatry
Western Psychiatry Institute and Clinic
University of Pittsburgh School of Medicine
Pittsburgh, Pennsylvania

Grune & Stratton

A Subsidiary of Harcourt Brace Jovanovich, Publishers
New York   London
Paris   San Diego   San Francisco   São Paulo
Sydney   Tokyo   Toronto

Library of Congress Cataloging in Publication Data
Main entry under title:

Psychopathology in the mentally retarded.

Bibliography.
Includes index.
1. Mentally handicapped—Mental health—Addresses,
essays, lectures. I. Matson, Johnny L. II. Barrett,
Rowland P. [DNLM: 1. Mental retardation—Complications.
2. Psychopathology. WM 300 P975]
RC451.4.M47P78   1982   616.89'00880826   82-11932
ISBN 0-8089-1511-8

Grune & Stratton, Inc.
111 Fifth Avenue
New York, New York 10003

Distributed in the United Kingdom by
Academic Press Inc. (London) Ltd.
24/28 Oval Road, London NW 1

Library of Congress Catalog Number 82-11932
International Standard Book Number 0-8089-1511-8
Printed in the United States of America

This book is dedicated to
Chris, Sarah, and Ethan Barrett and
Deann and Meggan Matson.

CONTENTS

FOREWORD

Mentally retarded people are vulnerable to the same range of behavior and emotional problems as the rest of us, but their difficulties have rarely been the subject of systematic study, and their proper treatment has always been a low priority for both medicine and psychiatry. This book represents the first comprehensive approach to the science of psychopathology in mentally retarded individuals. It is not meant to be a final word on the topic, but rather a new opening in an area that has been neglected for far too long.

Psychopathology is fundamentally a descriptive science. There is no substrate of pathologic anatomy or etiology to support its structure or to validate its contentions. Disorders are characterized by unique constellations of symptoms and signs; they are anteceded by certain risk factors or precipitating events, they run a predictable course, and they respond to treatment in a predictable way. For some disorders, especially the affective disorders and the schizophrenias, there are strong and compelling genetic correlates. Although the science of psychopathology has very little in the way of anatomic, physiologic, or etiologic foundations, at least some psychiatric disorders bear resemblance to "classical" medical disorders.

Beyond these traditional medical parameters, however, the proper study of psychopathologic disorders requires a far-reaching appreciation of the ecology of a patient's problem, circumstances or situations that can evoke or aggravate symptoms, the operant properties and adaptive qualities of pathologic behavior, the secondary effects of labelling and institutionalization, and the adaptive strengths and weaknesses of the patient himself.

Finally, because psychiatric disorders are basically behaviors, the study of these disorders requires careful measurement and analysis. Traditionally, psychiatrists have relied upon the patients' self-reports of symptoms and circumstances—most diagnostic procedures in psychiatry, and many of its therapies, are strongly language-based.

The study of psychiatric disorders in mentally retarded individuals requires a special understanding of the peculiar environments such persons have the misfortune to encounter, as well as a deep appreciation of the limited resources the mentally retarded can muster to cope with such environments. As a rule, medical people have not had the opportunities nor the incentives to develop such understandings. Psychiatrists are usually at a terrible loss when they have to contend with a nonverbal patient. There has been a tendency to neglect such patients. About two decades ago, however, behaviorally oriented psychologists began to fill this void, resulting in many contributions to behavioral psychology and dramatic improvements in the care of mentally retarded persons.

It is likely that specialists in the fields of medicine and psychiatry will turn increasingly toward the problems of mentally retarded and developmentally handicapped people. Doctors are bound to grow interested in the systematic analysis of behavior, the development of new behavior management techniques, the association between specific genetically determined syndromes (or of specific brain lesions) with specific behavioral syndromes, the proper cultivation of parents' groups and political allies, and a new focus on the rehabilitation model as a treatment strategy for high-level patients as well. While psychiatry has been cultivating its neurochemical and neuroanatomic aspects during the past generation, it has allowed its psychological side to lapse. Before long, psychiatists will take note of the new developments in behavioral, developmental, and cognitive psychology. When this happens, there will be a major transformation in our understanding of the origins and ecology of psychiatric disorders.

That is the future. Right now, though, the prospect is by no means so sanguine. Psychoactive drugs, especially the neuroleptics, are used widely among the retarded, but neither wisely nor well. The evidence that points to the damaging effects of such drugs accumulates at an alarming rate, and evidence to support their use is virtually nonexistent (there are still no scientific guidelines for their proper use).

If neuroleptics are prescribed in excess for retarded people, the antidepressants are used hardly at all. Affective disorders are grossly underdiagnosed in retarded people. This is probably because the caretaker's attention is more likely to be directed at the disturbing or disruptive behaviors. The patient who suffers quietly is simply overlooked. Retarded people have suffered in the past from the neglect and insouciance of medicine and psychiatry. The psychopharmacologic revolution has dealt them a new generation of suffering: the misapplicaton of ineffective drugs that limit their cognitive and rehabilitative potential and the denial of drugs which are likely to be helpful.

A midwestern state recently passed a law stating that no retarded person could receive a psychoactive drug unless he has an "official" psychiatric diagnosis. The consequence of this action was not a decrease in the use of psychoactive drugs, but rather a dramatic increase in the incidence of psychiatric disorders among the retarded. Such shams have not gone unnoticed, however, and federal judges are beginning to write the guidelines for diagnosis and drug treatment that the mental health "professionals" have so long eschewed. Now we are forced to face the issue, wrestle with it, and try to bring the strengths of modern psychiatry to bear in one of its most important arenas. This book is a worthy start; it does a good job of conveying the state of the art in 1982. It does an even better job of conveying the magnitude of what remains to be done.

C. Thomas Gualtieri, M.D.

Department of Psychiatry
The University of North Carolina
School of Medicine
Chapel Hill, North Carolina

PREFACE

The study of psychopathology in the mentally retarded population has traditionally received little emphasis from clinicians and applied researchers associated with either area of study. Despite the legal offensive across the past 20 years designed to improve the quality of life for mentally retarded persons, aspects of psychopathology—as they are manifested within this population—have been largely ignored. This appears to be a rather unfortunate circumstance since the empirical evidence gathered by recent studies conducted in Scandinavia and Western Europe, albeit limited, suggests that the incidence of psychopathology in the mentally retarded population is alarmingly high. Among these studies, several of them have reported rates four to six times greater than that observed in the population of intellectually nonimpaired persons.

The few books that have addressed the topic of psychopathology in the mentally retarded have been limited in scope and typically fail to reference empirical data. In the existing literature, a great deal of time and effort has been devoted to the description of therapeutic approaches found to be effective with intellectually nonimpaired clients, without mentioning that such treatments have no clearly demonstrated empirical basis as to the efficacy of the treatment when applied to the mentally retarded. Other differences, inherent within and between various subgroups of mentally retarded persons, also lend themselves to potential analogue error that makes it particularly important that we use the most precise and detailed clinical/scientific acumen available when making statements regarding the diagnosis, assessment, and treatment of psychopathology within this population. For example, the profoundly mentally retarded person may evince psychopathology in a distinctly different manner than the mildly mentally retarded person. Moreover, certain treatment modalities, such as cognitive behavior therapy, may be applicable for moderately and mildly mentally retarded individuals, but they would be useless for those clients in the severe and profound ranges of mental retardation. The use of least restrictive treatments may also arise as an issue that cannot be easily nor uniformly addressed across the various types of psychopathology, levels of mental retardation, and combinations thereof. And finally, the age of the person may be a highly pertinent variable with respect to treatment selection, particularly when combined with type of psychopathology and level of mental retardation.

We have prepared this volume with the intent of giving clinicians and applied researchers in the fields of psychopathology and mental retardation a clear view of the existing empirical data. We have also included discussions of future directions for research since in the case of many topic areas, such as affective disorders, documentation of what we do not know and what we need to know is as valuable as the comprehensive review of existing knowledge.

We have been fortunate in assembling a group of highly regarded professionals to author chapters in areas where their expertise is well known and respected. Our primary responsibility as editors was to encourage a comprehensive empirical review of topic areas pertinent to the fields of both psychopathology and mental retardation and to strive for consistency in terminology and organization across chapters.

Much remains to be studied in the area of psychopathology in the mentally retarded. This volume is relatively brief compared to what would have been compiled if the same topic areas were applied to the intellectually nonimpaired population. In the present volume, the reader will clearly see that the availability of empirically demonstrated treatment approaches is confined solely to the domains of pharmacotherapy and behavior therapy. We are hopeful that this book will serve to stimulate sufficient interest and research in the area of psychopathology in the mentally retarded, such that in a few years a second volume of much greater length and authority may be written. If that happens, the purpose of this book will have been thoroughly accomplished.

Johnny L. Matson
Rowland P. Barrett

CONTRIBUTORS

Basil Anton, Ph.D.
Department of Psychiatry
Case Western Reserve University Medical School
Cleveland, Ohio

Paul J. Bach, Ph.D.
Department of Psychiatry
University of Washington School of Medicine
Seattle, Washington

Rowland P. Barrett, Ph.D.
Department of Psychiatry
Western Psychiatric Institute and Clinic
University of Pittsburgh School of Medicine
Pittsburgh, Pennsylvania

Philip H. Bornstein, Ph.D.
Department of Psychology
University of Montana
Missoula, Montana

Stephen E. Breuning, Ph.D.
Department of Psychiatry
Western Psychiatric Institute and Clinic
University of Pittsburgh School of Medicine
Pittsburgh, Pennsylvania

Albert R. Cavalier, Ph.D.

Department of Psychological Services
Partlow State School and Hospital
Tuscaloosa, Alabama

Anthony Costello, M.D.

Department of Psychiatry
Western Psychiatric Institute and Clinic
University of Pittsburgh School of Medicine
Pittsburgh, Pennsylvania

Janet A. Kistner, Ph.D.

Department of Psychology
Florida State University
Tallahassee, Florida

Edward A. Konarski, Jr., Ph.D.

Department of Psychology
University of Alabama
Tuscaloosa, Alabama

Mark H. Lewis, Ph.D.

Biological Sciences Center
University of North Carolina School of Medicine
Chapel Hill, North Carolina

William E. MacLean, Jr., Ph.D.

Biological Sciences Center
University of North Carolina School of Medicine
Chapel Hill, North Carolina

Johnny L. Matson, Ph.D.

Department of Learning and Development
Northern Illinois University
DeKalb, Illinois

Duane G. Ollendick, Ph.D.
Clinical Services Unit
Zumbro Valley Mental Health Center
Rochester, Minnesota

Thomas H. Ollendick, Ph.D.
Department of Psychology
Virginia Polytechnic Institute and State University
Blacksburg, Virginia

Alan D. Poling, Ph.D.
Department of Psychology
Western Michigan University
Kalamazoo, Michigan

Raymond G. Romanczyk, Ph.D.
Department of Psychology
State University of New York
Binghamton, New York

one

Issues in Treating Emotional Disorders

••

Mark H. Lewis
William E. MacLean, Jr.

Emotional disturbance among mentally retarded persons is a problem of major proportion. It is, unfortunately, a problem that has been largely neglected and, consequently, poorly understood (Corbett, 1979). Relatively few empirical investigations of this important area have been conducted. Much of what is available in the literature is descriptive or anecdotal in nature and does not meet minimal methodological standards (Menolascino, 1970). What little sound empirical work is available has come largely from a small group of British investigators, notably Rutter and his colleagues (e.g., Rutter, 1971; also Corbett, 1977; Reid, 1980).

The lack of research addressing the problem of emotional disturbance in the mentally retarded has been dramatically illustrated by Heaton-Ward (1977). He noted that of the five International Congresses for the Scientific Study of Mental Deficiency (ICSSMD) held in the past 15 years, 1300 papers have been presented on a variety of aspects concerning mental retardation. Of these, only 40 were concerned with mental illness or its treatment. Half of these 40 reports involved autism and only 2 were concerned with psychosis in adult mentally retarded persons. The

The authors wish to acknowledge the support of Grants HD-07201 and HD-03110 in the preparation of this chapter.

reasons for such neglect are not clear. It may be due to ideological differences or a function of professional training. In any event, there is a dearth of reliable information on this topic.

The purpose of this chapter is to raise some of the numerous issues inherent in the treatment of emotionally disturbed mentally retarded individuals. Some of these are thorny issues, to be sure, and they defy easy solutions. For example, the question of how psychiatric symptoms may change as a function of intelligence level is not at all clear. Diagnostic criteria have been the subject of, at times, acrimonious debate within the field of psychiatry and clinical psychology. What constitutes appropriate indices of psychopathology becomes an even more confusing and frustrating issue when applied to mentally retarded persons. If, for example, the clinician or researcher is faced with assessing an emotional disorder without the benefit of access to language or intact thought processes, how is the diagnostic process affected? If, on the other hand, overt behavior becomes the standard, how does one discriminate what behavior is a function of limited intelligence and what behavior is due to "mental illness"?

Perhaps more basic is the issue of whether mentally retarded persons are at greater risk for emotional disturbance. If so, what are the mechanisms responsible for this? What role does brain damage play in the incidence of emotional disturbance among the mentally retarded? How will normalization and deinstitutionalization affect the mental health of these individuals?

A related issue is whether there are psychiatric syndromes specifically associated with mental retardation. Is the distribution of psychiatric maladies in the general population mirrored in the population of persons labeled mentally retarded?

Finally, several issues must be considered when discussing modes of treatment for disturbed mentally retarded individuals. For example, numerous questions have been raised recently concerning the efficacy of behavior management procedures as well as the effectiveness of pharmacotherapy. These habilitative or rehabilitative procedures are frequently applied to disturbed mentally retarded persons, often in combination with one another. How effective is each procedure? What are the consequences of using them in combination? Alternatively, does traditional psychotherapy have a place in the treatment of disturbed mentally retarded persons?

An attempt will be made to address these questions and highlight some of the issues relevant to the treatment of emotionally disturbed mentally retarded persons. A brief historical account of the relationship between mental retardation and mental health follows.

• HISTORY •

Prior to the 17th century, mental retardation as a handicapping condition was generally not distinguished from mental illness. Indeed, John Locke in 1690 made one of the earliest distinctions between mental retardation and mental illness: "Herein seems to be the difference between idiots and madmen, that madmen put wrong ideas together and reason from them but idiots make very few or no propositions and reason scarce at all." The critical feature is the *potential* for reasoning and complex thought, an ability that was not assumed to exist in the mentally retarded. This distinction is paramount, historically, because it set the precedent for all future conceptualizations of mental retardation.

The emphasis on mental retardation as a primary diagnostic entity created a separation in administrative structure that endures to the present day. Indeed, most states still have a Department of Mental Health and Mental Retardation or a division devoted exclusively to mental retardation services within some health-related megastructure. In some ways, particularly in the United States, the *and* in this title has the functional meaning of *or* in that the two phenomena have come to be seen as mutually exclusive. The recent emphasis on mental retardation, which was heralded by the infusion of tremendous amounts of political and financial support in the 1960s, has further delineated mental retardation as a self-contained biobehavioral condition, one separate from the mainstream of mental health.

The dichotimization of services has resulted, in part, from the nature of mental retardation. Because the habilitation of mentally retarded individuals involves education and behavior control, special education, psychology, and psychiatry have created their own regions of interest and influence in the habilitation process. The apparent reason for this division relates to the particular needs of the mentally retarded. By definition, their deficits are in intellectual and adaptive behavior; they have difficulty learning basic academic skills and basic social standards of behavior. It is little wonder that education and psychology have taken the lead in service delivery for the mentally retarded and that psychiatry has been relatively uninvolved. Indeed, special education and psychology have been at the forefront largely because of recent advances in applied behavior analysis, which have provided an effective technology for education and behavior training. Psychiatry, on the other hand, maintains that its roles include program administration, working with the parents, biomedical research aimed at delineating the various physiologic causes and concomitants of mental retardation syndromes, and psychopharmacologic treatment (Gualtieri, 1979; Wortis, 1977). Moreover, the insight-oriented psychodynamic approach frequently leaves something to be desired in the treatment of mental retardation. It could be that because retarded development is not a manifestation of an illness that can be cured, there is resistance among insight-oriented professionals to work with mentally retarded individuals. Shapiro (1979) reports that psychiatrists as a group have little contact with the mentally retarded and typically attribute a number of pathologic behaviors to the mental handicap rather than to a coexisting emotional disturbance. Gualtieri (1979) has observed that there are a number of reasons why psychiatrists are not very involved with the mentally retarded, not the least of which is that residents in psychiatry do not receive education and training in the area. This is not to say that professionals working from a behavioral perspective can or do provide the entire range of habilitative services. Indeed, the theoretical framework and strategies employed by the special educator or behavior analyst often ignore the emotional needs of mentally retarded clients.

Even in the training of professionals who work with mentally retarded clients there is a tendency to focus on disorders of cognitive development to the exclusion of emotional and social development. In some ways, because of the long-standing delineation between mental retardation and emotional disturbance, there is considerable resistance to integration of the two, particularly regarding service delivery. There is, of course, the additional factor that those trained in a behavioral/developmental mode are involved with more mentally retarded persons than those professionals whose expertise is in emotional disturbance. The potential exists, therefore, for an imbalance between habilitative or developmental services and mental health service delivery. There are at present no data which fully support these contentions. There is, however, a general feeling among professionals that the mental health needs of mentally retarded clients are often placed well below their educative and rehabilitative needs. It is open to question whether professional training is partly responsible for this state of affairs.

In summary, the separation of mental retardation services from the mental health service delivery system has resulted in a more concentrated administrative power and emphasis on education and rehabilitation as the primary needs of the retarded. The distinction also has had the effect of limiting the range of services available. Specifically, the contention has been that the mental retardation service delivery system at present is not generally responsive to the emotional problems of retarded individuals. Indeed, Reiss, Levitan, and McNally (1982) have contended that the emotionally-disturbed mentally-retarded may be one of the most underserved populations in this country. In effect, the distinction between mental health and mental retardation may deny mentally retarded individuals the full range of available services. This problem is not unique to mental retardation. In a recent article, McNett (1980) examined the availability of mental health services for individuals with a number of different handicaps (e.g., cerebral palsy, hearing impairment). These individuals receive primary services from an agency designed to meet their specific needs and as a result find themselves in a plight similar to the one just discussed for the mentally retarded. McNett indicated that many individuals with multiple needs could "fall through the cracks." Indeed, although the individuals receive comprehensive service delivery for their primary handicap, the linkages for ancillary services, such as mental health, are conspicuously absent. Although the mental health system may be responsive and willing, the issue becomes how the mental retardation professional can ensure that the client receives needed services. This issue is not unimportant (if prevalence data regarding emotional disturbance among the mentally retarded are to be believed) for a large number of retarded people are in need of more than habilitative and educational services.

• PREVALENCE •

The importance of considering emotional disturbance among mentally retarded persons is highlighted by a consideration of prevalence data. Almost without exception, epidemiological studies have supported the proposition of greater prevalence of psychiatric disorder among the mentally retarded than in the general population (e.g., Rutter, Graham, & Yule, 1970). For example, two early studies (Dewan, 1948; Weaver, 1946) examined military inductees or recruits found to be intellectually retarded according to the then current definition of mental deficiency. Of the 8000 inductees who were diagnosed as mentally retarded (IQ less than 75) and who underwent psychiatric examination, Weaver (1946) reported that 44 percent of the males and 38 percent of the females exhibited psychiatric problems. Dewan (1948) reported that 47 percent of the Canadian Army recruits diagnosed as mentally retarded were found by psychiatric examination to be emotionally unstable. This is in contrast to 20 percent of the inductees in a nonretarded control group found to be emotionally impaired. These early prevalence studies deserve attention as they were conducted with noninstitutionalized clients and involved a large number of subjects, thus avoiding the criticism of selection bias.

Most early studies, however, have involved institutionalized clients. Pollock (1944), for example, reported that of the 444 mentally retarded persons admitted to New York State hospitals in 1942, approximately 40 percent received a diagnosis of mental retardation with psychosis. Eighteen percent were considered to suffer from schizophrenia. Penrose (1966), also studying institutionalized mentally retarded persons, found that 16 percent were considered to be psychotic or neurotic. In a later study, Primrose (1971) examined reasons for hospital admission in Scotland and found that although only 8 percent were admitted for psychiatric illness, 50 percent were admitted for antisocial behavior. Because behavioral disturbances are probably an important factor in the decision to institutionalize an individual, these studies must be viewed with caution. Further, given that an inverse relationship exists between IQ and behavioral disturbances (Rutter, 1971) and between IQ and institutionalization, these estimates are probably inflated and do not adequately represent the prevalence of emotional disturbance among the population of persons diagnosed as mentally retarded. Finally, institutionalization may itself contribute to abnormal or aberrant behavior.

Chazan (1964), studying mildly mentally retarded children in an educational placement, determined the rate of maladjustment to be twice that of a control group of children attending regular class. The determination of emotional disturbance was made using the Bristol Social Adjustment Guides. A behavioral inventory was also used by Balthazar and English (1969) to determine the prevalence of emotional disorder among a delayed group. Two hundred eighty-eight severely and profoundly retarded institutionalized persons were rated on the Balthazar Scales of Adaptive Behavior. Sixteen percent were found to suffer from moderate to severe emotional and behavioral disturbance.

Chess and Hassibi (1970) studied 52 children aged 5 to 11 years. Each was living at home, was part of a middle-class family, and fell within an IQ range of 50 to 75. Twenty-one were found to have no psychiatric impairment whereas 13 were classified as having reactive behavior disorders including phobias, tantrums, and aggressive behavior. One was considered neurotic, one psychotic, and 11 showed signs of cerebral dysfunction including motility disturbances, compulsions, and perseverations. Psychiatric diagnoses were made on the basis of interviews with parents and teachers as well as direct observations of the child at home and in school.

This study is particularly useful in that it provides a description of the behavior of the children rather than simply a diagnosis. For example, 58 percent of the children were considered restless and excessively active whereas 52 percent engaged in stereotyped motor movements, 27 percent showed "unusual seeking of sensory experiences," 87 percent exhibited tantrums and aggressive behavior, 29 percent engaged in obsessional behavior, and 19 percent engaged in stereotyped play activity.

In the now classic Isle of Wight studies (Rutter, Tizard, Yule, Graham, & Whitmore, 1976; Rutter, Tizard, & Whitmore, 1970; Rutter, 1971),

Rutter and his associates found that 30 percent of the intellectually retarded children in a 9-, 10-, and 11-year-old cohort (N = 2199) were rated as disturbed by parents and 42 percent were so rated by teachers. This represents five to six times the rate of emotional disturbance seen in a randomly selected control group (5.4%). In a subgroup of severely retarded children (IQ less than 50), 50 percent showed evidence of psychiatric disorder compared with 7 percent in the general population. Emotional disturbance was determined by standardized interviews with parents and by psychiatric examination. The Isle of Wight findings are by far the best data available on the problem of prevalence. The use of control groups, the use of multiple measures, and the attempt to establish the reliability and validity of measuring instruments make these investigations landmark studies and a rich source of information.

In a survey of 100 mentally retarded children referred to a psychiatric clinic (Phillips & Williams, 1975), 38 percent were diagnosed as psychotic, 10 percent were classified as neurotic, 52 percent exhibited behavioral disorders, and 32 percent were categorized as having personality disorders. Only 26 percent were deemed to be free of psychiatric disorder. Among the nonpsychotic children, the three major symptom clusters noted by parents were aggression (44%), poor social relations (43%), and developmental lags (44%). Developmental lags included inactivity, speech lags, toilet problems, and sleeping and eating disturbances. Comparisons with a control group of emotionally disturbed nonretarded children suggested little difference in the kind of psychopathology seen in children of average intelligence. These data must also be viewed with caution as prevalence rates were determined using clients referred to a psychiatric clinic, despite the fact that the clinic provided a wide range of services to mentally retarded clients.

Using the multiaxial classification scheme developed by Rutter and his colleagues (Rutter, Lebovici, Eisenberg, Sneznevskij, Sadoun, Brooks, & Lin, 1969), Corbett (1977) surveyed severely retarded children under the age of 14 years living in an area of South London. These were 140 noninstitutionalized children having an IQ less than 50. Of the 43 percent classified as emotionally disturbed, 17 percent were considered psychotic and 4 percent were diagnosed as hyperkinetic. Severe stereotypies and pica (10%), neurotic disorders (4%), and conduct disorders (4%) were also in evidence.

The available studies lead to the inescapable conclusion that emotional disorders are much more common among mentally retarded persons than in the general population. This conclusion is based on investigations using very different patient samples and very different methodologies.

• Intelligence •

Having established the substantially increased likelihood of emotional disturbance among mentally retarded persons, the question that emerges is to what can such an increase be attributed. The obvious variable to consider is, of course, intelligence.

The Isle of Wight studies have indicated that there is a strong association both between low IQ and psychiatric disorder and individual items of deviant behavior such as fighting, poor concentration, and stuttering (Rutter et al., 1976). Further, the association between IQ and psychiatric disorder holds across the full range of IQ, not just at the lower end of the IQ distribution (Ryle, Pond, & Hamilton, 1965). Moreover, the association between IQ and individual items of deviant behavior also holds across the full range of IQ scores, although a significant departure from linearity was noted at the very low end of the IQ distribution (Ryle et al., 1965). Additionally, individual items of deviant behavior were correlated with low IQ for children who did not suffer from a diagnosable psychiatric disorder (Rutter, Graham, & Yule, 1970).

• Sensory Disorders •

A further issue to consider when contemplating the relationship between psychiatric disorder and mental retardation is the role played by handicapping conditions ancillary to the primary diagnosis of mental retardation. For example, sensory disorders often accompany mental retardation. Whether such handicapping conditions place the retarded individual at greater risk for psychiatric disturbance has not been studied in any detail. It is known, however, that sensory handicaps do increase the risk of emotional disturbance. For example, reported rates of emotional disorder vary widely among the hearing impaired, but typically these rates are higher than in the general population (Freeman & Malkin, 1977). Although deafness is associated with an increased prevalence of behavioral difficulties, most hearing impaired children did not present serious psychiatric problems (Freeman & Malkin, 1977). In the Isle of Wight studies, Rutter, Graham, and Yule, (1970) found that the rate of emotional disorder among deaf children was approximately 15 percent compared to a rate of roughly 7 percent for the general population aged 10 and 11 years.

The relationship between visual impairment and emotional disturbance, however, is not as clear. Estimates of the prevalence of behavioral disorders in visually impaired children range from proportions comparable to that found in the general population to as high as one-third (Jan, Freeman, & Scott, 1977). The one point about which there is agreement, however, is that stereotyped mannerisms are much more common in the blind and even more prevalent in visually impaired persons with low IQs. Interestingly, stereotyped mannerisms appear to be most common in children with retrolental fibroplasia (Jan, et al., 1977). In studies, reported by Jan, et al. (1977), mental retardation occurred in 27 percent of the blind persons studied and in 10 percent of the partially sighted and was accompanied by a high rate of behavioral disturbance and developmental problems including stereotypies.

The prevalence of psychiatric problems in blind children on the Isle of Wight was approximately 17 percent, a figure roughly comparable to the rate found for deaf children. Seven percent represents the comparison standard or prevalence rate of emotional disturbance in the age-matched childhood population (Rutter, Graham & Yule, 1970).

• Reading Retardation •

Rutter et al. (1976) have reported that studies of 10-year-old children on the Isle of Wight indicated a strong positive correlation between reading retardation and psychiatric disturbance, specifically conduct disorder. Specific reading retardation was defined as at least 28 months below the reading level predicted for age and IQ. These children were of average intelligence and constituted 4 percent of the island's population. Of the 9–11 year olds with specific reading retardation, approximately one-third showed significant antisocial behavior. This result was replicated in a later study of 10 year olds from London (Berger, Yule, & Rutter, 1975). Interestingly, Rutter reports (Rutter et al., 1976) that when examining the 14-year-old Isle of Wight cohort, the same correlation was seen but only when the psychiatric disorder was evident from earlier childhood. This was not the case, however, when the psychiatric disorder manifested itself during adolescence. Two hypotheses emerge from this work: (1) that classroom failure may result in increased vulnerability to psychiatric disorder or (2) that emotional problems and cognitive deficits may stem from a common source.

• Speech and Language Retardation •

In a recent review, Cantwell and Baker (1977) concluded that children with speech and language disorders were at risk for psychiatric disturbance. They reached such a conclusion, however, with the disclaimer that the available studies suffer from a number of methodological deficiencies including a failure to consider associated conditions such as brain damage and intellectual retardation, problems in definition, the reliability and validity of measuring instruments, and sampling bias. Despite these problems, additional conclusions were tentatively drawn. First, the types of psychiatric disorder documented are typically the same as seen in children from the general population. Second, language disorders seem to be more highly correlated with emotional disturbance than speech disorders. Children with receptive language disorders are, in turn, more at risk than children with pure expressive language disorders. Finally, comprehension deficits have been reported to be associated with autistic like impairment of social relationships.

More recently, Cantwell, Baker, and Mattison (1980) examined 100 children aged 2 to 13 years who were being seen at a community speech and hearing clinic. Fifty-three percent were judged to have a definable psychiatric illness, using interviews and parent and teacher rating scales. Comparisons of the emotionally disordered group versus the psychiatrically well group indicated that significantly more of the former group suffered from abnormalities of language. No significant differences between groups were noted in IQ, medical or biological factors, or family disorders.

• Neuroepileptic Disorders •

The prevalence of epilepsy increases rather dramatically with the severity of retardation. Corbett, Harris, and Robinson (1975) have suggested that approximately 1 percent of the normal population suffers from this disorder, 3–6 percent of the mildly and moderately retarded are afflicted, and 20 percent of the severely retarded are subject to seizures. For example, in one study 32 percent of a sample of 155 children with an IQ less than 50 had a history of seizures, with 10 percent having had at least one seizure the previous year (Corbett & Harris, 1974).

These data take on considerable significance given that epilepsy, and particularly temporal lobe epilepsy, has been associated with an increase in susceptibility to behavioral disturbance. This positive relationship apparently holds true for both intellectually retarded persons and children of normal intelligence. For example, in the Isle of Wight studies the rate of psychiatric disorders among children with neuroepileptic conditions was approximately one-third in comparison to a prevalence rate of roughly 6 percent for the general population (Rutter, Graham & Yule, 1970). The rate of behavioral disturbance was highest in children with neurological disorders accompanied by seizures (58%) and lowest in children with uncomplicated or idiopathic epilepsy (29%).

Eyman, Moore, Capes, and Zachofsky (1970) reached a similar conclusion from their study of the mentally retarded persons residing in three different hospitals. They reported that behavioral disturbances were significantly more common in those mentally retarded persons with a history of seizures than in those without seizures. Specifically, hyperactivity and aggressive behavior occurred significantly more often in epileptic subjects.

• Organic Brain Dysfunction •

The high rate of psychiatric disturbance associated with neuroepileptic conditions raises the issue of the role of brain damage in behavioral disturbance. Once again turning to the Isle of Wight data, psychiatric disorder was approximately twice as common among children with chronic physical disorders not involving the brain as found in children serving as control subjects (Graham & Rutter, 1968; Rutter, 1977). For children with neuroepileptic conditions, the rate was almost five times that of controls; that is, psychiatric difficulties were much more common when the physical disability involved brain damage. Parenthetically, IQ differences were not responsible for the high rate of behavioral disturbance among neuroepileptic children, as they exhibited a typical IQ distribution. Moreover, for those children having a measured IQ greater than 68, the rate of psychiatric disorders was still more than twice that seen for children with physical disorders not involving the brain (Graham & Rutter, 1968; Rutter, 1977). These data suggest that psychiatric disorder is more closely linked to brain lesions than to the presence of a physical handicap per se.

Additionally, most brain-damaged children on the Isle of Wight exhibited the spectrum of behavioral disorders typical of behaviorally disturbed children without brain damage (Rutter, Graham, & Yule, 1970). These data contradict the traditional notion that such symptoms as restlessness, impulsivity, attention deficits, and an increase in activity are manifestations of brain dysfunction and should be overrepresented in the brain damaged group. Rutter (1977) has concluded that such symptoms as impulsivity and hyperactivity are common features of psychiatric disorder and not indicative of brain damage per se.

The relevance of the relationship between psychiatric problems and central nervous system (CNS) insult is difficult to overestimate given the relationship between mental retardation and brain damage (Baumeister & MacLean, 1979). That is, one might easily defend the position that insult to the central nervous system is responsible for both the intellectual retardation and the psychiatric disorder. Psychiatric problems have been found to be more common in mentally retarded children with neurological abnormalities, for example, than in retarded children without evidence of such abnormality (Rutter, 1971).

It has been the traditional professional lore that mentally retarded persons can be categorized as "organics" or "cultural-familials." That is, mental retardation workers have viewed retarded persons as a dichotomous group, approximately 20 percent of whom were retarded because of some biological dysfunction and 80 percent as a result of environmental influences. Such a view is probably without a great deal of merit. Post-mortem studies, reviewed recently by Baumeister and MacLean (1979), lead to the view that CNS insult in varying degrees is almost always associated with mental retardation, even mild mental retardation.

• EVIDENCE FOR A PSYCHOPATHOLOGY OF • MENTAL RETARDATION

A major question raised by the prevalence studies concerns the relative distribution of diagnostic categories among retarded versus nonretarded persons. Are psychiatric problems seen in the general population similarly represented in the population diagnosed as mentally retarded? Are there behavioral deviations that are characteristic of retarded persons? We might thus pose the question: Is there a psychopathology of mental retardation?

It is generally accepted that the full spectrum of psychiatric disorders is represented among the mentally retarded (Rutter, 1977). Although the behavioral disturbances described in mentally retarded individuals appear to be similar to those found in the population at large, several psychiatric disorders are represented disproportionately, notably autism and hyperkinesis.

• Autism •

Early views of autism by Kanner and others (e.g., Kanner, 1943) included the notion that autistic children were not mentally retarded. If IQ scores indicated subnormal intelligence, it was thought that either the test was unreliable or the autistic syndrome was masking the true abilities of the child. The present view recognizes that a high number of autistic children are, in fact, severely mentally retarded. (It is important to note at this point that no causal relationships are being suggested.) Rutter and Lockyer (1967), for example, found that of 63 autistic children studied, 10 were untestable and 51 percent of the remaining 53 had IQs less than 50. Chess (Chess, Korn, & Fernandez, 1971) has found similar results. In her study of children with congenital rubella who were diagnosed as autistic, 50 percent had an IQ less than 50. Of the behavior of autistic children considered bizarre, stereotypy and self-injury occurred significantly more often in those children with an IQ less than 60.

Recently, Bartak and Rutter (1976) compared autistic children of normal intelligence with autistic children who were concurrently mentally retarded. Their results suggested that among other things a lack of emotional expression was twice as common in the mentally-retarded autistic group whereas deviant social responses such as smelling and inappropriately touching the interviewer occurred six to seven times more frequently. Resistance to environmental change and attachments to odd objects were observed to be twice as common in mentally-retarded autistic clients. Somewhat surprisingly, head and finger stereotypies were found much more frequently in the mentally retarded group and rocking did not differ between groups. The nonretarded autistic group exhibited a significantly greater incidence of pronomial reversals, undue sensitivity to noise, and ritualistic behavior.

• Hyperkinesis •

Although hyperactivity can occur in children of all ranges of measured intelligence, it manifests itself much more often in mentally retarded persons (Pond, 1961). For example, after exclusion of brain damaged and mentally retarded children, hyperkinesis was diagnosed only once in over 2000 children residing on the Isle of Wight (Ryle, Pond, & Hamilton, 1965). In a different population, Rutter, Graham, and Yule, (1970) found that 4 of 99 neuroepileptic children in school and 5 of 38 severely mentally retarded children were considered hyperkinetic. The reasons for the strong association between mental retardation and hyperkinesis are not clear at this point. Hyperactivity in animals can be seen following a variety of physiological perturbations in the CNS (Mailman, Lewis, & Kilts, 1981). Such results attest to its nonspecificity. Both intellectual deficiency and hyperkinesis may be general effects of CNS insult. Being mentally retarded, however, puts one at risk for this psychiatric disorder, just as it does for autism.

• Disintegrative Psychosis of Childhood •

Disintegrative psychosis is a degenerative disorder first described by Heller some 50 years ago, hence often referred to as Heller's syndrome (Malamud, 1959). It is almost always associated with mental retardation. Children suffering from such a disorder typically display normal development for the first three to four years. The onset of the disease is typified by behavior changes that include increased irritability, anxiety, hyperactivity, and destructive behavior (Malamud, 1959; Rutter, 1971). Over a period of several months children so afflicted display a marked regression in adaptive behavior, losing even basic functions such as toileting and feeding. They also develop movement disorders including stereotypies. Severe emotional disturbance is typical in the latter stages of this disorder (Corbett, Harris, Taylor, & Trimble, 1977).

• Specific Aberrant Behaviors •

While the full spectrum of psychiatric disorders is represented among the mentally retarded, there are distinctive aberrant behaviors that are characteristically, if not exclusively, exhibited by lower functioning mentally retarded persons. Such deviant behavior includes stereotypy, self-injurious behavior (SIB), pica, coprophagy, and rumination. We wish to raise the issue of whether such behavior should be considered sufficent evidence to warrant a diagnosis of emotional disturbance (see Corbett, 1979; Rutter, 1971). Clearly, the frequency of this behavior among some mentally retarded persons versus the general population warrants such labels as aberrant or deviant. Whether such behavior is symptomatic of psychosis, for example, is quite another issue. One could argue that such behavior differs in form and frequency quite dramatically from anything in the repertoire of most people and that etiology or associated conditions are irrelevant. Conversely, it may be that stereotypy and SIB, for example, are simply movement disorders and are not correlated with cognitive or affective indices of emotional disturbance.

• EMOTIONAL VARIABLES AND EMOTIONAL • DISTURBANCE

Having reviewed the prevalence data and concluded that mentally retarded individuals are, in fact, significantly more likely to manifest emotional disturbance, one is left with the question of whether additional factors are responsible for the disproportionate number of disturbed mentally retarded individuals. For example, Rutter et al. (1976) report that intellectual retardation among the children of the Isle of Wight was more prevalent in families with unskilled or semiskilled workers as parents. It is probably very likely that environmental factors such as socioeconomic status are important in view of their reported relationship to emotional disturbance in the population as a whole (see Kisker, 1977, for a review). Indeed, a host of sociocultural factors such as parental attitudes, child-rearing practices, family psychopathology, cultural practices, and social environment characteristics, not to mention physiological and genetic factors, contribute significantly to emotional development. Therefore, each has the potential for adversely affecting an individual's emotional development. When several of these risk factors are present in any individual case, their intercorrelations greatly hinder the task of making specific causal inferences.

An additional factor, one still of significance for some mentally retarded individuals, is that if institutionalization. The bulk of the data suggest that institutionalized mentally retarded people manifest maladaptive behavior to a greater degree than those who reside in the community or their own home (Eyman & Call, 1977). Although it is not clear whether people are institutionalized because they manifest behavior problems or they develop the behavioral disturbances as a result of their institutional-ization, it is significant that there is an association.

It is generally held that as an individual's ability to adapt is chal-lenged by his or her environment, the potential for stress, and perhaps emotional disturbance, increases. The implications of this observation for the outcome of the present normalization/deinstitutionalization move-ment are unclear. On the one hand, proponents of normalization would argue that deinstitutionalization would actually decrease the prevalence of emotional disturbance simply because mentally retarded persons would be living in a more appropriate setting, a setting that would not tend to produce maladaptive behavior. On the other hand, the individual who resides in the community will be constantly challenged by a more com-plex environment. The resulting stress could very well increase the preva-lence of emotional disturbance. There are some data to support this hy-pothesized outcome.

Several theoretical perspectives on the development of children's self-concept emphasize the contribution of the environment to that proc-ess. Social comparison theory (Festinger, 1954) purports that people, when confronted with situations where objective references of compari-son are unavailable, will look to significant others in the environment as a source of comparison. When an individual is confronted daily with situa-tions that are beyond his or her intellectual or social/adaptive abilities and in which significant others cope readily, one might expect emotional prob-lems to surface. Smith and his colleagues have demonstrated such an ef-fect using the self-concept of nonretarded children with learning problems (Rogers, Smith, & Coleman, 1978; Smith, Dokecki, & Davis, 1977). They found that children in self-contained classrooms actually had higher self-concepts than their regular classroom counterparts. The children in the self-contained classes presumably used their classmates as a standard and, therefore, enjoyed higher self-concepts in relation to their counter-parts in regular classes whose comparison group included children of greater academic ability. The data for mentally retarded children are very similar. Schurr, Towne, and Joiner (1972) found that educable mentally retarded (EMR) children, although labeled and placed in a self-contained EMR class program, had higher self-concepts while in the EMR program than before the group had been labeled and then placed in the self-con-tained class. When the same group was eventually mainstreamed to the regular classroom, their self-concepts decreased. Although not directly applicable to emotional disturbance, these results suggest that social comparison theory can explain, at least partially, an individual's behavior. The naturalistic experiment created by the normalization movement has provided an opportunity for examining the role of social comparison as a determinant in the emotional disturbance of the mentally retarded.

• Personological Variables •

Although there are a number of factors presumed to impact on the development of emotional disturbance among the mentally retarded, one factor that remains relatively uninvestigated is personality development. Although there have been a number of fairly well-articulated theories of personality development among nonretarded individuals, the direct translation of these theories to the mentally retarded has been slow and at times unwieldy. In fact, what little research has been reported clusters around a number of behavioral attributes of developmentally immature (children) and delayed individuals. The importance of investigating personality factors lies in the relationship of these constructs to the psychosocial adjustment of the individual. Given their difficulties with performance, both cognitive and social, it is not surprising that mentally retarded individuals approach these situations with a high degree of wariness. Indeed, their responses tend to vary in degree or quality rather than type so that there is little need for a separate psychology of mental retardation.

Before elaborating further the possible role of personality factors in the emotional disturbances of the mentally retarded, perhaps something should be said about personality in general. Cromwell (1967) proposed a reasonable approximation to a definition. He indicated that the term *personality* "refers to the recurring, long-term aspects of behavior that characterize individual differences among people." This definition has a great deal of intuitive appeal because of its reliance on the enduring behavioral qualities of people rather than isolated behaviors. In addition, Cromwell's perspective places personality in the realm of individual differences.

Personality, whether described in terms of traits, needs, or types, presents a problem in assessment. Whatever the theory, the information is usually obtained by three basic paradigms. Bloom (1964) describes these as (1) the rating of an individual by an assessor on a particular scale, (2) unconscious self-revelation through incidental report or projective technique, and (3) a self-report measure where the individual usually completes a questionnaire that is designed to elicit honest responses. Considerable error is inherent in each type of measure, which makes use of the measures somewhat risky even for nonretarded populations. The cognitive limitations of mentally retarded individuals make the use of projectives and self-report measures even more tenuous. Gardner (1968), in a review of the personality research with mentally retarded subjects, enumerates the problems in assessing personality status as "limited language skills (reading, verbal, and conceptual-cognitive deficits), limitations in self-perception and those of time-boundedness and stimulus-boundedness." These limitations are most probably manifestations of the mentally retarded individual's cognitive deficit and represent a real nemesis to conventional assessment methods. This is not to say that questionnaires and self-report measures are inappropriate. The limitations should, however, be taken into consideration in designing assessment instruments and in interpreting the results.

Without reviewing the personality literature in its entirety, a major issue arises with regard to the focus of this chapter, specifically, whether there are personality constructs that predispose a mentally retarded individual to emotional disturbance. The answer is a resounding maybe. Although a large number of personality concepts have been elucidated, no author has articulated the relationship between these findings and emotional disturbance. However, the intuitive relationship makes it reasonable to entertain a potential association between the personality of the individual and emotional disturbance.

For years, mentally retarded individuals were considered to have highly stereotyped personality profiles that in some ways made the question of personality research with mentally retarded subjects unnecessary. Heber (1964) concluded that

> Not one of such commonly purported attributes of the retarded as passivity, anxiety, impulsivity, rigidity, suggestibility, a lack of persistence, immaturity, withdrawal, low frustration tolerance, unrealistic self-concept, . . . can be either substantiated or refuted on the basis of available research data. (p. 319)

This was, of course, an improvement from previous stereotyped viewpoints which held that the mentally retarded were "essentially immoral, degenerate, and depraved" (Zigler & Harter, 1969). It was not until the early 1960s that the stereotyped views were challenged. The personality literature has evolved from two major perspectives: Zigler's motivational hypothesis and Cromwell's adaptation of Rotter's social learning theory.

As Zigler (1973) has noted, our thinking regarding the personality of individuals labeled intellectually retarded has been stereotyped and trite. This unfortunate state of affairs is due in part to what Zigler has characterized as the cognitive deterministic approach. In his words, "cognitive deficiency makes one impervious to those environmental events known to be central in the genesis of the personality of individuals of normal intellect" (Zigler, 1973, p. 237). This assumption has contributed to the dearth of personality investigation and to the general neglect of the affective needs of the mentally retarded person. Zigler has been instrumental in the challenge of the cognitive deterministic viewpoint. He reviews numerous incidences in which personality and motivational factors are presumably in operation and account for as much variance as the cognitive abilities of retarded subjects.

Zigler's group has set about to investigate the role of personological/motivational variables in the context of traditional laboratory performance tasks. A common thread is readily apparent through all of Zigler's work. The common assumption is the importance of the life history of the individual in dictating what will be seen in any one particular sample of behavior. An individual's life experience, according to Zigler, is of paramount importance in the performance of mentally retarded subjects on any task. Zigler, because of his commitment to matching on developmental level (most commonly expressed in terms of mental age), has been able to isolate fairly reliably a set of constructs which at present appear to account for motivational differences between retarded and nonretarded subjects of the same developmental level. These constructs have been elaborated in detail elsewhere (Balla & Zigler, 1979; Zigler, 1973). The constructs such as positive and negative reaction tendencies, expectancies of success and failure on performance, outer directedness, and reinforcer preference may play an important role in the adjustment of the mentally retarded individual to his or her environment and, therefore, have a direct impact on the psychosocial functioning of the individual. It remains to be seen whether poor adjustment, as defined by various descriptions, would necessarily lead to emotional disturbance.

Cromwell's (1963) social learning treatment of mental retardation also emphasizes the history of the individual. Cromwell has elaborated the expectancy for success construct with regard to the individual's behavior. One conceptualization of the expectancy construct, locus of control, has been fairly well established in the literature as the generalized perception of a connection between an individual's behavior and subsequent events. Mentally retarded persons typically have extreme difficulty with an accurate perception of contingency, unless explicit and temporally close, and thus they frequently feel at the mercy of their environment. In other words, the mentally retarded may have a higher expectancy for failure than their nonretarded peers. Cromwell and his associates have provided some evidence that mentally retarded individuals have a tendency to be more motivated to avoid failure than to achieve success. Some workers have suggested that the mentally retarded person's expectancy for failure will lead to greater manifestations of frustration (Viney, Clarke, & Lord, 1973).

DeVellis (1977) has asserted that the behavior of many institutionalized mentally retarded individuals is surprisingly similar to the learned helplessness phenomenon described by Seligman (1975). Given the pervasive deficits in learning, and therefore, in perceiving contingency in general, it seems highly plausible that mentally retarded individuals could be at risk for learned helplessness and that this could very well be manifested in a variety of emotional problems.

In summary, relatively little is known about personality development among mentally retarded individuals, and even less is known about the relationship between personality factors and emotional disturbances. Clearly, this is a question that merits further investigation.

• ASSESSMENT AND DIAGNOSIS •

The chapter by Costello in this volume will address the diagnostic/ assessment process in detail; however, it is important to highlight some of the issues and potential caveats of what has evolved into a rather complicated topic. In fact, the term *emotional disturbance* has come to subsume a number of disparate clinical phenomena which are presumed to represent pathological functioning. Emotional disturbance can be considered the modern-day analog to the controversial term *mental illness*, which has elicited a plethora of ideological battles among various professionals. The conceptualization of disturbed behavior as an illness, and thus falling under the purview of the medical profession, succeeded in shifting the purported etiology from demons, evil spirits, witchcraft, and the like to a natural cause. The definition of emotional disturbance as an "illness," however, resulted in the establishment of the medical model of diagnosis and treatment. Less emphasis was placed on emotional disturbance as a violation of social standards of overt behavior, thought, affective expression, or interpersonal interaction.

Albee (1969), among others, has spirited the movement away from the illness model and makes quite an eloquent case for a social-developmental model that stems from a continuity perspective of mental disorders. Albee contends that there is a continuity between "normal" and "abnormal" behavior: "disturbed behavior reflects the results of social-developmental learning in pathological social environments (rather than intrapersonal sickness)" (p. 876). The social-developmental model described by Albee represents a reasonable alternative to an illness or pathological model and is consistent with the particular orientation of this volume.

The crux of the diagnostic/assessment problem is bound up in the very nature of mental retardation; that is, it is difficult to discern what disturbances of behavior are the direct result of emotional problems and which are the result of subnormal intellectual functioning. One potential answer is that all mentally retarded individuals manifest some degree of emotional disturbance. Another less than satisfactory possibility is that mentally retarded individuals cannot be emotionally disturbed. Clearly, there is a middle ground where the two phenomena can coexist. It is the task of the service provider to arrive at some set of acceptable criteria for delineating emotional disturbance in mentally retarded individuals. This has not been an easy process for the practitioner who faces the same task with the nonretarded individual. However, there is general agreement among professionals as to what particular behaviors are associated with rather specific nosological categories. The critical factor is the intellectual functioning level of the individual. As the person becomes less able to relate in a verbal manner, behavior becomes the point of analysis and the diagnostician becomes less able to use traditional measures of emotional functioning such as projective tests and clinical interviews. Rather, direct behavioral observations by the evaluator and the reports of the parents, teachers, and staff are given more weight. The potential for misdiagnosis or failure to identify emotional disturbance, therefore, increases. Corbett (1979) has indicated that accurate diagnoses are more of a problem for mentally retarded adults because only the more severely disturbed individuals are identified. Emotional disturbances of mentally retarded children, on the other hand, are qualitatively similar to those of their nonretarded peers, although they are more prevalent in the mentally retarded group (Corbett, 1979). An additional difference is that a disproportionate number of mentally retarded individuals are autistic. Further, mentally retarded individuals frequently manifest significant medical problems which may have important psychological components. Corbett has contended that the present diagnostic scheme does not have the predictive value for mentally retarded individuals that it reportedly has for nonretarded individuals.

The fact that mental health services are not routinely available for the mentally retarded may be due, in part, to zealous service workers who have stressed that the mentally retarded are not mentally ill. Furthermore, previous psychiatric nosological schemas also tended to perpetuate the view that the two phenomena were, indeed, mutually exclusive. A multiaxial classification of mental disorders has evolved which permits documentation of a number of relevant characteristics. The multiaxial system was originally advocated in the diagnosis of childhood disorders by Rutter et al. (1969) and has been recently elaborated and incorporated into the DSM-III (American Psychiatric Association, 1980). The system proposed by Rutter et al. (1969) contains three axes. The first describes the clinical psychiatric syndrome, the second axis records the individual's level of intellectual functioning, and the third notes any associated factors or etiological data. The DSM-III scheme contains five axes. These include the following:

- Axis I   Clinical syndromes, conditions not attributable to a mental disorder that are a focus of attention or treatment (V. Codes), additional codes.
- Axis II   Personality disorders, specific developmental disorders.
- Axis III   Physical disorders and conditions.
- Axis IV   Severity of psychosocial stressors.
- Axis V   Highest level of adaptive functioning past year.

In the specific case of a mentally retarded individual, who also manifests significant emotional disturbance, both phenomena would be entered under Axis I. In other words, the conditions can coexist in the DSM-III classification schema.

The multiaxial system permits the diagnostician to transmit a large amount of clinically useful information about the functioning of an individual and should promote treatment programs designed to meet the total needs of the mentally retarded individual.

• TREATMENT METHODS •

There are a number of issues to be considered in any discussion of treatment methods for disturbed mentally retarded persons. We will divide treatment methods into three major categories: pharmacotherapy, behavior therapy, and psychotherapy. Each of these treatment methods has been used frequently with retarded clients exhibiting behavioral disturbances and each is accompanied by its own set of issues.

• Pharmacotherapy •

The effects of drugs on mentally retarded persons will be detailed in the chapter by Breuning, Ferguson, Davidson, and Poling, but some of the more pertinent issues will be raised here. First, it should be noted that as many as 50 percent of institutionalized mentally retarded persons are receiving psychotropic medication (Lipman, 1970; Sprague & Baxley, 1978). The most frequently prescribed psychotropics are antipsychotic drugs, notably thioridazine and chlorpromazine (phenothiazines) and haloperidol (a butyrophenone). Although antianxiety agents (e.g., diazepam, chlordiazepoxide) and stimulants (e.g., methylphenidate) are also used clinically, their frequency of use if far below that of the antipsychotics.

A large number of studies is available in the literature on the effects of antipsychotic drugs with mentally retarded subjects, however, most of these have major methodological weaknesses (Aman & Singh, 1980; Sprague & Werry, 1971). In many cases such weaknesses make these studies essentially uninterpretable. Studies that have used adequate experimental controls have generated equivocal results. It does appear, however, that antipsychotics may be efficacious in controlling aggression, excessive motor activity, and perhaps, stereotyped behavior.

This conclusion is tempered, however, by the results of a recent review of the efficacy of thioridazine with the mentally retarded (Aman & Singh, 1980). Thioridazine, it will be recalled, is the most frequently prescribed antipsychotic for use with disturbed mentally retarded persons. Aman and Singh (1980) have concluded that the only category of behavior that seems to be affected by thioridazine is stereotypies, and this effect has not been well established. Furthermore, the clinical significance of the reported data is open to question.

In addition to efficacy, there are a number of other issues to be considered regarding the use of antipsychotics in mental retardation. These considerations are elaborated in the following sections.

• *State Dependent Learning* •

Psychotropic drugs are generally thought to act as unconditioned stimuli. They can also act as discriminative stimuli, as in the case of state dependent learning (SDL). If learning that occurs in a drug state does not generalize to a nondrug condition, or conversely, learning in a nondrug condition is not retained in a drug state, then SDL is said to have occurred. Early investigations of SDL were conducted with children receiving stimulant medication. These studies were not able to demonstrate dissociated learning (e.g., Aman & Sprague, 1974), although later investigations have reported SDL (Shea, 1977; Swanson & Kinsbourne, 1976). The demonstration of SDL may depend on the use of "responders" as subjects. That is, SDL may occur only with those children whose performance improves following administration of stimulant medication (Shea, 1977).

Surprisingly, we have not found any studies in the literature examining SDL in humans receiving antipsychotic drugs. Several animal investigations, however, have demonstrated dissociated learning with chlorpromazine (Downey, 1975; Otis, 1964). It is not clear if SDL is a clinically important problem for mentally retarded individuals receiving psychotropic medication. Certainly, SDL will be determined, in part, by such factors as behavioral tolerance, the nature of the task, and the dose used.

• *Drug Effects on Reinforced Behavior* •

Dose-dependent decreases in the rate of operant responding following administration of antipsychotic drugs have been demonstrated in both animals and humans (Breuning & Davidson, 1981; Breuning, Ferguson,

Davidson, & Poling, Hollis & St. Omer, 1972; McMillan & Leander, 1976). This suppression of reinforced behavior by antipsychotics has important consequences for mentally retarded individuals receiving such drugs. It is well known that antipsychotics may exert a potent sedative effect. Perhaps more important, a major effect of antipsychotic administration is the interruption of dopamine transmission by blockade of postsynaptic receptor sites. Dopamine-containing pathways have been shown recently to be a primary substrate for reward (e.g., Stein, 1978). If dopamine is important in the mediation of reward, antipsychotics might "short-circuit" reward mechanisms, thereby reducing the reward value of various stimuli. Studies by Hollis and St. Omer (1972) as well as Breuning and coworkers (Breuning & Davidson, 1981; Breuning et al., in press) lend support to the notion that antipsychotics may antagonize conditioned reinforcement.

• Drug Effects on Stimulus Control •

Another issue to be considered in the use of pharmacotherapy with mentally retarded persons is the effect of psychotropic drugs on stimulus control. Because sound human studies are lacking, we must generate hypotheses based on animal data. Animal studies have shown that behavior under strong stimulus control is much less likely to be disrupted by psychoactive agents than is behavior under weak stimulus control (Moerschbaecher & Thompson, 1980). That is, increased responding in the nonreinforcement condition S^Δ following drug administration is observed only if baseline rates of responding in the S^Δ condition were not asymptotic to zero (Thompson, 1978). Establishment of strong stimulus control in naturalistic settings is, of course, quite difficult with lower functioning retarded persons. The extent to which psychotropic drugs disrupt stimulus control is an important clinical question.

• Drug Effects on Aversively Motivated Behavior •

One of the earliest documented effects of antipsychotics on behavior is the selective attenuation of avoidance responding at doses that do not affect escape behavior (Courvoisier, Fournel, Duerot, Kolsky, & Koetschet, 1953; Fibiger, Zis, & Phillips, 1975; Niemegeers, Verbruggen, & Janssen, 1969). Apparently, the specific mechanism of this effect is the inability of the animal to initiate responses in the presence of the conditioned stimulus (Beninger, Mason, Phillips, & Fibiger, 1980a, 1980b).

To what degree the behavior of developmentally disabled persons is governed by avoidance contingencies is, of course, open to discussion. Further, almost nothing is known about how such avoidance behavior in retarded persons might be affected by antipsychotics. Nevertheless, animal data make such questions important ones to consider when treating mentally retarded clients.

• *Side Effects* •

A great deal has been written about the potential adverse effects of antipsychotic drugs. Winsberg and Yepes (1978) have described three classes of acute side effects that follow administration of neuroleptics. Apathy, drowsiness, and lethargy are among the so-called treatment-emergent effects included in their first category. Anticholinergic effects such as dry mouth, blurring of vision, urinary retention, and abdominal pain constitute a second category. The final category includes extra-pyramidal symptoms (EPS) which involve akathisia, dystonic reactions, and parkinsonianlike symptoms.

Long-term side effects of antipsychotics have received a great deal of attention recently largely because of the disorder of tardive dyskinesia (TD). TD describes a set of involuntary movements typically seen following neuroleptic withdrawal. Choreoathetoid movements, buccal-lingual movements, motor restlessness, abnormal posturing, and ataxia are among the defining characteristics of this syndrome (Gualtieri, Barnhill, McGimsey, & Schell, 1980).

Prior to the onset of TD, are the so-called withdrawal emergent symptoms (Polizos, Engelhardt, Hoffman, & Waizer, 1973). These include oral dyskinesias, abnormal involuntary movements, and sometimes nausea and vomiting. Withdrawal from antipsychotics may also result in behavioral deterioration including hyperactivity, agitation, and even psychotic behavior (Caine, Margolin, Brown, & Ebert, 1978; Chouinard & Jones, 1980; Polizos et al., 1973). Such behavior is usually explained as the result of compensatory neural changes resulting from chronic antipsychotic use. Chronic antipsychotic treatment presumably renders mesolimbic and mesocortical dopamine receptors supersensitive, as well as cells in the nigrostriatal pathway. It is not clear if behavioral deterioration in the mentally retarded following chronic neuroleptic treatment is a reliable phenomenon or if it is due to dopamine receptor supersensitivity or to the manifestation of a preexisting condition. The development of behavioral supersensitivity in mentally retarded persons receiving chronic neuroleptics has not been demonstrated in an unequivocal way.

• *Drug Effects on Learning and Memory* •

Surprisingly few studies are available documenting the effect of psychotropic drugs on learning and memory in mentally retarded persons. Of the investigations that have appeared in the published literature, many have assessed drug effects on standardized intelligence tests. IQ tests, however, are not sensitive indicators of drug effects (Breuning & Davidson, 1981; Sprague & Werry, 1971). On the basis of animal data and work with other clinical populations, it is likely that use of antipsychotics will result in decrements in learning. A recent study by Wysocki, Fuqua, Davis, and Breuning (1981) is one of a few studies examining this issue with mentally retarded subjects. Here, using a delayed match-to-sample task, these workers demonstrated an increased accuracy at longer delay values with each dose reduction with the greatest delay reached only after a 0 mg dose.

Pharmacotherapy—Behavior Therapy Interactions

Psychotropic medications are widely prescribed for mentally retarded persons. The widespread application of behavior management programs has also been well documented. Data analyzing the interaction of these two modes of treatment, however, are extraordinarily sparse (Shroeder, Lewis, & Lipton, in press), despite a number of reports demonstrating the importance of environmental factors in the mediation of drug response. In a recent review of the use of drugs with mentally retarded persons, Sprague and Baxley (1978) have termed the lack of studies examining the interaction of psychotropic medications and behavior management programs "deplorable."

• Behavior Therapy •

There are countless demonstrations in the literature of the utility of applying operant conditioning principles to the habilitation of the mentally retarded (for recent reviews see Schroeder, Mulick, & Schroeder, 1979; Whitman & Scibak, 1979). Despite the power of this technology there are a number of issues to consider regarding the widespread application of applied behavior analysis to mental retardation. As the use of behavior management procedures will be treated in great detail later in this volume, only important considerations will be introduced when evaluating behavior modification as a treatment regimen.

Of major importance to the effective treatment of the mentally retarded is the problem of generalization and maintenance of treatment gains. For example, in a recent report Bates and Wehman (1977) reviewed 56 studies using behavior management procedures with retarded persons. Only 29 percent of these provided maintenance and generalization data. The fact that maintenance and generalization are not typically demonstrated is further highlighted by the fact that only 3 of the 56 studies reviewed by Bates and Wehman reported longer than three months follow-up.

Single-subject designs, particularly reversal designs, are typically used to evaluate the effects of behavior management procedures (Bates & Wehman, 1977). Although these designs are quite powerful in detecting changes in behavior over time (Sidman, 1960), their use is accompanied by several distinct disadvantages. For one, because of the problem of order effects or multiple-treatment interference (Campbell & Stanley, 1966), it becomes almost impossible to compare different treatment techniques (e.g., differential reinforcement of other behaviors (DRO) versus time-out) or the components of any one treatment package. Being restricted, methodologically, to the use of one independent variable is certainly a drawback. In order to compare the relative efficacy of various treatments, greater use of group designs is probably necessary.

Yet another issue which must be considered is the analysis of both positive and negative collateral behaviors (Sajway, Twardosz, & Burke, 1972). The degree to which collateral behaviors are induced by treatment procedures must be considered in evaluating the effectiveness of the behavior management program. Schroeder (Schroeder et al., 1979) has noted that collateral behavior has been observed in a wide range of contexts and with most procedures that attempt to suppress high rates of aberrant behavior. For example, Rollings, Baumeister, and Baumeister (1977) observed increases in self-injurious behavior when they attempted to punish stereotyped mannerisms with an overcorrection procedure.

Another issue to which we draw the reader's attention is the efficacy of various behavior management procedures. That is, what is the extent and rate of suppression of various behavior modification techniques relative to specific behaviors targeted for deceleration. Insufficient data exist on this subject although the combination of punishment plus reinforcement of incompatible behavior seems to be a powerful one (Forehand & Baumeister, 1976) resulting in rapid suppression.

The efficiency, including cost efficiency, of various behavioral treatments will necessarily be linked to their frequency of use in various settings. For example, few reports are available documenting successful use of behavior management in homes or vocational settings (e.g., Bates & Wehmann, 1977). More often, published reports include interventions conducted in an institutional setting or a classroom environment. With the advent of deinstitutionalization and the normalization movement, it is important to demonstrate the efficiency of these procedures in home and workshop environments.

Related to this issue is the need to establish the effectiveness of behavioral techniques when they are used by paraprofessionals or parents. Numerous reports are available documenting training efforts with such groups (e.g., Gardner, 1972). Detailed accounts of specific training procedures are largely lacking, however, making replication difficult (Whitman & Scibak, 1979).

• Psychotherapy •

The evolution of service delivery patterns and practices with mentally retarded persons has rendered psychotherapy an endangered species among currently available habilitative procedures. This is partly because of a number of assumptions which have more or less empirical validity. For example, Sternlicht (1966) has suggested that psychotherapy is little used because the assumption is made that mentally retarded persons lack the intelligence necessary for insight and are deficient in their ability to abstract and use verbal mediators. The inability of many mentally retarded individuals to generate effective verbal mediators is supported by basic experimental research (e.g., Borokowski & Johnson, 1968) and is a popular objection to the use of psychotherapy. As a consequence of this deficiency, Gardner (1971) has suggested that the mentally retarded exhibit a lack of verbal control over nonverbal behavior. From a behavioral point of view such a lack of control makes verbally oriented therapy less than useful. In Gardner's (1971) view, the development of verbal behavior as cues for nonverbal, overt behavior is critical for successful treatment.

Sternlicht (1966) has cited other reasons for not making psychotherapy services available to the mentally retarded, including their deficiency in realizing the sources and consequences of behavior, and inability to adjust to the needs of others and understand the purposes of therapy.

The unavailability of psychotherapeutic services for the mentally retarded with behavioral disorders is, according to Phillips (1966), due to "misconceptions." Among these are that behavioral or emotional problems are a function of mental retardation rather than of interpersonal relations; emotional disorders in mentally retarded persons differ from those seen in the nonretarded population; and the cause of behavior disorders is brain damage.

An additional reason for the all-too-frequent failure to consider psychotherapy for the emotionally disturbed mentally retarded is the unavailability of appropriately trained therapists. Most therapists are trained in verbally loaded, intellectually oriented therapeutic techniques and are thus reluctant to work with mentally retarded clients. Additionally, the assumption that therapuetic gains will be few and far between also adds to the unwillingness of therapists to work with mentally retarded clients.

Before discussing how psychotherapeutic procedures have been used with the mentally retarded, the term psychotherapy should be defined. Bialer (1967) proposed the following definition:

> the systematic utilization of psychological techniques, chief of which is a close interpersonal relationship, by a professionally trained therapist in order to help individuals who need or seek assistance in the amelioration of their emotional or behavioral problems. (p. 139)

This definition is useful in that it does not limit psychotherapy to classical procedures designed to bring about personality change. Nor does it require the exclusive use of verbal techniques or awareness of therapeutic dynamics. It allows instead for other helping techniques to be included, techniques which may be more applicable to intellectually deficient persons.

There are several verbal techniques that have been advanced by Robinson and Robinson (1976) as potentially useful with mentally retarded clients. These include catharsis, reassurance, support, advice, alternative guidance, directed discussion, reflection and classification of feelings, interpretation, and psychodrama. The procedures are relatively self-explanatory and require of the client a wide range of abilities that varies along a continuum from abstract to concrete.

In addition to verbally loaded techniques, a wide variety of nonverbal techniques is available to therapists. These techniques represent extensions of therapeutic procedures developed for children who may also be limited in their verbal communication skills. Sternlicht (1977) has provided a compendium of such procedures. Among these are dance therapy, finger painting, clay modeling, play therapy, and even shadow and balloon therapy.

Outcome studies evaluating the efficacy of psychotherapy with mentally retarded persons are largely lacking. Clinical results typically have not been based on well-controlled, empirical investigations. The problems usually associated with psychotherapy outcome research are even more salient when applied to mentally retarded clients. Process and outcome variables have not been defined, appropriate controls are difficult to establish, and methods of evaluation are often vague and lack reliability. While Sternlicht (1977) has pointed to the relative effectiveness of nonverbal, directive approaches, there still remains the basic challenge of demonstrating efficacy.

For instance, in one of the best controlled studies of psychotherapy with mentally retarded persons (Humes, Adamczyk, & Myco, 1969), group counseling was compared with a control condition using adolescents in a special education class with an IQ range of 53 to 77. The counseled group received significantly better teacher ratings and therapist ratings (California Test of Personality) when compared with the noncounseled group. Self-concept measures plus the subjects' sociometric ratings of their classmates, however, did not significantly differ. It is quite possible, though, that increases in counselor and teacher ratings were due to the use of "nonblind" raters. Further, little information is available regarding the validity or reliability of the measuring scales used.

Other studies conducted in the last decade or so have also indicated some support for the efficacy of therapy or counseling over control conditions (Bozarth & Roberts, 1970; Mann, Beaber, & Jacobson, 1969; Silvestri, 1977; Zisfein & Rosen, 1974). Methodological weaknesses, however, including the reliability of assessment instruments, the use of raters blind to the treatment condition, and nonrandom assignment to treatment condition, make interpretation difficult.

• CONCLUSIONS •

Emotional disturbance among persons diagnosed as mentally retarded is a problem of major proportion. The magnitude of the problem is clearly borne out by existing prevalence data. Despite this, relatively little research has been conducted on various parameters of the problem. For example, little is known about factors that may predispose the mentally retarded individual to emotional disturbance. Furthermore, current service delivery systems appear to lack the capability of providing mental health services to mentally retarded clients, despite a legally guaranteed right to mental health services. The unavailability of such services seems due to a multiplicity of factors, including the bureaucratic structure of health agencies, prevailing ideologies, disciplinary spheres of influence, and professional training practices.

Lack of research into the problem of emotional disturbance in mental retardation has allowed a number of assumptions to go unchallenged: to wit, severely and profoundly mentally retarded people cannot be emotionally disturbed, or behavioral disturbances are the result of cognitive deficiencies. Moreover, the lack of an acceptable system of classification of psychiatric disorders in mental retardation and the difficulty in applying standard psychiatric diagnoses to handicapped persons has further complicated the problem. Considerable confusion exists as to whether certain aberrant behaviors are a manifestation of emotional disorder or cognitive deficiency. Although it is generally agreed in the literature that the mentally retarded exhibit the full spectrum of psychiatric disorders observed in the general population, there does seem to be a cluster of aberrant behaviors overrepresented in the mentally retarded population. The implications of such observations are difficult to determine.

Existing treatment regimens for disturbed, mentally retarded persons generally involve the use of either pharmacotherapy, behavior therapy, or some combination of the two. The efficacy of pharmacotherapy (antipsychotics) has not been established. Indeed, recent reviews have demonstrated that not only does the efficacy of antipsychotics remain to be established but significant negative effects in performance and behavior may result from their use. Further, few data are available documenting the interaction of pharmacotherapy and behavior therapy. Although the power of behavior modification procedures has been amply demonstrated, several issues remain concerning their use with disturbed, mentally retarded individuals. Some of these are methodological and others involve such important issues as generalization and maintenance.

Taken as a whole, emotional disturbance in mental retardation is a problem that requires a great deal more and better research. In turn, such research can provide an empirical base for more and better services for disturbed, mentally retarded clients. Changes in the service delivery system will require not only a broader empirical base but major changes in the structure of health care agencies, professional training programs, and traditional disciplinary boundaries.

• REFERENCES •

Aman, M. G., & Singh, N. N. The usefulness of thioridazine for treating child-hood disorders—Fact or folklore? *American Journal of Mental Deficiency,* 1980, *84,* 331–338.

Aman, M. G., & Sprague, R. L. The state-dependent effects of methylphenidate and dextroamphetamine. *Journal of Nervous and Mental Disease,* 1974, *158,* 268–279.

American Psychiatric Association (Task Force on Nomenclature and Statistics). *Diagnostic and statistical manual of mental disorders* (3rd ed., DSM-III). Washington, D.C.: APA, 1980.

Albee, G. W. Emerging concepts of mental illness and models of treatment: The psychological point of view. *American Journal of Psychiatry,* 1969, *125,* 870–876.

Balla, D., & Zigler, E. Personality development in retarded persons. In N. R. Ellis (Ed.). *Handbook of mental deficiency, psychological theory and research* (2nd ed.). Hillsdale, N.J.: Lawrence Erlbaum, 1979.

Balthazar, E. E., & English, G. E. A system for the social classification of the more severely mentally retarded. *American Journal of Mental Deficiency,* 1969, *74,* 361–368.

Bartak, L., & Rutter, M. Difference between mentally retarded and normally intelligent autistic children. *Journal of Autism and Childhood Schizophrenia,* 1976, *6,* 109–120.

Bates, P., & Wehman, P. Behavior management with the mentally retarded: An empirical analysis of the research. *Mental Retardation,* 1977, *15,* 9–12.

Baumeister, A. A., & MacLean, W. E., Jr. Brain damage and mental retardation. In N. R. Ellis (Ed.), *Handbook of mental deficiency* (2nd ed.). Hillsdale, N.J.: Lawrence Erlbaum, 1979.

Beninger, R. J., Mason, S. T., Phillips, A. G., & Fibiger, H. C. The use of conditioned suppression to evaluate the nature of neuroleptic-induced avoidance deficits. *Journal of Pharmacology and Experimental Therapeutics,* 1980a, *213,* 623–627.

Beninger, R. J., Mason, S. T., Phillips, A. G., & Fibiger, H. C. The use of extinction to investigate the nature of neuroleptic-induced avoidance deficits. *Psychopharmacology,* 1980b, *69,* 11–18.

Berger, M., Yule, W., & Rutter, M. Attainment and adjustment in two geographical areas. II. The prevalence of specific reading retardation. *British Journal of Psychiatry,* 1975, *126,* 510–519.

Bialer, I. Psychotherapy and other adjustment techniques with the mentally retarded. In A. A. Baumeister (Ed.), *Mental retardation.* Chicago: Aldine, 1967.

Bloom, B. S. *Stability and change in human characteristics.* New York: Wiley, 1964.

Borokowski, J. G., & Johnson, L. O. Mediation and the paired–associate learning of normals and retardates. *American Journal of Mental Deficiency*, 1968, *72*, 610–613.

Bozarth, J. D., & Roberts, R. R. Effectiveness of counselor-trainees with mentally retarded sheltered workshop clients. *Training School Bulletin*, 1970, *67*, 119–122.

Breuning, S. E., & Davidson, N. A. Effects of psychotropic drugs on the intelligence test performance of mentally retarded adults. *American Journal of Mental Deficiency*, 1981, *85*, 575–579.

Breuning, S. E., Ferguson, D. G., Davidson, N. A., & Poling, A. D. Effects of thioridazine on the intelligence of mentally retarded drug responders. *Archives of General Psychiatry*, in press.

Caine, E. D., Margolin, D. I., Brown, G. L., & Ebert, M. H. Gilles de la Tourette's syndrome, tardive dyskinesia, and psychosis in an adolescent. *American Journal of Psychiatry*, 1978, *135*, 241–243.

Campbell, D. T., & Stanley, J. C. *Experimental and quasi-experimental designs for research.* Chicago: Rand McNally, 1966.

Cantwell, D. P., & Baker, L. Psychiatric disorder in children with speech and language retardation: A critical review. *Archives of General Psychiatry*, 1977, *34*, 583–591.

Cantwell, D. P., Baker, L., & Mattison, R. E. Psychiatric disorders in children with speech and language retardation. *Archives of General Psychiatry*, 1980, *37*, 423–426.

Chazan, M. The incidence and nature of maladjustment among children in schools for the educationally subnormal. *British Journal of Educational Psychology*, 1964, *34*, 292–304.

Chess, S., & Hassibi, M. Behavior deviations in mentally retarded children. *Journal of the American Academy of Child Psychiatry*, 1970, *9*, 282–297.

Chess, S., Korn, S. J., & Fernandez, P. B. *Psychiatric disorders of children with congenital rubella.* New York: Brunner/Mazel, 1971.

Chouinard, G., & Jones, B. D. Neuroleptic-induced supersensitivity psychosis: Clinical and pharmacological characteristics. *American Journal of Psychiatry*, 1980, *137*, 16–21.

Corbett, J. A. Mental retardation—Psychiatric aspects. In M. Rutter & L. Hersov (Eds.), *Child psychiatry: Modern approaches.* Oxford: Blackwell Scientific Publications, 1977.

Corbett, J. A. Psychiatric morbidity. In F. E. James & R. B. Snaith (Eds.), *Psychiatric illness and mental handicap.* London: Gaskell, 1979.

Corbett, J. A., & Harris, R. Epilepsy in children with severe mental handicap. Institute for Research into Mental and Multiple Handicap. Symposium No. 16. London, 1974.

Corbett, J. A., Harris, E., & Robinson, R. Epilepsy. In J. Wortis (Ed.), *Mental retardation and developmental disabilities* (vol. 7). New York: Brunner/Mazel, 1975.

Corbett, J. A., Harris, R., Taylor, E., & Trimble, M. Progressive disintegrative psychosis of childhood. *Journal of Child Psychology and Psychiatry*, 1977, *18*, 211–219.

Courvoisier, S., Fournel, J., Ducrot, R., Kolsky, M., & Koetschet, P. Propriétés pharmacodynamiques du chlorhydrate de chloro-3 (diméthyl-amino-3'-propyl)-10 phénothiazine (4.560 R.P.) *Archives Internationale Pharmacodynamie*, 1953, *92*, 305–361.

Cromwell, R. L. A social learning approach to mental retardation. In N. R. Ellis (Ed.), *Handbook of mental deficiency, psychological theory and research.* New York: McGraw-Hill, 1963.

Cromwell, R. L. Personality evaluation. In A. A. Baumeister (Ed.), *Mental retardation, appraisal, education and rehabilitation.* Chicago: Aldine, 1967.

DeVellis, R. F. Learned helplessness in institutions. *Mental Retardation*, 1977, *15*, 10–13.

Dewan, J. G. Intelligence and emotional stability. *American Journal of Psychiatry*, 1948, *104*, 548–554.

Downey, D. State dependent learning with centrally and non-centrally active drugs. *Bulletin of the Psychonomic Society*, 1975, *5*, 281–284.

Eyman, R. K., & Call, T. Maladaptive behavior and community placement of mentally retarded persons. *American Journal of Mental Deficiency,* 1977, *82*, 137–144.

Eyman, R. K., Moore, B. C., Capes, L., & Zachofsky, T. Maladaptive behavior of institutionalized retardates with seizures. *American Journal of Mental Deficiency*, 1970, *74*, 651–659.

Festinger, L. A theory of social comparison processes. *Human Relations*, 1954, *2*, 117–140.

Fibiger, H. C., Zis, A. P., & Phillips, A. G. Haloperidol-induced disruption of conditioned avoidance responding: Attenuation by prior training or by anticholinergic drugs. *European Journal of Pharmacology*, 1975, *30*, 309–314.

Forehand, R., & Baumeister, A. A. Deceleration of aberrant behavior among retarded individuals. In M. Hersen, R. M. Eisler, & P. M. Miller (Eds.), *Progress in behavior modification* (Vol. 2). New York: Academic Press, 1976.

Freedman, R. D. & Malkin, S. F. A comparison of the psychosocial problems of deaf, of visually inpaired, and of non-handicapped children. *Developmental Medicine and Child Neurology,* 1977, *19*, 111.

Gardner, J. M. Teaching behavior modification to non-professionals. *Journal of Applied Behavior Analysis*, 1972, *5*, 517–521.

Gardner, W. I. *Behavior modification and mental retardation.* Chicago: Aldine, 1971.

Gardner, W. I. Personality characteristics of the mentally retarded: Review and critique. In H. J. Prehm, L. A. Hamerlynck, & J. E. Crosson (Eds.), *Behavior research in mental retardation.* Eugene: University of Oregon Press, 1968.

Graham, P., & Rutter, M. Organic brain dysfunction and child psychiatric disorder. *British Medical Journal*, 1968, *3*, 695–700.

Gualtieri, C. T. Psychiatry's disinterest in mental retardation. *Psychiatric Opinion,* May, 1979, pp. 26–30.

Gualtieri, C. T., Barnhill, J., McGimsey, J., & Schell, D. Tardive dyskinesia and other movement disorders in children treated with psychotropic drugs. *Journal of the American Academy of Child Psychiatry*, 1980, *19*, 491–510.

Heaton-Ward, A. Psychosis in mental handicap. *British Journal of Psychiatry*, 1977, *130*, 525–533.

Heber, R. Research on personality disorders and characteristics of the mentally retarded. *Mental Retardation Abstracts*, 1964, *1*, 304–325.

Hollis, J. H., & St. Omer, V. V. Direct measurement of psychopharmacological response: Effects of chlorpromazine on motor behavior of retarded children. *American Journal of Mental Deficiency*, 1972, *76*, 397–407.

Humes, C., Adamczyk, J., & Myco, R. A school study of group counseling with educable retarded adolescents. *American Journal of Mental Deficiency*, 1969, *74*, 191–195.

Jan, J. E., Freeman, R. D., & Scott, E. P. (Eds.): *Visual impairment in children and adolescents*. New York: Grune & Stratton, 1977.

Kanner, L. Autistic disturbances of affective contact. *The Nervous Child*, 1943, *2*, 217–250.

Kisker, G. W. *The disorganized personality* (3rd ed.). New York: McGraw-Hill, 1977.

Lipman, R. S. The use of psychopharmacological agents in residential facilities for the retarded. In F. J. Menolascino (Ed.), *Psychiatric approaches to mental retardation*. New York: Basic Books, 1970.

Mailman, R. B., Lewis, M. H., & Kilts, C. D. Animal models related to developmental disorders: Theoretical and pharmacological analyses. *Applied Research in Mental Retardation*, 1981, *2*, 1–12.

Malamud, N. Heller's disease and childhood schizophrenia. *American Journal of Psychiatry*, 1959, *116*, 215–218.

Mann, P. H., Beaber, J. O., & Jacobson, M. D. The effect of group counseling on educable mentally retarded boys' self concepts. *Exceptional Children*, 1969, *35*, 359–366.

McMillan, D. E., & Leander, J. D. Effects of drugs on schedule-controlled behavior. In S. D. Glick & J. Goldfarb (Eds.), *Behavioral pharmacology*. St. Louis: Mosby, 1976.

McNett, I. Part II: Mental health services for handicapped fall between agencies. *APA Monitor*, 1980, *11*, 15.

Menolascino, F. J. (Ed.). *Psychiatric approaches to mental retardation*. New York: Basic Books, 1970.

Moerschbaecher, J. M., & Thompson, D. M. Effects of D-amphetamine, cocaine, and phencyclidine on the acquisition of response sequences with and without stimulus fading. *Journal of the Experimental Analysis of Behavior*, 1980, *33*, 369–381.

Niemegeers, C. J., E., Verbruggen, F. J., & Janssen, P. A. J. The influence of various neuroleptic drugs on shock avoidance responding in rats. *Psychopharmacologia*, 1969, *16*, 161–174.

Otis, L. S. Dissociation and recovery of a response learned under the influence of chlorpromazine or saline. *Science*, 1964, *143*, 1347–1348.

Penrose, L. S. The contribution of mental deficiency research to psychiatry. *British Journal of Psychiatry*, 1966, *112*, 747–755.

Phillips, I. Children, mental retardation and emotional disorder. In I. Phillips (Ed.), *Prevention and treatment of mental retardation*. New York: Basic Books, 1966.

Phillips, I., & Williams, N. Psychopathology and mental retardation: A study of 100 mentally retarded children. I: Psychopathology. *American Journal of Psychiatry*, 1975, *132*, 1265–1271.

Polizos, P., Engelhardt, D., Hoffman, S., & Waizer, J. Neurological consequences of psychotropic drug withdrawal in schizophrenic children. *Journal of Autism and Childhood Schizophrenia*, 1973, *3*, 247–253.

Pollock, H. M. Mental disease among mental defectives. *American Journal of Psychiatry*, 1944, *101*, 361.

Pond, D. A. Psychiatric aspects of epileptic and brain-damaged children. *British Medical Journal*, 1961, *2*, 1377–1382, 1454–1459.

Primrose, D. A. A survey of 502 consecutive admissions to a subnormality hospital from 1st January 1968 to 31st December 1970. *British Journal of Mental Subnormality*, 1971, *32*, 25–28.

Reid, A. H. Psychiatric disorders in mentally handicapped children: A clinical and follow-up study. *Journal of Mental Deficiency Research*, 1980, *24*, 287–297.

Reiss, S., Levitan, G. W., & McNally, R. J. Emotionally disturbed mentally retarded people. *American Psychologist*, 1982, *37*, 361–367.

Robinson, N.M., & Robinson, H. B. *The mentally retarded child* (3rd ed.). New York: McGraw-Hill, 1976.

Rogers, C. M., Smith, M. D., & Coleman, J. M. Social comparison in the classroom: The relationship between academic achievement and self-concept. *Journal of Educational Psychology*, 1978, *70*, 50–57.

Rollings, J. P., Baumeister, A., & Baumeister, A. The use of overcorrection procedures to eliminate stereotyped behaviors in retarded individuals. *Behavior Modification*, 1977, *1*, 29–46.

Rutter, M. Brain damage syndromes in childhood: Concepts and findings. *Journal of Child Psychology and Psychiatry*, 1977, *18*, 1–21.

Rutter, M. Emotional disorder and educational underachievement. *Archives of Diseases of Childhood*, 1974, *49*, 249–256.

Rutter, M. Psychiatry. In J. Wortis (Ed.), *Mental retardation: An annual review* (Vol. 3). New York: Grune & Stratton, 1971.

Rutter, M., Graham, P., & Yule, W. *A neuropsychiatric study in childhood*. Clinics in Developmental Medicine. Nos. 35/36. London: SIMP/Heinemann, 1970.

Rutter, M., Lebovici, S., Eisenberg, L., Sneznevskij, A. V., Sadoun, R., Brooks, E., & Lin, T. Y. A tri-axial classification of mental disorders in childhood. *Journal of Child Psychology and Psychiatry*, 1969, *10*, 41–61.

Rutter, M., & Lockyer, L. A five to fifteen year follow-up study of infantile psychosis—1. Description of sample. *British Journal of Psychiatry*, 1967, *113*, 1169–1182.

Rutter, M., Tizard, J., & Whitmore, K. (Eds.). *Education, health and behaviour*. London: Longman, 1970.

Rutter, M., Tizard, J., Yule, W., Graham, P., & Whitemore, K. Research report: Isle of Wight studies, 1964–1974. *Psychological Medicine,* 1976, *6,* 313–332.

Ryle, A., Pond, D. A., & Hamilton, M. The prevalence and patterns of psychological disturbance in children of primary age. *Journal of Child Psychology and Psychiatry,* 1965, *6,* 101–113.

Sajway, T., Twardosz, S., & Burke, M. Side effects of extinction procedures in a remedial school. *Journal of Applied Behavior Analysis,* 1972, *5,* 163–175.

Schroeder, S. R., Lewis, M. H., & Lipton, M. A. Interactions of pharmacotherapy and behavior therapy among children with learning and behavioral disorders. In K. Gadow & I. Bialer (Eds.), *Advances in learning and behavioral disabilities* (Vol. 2). Greenwich, Conn.: JAI Press, in press.

Schroeder, S. R., Mulick, J. A., & Schroeder, C. S. Management of severe behavior problems of the retarded. In N. R. Ellis (Ed.), *Handbook of mental deficiency* (2nd ed.). Hillsdale, N.J.: Lawrence Erlbaum, 1979.

Schurr, K. T., Towne, R. C., & Joiner, L. M. Trends in self-concept of ability over 2 years of special class placement. *Journal of Special Education,* 1972, *6,* 161–166.

Seligman, M. E. P. *Helplessness: On depression, development, and death.* San Francisco: Freeman, 1975.

Shapiro, A. Psychiatric illness in the mentally handicapped: An historical survey. In F. E. James & R. P. Snaith (Eds.), *Psychiatric illness and mental handicap.* London: Gaskell, 1979.

Shea, V. T. State-dependent learning in children receiving methylphenidate. Unpublished doctoral dissertation, University of North Carolina at Chapel Hill, 1977.

Sidman, M. *Tactics of scientific research.* New York: Basic Books, 1960.

Silvestri, R. Implosive therapy treatment of emotionally disturbed retardates. *Journal of Consulting and Clinical Psychology,* 1977, *45,* 14–22.

Smith, M. D., Dokecki, P. R., & Davis, E. E. School-related factors influencing the self-concepts of children with learning problems. *Peabody Journal of Education,* 1977, *54,* 185–195.

Sprague, R. L., & Baxley, G. B. Drugs used for the management of behavior in mental retardation. In J. Wortis (Ed.), *Mental retardation* (Vol. 8). New York: Brunner/Mazel, 1978.

Sprague, R. L., & Werry, J. S. Methodology of psychopharmacological studies with the retarded. In N. R. Ellis (Ed.), *International review of research in mental retardation* (Vol. 5). New York: Academic Press, 1971.

Stein, L. Reward transmitters: Catecholamines and opioid peptides. In M. A. Lipton, A. DiMascio, & K. F. Killam (Eds.), *Psychopharmacology: A generation of progress.* New York: Raven Press, 1978.

Sternlicht, M. Issues in counseling and psychotherapy with mentally retarded individuals. In I. Bialer & M. Sternlicht (Eds.), *The psychology of mental retardation: Issues and approaches.* New York: Psychological Dimensions, 1977.

Sternlicht, M. Psychotherapeutic procedures with the retarded. In N. R. Ellis (Ed.), *International review of research in mental retardation.* New York: Academic Press, 1966.

Swanson, J. M., & Kinsbourne, M. Stimulant-related state-dependent learning in hyperactive children. *Science,* 1976, *192,* 1354–1357.

Thompson, D. M. Stimulus control and drug effects. In D. E. Blackman & D. J. Sanger (Eds.), *Contemporary research in behavioral pharmacology.* New York: Plenum Press, 1978.

Viney, L. L., Clarke, A. M., & Lord, J. Resistance to extinction and frustration in retarded and nonretarded children. *American Journal of Mental Deficiency,* 1973, *78,* 308–315.

Weaver, T. R. The incidence of maladjustment among mental defectives in military environment. *American Journal of Mental Deficiency,* 1946, *51,* 238–246.

Whitman, T. L., & Scibak, J. W. Behavior modification research with the severely and profoundly retarded. In N. R. Ellis (Ed.), *Handbook of mental deficiency* (2nd ed.). Hillsdale, N.J.: Lawrence Erlbaum, 1979.

Winsberg, B. G., & Yepes, L. E. Antipsychotics (major tranquilizers, neuroleptics). In J. S. Werry (Ed.), *Pediatric psychopharmacology.* New York: Brunner/Mazel, 1978.

Wortis, J. Introduction: The role of psychiatry in mental retardation services. In J. Wortis (Ed.), *Mental retardation and developmental disabilities* (Vol. 9). New York: Brunner/Mazel, 1977.

Wysocki, T., Fuqua, W., Davis, V. J., & Breuning, S. E. Effects of thioridazine (Mellaril) on titrating delayed matching-to-sample performance of mentally retarded adults. *American Journal of Mental Deficiency,* 1981, *85,* 539–548.

Zigler, E. The retarded child as a whole person. In D. K. Routh (Ed.), *The experimental psychology of mental retardation.* Chicago: Aldine, 1973.

Zigler, E., & Harter, S. Socialization of the mentally retarded. In D. A. Goslin and D. C. Glass (Eds.), *Handbook of socialization theory and research.* New York: Rand McNally, 1969.

Zisfein, L., & Rosen, M. Effects of a personal adjustment training group counseling program. *Mental Retardation,* 1974, *12,* 50–53.

two

Assessment and Diagnosis of Psychopathology

Anthony Costello

The concept of mental retardation, as it is commonly employed in psychiatry, is often misleading despite its attractive simplicity. Services and funding have generally been devised on the assumption that mental retardation and mental illness are distinct conditions that do not overlap, an assumption which is hard to reconcile with the evidence. Not only do the mentally retarded show patterns of emotional as well as cognitive development that are qualitatively different from those of normal development, but the identification of mental retardation is often prompted not by cognitive disabilities but by unusual or troublesome behavior. Moreover, there is no reason to suppose that mental retardation guarantees mental health. Indeed, there is much evidence to suggest that the causes of mental retardation are associated with an increased prevalence of mental illness. The manifestations of mental illness in the mentally retarded obviously depend on the level of ability (Hayman, 1939; Heaton-Ward, 1977); psychiatric disorder is still detectable, however, even in the most profoundly mentally retarded individuals.

The boundary is further confused by mental illness occasionally masquerading as mental retardation. Although it is well recognized that certain psychiatric disorders are a severe handicap to normal mental functioning, the symptoms and psychopathology that would suggest the diagnosis can easily be overlooked by the unwary clinician. This is particularly true of the chronically psychotic patient, and to a lesser extent of the individual of low-normal intellectual ability who is suffering from depression. Many patients with chronic schizophrenia who are returned to the community after prolonged institutionalization, though they no longer present florid symptoms, have such impaired thought processes that their functioning in daily life is poor. Such individuals will typically perform poorly on standardized intelligence testing. Similarly, normal mental functioning may be inhibited by depressive retardation, and if depressed mood is not a striking feature of the affective disorder, an impression of mental retardation may easily be obtained.

Conversely, if the mental health worker fails to recognize the evidence of past low intellectual functioning, a mentally retarded individual with relatively minor emotional problems may be assessed as more seriously psychiatrically impaired than is the actual case. The mentally retarded individual may be less susceptible to the social influences that usually modify psychiatric symptomatology and may appear to be floridly disturbed. The picture may be further confused by overly energetic physical treatments for what is presumed to be depressive retardation or schizophrenic withdrawal. It is not uncommon to find that the mentally retarded individual shows quite disturbed behavior in response to stress, but that such disturbance is transient.

In children the boundaries are also difficult to define. The group of disorders now classified as pervasive developmental disorders, which includes early infantile autism, childhood psychosis, childhood schizophrenia, and the condition sometimes known as symbiotic psychosis, is a very heterogeneous one. Among these children there is a relatively "pure" group, that of early infantile autism, consisting of children who are quite distinct from the common picture of developmental delay. Indeed, within this group there may be children of normal or superior intelligence, though the practical difficulties of psychologically testing such children often lead to an underestimate of ability, and the child's adaptive functioning is usually poor. In many cases, psychometric assessment is not helpful (Moor, 1968). Although this group is markedly distinctive, the diagnostic boundaries are not sharply drawn, and the distribution from classic autism to straightforward mental retardation through those retarded children who present many but not all of the clinical features of autism, is probably a relatively even one. The rarity of autism and the frequency with which the diagnosis is overlooked make it difficult to obtain good information. Epidemiological studies (e.g., Lotter, 1966) have necessarily resorted to somewhat arbitrary criteria to exclude such borderline cases. Children with severe perceptual or language problems may also be difficult to distinguish from the mentally retarded and may show some of the behaviors that characterize pervasive developmental disorders. In addition, unusual behavior among children diagnosed as mentally retarded is often accepted as an intrinsic feature of the developmentally handicapped, and thus quite extreme psychopathology may remain ignored.

• ASSOCIATION OF MENTAL RETARDATION WITH • MENTAL ILLNESS

The frequency with which mental illness occurs in a mentally retarded population is difficult to assess because of the many problems of definition, identification, and sampling. Among children referred to psychiatrically oriented clinics for the mentally retarded, the range of emotional disturbance has been estimated between 7 (Philips & Williams, 1975) and 25 percent (Menolascino, 1968). Institutionalized series yield a much higher rate, up to 40 percent or more (Haracopos & Kelstrup, 1978). Among adults, the range within a hospital population has been variously estimated between 13 and 59 percent (Forrest & Ogunremi, 1974; Pollock, 1944; Browne, Gunzberg, Johnston-Hannah, MacColl, Oliver, & Thomas, 1971; Craft, 1959; Leck, Gordon, & McKeown, 1967; Williams, 1971). Even conservative criteria suggest a rate of about 13 percent among mentally retarded adults attending a community training center (Ballinger & Reid, 1977). One problem is that personality disorder, or what might more loosely be termed difficult behavior associated with a severe functional handicap, is not always easy to distinguish from classic psychiatric disorder, and it is a moot point whether this distinction should be made. Craft (1959), who attempted to make this distinction, estimated that the rate of mental illness in the hospital population was only 7 percent, whereas the rate of personality disorder might be as high as 33 percent. A consistent theme running through these studies is that the rate of psychiatric disorder in institutionalized populations tends to be much higher than that found in the community. Since the rates for institutionalized children and adults do not differ greatly, it is reasonable to infer that these reflect referral biases and that hospitalization or other institutional care for the moderately and severely mentally retarded is much more likely if behavioral problems coexist, just as the identification of mild mental retardation is much more likely to occur in the presence of behavioral disturbance.

Epidemiologic studies that have attempted to sample the whole population have not often tackled the question of whether mental retardation and mental illness are associated. Some studies of psychiatric epidemiology have begged the question by excluding cases of mental retardation. When truly complete sampling has been attempted, it appears that an intelligence quotient below 70 may be associated with a three- to four-fold increase in the rate of psychiatric abnormality (Rutter, Tizard, & Whitmore, 1970). Evidence for adults rests entirely on identified patients but strongly suggests that this finding in children applies to adults as well. This presumably reflects both the biological associations of mental retardation and the social and environmental disadvantages often attached to the handicap.

For the practitioner, it is difficult to avoid the conclusion that the provision of services for the mentally retarded must accommodate the need that many also have for psychiatric treatment. From the studies cited it is equally clear that although the proportions of patients suffering from anxiety disorders, affective disorders, psychoses, or other psychiatric conditions vary a great deal from one sample to another, depending on the population reviewed and the diagnostic criteria used, highly significant numbers of every sort of mental disorder will be found within any group of mentally retarded patients.

It has been fashionable in recent years to decry some attempts to make individual assessment on the grounds that assessment tools are so imperfect that spurious labeling can occur to the disadvantage of the individual. Saddling an individual with the diagnosis of both psychiatric disorder and mental retardation may provide an excuse for each treatment system for the two categories of disability to exclude the patient on the grounds that they lack the resources for this type of patient. These are not problems of assessment or labeling but of defective system design. Some caution may, of course, have to be exercised in allowing the diagnosis made as a result of psychiatric assessment to enter into the public domain. The validity or usefulness of such an assessment should not be vitiated by these considerations.

• SPECIFIC PSYCHIATRIC SYNDROMES IN MENTAL • RETARDATION

Unipolar affective disorder in the mentally retarded is often difficult to diagnose, but loss of appetite, slowing of motor movement and activity, and sleep disturbance should alert one to the possibility. Mood changes such as sullenness or irritability are more likely to be observed than frank sadness (Reid, 1972a). Bipolar affective disorder is more readily recognized because of the cyclical changes in mood and behavior (Reid, 1972a; Reid & Naylor, 1976; Heaton-Ward, 1977). Irritability and assaultive behavior are more common in the manic phase, although the classic gradiosity and impulsiveness of mania may be encountered.

Schizophrenia is a difficult psychiatric diagnosis to make in the severely mentally retarded, and many of the major criteria cannot be elicited if the IQ is much below 45 (Reid, 1976). The history of the association between schizophrenia and mental retardation is a long one and is well reviewed by Reid (1972b). Many of the classic cases would probably not be considered schizophrenic today, particularly since the emphasis on motor symptoms and catatonia has waned. Such phenomena are now rarely seen in patients of normal cognitive ability and may well have been in part a consequence of institutional care. In the mentally retarded, delusional material tends to be simple, often florid, and occasionally may compensate rather obviously for the patient's handicap. Since ideas of thought control, insertion, withdrawal, and so on may be too sophisticated for such patients, and thought disorder may be difficult to elicit, differentiation from the elation and gradiosity of mania may not be easy. Blunting of affect and schizophrenic withdrawal, though apparent to those who are sufficiently familiar with the patient, may also be very difficult to assess. Hallucinations may be the most helpful symptoms in raising the suspicion of schizophrenia; of course, they may also be difficult to elicit, and care should be taken to avoid the interpretation of misunderstandings or perceptual distortions as hallucinatory material.

Although the full range of anxiety disorders is seen in the mentally retarded, such diagnoses are commonly not recognized or are managed by nonpsychiatric techniques. The distinction between the concept of anxiety disorder and the rival interpretation of habit disorder is, in any case, a difficult one to make in theory and in practice it is unimportant because behavioral (operant) techniques are usually very effective in the reduction of symptoms. It is important to note that the incidence and intensity of fears and phobias are higher in the mentally retarded than in normal adults and commensurate with those in children of comparable mental age (Duff, LaRocca, Lizzet, Martin, Pearce, Williams, & Peck, 1981). This finding is especially relevant when discharge from institutional care is attempted. Although psychotherapy has been offered for many years to the mentally retarded (see Burton, 1954), supportive therapy and reassurance have the most valuable contribution to make, and so the niceties of differential diagnosis in the anxiety disorders are often not of great practical importance.

More florid types of anxiety disorder, such as conversion hysteria and obsessive–compulsive disorders, may be encountered and may be among the most difficult conditions the psychiatrist has to manage in the mentally retarded. Simple suggestion and psychological manipulation may remove the symptoms of conversion hysteria, but the cognitive techniques that have been used for the troublesome thoughts of obsessive–compulsive disorder in patients of normal intellectual ability are difficult to put into practice with the mentally retarded, although behavioral techniques will succeed with certain compulsive behaviors (Foa & Steketee, 1979).

• THE FUNCTION OF ASSESSMENT •

Psychiatric assessment can serve several purposes. The most important goal should be to identify conditions that may respond to treatment.

The assessment of psychopathology, however, is relevant to other purposes that are not usually considered a psychiatrist's domain. The adaptive functioning of a mentally retarded individual is usually assessed by using a standardized instrument, of which there are many examples (see Shapiro & Barrett, 1982; Walls, Werner, Bacon, & Zane, 1977). Such scales very properly emphasize achievements rather than problems or deficits, but both the fixed schedule of times and conventional scoring techniques allow many qualitative features to escape attention. A systematic review of those features usually described as psychopathology may strengthen such an assessment and make it more realistic, though psychiatric assessment cannot substitute for the standardized assessment of functional adaptation. An experienced clinician can usually give a well-informed guess on the level of adaptive ability of a patient, but the interaction between psychopathology and apparent ability is such that neither can be assessed if both are unknowns. The dangers of circularity in this argument make it essential to structure both the assessment of psychopathology and that of functional adaptation.

The dynamics of adaptation need to be considered, as well. Current adaptive functioning may depend on, or be limited by, the emotional environment. An individual's proven capacity to tolerate change must be assessed since this is the only reliable guide to that person's possible response to future change. Certain aspects of daily living are known to be particularly difficult for some mentally retarded people with psychiatric disorders. For example, inconsistent daily timetables may disturb an autistic adolescent or adult to the point that behavioral training breaks down. With a firm and consistent timetable, the same individual may show quite acceptable social behavior. The parent or caretaker who is intolerant of repetitive questioning or of unresponsiveness from the mentally retarded individual, may by ill-judged attempts to normalize behavior provoke a catastrophic reaction. These qualitative aspects of the patient's functional adaptation must be assessed to complement the more normal and structured aspects of both psychiatric and cognitive assessment in the mentally retarded.

The patient's vulnerability to future stress is often important but difficult to assess. This may be a critical factor when a change of accommodation or care is planned. Past experience may be the best guide. Unusual changeability of mood deserves careful assessment because mood changes ascribed to environmental change may, in fact, be spontaneous and reflect either a cyclothymic personality or clear-cut bipolar affective disorder.

It may also be important to assess deterioration. Though much of the deteriorated behavior in the mentally retarded can be explained by the adverse characteristics of the care they receive and is potentially reversible, there is a significant rate of superimposed and progressive presenile dementia to be found among the mentally retarded.

• APPROACHES TO ASSESSMENT •

Assessment cannot be compressed into a rigid mold. Techniques appropriate to the assessment of an individual who is a candidate for psychiatric treatment may not meet the needs of a school principal wishing to find the appropriate classroom placement for a child or those of an agency team charged with selecting individuals who would best succeed at living in the community with minimal support. The act of assessment necessarily implies the development of appropriate policies to use the assessment. Clarity here is vital, since the use of an inappropriate assessment strategy can be misleading. As yet, even those instruments that have to some extent been standardized and might be used to compare one population with another, have necessarily been developed on small populations, and thus the comparisons lack rigor. Despite this limitation, such instruments may be very effective for internal comparisons within a restricted setting and may, for example, be used to screen clients for more detailed assessments.

Before considering the techniques of assessment, it is important to remember that good assessment will usually demand the pooling of several different sources and types of information. The mentally retarded, like everyone else, show different behaviors in response to different situations, a trivial and obvious point that nevertheless is easily overlooked. Moreover, different informants have different biases. For example, what is acceptable behavior to the staff of a large institution may be highly disturbing to the family in the natural home setting. In the psychiatric assessment of the mentally retarded, it is common to find that the history and description of behavior obtained from others is distorted both by exceptional sensitivity to specific behaviors and by the familiarity of long experience. On the whole the latter is the more serious, for significant behavior can be overlooked or tolerated by experienced staff, and thus the patient is deprived of the opportunity for treatment. Assessment, therefore, should not rely on a single informant, and should preferably include *direct observation* in as wide a variety of settings as possible. Although the profoundly mentally retarded individual may not be able to contribute much, self-report by the mild and moderately mentally retarded individual is also an essential part of the assessment.

• CLINICAL ASSESSMENT •

The classic psychiatric inquiry is usually based on the medical model, in which the history of the patient's complaint and other symptoms elicited by inquiry is recorded before the physician proceeds to a physical examination, and leads eventually to investigations which elaborate, confirm, or make improbable the diagnosis suggested by the history. Despite attempts to codify a mental status examination, the psychiatrist is also heavily influenced not only by what the patient reports but by the manner in which he or she reports it as well. Consider, for example, a patient who complains of a loss of appetite and weight, disturbed sleep, and lack of energy, but states that his or her mood is normal. If the individual seems reluctant to speak and moves slowly, looks miserable, and is unable to respond with a smile, the psychiatrist is likely to decide that the patient is depressed. If the patient, while expressing appropriate concern, presents the symptoms briskly and willingly, and can at least present a wry humor about his or her condition, the psychiatrist will be more willing to consider a possible physical cause. Although the mental status can be considered one aspect of the assessment, it is often observed mainly in the course of eliciting the history of the problem, and formal examination is only used to confirm or refine these observations.

Hence arises the difficulty that many psychiatrists have in assessing the psychiatric status of the more severely mentally retarded population. The formal assessment of mental status in the absence of history is both a difficult and an unfamiliar task, but unwary psychiatrists have been led to believe that a mentally retarded patient can report little about his or her own condition. Even when a moderately mentally retarded patient is assessed, it is wise to adopt a style common in child psychiatry and to take the history from the patient and another informant together, encouraging the patient to contribute comment or corrections as he or she wishes. At the lesser levels of mental retardation (i.e., mild), the patient can and should contribute most of the history, though it is essential (and sensible) to seek some report from knowledgeable others for corroboration, as is usual in psychiatric assessment. Indeed, it should be remembered that psychiatric illness may prompt the patient to express ideas which, when he or she is well, might seem beyond the patient's understanding (Reid, 1972a).

In assessing the more severely mentally retarded, it is difficult to put too much emphasis on the importance of assessment over time. Only prolonged observation of behavior, weight, sleep changes, and so on, will reveal recurrent affective disorder in those with severely impaired language. The limitations of a single assessment must be recognized and respected. Such observation is best carried out by those who know the patient well and see him or her often, preferably using one of the standardized scales described in the following paragraphs.

Even with the reservations already stated, the clinical assessment of mental status in an unfamiliar mentally retarded patient may be very difficult. Although adequate psychometric reports may be available, it is best to explore current intellectual functioning, orientation, and awareness, since clinical interviewing may reveal new qualitative aspects of intellectual functioning and unexpected discrepancies from previous assessment. Such an exploration may also reveal delusional ideas that would otherwise remain hidden.

Observation of unusual mannerisms and posturing in the severely and profoundly mentally retarded is rarely contributory, particularly if the patient has been in institutional care for some time. Many odd mannerisms, behavioral stereotypies, and even catatonia can occur in isolation in the more severely mentally retarded. Since Kraepelin's original work it has been suggested that these are signs of schizophrenia, but most experts now share Penrose's doubts about the significance of such signs (Penrose, 1963).

Because of the difficulties of assessing the significance of both verbal and nonverbal behavior in the most severely developmentally handicapped, it is probably best to describe the behavior as objectively as possible but without resort to technical terms. If this is done, the psychiatrist provides descriptive benchmarks, against which further progress may be measured, without inviting diagnostic confusion.

Quantification of the disability should always be attempted. The simplest technique is to compare the patient with those of one's own previous clinical experience. To say the patient is significantly depressed is not particularly helpful, but to say that the patient is "at least as depressed as 80 percent of those patients of normal ability whom I have treated as outpatients," or that "most patients I've seen who are as depressed as this have had to be admitted to a hospital" is useful to nonpsychiatrically trained staff. The adaptive functioning scale in DSM-III is not well suited for this purpose but does suggest criteria that can be used as models for the measurement of the added disability of psychiatric disorder in the mentally retarded.

Finally, it is helpful to make sure that omissions are as significant as statements of positive findings by using a standardized checklist of symptoms and signs with which the assessment can be recorded. Several such instruments are in common use (e.g., Mezzich, Dow, Rich, Costello, & Himmelhoch, 1981) and make it possible to record in a narrative report only the detail needed to substantiate positive findings. Although there is research potential in a widely used format, many clinicians will prefer to develop their own system adapted to the needs of a specific patient population. Mezzich et al. (1981) outline some of the details which need to be considered if this is to be attempted.

• STANDARDIZED ASSESSMENTS •

Standardized assessment may be used by a trained psychiatrist, but if suitably devised it can also be used by other staff using their own reports or reports by knowledgeable informants, to assess the status of the patient compared with the normative population and to provide a potential measure of change. Higher functioning patients may themselves provide verbal reports that can contribute to the behavioral assessment.

Daniels and Stewart (1972) report the use of a series of self-report scales for young adults in the IQ range 50–80 (mean IQ 64.5) to assess the relationship between self-concept, vocational adjustment, and perceived parental behavior, although the items were adjusted to be readable at a fourth-grade level and were read to the subject by the interviewer. The Laurelton Self-Concept Scale (Guthrie, Butler, & Garow, 1961) has, of course, been widely used with mildly to moderately mentally retarded subjects, and factor analysis (Harrison & Budoff, 1971) suggests that much of the content of this scale taps psychiatrically relevant concepts. The relationship of this and other similar scales to clinical assessment is still uncertain.

Although the use of patients' relatives and other nonprofessional caretakers as informants is relatively unexplored, it appears to have considerable potential. The Child Behavior Checklist (Achenbach & Edelbrock, 1981), which is completed by parents, has been used successfully on a group of mild to moderately mentally retarded children (Edelbrock, 1981), and it seems likely that such instruments as the John Hopkins symptom checklist (SCL 90) or the Health Screening Questionnaire (Goldberg, Rickels, Downing, & Hesbacher, 1976) could be used successfully on a comparable adult population using informants who know the subject well enough to be able to corroborate his or her own report.

For planning purposes the relatively crude data provided by Kushlick's (Kushlick, Blanden, & Cox, 1973) Social and Physical Incapacity (SPI), and Social and Speech, Self-Help and Literacy (SSL) scales, may be sufficient (Kushlick & Cox, 1967; Kushlick, 1975). Although the behavioral information contained is very restricted and does not address specific psychiatric problems, the scales have proved useful in the assessment of patients in a large population sample when services were reorganized. Personal experience suggests that most of the psychopathology encountered in the moderately to profoundly handicapped is among those individuals with high behavior disorder scores on the SPI, and so the scales could be used as a quick screening test. A more detailed scale for the evaluation of the specific behaviors of severely mentally retarded individuals, using community respondents, is not yet available.

More instruments are available when the staff of hospitals, schools, or other institutions can act as informants, although the choice is still limited. Moore, et al. (1968) describe a "census" form which includes 21 behavioral items, each rated on a four-point frequency scale, which proved feasible to administer to the combined populations of 19 institutions across 13 states. The scale was adapted to measure current status by James, Spencer, and Hamilton (1975) and in this form proved sensitive enough to identify behavioral changes that occurred when patients were moved from one institution to another. It should be noted that these and similar scales, although they will measure gross changes in a disturbed population, are essentially screening devices and unlikely to be sensitive to the measurement of subtle behavioral change in individuals.

Many instruments devised for patients attending or residing in institutions are either unstandardized or standardized on a small population. Even the AAMD Adaptive Behavior Scales (Nihira, Foster, Shellhaas, & Leland, 1974), standardized on a much larger population than is often the case, are based on small numbers in many of the age–sex cells in the standardization sample. The AAMD scale has been criticized for difficulties in administration and scoring (Sparrow & Cichetti, 1978), perhaps because it requires definite statements to be made about areas of behavior in which genuine uncertainty can exist. This has been overcome in other instruments by interviewing the informant, when greater consistency can be obtained at the expense of staff time (e.g., Sparrow & Cichetti, 1978). Since there are many occasions when the comparisons to be made by the scale require good test–retest reliability rather than exportability or the ability to compare one population with another, consistent local ad hoc rules may overcome this difficulty. Even relatively simple ad hoc scales, if carefully administered, can be useful for measuring change in disturbed behavior (e.g., Hunter & Stephenson, 1963; Al-Kaisi & McGuire, 1974).

If a skilled clinician or specifically trained behavioral–psychiatric interviewer is available, more refined instruments can be used. For children the most sophisticated is probably the scale for the Diagnosis of Psychotic Behavior in Children (Haracopos & Kelstrup, 1978), which relies on a schedule sent to the adult who has closest contact with the child. The schedule is completed after three weeks' observation, and the informant is interviewed by the clinician. The target behaviors addressed by the DIPBEC are largely restricted to those of psychotic children, so that other psychiatrically abnormal behavior seen in the mentally retarded may be excluded.

An alternative structured interview schedule, the Children's Handicap, Behavior and Skills (HBS) Schedule, has been devised by Wing and Gould (1978) for use with mentally retarded or psychotic children. Unfortunately, the authors state that their own training program is essential for the adequate use of this schedule, which restricts its availability. They also advise that it be used in conjunction with observation of the child, although an observation system is not provided.

When skilled clinicians are available to make the assessment, clinical skills may be utilized to elicit aspects of behavior and the history that may not emerge from more structured interviewing and observation. The value of such assessments for research and the evaluation of programs and treatment, however, may be increased by the use of ratings. Thus, Ballinger, Armstrong, Presly, and Reid (1975) have shown that the Manifest Abnormalities Scale of Goldberg's Clinical Interview Schedule (Goldberg et al., 1976) can be applied to the assessment of the severely mentally retarded with little modification. Reid and his colleagues (Reid, Ballinger, & Heather, 1978) incorporated this into an assessment procedure in which nurses' ratings and ratings made from hospital records were combined with the Manifest Abnormalities Scale to develop a cluster analysis of behavioral syndromes in a population of severely and profoundly mentally retarded adults in institutional care.

Even when direct assessment of the patient is not possible, it should not be forgotten that official institutional records may still contain enough archival material to allow meaningful ratings of behaviors and skills. Another example of this approach is that of Vogel, Kin, and Meshorer (1969), in which it was possible to predict successful functioning after institutional release and changes in adaptive behavior under conditions of environmental enrichment or deprivation.

Direct observation is, of course, a powerful tool for the assessment of behavioral change, and the many techniques of time and event sampling that have been developed in recent years, particularly to evaluate behavioral treatment, are too extensive to review here (see Shapiro & Barrett, 1982). When the course of an individual patient is being followed and target behaviors can be specified, these methods offer a straightforward technology that is usually much more sensitive than any techniques designed to compare the individual with a reference population.

• CONCLUSION •

The assessment of individuals is most valuable when based on firsthand knowledge collected over a period of time (Medynska & Kuzak, 1974) or based on detailed information from knowledgeable informants who have daily contact with the person being assessed. It is not unusual to ask a consultant to assess a patient on the basis of a single examination, which is inevitably less satisfactory. Both single assessments and observation over time can be strengthened considerably by the use of systematic measurements, and a wide variety have been reviewed in this chapter. Given the difficulties of psychiatric diagnosis in the mentally retarded, it is desirable to make as much use as possible of objective measurement. Only this approach will allow the psychiatrist to disentangle the relative contribution of transient psychiatric disorder and basic disabilities to the current functioning of the individual, for only measurement will allow any reliable empirical appraisal of the effects of specific treatments.

The specific contribution of the powerful psychopharmacologic agents presently available to improve behavior in the mentally retarded population is still unclear, but many professionals now suspect that such drugs are being misused (Lipman, 1970; Sprague & Baxley, 1978; Gualtieri & Hawk, 1980; Hughes, 1977). This problem can only be resolved by a much more careful evaluation of drug effects, such as is detailed by Breuning and Poling in the ensuing chapter on pharmacotherapy, to which good psychiatric assessment can make an important contribution. Careful behavioral assessment, such as that detailed by Shapiro and Barrett (1982), is also required for planning and programmatic change, and the techniques reviewed can be applied to these problems as well. The contribution of psychiatry to the contemporary problems of mental retardation is so poorly developed that there is ample space for a more modern and critical approach to this challenge.

• REFERENCES •

Achenbach, T. M., & Edelbrock, C. S. Behavioral problems and competencies reported by parents of normal and disturbed children aged four through sixteen. *Monographs of the Society for Research in Child Development*, 1981, *46*, (1, Serial No. 188).

Al-Kaisi, A. H., & McGuire, R. J. The effect of sulthiame on disturbed behaviour in mentally subnormal patients. *British Journal of Psychiatry*, 1974, *124*, 45–49.

Ballinger, B. R., Armstrong, J., Presly, A. S., & Reid, A. H. Use of a standardized psychiatric interview in mentally handicapped patients. *British Journal of Psychiatry*, 1975, *127*, 540–544.

Ballinger, B. R. & Reid, A. H. Psychiatric disorder in an adult training centre and a hospital for the mentally handicapped. *Psychological Medicine*, 1977, *7*, 525–528.

Browne, R. A., Gunzberg, H. C., Johnston-Hannah, L. G. W., MacColl, K., Oliver, B., & Thomas, A. Symposium on the "Hospitalized" patient in the community. *British Journal of Mental Subnormality*, 1971, *17*, 7–24.

Burton, A. Psychotherapy with the mentally retarded. *American Journal of Mental Deficiency*, 1954, *58*, 486–489.

Craft, M. Mental disorder in the defective: A psychiatric survey among in-patients. *American Journal of Mental Deficiency*, 1959, *64*, 829–834.

Daniels, L. K., & Stewart, J. A. The use of verbal self-reports with the educable mentally retarded. *Training School Bulletin*, 1972, *68*, 212–216.

Duff, R., LaRocca, J., Lizzet, A., Martin, P., Pearce, L., Williams, M., & Peck, C. A comparison of the fears of mildly retarded adults with children of their mental age and chronological age matched controls. *Journal of Behavior Therapy and Experimental Psychiatry*, 1981, *12*, 121–124.

Edelbrock, C. S. Personal communication, 1981.

Foa, E. B., & Steketee, G. S. Obsessive–compulsives: Conceptual issues and treatment interventions. In M. Hersen, R. M. Eister, & R. Miller (Eds.), *Progress in behavior modification* (Vol. 8). New York: Academic Press, 1979.

Forrest, A. D., & Ogunremi, O. O. The prevalence of psychiatric illness in a hospital for the mentally handicapped. *Health Bulletin*, 1974, *32*(5), 199–202.

Goldberg, D. P., Rickels, K., Downing, R., & Hesbacher, P. A comparison of two psychiatric screening tests. *British Journal of Psychiatry*, 1976, *129*, 61–67.

Gualtieri, C. T., & Hawk, B. Tardive dyskinesia and other drug-induced movement disorders among handicapped children and youth. *Applied Research in Mental Retardation*, 1980, *1*, 55–69.

Guthrie, G., Butler, A., & Garow, L. Patterns of self-attitudes of retardates. *American Journal of Mental Deficiency*, 1961, *66*, 222–229.

Haracopos, D., & Kelstrup, A. Psychotic behavior in children under the institutions for the mentally retarded in Denmark. *Journal of Autism and Childhood Schizophrenia*, 1978, *8*(1), 1–12.

Harrison, R. H., & Budoff, M. A factor analysis of the Laurelton Self-Concept Scale. *American Journal of Mental Deficiency*, 1971, *76*:4, 416–459.

Hayman, M. The interrelations of mental defect and mental disorder. *Journal of Mental Science*, 1939, *85*, 1183–1193.

Heaton-Ward, A. Psychosis in mental handicap. *British Journal of Psychiatry*, 1977, *130*, 525–533.

Hughes, P. S. Survey of medication in a subnormality hospital. *British Journal of Mental Subnormality*, 1977, *23*, 88–94.

Hunter, H., & Stephenson, G. M. Chlorpromazine and Trifluoperazine in the treatment of behavioural abnormalities in the severely subnormal child. *British Journal of Psychiatry*, 1963, *109*, 411–417.

James, F. E., Spencer, D. A., & Hamilton, M. Immediate effects of improved hospital environment on behaviour patterns of mentally handicapped patients. *British Journal of Psychiatry*, 1975, *126*, 577–581.

Kushlick, A. Epidemiology and evaluation of services for the mentally handicapped. In M. J. Begab and J. A. Richards (Eds.), *The mentally retarded and society*. Baltimore: University Park Press, 1975.

Kushlick, A., Blunden, R., & Cox, G. A method of rating behaviour characteristics for use in large scale surveys of mental handicap. *Psychological Medicine*, 1973, *3*, 466–478.

Kushlick, A., & Cox, G. The ascertained prevalence of mental subnormality in the Wessex Region on 1st July, 1963. In *Proceedings of the First Congress of the International Association for the Scientific Study of Mental Deficiency* (Montpelier). St. Lawrence's Hospital: Caterham, September, 1967.

Leck, I., Gordon, W. L., & McKeown, T. Medical and social needs of patients in hospital for the mentally subnormal. *British Journal of Preventative Social Medicine,* 1967, *21*, 115–121.

Lipman, R. S. The use of psychopharmacological agents in residential facilities for the retarded. In F. J. Menolascino (Ed.), *Psychiatric approaches to mental retardation.* New York: Basic Books, 1970.

Lotter, V. Epidemiology of autistic conditions in young children: I. Prevalence. *Social Psychiatry,* 1966, *1*, 124–137.

Medynska, L., & Kuzak, K. Psychotic disturbances in mentally retarded youths. *Psychiatria Polska,* 1974, *8*, 301–306.

Menolascino, F. J. Emotional disturbances in mentally retarded children. *Archives of General Psychiatry,* 1968, *19*, 456–464.

Mezzich, J. E., Dow, J. T., Rich, C. L., Costello, A. J., & Himmelhoch, J. M. Developing an efficient information system for a comprehensive psychiatric institute: II. Initial evaluation form. *Behavior Research Methods and Instrumentation,* 1981, *13*(4), 464–478.

Moor, L. Criteres psychologiques des psychosis chez oligophrenes. *Revue de Neuropsychiatrie Infantile,* 1968, *16*, 211–217.

Moore, B. C., Thuline, J. C., & Capes, L. Mongoloid and non-mongoloid retardates: A behavioral comparison. *American Journal of Mental Deficiency,* 1968, *83*, 433–436.

Nihira, K., Foster, R., Shellhaas, M., & Leland, J. *AAMD Adaptive Behavior Scale* (Rev. ed.). Washington, D.C.: American Association on Mental Deficiency, 1974.

Penrose, L. S. *A clinical and genetic study of 1280 cases of mental defect.* London: Institute for Research into Mental and Multiple Handicap, 1963.

Philips, I., & Williams, N. Psychopathology and mental retardation. A study of 100 mentally retarded children: I. Psychopathology. *American Journal of Psychiatry,* 1975, *132*(12), 1265–1271.

Pollock, H. M. Mental disease among mental defectives. *American Journal of Psychiatry,* 1944, *101*, 361–363.

Reid, A. H. Psychoses in adult mental defectives: I. Manic depressive psychosis. *British Journal of Psychiatry,* 1972a, *120*, 205–212.

Reid, A. H. Psychoses in adult mental defectives: II. Schizophrenic and paranoid psychoses. *British Journal of Psychiatry,* 1972b, *120*, 213–218.

Reid, A. H. Psychiatric disturbances in the mentally handicapped. *Proceedings of the Royal Society of Medicine,* 1976, *69*, 509–512.

Reid, A. H., Ballinger, B. R., & Heather, B. B. Behavioural syndromes identified by cluster analysis in a sample of 100 severely and profoundly retarded adults. *Psychological Medicine,* 1978, *8*, 399–412.

Reid, A. H., & Naylor, G. J. Short-cycle manic depressive psychosis in mental defectives: A clinical and physiological study. *Journal of Mental Deficiency Research,* 1976, *20*, 67–76.

Rutter, M., Tizard, J., & Whitmore, K. *Education, Health and Behavior.* London: Longman, 1970.

Shapiro, E. S., & Barrett, R. P. Behavioral assessment of the mentally retarded. In J. L. Matson & F. Andrasik (Eds.), *Treatment issues and innovations in mental retardation.* New York: Plenum Press, 1982.

Sparrow, S. S., & Cicchetti, D. V. Behavior rating inventory for moderately, severely, and profoundly retarded persons. *American Journal of Mental Deficiency,* 1978, *82*(4), 365–374.

Sprague, R., & Baxley, G. Drugs used for the management of behavior in mental retardation. In J. Wortis (Ed.), *Mental retardation* (Vol. 10). New York: Brunner/Mazel, 1978.

Vogel, W., Kin, K. J., & Meshorer, E. Determinants of institutional release and prognosis in mental retardates. *Journal of Abnormal Psychology,* 1969, *74*(6), 685–692.

Walls, R. T., Werner, T. J., Bacon, A., & Zane, T. Behavior checklists. In J. D. Cone & R. P. Hawkins (Eds.), *Behavioral assessment: New directions in clinical psychology.* New York: Brunner/Mazel, 1977.

Williams, C. E. III–A study of the patients in a group of mental subnormality hospitals. *British Journal of Mental Subnormality,* 1971, *17,* 29–41.

Wing, L., & Gould, J. Systematic recording of behaviors and skills of retarded and psychotic children. *Journal of Autism and Childhood Schizophrenia,* 1978, *8*(1), 79–97.

three

Current Models of Psychopathology

••

Edward A. Konarski, Jr.
Albert R. Cavalier

Theories of psychological disturbance have contributed to an understanding of the dynamics of psychopathology, led to the development of various psychotherapeutic techniques, and guided researchers at both basic and applied levels. Traditionally, these theories were on a large scale and attempted to account for normal as well as abnormal functioning (e.g., Erikson, 1950; Freud, 1966; Lewin, 1935; Sullivan, 1940). In recent times, the support of these grand models appears to be declining as theorists have tended to limit their range of coverage to specific abnormal conditions (e.g., autism, phobia, schizophrenia, stereotypic behavior, self-injurious behavior). In addition, recent theories tend to have a behavioral rather than a psychodynamic orientation (Baumeister & Rollings, 1976; Singh, 1981).

Only a few of these smaller theories were designed to address the special consideration of mental retardation. Typically, mental retardation has been seen simply as a specific pathology and interpreted as such in light of the particular theory (e.g., Pearson, 1942; Lewin, 1935). Although theories using this approach may mention specific psychological disturbances of the mentally retarded, they do not usually speak to this issue.

The authors' review of the relevant literature confirms this idea. Although some practitioners have developed theoretical models for treating psychological disturbances in the mentally retarded (e.g., Sternlicht, 1977), few formal theories concerning the *development* of psychological disturbance in this population could be found. Recent theorizing has, instead, been limited to post hoc speculation on individual cases or to the adaption and application of the large-scale theories developed for use with intellectually normal populations.

One reason comprehensive theories have not been developed and tested may be the often-reported finding that retarded individuals manifest essentially the same emotional disorders as nonretarded persons (e.g., Menolascino, 1969; Philips, 1967). This finding has led to the conclusion that these disturbances may be due to similar factors across the populations (Philips & Williams, 1977), with the retarded simply being more susceptible to their effects (Menolascino, 1977). Hence, practitioners may have felt it sufficient to rely on adapted versions of past theories (e.g., Sternlicht, 1976) which have proven adequate with intellectually normal populations.

An apparently overlooked potential shortcoming of this approach is its failure to recognize the fact that, probably because of their cognitive deficits, retarded individuals sometimes adapt and react to environmental events differently from their nonretarded peers (see Ellis, 1979). Therefore, although mentally retarded individuals display many of the same disturbances as others and many of the same potential etiological factors appear to be involved, it may not be safe to conclude that the dynamics leading to psychological disturbances in the mentally retarded are identical to those in nonretarded individuals. Ultimately, this theoretical confusion seems to result from the often entangled, descriptive labels of mental retardation and mental illness and the similarity of the factors that have been postulated to account for their development.

This chapter will review two dominant psychological models for explaining and treating abnormal behavior in the mentally retarded, namely, the psychoanalytic (Freud, 1966) and behavioral (e.g., Agras, Kazdin, & Wilson, 1979) approaches. After the models are outlined, the specific adaptations of the models to psychopathology in the retarded will be discussed. A hypothetical case of psychological disturbance in a mentally retarded person will then be analyzed from the perspective of each of these approaches.

• PSYCHOANALYTIC MODEL •

The psychoanalytic approach to understanding abnormal behavior (Freud, 1966) borrows the disease concept of psychopathology from the medical model (see Craighead, Kazdin, & Mahoney, 1981). However, whereas the medical model attributes the symptoms of abnormality to physiological causes, intrapsychic conflict is seen as the root of all problems in the psychoanalytic model (Brenner, 1974). This conflict results from the dynamic interaction of the three components of the mind: the id, ego, and superego. In essence, this dynamic interaction is hypothesized to produce abnormal behavior just as a disease results in symptoms.

• Basic Assumptions •

The two fundamental hypotheses of the psychoanalytic model of behavior are "the principle of psychic determinism, or causality, and the proposition that consciousness is an exceptional rather than a regular attribute of psychic processes" (Brenner, 1974, p. 2). The first principle holds that nothing in the mind happens by chance, that is, all psychic events are the result of those which preceded it. Therefore, all psychic events are important and have significance no matter how unrelated or meaningless they appear on the surface. Furthermore, behavior, whether normal or symptomatic of psychic trauma, is considered the result of these psychic events. The fact that a person might be unaware of the impact of these events on his or her behavior does not minimize their importance. This idea is related to the second fundamental hypothesis; that is, in psychoanalytic theory, the conscious aspect of the mind is the least critical level of consciousness for understanding human behavior because the dynamic interactions controlling behavior take place primarily at the unconscious level. In essence, we are typically unaware of the factors controlling our everyday behavior. This idea contrasts sharply with many other theories of behavior (Brenner, 1974). The only way to determine these unconscious processes according to the psychoanalytic model, is through the indirect techniques developed from psychoanalysis, such as free association and dream analysis.

• Psychic Energy •

Freud viewed the mind as a closed system driven by inborn psychological energy, which he referred to as drives (Brenner, 1974). These drives produce a state of psychic excitation which results in psychic functioning and, ultimately, behavior. This functioning typically results in the cessation of the excitation.

Freud (1966) postulated two basic human drives, the sexual or erotic aspect of functioning and the aggressive or destructive aspect. Although he distinguished between them, he made it clear that all behaviors are a product of the effects of both. There is no place in Freudian theory for a behavior resulting exclusively from the sexual or aggressive drive, but there are situations in which one drive may dominate the other (Brenner, 1974).

Each drive generates a type of psychic energy. The sexual drive results in energy called libido, whereas the aggressive drive produces energy sometimes referred to as *destrudo* or *thanatos* (Robinson & Robinson, 1965) but usually just called aggressive energy (Brenner, 1974). Both types of energy are present at birth and immediately begin to affect psychic functioning. They remain present and virtually unchanged throughout a person's life; however, they find expression in different ways at different times, thus leading to the Freudian concept of stages of development. The major stages of development, in order, are the oral, anal, phallic, and genital. These stages are named for the primary area of the body through which the person seeks to satisfy the drive energy.

• *Psychic Apparatus* •

Although Freud developed several conceptualizations of the mind, his latest, referred to as the structural hypothesis (Bemporad, 1980), is the most familiar. In it, he postulated three basic structures of the mind defined according to their unique contents and functions. He called these three basic structures the id, ego, and superego.

The id is present at birth and is the source of all psychic energy throughout life. It operates according to the pleasure principle, meaning it demands immediate satisfaction of its drives, is illogical, has little regard for reality, and is self-centered. The id undergoes little developmental change.

The ego is that aspect of the mind concerned with one's relationship to the environment (Brenner, 1974). It operates according to the reality principle in its attempts to adapt to the environment. It is the rational aspect of our mind which carries on many of our basic intellectual functions and allows us to perceive the consequences of our behavior (Robinson & Robinson, 1965). Its relationship to the id is that of executant of the drives (Brenner, 1974). However, a normally functioning ego will satisfy the demands of the id in socially acceptable ways.

The ego begins differentiation from the id because of the effects of the external environment within the first six months after birth and continues to develop throughout life, although it is well-developed by about the age of two to three years. The ego attains its own unique character and power through development of control over motor functioning, the acquisition of memories, thought, and affect. However, perhaps the most significant mechanism of ego development, especially early in life, is identification. This involves a person "becoming like something or someone in one or several aspects of thought or behavior" (Brenner, 1974, p. 41).

The superego is the self-evaluative aspect of the mind, sometimes referred to as the conscience (Robinson & Robinson, 1965). However, in addition to performing this function, the superego also contains our ideal aspirations of the way things should be. In short, it functions as the moral aspect of the mind. As with the previous structures, it performs these functions at the unconscious level. It begins its differentiation from the ego early in life, with its primary development occurring as a result of the Oedipal complex during the phallic stage. The Oedipal complex involves two deep emotions of the child. The first is an intense desire for a love relationship with the opposite-sex parent, and the second is hate and a desire to eliminate the same-sex parent. Practical circumstances prohibit fulfillment of these desires, and resolution is achieved through their repression and identification with both parents (Brenner, 1974). Through identification, the child adopts the moral aspects of the parents and their ideal aspirations about the world.

• Anxiety and the Defense Mechanisms •

Anxiety is a biologically based uncomfortable state that, consistent with the pleasure principle, a person works to avoid. According to Brenner (1974), it results from an influx of stimulation, typically from the id that the ego cannot immediately handle (traumatic anxiety) or from events that predict the onset of this influx (signal anxiety).

The defense mechanisms are functions used by the ego to guard against anxiety. They operate at the unconscious level, deny or distort reality, and are generally successful in reducing anxiety. The development and maintenance of the defense mechanisms requires a large investment of the energy the ego has appropriated for its use from the id.

Individuals sometimes employ many different defense mechanisms (see Brenner, 1974; Robinson & Robinson, 1965). Some, such as denial, regression, repression, and isolation, are considered immature and primitive whereas projection, sublimation, and reaction formation are characterized as mature defense mechanisms (Robinson & Robinson, 1965). It is important to acknowledge that use of defense mechanisms does not necessarily imply psychopathology, for they are also characteristic of normal psychic functioning.

• Psychopathology •

The psychoanalytic model describes no sharp division between abnormal and normal behavior. As stated, all individuals rely on defense mechanisms, and it is assumed that no one escapes the entire developmental sequence without encountering some sort of trauma. The subjective guidelines of the degree to which a person can experience pleasure and adapt to the environment have been suggested as criteria for determining normality or abnormality (Brenner, 1974).

Abnormal behavior itself is best understood as an indication of disturbance within the psychic apparatus in terms of either structure or function (Brenner, 1974). The etiology of this psychic disturbance lies in constitutional and experiential factors beginning very early in life as the child passes through the stages of psychosexual development (Brenner, 1974). Each stage produces its own unique challenges as the drive energy seeks expression in different ways and reality places different demands on the child. Therefore, there are many potential factors which might contribute to a disturbance in development. Essentially, the child must develop an ego and, later, a superego, capable of satisfying the drives of the id but only in conjunction with the demands of reality. An ego incapable of effectively developing and using mature defense mechanisms while adapting to reality, or an over- or under-developed superego, will produce an imbalance in the structure. Ultimately, this will result in some abnormal behavior, the extent of the abnormality being related to the size of the disturbance.

The psychoanalytic model also postulates that disturbances at each stage of development result in character disorders specific to that stage. In brief, a person fixated (i.e., showing little psychic development beyond a certain point) at the oral stage will develop the character traits of excessive passivity and dependency. One fixated at the anal stage is a possessive, obstinate, and miserly person, and an individual fixated at the phallic stage will likely have disturbed heterosexual relationships among other neurotic symptoms (Bemporad, 1980).

• Implications for the Mentally Retarded •

It appears that the basic drives postulated by psychoanalysts for non-retarded persons remain essentially the same in the mentally retarded (Robinson & Robinson, 1976). Furthermore, the flow of psychic energy across the stages of development remains the same. However, it has been postulated that retarded children go through these stages more slowly (Sternlicht, 1976) and show poorer resolution of the conflicts present at each stage (Robinson & Robinson, 1965). The slow progress through the stages results not only from the child's delayed cognitive development but also from the overall delay with which the mentally retarded child abandons primitive modes of behavior (Robinson & Robinson, 1965). The mentally retarded child appears more prone to fixation at a particular stage, which makes less energy available for later resolution of conflicts.

It seems clear that psychopathology associated with mental retardation from the psychoanalytic perspective is primarily a deficit in ego functioning (Balthazar & Stevens, 1975; Pearson, 1942; Robinson & Robinson, 1965; Sternlich, 1976). This defective functioning results from inadequate ego development very early in life produced by the child's cognitive deficits which severely limit reality testing, the anticipation of the consequences of behavior, and the development of higher cognitive functions such as language.

The deficient ego finds itself with the difficult task of facing the demands of reality while controlling the drive energy of the id, which presumably remains intact in the mentally retarded (Pearson, 1942). To do this, mentally retarded persons have an increased need for defense mechanisms, however, they do not use them very effectively (Balthazar & Stevens, 1975) and tend to rely on the more primitive ones (Robinson & Robinson, 1965).

The abnormal development of the ego adversely affects superego development. Rather than developing the capacity to perform its evaluative function in line with reality, it remains immature, inflexible, and unduly harsh throughout life (Robinson & Robinson, 1965). These characteristics establish the superego as one more source of difficulty for the ego of the mentally retarded person.

• Psychopathology and Mental Retardation •

Comparing the previous sections on psychopathology and implications for the mentally retarded, it is readily apparent that the psychoanalytic model would predict a high rate of emotional disorder and adjustment problems in mentally retarded persons. From the psychoanalytic viewpoint, the mentally retarded child is highly susceptible to all forms of psychopathology. In fact, one theorist believes that many of the behavioral correlates of mental retardation (e.g., rigidity, impulsivity, distractibility) reflect inadequate ego development as much as they do mental retardation (Sternlicht, 1976).

There has been no shortage of theoretical suggestions concerning the development of psychological disturbance in the mentally retarded from the psychoanalytic perspective. For self-injurious behavior alone, Baumeister and Rollings (1976) listed four different psychodynamic interpretations and Singh (1981) listed as many for rumination. It appears that the number of disruptive factors surrounding the development of the mentally retarded personality offers the psychodynamic theorist many options for interpreting the variety of pathologies associated with this population. Rather than review all of these, this section will summarize the more general conditions of the mentally retarded which have been implicated by psychoanalysts as particularly critical in the development of psychological disturbance and review some examples of specific disorders often associated with the mentally retarded.

Immediately after birth, many factors arise in the life of the mentally retarded child which have been theoretically linked by the psychoanalytic model to the development of psychological disturbance. The first, and most important, category of these factors are those which affect the child's interaction with his or her parents. Factors that are potentially detrimental to this interaction include the suggestions of Sternlicht and Deutsch (1972) that parents of the mentally retarded may show overt rejection of the child, generally provide less love and support, often feel guilty over the condition of the child, and tend to foster the dependent behavior of the child. Other factors that may interfere with normal parent–child interactions include the findings that parents of mentally retarded children perceive them as younger (Sternlicht, 1976), view them more negatively (Waisbren, 1980), and may be more likely to engage in child abuse (Frodi, 1981).

A second category of factors are those which disrupt general familial interactions. An example of these factors is the increased familial stress resulting from having a mentally retarded child (Friedrich & Friedrich, 1981). Evidence for this stress is given by statistics which show that the divorce rate for parents of mentally retarded children is three times that of other parents and their suicide rate is twice the national average (see Sternlicht & Deutsch, 1972).

Any of these factors could easily be viewed by the mentally retarded child as reflecting a lack of love and acceptance that, it has been hypothesized (Pearson, 1942), causes undue insecurity and anxiety in the mentally retarded child and leaves the child to cope with life differently from the normal child. These feelings are no doubt compounded by the child's perception of his or her own shortcomings and failures and by repeated negative social interactions.

All these potentially ego-crippling experiences have been hypothesized at one time or another as producing a variety of psychological problems. The weakened ego of the mentally retarded person has been suggested as the source of the rigid and stereotyped behavior often seen by this population. For example, repetitive behavior has been viewed as the ego's attempt to maintain an illusion of strength by minimizing the threat of unknown or challenging situations through limiting its boundaries of operation (Sternlicht, 1976). It has also been suggested that rigid behavior patterns might result from the weakened ego's attempt to avoid the super-ego's reprimands for failure by continuing to operate only in those situations in which success is likely (Sternlicht, 1976). These interpretations lead to the conclusion that repetitive, rigid behavior is really a reflection of the ego's attempt to maintain its own integrity.

Alternatively, repetitive behavior of the mentally retarded has been viewed as the expression of an obsessive-compulsive reaction (Sternlicht & Deutsch, 1972). A comprehensive dynamic interpretation of rigidity based on the lack of differentiation of the mentally retarded person has also been suggested by Lewin (1936) and Kounin (1941).[1]

Some of the ego-weakening experiences described have also been

---

[1] For another review of psychodynamic interpretations of stereotypic behavior, the reader is referred to Baumeister (1978).

suggested as causes for the emotional withdrawal sometimes shown by mentally retarded persons (Sternlicht & Deutsch, 1972), the extreme manifestation of which is the development of a schizophrenic reaction. In particular, patterns of repeated rejection and isolation such as might occur in a poorly managed institution have been identified as factors leading to a flat emotional response and apathy on the part of the mentally retarded individual (Goldfarb, 1945). Also, in situations in which this pattern of rejection exists, either at home or in an institution, theorists have suggested that mentally retarded persons may develop a depressive reaction (Sternlicht & Deutsch, 1972). It has also been indicated that this reaction may result from the mentally retarded person's preoccupation with feelings of worthlessness and thoughts of their own shortcomings. Suggested behavioral correlates of this depression are a neglect of self-care responsibilities and sometimes antisocial behavior as a defense against the depression (Berman, 1967). Sternlicht and Deutsch (1972) also suggested that despair may result from repeated rejection, leaving the mentally retarded person void of motivation to continue appropriate interaction with the social environment.

Finally, with regard to ego deficits, the mentally retarded child's underdeveloped ego is often seen as unable to satisfy the instinctual sexual and aggressive urges of the id according to the reality principle because of its inability to use mature defense mechanisms such as sublimation. This results in impulsive behavior and an inability to delay gratification of these drives (Sternlicht & Deutsch, 1972), thus accounting for the high incidence of aggressive behaviors in the mentally retarded and the expression of primitive and immediate modes of sexual satisfaction (e.g., public masturbation). It has also been suggested that a weak superego will likely result in a highly impulsive personality incapable not only of delaying the gratification of impulses but also of assessing the consequences of behavior. This situation also might account for the overt expression of aggressive energy often seen in mentally retarded individuals (Sternlicht, 1976).

A particular source of psychopathology in the mentally retarded is slowness of their passage through and their poor resolution of the stages of psychosexual development. In part, this is no doubt due to their cognitive deficits, however, parental fostering of infantile and dependent behavior could also be a significant factor. The tendency toward fixation at the early levels of development results in the persistence of infantile modes of satisfaction and interaction with the environment and the development and maintenance of so-called immature defense mechanisms (Robinson & Robinson, 1965). One of the most damaging results of this situation in the mentally retarded is that the maintenance of these primitive defense mechanisms requires a large amount of psychic energy, which leaves little energy for the development of mature defense mechanisms and higher order cognitive functions. It appears, therefore, that immature psychic functioning only compounds the deficits already present in the mentally retarded person. Another obvious result of fixation at early levels is the development of the negative character traits mentioned earlier as symptomatic of these infantile stages.

In summary, specific psychopathologies of the mentally retarded have attracted the attention of psychoanalytic theorists. However, in the absence of research support for these interpretations, they must be considered as merely speculative of the dynamics underlying the development of psychological disturbance in this population.

• THE BEHAVIORAL MODEL •

The behavioral model of psychopathology is heavily dependent on the laboratory investigations of Thorndike (1911), Pavlov (1927), and Skinner (1938) and on the applied work of countless therapists since their time. The rise of the behavioral model was a result of the interaction of various philosophical positions and a reaction to various aspects of the medical and psychoanalytical models.

• Basic Assumptions •

Two fundamental characteristics of the behavioral model are (1) a psychological model of human behavior grounded on scientifically established learning principles and (2) critical evaluation of the therapeutic outcome of intervention efforts through scientific methodology (Agras et al., 1979). The behavioral model differs from the others primarily in its conception of the causes of abnormal behavior and the implications for intervention. Whereas the medical and psychoanalytic models view abnormal behavior as merely symptomatic of underlying problems (see Craighead et al., 1981), the behavioral model holds that it is learned, maintained, and displayed by the same principles as normal behavior, some limited exceptions notwithstanding. The behavioral model is not concerned with underlying internal causes of behavior such as repressed desires, minimal brain dysfunction, or low ego strength. The focus is instead on the abnormal behavior itself, and intervention involves manipulation of the contemporary determinants of behavior.

Today, the behavioral model is undergoing change and growth in both nature and scope.

> Clinical practice reflects the development of new techniques and the modification of existing methods; the range of procedures and problems that are

being researched shows exponential growth, and theoretical views, often sharply conflicting, are the subject of lively debate. (Agras et al., 1979, p. 2)

The behavioral model subsumes a variety of different approaches which share the previously mentioned characteristics and assumptions, including applied behavior analysis derived primarily from the work of Skinner (1953), a neobehavioristic mediational model derived primarily from the work of Eysenck (1959) and Wolpe (1958), social learning theory based on the work of Bandura (1977a, b), and cognitive behavior modification based on the work of Beck (1976), Ellis (1970), Mahoney (1974), and Meichenbaum (1977). The efficacy of intervention efforts from these approaches has been demonstrated, in varying degrees, with a variety of problems, including anxiety and phobic reactions; obsessive-compulsive disorders; sexual dysfunctions; transsexualism; exhibitionism; fetishism; marital discord; alcoholism; cigarette smoking; drug use; psychotic disorders; hyperactivity; autism; delinquency; stereotypy; limited self-care; social; communication; gross and fine motor; vocational, recreational, educational, and practical living skills; hypertension; insomnia; self-injury; anorexia nervosa; unemployment; theft; pollution control; and energy conservation.

The behavioral approach most common to the mentally retarded is applied behavior analysis (Baer, Wolf, & Risley, 1968). The central tenets of this approach are that (1) the appropriate focus of study is observable behavior, (2) behavior is a function of its consequences, and (3) the primary area of intervention is the conditions maintaining the presence or absence of the behavior in question. Treatment techniques are derived from operant conditioning principles such as reinforcement, discrimination, generalization, extinction, punishment, response differentiation, and shaping.

In the behavioral approach, the development of a child's motor, perceptual, communicative, intellectual, emotional, and social abilities is a function of progressive changes in the child's interactions with the environment. Behavioral repertoires evolve through complex and multifaceted environmental conditioning. Increasingly sophisticated response classes are controlled by stimulus classes through discrimination and generalization (Bijou & Baer, 1966). Individual differences are based on variations in discriminative stimulus history and reinforcement schedule history. Personality development in particular depends on experience with a variety of stimuli in the presence of which some behaviors are reliably reinforced and in the absence of which those behaviors are not reinforced (Hogg, 1976). For behavior that society labels "normal," the succession of interactions with one's environment is more or less typical for one's culture.

In this behavioral approach, psychopathology represents the absence of adaptive behaviors or the presence of maladaptive behaviors which have been shaped by historical events and maintained by contemporary setting events. That some behaviors are labeled "retarded" and some "emotionally disturbed" is a matter of practical convenience. All are acquired by the same principles, and the implications for remediation are the same. The applied behavior analysis of mental retardation focuses on the processes that prevent, limit, or delay the formation of stimulus-response relationships.

> For the retarded individual, social, physical, and biological conditions of development deviate in the direction of slowing down the pace of successive interactional changes—the more extreme the curtailment of opportunities, the more extreme the retardation. (Bijou, 1966, p. 2)

• Implications for the Mentally Retarded •

The specific form of the behavior pathology for a particular mentally retarded person is a function of four classes of interactions between person and environment (Bijou, 1966). First, a person with abnormal anatomical structure and physiological functioning may have altered stimulus function or response function, with adverse effects on the stimulus-response relationships and the behavioral repertoire. Depending on the type of biological abnormality, the type and amount of opportunities to interact with stimuli essential for normal development will be restricted and some responses will be limited, and others will be impossible. Physical abnormalities can also produce abbreviated or altered interactions with other persons, thereby restricting important social and intellectual stimulation.

Second, abnormal behavior could result from inadequate reinforcement and discrimination histories.

> On the one hand, interactions with environmental events which reinforce, discriminate, and interrelate varieties of culturally serviceable behaviors are expected to produce individuals with large repertoires of socially, intellectually, and vocationally valuable (highly reinforcible) behaviors. . . . On the other hand, environments with meager opportunities for reinforcement, discrimination, and the development of complex stimulus-response chains are expected to produce children with limited repertoires of socially serviceable behaviors. (Bijou, 1966, p. 10)[2]

Inadequate histories result from reinforcement which is infrequent and

---

[2]Reprinted with permission from Bijou, S. W. A functional analysis of retarded development. In N. R. Ellis (Ed.), *International review of research in mental retardation* (Vol. 1). New York: Academic Press, 1966.

insufficient, reinforcement which is absent or administered noncontingently, and limited stimulus-response opportunities. Failure to develop new chains of behavior and to maintain already acquired behavior not only restricts the behavioral repertoire but also precludes the "behavior elaborations" necessary for adequate adjustment. And if opportunities for functional responses are curtailed, either by abnormal parental practices or by too few effective and available people and things, the probability that a child will remain physically uncoordinated, intellectually limited, emotionally immature, and socially unskilled is heightened (Bijou, 1966).

Third, punishment that is inappropriate, severe, or inconsistent may modify functional behavior so that its effectiveness is impaired and may suppress ongoing behavior and strengthen avoidance or withdrawal. These behaviors may be building blocks for further adaptive behavior development, and the situations avoided may include components necessary for proper adjustment. Consequently, development may be retarded and maladjusted behaviors may emerge.

Fourth, inappropriate or maladaptive behavior may develop through contingent reinforcement, such as when a parent attends to a child exhibiting a bizarre gesture or vocalization. If the behavior is aversive to the parent and attending to the behavior reduces that episode, the behavior is positively reinforced by the parents' attention and the attending behavior is negatively reinforced by the termination of the child's behavior. Learning of socially appropriate and more functional behaviors would be reduced and interactions with other people would be discouraged (Bijou, 1966; Bucher & Lovaas, 1968; Forehand & Baumeister, 1976).

The following are descriptions and explanations of some typical pathological behavior patterns of mentally retarded persons in terms of the behavioral approach.

• *Dependency* •

The behavior of many mentally retarded individuals is characterized by a continual beckoning for help or attention from their care givers and a failure to initiate any other actions without direct instruction or assistance. This dependent behavior can be defined as "persistently recurring behavior characterized by the seeking of others and by a lack of achievement or success, which has been caused by an earlier history of reinforcement for seeking others, concurrent with a lack of reinforcement for competence" (Gavalas & Briggs, 1966, p. 101). Normally, children receive reinforcers for approaching their parents and others for competent or adaptive behavior in other situations. Consequently, they behave according to particular concurrent schedules of reinforcement. Dependent behavior emerges when a person's approaches to care givers are reinforced but competent behavior in other situations is ignored or unnoticed. Over time, previously neutral stimuli in the environment become associated with the competent behavior and become discriminative for the associated periods of nonreinforcement. As a result, the frequency of competent behavior decreases, thereby reducing the future probability of obtaining reinforcement for independent accomplishment, while the frequency of behavior directed toward obtaining reinforcement from caregivers increases (Gavalas & Briggs, 1966).

• Self-Injury •

One of the most distinctive and heart-rendering aspects of some mentally retarded persons' functioning is the variety of ways and intensity with which they inflict injury on themselves. Skinner (1953) indicated that an aversive stimulus could function as a conditioned positive reinforcer if it was reliably associated with, and consequently discriminative for, positive reinforcement. In this way, the aversive stimulus can become positively reinforcing.

Research with both animal and human subjects indicates that the initial occurrence of self-injurious behavior may be an unconditioned response which is subsequently shaped by operant reinforcement (Frankel & Simmons, 1976). Naturalistic observations indicate that a low frequency of self-injurious behaviors occurs in the general population of humans (de Lissovoy, 1961; Kravitz, Rosenthal, Teplitz, Murphy, & Lesser, 1960). A mentally retarded person with few competent means of obtaining reinforcement who exhibits unconditional emotional responses that cause self-injury and pain has a high probability of being reinforced by the immediate and intense attention of a nearby care giver. Over time, pain becomes discriminative for reinforcement (Ferster, 1961), the mentally retarded person's tolerance for pain increases (Feirstein & Miller, 1963), and the speed and intensity of the care giver's response to the behavior decreases. Consequently, the intensity of the self-injurious behavior increases and the cycle repeats itself (Lovaas & Simmons, 1969). If this process is accomplished through intermittent schedules of positive reinforcement, then the self-injurious behaviors would be in evidence over considerable periods of time without additional reinforcement (Baumeister & Rollings, 1976).

• Aggression •

Aggressive behavior is a constant problem in many mentally retarded persons in residential facilities which requires valuable time from staff and causes great disruption for the victims (Forehand & Baumeister, 1976). It is proposed that the majority of aggressive behaviors are initially elicited as emotional responses to unpredictable and quickly developing conditions and are operantly shaped by the direct and indirect effects of the acts. Some typical eliciting conditions are temper tantrums, an aggressive act directed toward the person, and creation of an aversive situation by another person. For some individuals, these aggressive behaviors result in positive consequences; for example, the aversive stimulus may be terminated, the aggressive individual may avoid the person in question, a desirable object may be acquired, or considerable attention may be gained from the staff. For persons who have few adaptive or prosocial behaviors to acquire potent reinforcers, the success of these initial aggressive responses is dramatic. Through avoidance and escape conditioning or positive reinforcement, the likelihood of aggressive behavior increases and is maintained. As this process develops, there is reduced probability of adaptive behaviors being learned or becoming as successful as the aggressive behaviors (Bostow & Bailey, 1969; Nordquist & Wahler, 1973).

• *Stereotypy* •

Stereotyped behaviors are highly consistent and repetitious motor or posturing behaviors which are not directly harmful or disruptive to others (Baumeister & Forehand, 1973; Forehand & Baumeister, 1976). They have been observed in approximately 65 percent of the institutionalized mentally retarded (Kaufman & Levitt, 1965). When engaging in stereotyped behaviors, mentally retarded persons are less responsive to environmental events and consequently have reduced opportunities to advance their behavioral repertoires (Koegel & Covert, 1972; Lovaas, Litrownik, & Mann, 1971).

In accounting for stereotyped behaviors, reinforcement is considered to be a result of inward-directed or outward-directed behaviors (Foxx & Azrin, 1973). Reinforcers for inward-directed activities are tactile, proprioceptive, and sensory stimuli, whereas reinforcers for outward-directed activities are usually tangible and social stimuli along with the other reinforcers. Since the outward behaviors typically require more effort and are more sophisticated, mentally retarded persons are less likely to display them at a level of competence sufficient to receive reinforcement. Although the reinforcement for the simple inward behaviors is less potent, it is reinforcement nonetheless. In actuality, frequent and bizarre stereotyped behaviors often receive considerable social reinforcers from care givers. Replacing the inward behaviors with appropriate outward behaviors becomes more difficult as the inward behaviors accumulate a long history. In addition, the more severe the retardation—that is, the more extensive the behavioral deficits—the lower the likelihood of outward behaviors being reinforced and shaped. Over time, stereotyped behaviors dominate because of the absence of competing outward behaviors (Azrin, Kaplan, & Foxx, 1973).

• AN ILLUSTRATIVE CASE •

Joe is a 20-year-old moderately retarded adult living at home with his parents in a middle-class community located in a small midwestern city. His mother has taken primary responsibility for raising him. She quit her job as a schoolteacher when Joe received his diagnosis of mental retardation soon after birth. Since that time she has been active in local advocacy groups for the mentally retarded and has enrolled Joe in several special programs through the years. Joe's father is a salesman for a large manufacturing company. He earns a comfortable income but is very busy and is necessarily away from home two or three days a week. Joe also has an older sister who was recently married and moved to another town.

Joe was a low-birth-weight baby and experienced some major medical complications soon after birth. Since that time he has had no major medical problems. His overall development was delayed since birth. He sat up, walked, and was toilet trained later than the typical age for such milestones. His speech development has been particularly disturbed. Joe's expressive language is very limited and he rarely communicates verbally with others, however, his receptive language is adequate. He attended special public school classes until his 18th birthday, at which time he was enrolled in the local association for retarded citizens' adult training program which he continues to attend.

Joe made adequate progress through school and presented no behavior problem, although he was often slow to comply with teachers' demands, sometimes mouthed his fingers, and engaged in a greater than average amount of rocking behavior. His mother had no major complaints about his behavior other than his occasional finger mouthing. He spent his time at home playing in the back yard (sometimes with his sister, if she was home), in the den watching TV or listening to music, or accompanying his mother while she ran errands. Occasionally, he attended a special event for mentally retarded persons in the community (e.g., field trip) or accompanied his parents on an activity (e.g., movie, sight-seeing, shopping).

Joe began having problems around the time he graduated from public school and started in the local adult training school. At about this time, his sister was married and left home. At the school, he began refusing to comply with the instructions of his teachers. He spent long periods of time sitting in his chair rocking back and forth, sucking his thumb, and staring out the window. Of the six hours he spent at school, approximately one-half were spent engaging in these behaviors. Pleading by the teachers did little to distract him from this activity.

When teachers spoke to Joe's mother about his behavior, she reported that he was also displaying the very same behaviors at home to a greater degree than he ever had before. She also indicated he was spending very little time outside of his room and much less time outside of the house and was becoming increasingly unwilling to attent special events in the community.

When any of his teachers attempted to guide him physically to appropriate activities, Joe reacted by trying to bite the teacher. If the person persisted in attempting to guide him physically Joe would fall on the floor, cry, and resist attempts to be helped up, and sometimes slapped his left cheek with his right hand. One time he hit himself hard enough to cut his lip. At home, he showed similar reactions to physical guidance from his mother except that he did not attempt to bite her. His mother was also very concerned because Joe was beginning to have occasional toileting accidents at home, as well, a problem which had not manifested itself at school.

Finally, although Joe's social interactions had always been minimal, they were now essentially nonexistent. His only social interactions occured with his teachers and parents.

• JOE: A PSYCHODYNAMIC PERSPECTIVE •

The recent changes in Joe's life (i.e., loss of his sister from home; graduation from his old school; starting at the adult training program) disrupted his accustomed life-style and forced him to adapt to a new life situation. The increase in his undesirable behaviors are symptomatic of the inability of his ego to make mature adaptations to these changes. His specific inappropriate behaviors, such as aggression, noncompliance, crying, stereotypy, and isolation, appear to reflect the use of primitive defense mechanisms to reduce the anxiety and insecurity no doubt created by all the sudden changes over which he had no control.

The source of Joe's ego deficits are likely due largely to his parental interactions early in life and general familial interactions throughout his life. The brief description of the case indicates his mother quit her job as a schoolteacher to care for Joe. Although her actions might have been motivated by many factors, it may be that she experienced some guilt as a result of Joe's condition. If this were true, her taking responsibility for his care may have been motivated as much by a need to ease her guilt as by her love and concern for Joe. It should be noted that she apparently continued to work after giving birth to Joe's older sister, of normal intelligence, who it is assumed she also loved, which perhaps suggests special guilt feelings over Joe. If this was the case, she may have overindulged Joe with her mothering to atone for her guilt. Furthermore, his medical complications very early in life may have led her to be even more overprotective and anxious about his care.

The combination of these factors may have produced mother–child interactions that fostered dependence in Joe and communicated his mother's guilt to him, which would likely inhibit his ego development. His particular aberrant behaviors indicate fixation of development and failure to resolve the conflicts characteristic of the oral and anal stages. Support for this comes from Joe's regression to such infantile modes of satisfaction and control as thumb-sucking, toilet accidents, rocking, and biting when confronted with his new life situation.

Joe's social withdrawal and failure to comply with demands may also be interpreted as an infantile method of "getting even" with the people who he perceives as being responsible for his situation, namely, his mother and the teachers at the training center. His self-abuse may also accomplish a similar function by attempting to create guilt in others over his hurting himself. Alternatively, this behavior might be his attempt to establish his sense of self, which is likely severely lacking due to his deficient ego development.

Additionally, it appears that virtually all his life experiences, with the possible exception of school, were within the protective realm of his family, for no peer interactions or friendships outside the family are mentioned in the case description. He has obviously led a sheltered, protected life which provided his ego with little opportunity to develop and express itself. His ego weaknesses now become glaring in the light of new life demands far removed from the safety of the family.

Other evidence for disturbed ego development early in life is Joe's slowed speech. If development is deficient early in life, the ego will not likely master such a higher order function as language for its energy will be consumed by attempts to manage the basic psychic apparatus and its functioning.

The account of Joe's history and his present behavior also suggests maladaptive superego development, probably resulting from poor resolution of the Oedipal complex. The case description indicates little, if any, interaction with his father. This was probably due in part to the father's frequent business trips but also, perhaps, to his rejection of Joe. He may, therefore, have not functioned as an ideal identification figure for Joe, which is a basic requirement for solving this complex.

Joe's present aggressive behaviors, for example, might indicate a superego incapable of judging the consequence of his actions or unable to chastize the ego for allowing the direct expression of aggressive energy. His repetitive behavior and retreat to his room, however, may reflect an overdeveloped superego; they could be a defense by Joe's ego from the superego's reprimands for his failure to master his current life situation. Since the training center is no doubt the source of many new and frustrating demands, Joe minimizes the possibility of failure by limiting his range of operations and not participating in the activities.

• JOE: A BEHAVIORAL PERSPECTIVE •

Different therapists operating under the behavioral approaches used most often with the mentally retarded may emphasize different aspects of Joe's case and choose different points of intervention. This is no doubt a result of both the gaps in the information a therapist has about any case and the different complex of contingencies that shape different therapists' professional development. Consequently, the following explanation is just one of many possible behavioral diagnoses. Also, to be sure, before any behavioral practitioner intervened, he or she would require many more bits of information about the environmental contingencies in Joe's life.

Some of Joe's distinctive characteristics, his finger mouthing and body rocking, probably started as exploratory behavior and were maintained at some low operant level by the inward reinforcing stimuli. It is probable that these behaviors received occasional reinforcement in the form of parental attention, as the account specified that his mother had "complaints" about his finger mouthing. His parents and sister apparently were the source of many diverse reinforcers. These included enjoyable backyard activities, indoor activities, community outings, companionship, and affection. Joe's moderate level of retardation indicates that there were a number of behaviors for which his competence probably received favorable attention.

His speech problems probably were the source of some difficulty and awkwardness in his interactions with others outside the home and for which reinforcers were less readily available and potentially reinforcing activities were less than successful. These limitations were most likely very mild in the home, where the general attitude was more accepting and patient and the individuals were more sensitive communicators. Outside the home, these limitations were probably the cause of the infrequence of Joe's verbal communication with others. Over time, it could be expected that people's increasing familiarity with Joe, along with growing friendships, would lessen these communication limitations. Joe probably had come to feel fairly comfortable in his special public school classes.

A confluence of factors probably contributed to the emergence of and increase in Joe's problem behaviors. Graduating from public school terminated a very familiar situation, a variety of reinforcers, a number of reinforcing activities, a complex of well-learned discriminative stimuli, and familiar schedules of reinforcement and scattered a number of reinforcing and sensitive people. Starting in the adult training school presented a very unfamiliar situation, with strange tasks requiring uncertain competencies in strange surroundings with unknown schedules of reinforcement and unfamiliar people. His home situation also was altered; his sister had married and was no longer readily available. Undoubtedly, the very comforting and reinforcing situation that she sometimes offered, particularly in difficult times, left with her.

In the new situation, more demanding and sophisticated behaviors would be the first to drop out of the repertoire. Consequently, Joe began refusing to comply with instructions. This noncompliance was also probably associated in the past with some moderate degree of attention and cajoling from others. Joe's more inward-directed behaviors, that is, body rocking and finger mouthing, increased most likely because of the low level of competence they require and the certainty of their association with inward reinforcing stimuli. If these behaviors, along with staring out the windows, also helped to avoid the more aversive situation that the new tasks presented, avoidance conditioning was most likely operating. Pleading by his teachers, while well intentioned, probably served only to reinforce these counterproductive behaviors.

The increase in these behaviors generalized to the home, which had become a somewhat less outwardly reinforcing situation because of his sister's absence. The environment that was most familiar and comforting would be the one in which Joe could be expected to spend a large proportion of this time, thus explaining his almost constant presence in his own room. At this point, more emotional behaviors could be expected in Joe, and his poor verbal skills probably became more tentative. As a result, the effort involved in community outings and social interaction was probably no longer worth the small, if any, reinforcement he received.

Joe's biting the teacher who attempted to physically force him to attend activities most likely had the desired effect of terminating the attempt and avoiding the forthcoming aversive situation. More persistent attempts at physical guidance probably produced more extreme emotional behaviors such as crying and face slapping which, no doubt, would be reinforced by the immediate attempts to stop these actions and console him. Joe generalized these behaviors to his home but obviously discriminated between his mother and all others and did not display his aggressive behavior toward her. Toileting accidents at home most likely increased his mother's sympathy and efforts to comfort Joe, without producing the aversive embarrassment that would most likely result if these behaviors occurred at the adult training school. Without intervention, this whole regressive cycle would very likely continue.

• REFERENCES •

Agras, W. S., Kazdin, A. E., & Wilson, G. T. *Behavior therapy: Toward an applied clinical science.* San Francisco: Freeman, 1979.

Azrin, N. H., Kaplan, S. J., & Foxx, R. M. Autism reversal: Eliminating stereotyped self-stimulation of retarded individuals. *American Journal of Mental Deficiency*, 1973, *78*, 241–248.

Baer, D. M., Wolf, M. M. & Risley, T. R. Some current dimensions of applied behavior analysis. *Journal of Applied Behavior Analysis*, 1968, *1*, 91–97.

Balthazar, E. E., & Stevens, H. A. *The emotionally disturbed, mentally retarded: A historical and contemporary perspective.* Englewood Cliffs, N.J.: Prentice-Hall, 1975.

Bandura, A. Self-efficacy: Toward a unifying theory of behavioral change. *Psychological Review*, 1977, *84*, 191–215.

Bandura, A. *Social learning theory.* Englewood Cliffs, N.J.: Prentice-Hall, 1977b.

Baumeister, A. A. Origins and control of stereotyped movements. In C. E. Meyers (Ed.), *Quality of life in severely and profoundly mentally retarded people: Research foundations for improvement. Monograph of the American Association on Mental Deficiency,* 1978, 3.

Baumeister, A. A., & Forehand, R. Stereotyped acts. In N. R. Ellis (Ed.) *International review of research in mental retardation* (Vol 6). New York: Academic Press, 1973.

Baumeister, A. A., & Rollings, J. P. Self-injurious behavior. In N. R. Ellis (Ed.), *International review of research in mental retardation* (Vol. 8). New York: Academic Press, 1976.

Beck, A. T. *Cognitive therapy and the emotional disorders.* New York: International Universities Press, 1976.

Bemporad, J. R. *Child development in normality and psychopathology.* New York: Brunner/Mazel, 1980.

Berman, M. I. Mental retardation and depression. *Mental Retardation,* 1967, *5,* 19–21.

Bijou, S. W. A functional analysis of retarded development. In N. R. Ellis (Ed.), *International review of research in mental retardation* (Vol. 1). New York: Academic Press, 1966.

Bijou, S. W., & Baer, D. M. Operant procedures and child behavior and development. In W. K. Honig (Ed.), *Operant behavior: Areas of research and application.* New York: Appleton Century Crofts, 1966.

Bostow, D. E., & Bailey, J. B. Modifications of severe disruptive and aggressive behavior using brief timeout and reinforcement procedures. *Journal of Applied Behavior Analysis,* 1969, *2,* 31–37.

Brenner, C. *An elementary textbook of psychoanalysis* (Rev. ed). Garden City, N.Y.: Anchor Books, 1974.

Bucher, B., & Lovaas, O. I. Use of aversive stimulation in behavior modification. In M. R. Jones (Ed.), *Miami symposium on the prediction of behavior, 1967: Aversive stimulation.* Coral Gables, Fla.: University of Miami Press, 1968.

Craighead, W. E., Kazdin, A. E., & Mahoney, M. J. *Behavior modification: Principles, issues, and applications* (2nd ed.). Boston: Houghton Mifflin, 1981.

de Lissovoy, V. Headbanging in early childhood: A study of incidence. *Journal of Pediatrics,* 1961, *58,* 803–805.

Ellis, A. *The essence of rational psychotherapy: A comprehensive approach to treatment.* New York: Institute for Rational Living, 1970.

Ellis, N. R. *Handbook of mental deficiency, psychological theory, and research.* Hillsdale, N.J.: Lawrence Earlbaum, 1979.

Erikson, E. H. *Childhood and society.* New York: Norton, 1950.

Eysenck, H. J. Learning theory and behavior therapy. *Journal of Mental Science,* 1959, *195,* 61–75.

Feirstein, A. R., & Miller, N. E. Learning to resist pain and fear: Effects of electric shock before versus after reaching goal. *Journal of Comparative and Physiological Psychology,* 1963, *56,* 797–800.

Ferster, C. B. Positive reinforcement and behavior deficits of autistic children. *Child Development,* 1961, *32,* 437–456.

Forehand, R., & Baumeister, A. A. Deceleration of aberrant behavior among retarded individuals. In M. Hersen, R. M. Eisler, & P. M. Miller (Eds.), *Progress in behavior modification*. New York: Academic Press, 1976.

Foxx, R. M., & Azrin, N. H. The elimination of autistic self-stimulatory behavior by overcorrection. *Journal of Applied Behavior Analysis*, 1973, *6*, 1–14.

Frankel, F., & Simmons, J. Q., III. Self-injurious behavior in schizophrenic and retarded children. *American Journal of Mental Deficiency*, 1976, *80*, 512–522.

Freud, S. *Complete introductory lectures on psychoanalysis*. New York: Norton, 1966.

Friedrich, W. N., & Friedrich, W. L. Psychosocial aspects of parents of handicapped and nonhandicapped children. *American Journal of Mental Deficiency*, 1981, *85*, 551–553.

Frodi, A. M. Contribution of infant characteristics to child abuse. *American Journal of Mental Deficiency*, 1981, *85*, 341–349.

Gavalas, R. J., & Briggs, P. F. Concurrent schedules of reinforcement: A new concept of dependency. *Merrill-Palmer Quarterly of Behavior and Development*, 1966, *12*, 97–121.

Goldfarb, W. Effects of psychological deprivation in infancy and subsequent stimulation. *American Journal of Psychiatry*, 1945, *102*, 18–33.

Hogg, J. The experimental analysis of retarded behaviour and its relation to normal development. In M. P. Feldman & A. Broadhurst (Eds.), *Theoretical and experimental bases of the behaviour therapies*. London: Wiley, 1976.

Kaufman, M. E., & Levitt, H. A study of three stereotyped behaviors in institutionalized mental defectives. *American Journal of Mental Deficiency*, 1965, *69*, 467–473.

Koegel, R. L., & Covert, A. The relationship of self-stimulation to learning in autistic children. *Journal of Applied Behavior Analysis*, 1972, *5*, 381–387.

Kounin, J. Experimental studies of rigidity. *Character & Personality*, 1941, *9*, 251–282.

Kravitz, H., Rosenthal, V., Teplitz, Z., Murphy, J. B., & Lesser, R. E. A study of head-banging in infants and children. *Diseases of the Nervous System*, 1960, *21*, 203–208.

Lewin, K. *A dynamic theory of personality*. New York: McGraw-Hill, 1935.

Lovaas, O. I., Litrownik, A., & Mann, R. Response latencies to auditory stimuli in autistic children engaged in self-stimulatory behavior. *Behaviour Research and Therapy*, 1971, *9*, 39–49.

Lovaas, O. I., & Simmons, J. Q. Manipulation of self-destruction in three retarded children. *Journal of Applied Behavior Analysis*, 1969, *2*, 143–157.

Mahoney, M. J. *Cognition and behavior modification*. Cambridge: Ballinger, 1974.

Meichenbaum, D. *Cognitive behavior modification*. New York: Plenum Press, 1977.

Menolascino, F. J. *Challenges in mental retardation: Progressive ideology and services*. New York: Human Sciences Press, 1977.

Menolascino, F. J. Emotional disturbances in mentally retarded children. *American Journal of Psychiatry*, 1969, *126*, 54–62.

Nordquist, V. M., & Wahler, R. G. Naturalistic treatment of an autistic child. *Journal of Applied Behavior Analysis*, 1973, *6*, 79–87.

Pavlov, I. P. *Conditioned reflexes* (G. V. Anrep, Ed. and Trans.). London: Oxford University Press, 1927.

Pearson, G. H. J. The psychopathology of mental defectives. *Nervous Child*, 1942, *2*, 9–20.

Philips, I. Psychopathology in mental retardation. *American Journal of Psychiatry*, 1967, *124*, 29–35.

Philips, I., & Williams, N. Psychopathology in mental retardation: A study of 100 mentally retarded children. In S. Chess, & A. Thomas (Eds.), *Annual progress in child psychiatry and child development, 1976*. New York: Brunner/Mazel, 1977.

Robinson, H. B., & Robinson, N. M. *The mentally retarded child: A psychological approach*. New York: McGraw-Hill, 1965.

Robinson, N. M., & Robinson, H. B. *The mentally retarded child* (2nd ed.). New York: McGraw-Hill, 1976.

Singh, N. N. Rumination. In N. R. Ellis (Ed.), *International review of research in mental retardation* (Vol. 10). New York: Academic Press, 1981.

Skinner, B. F. *Science and human behavior*. New York: The Free Press, 1953.

Skinner, B.F. *The behavior of organisms: An experimental analysis*. New York: Appleton Century, 1938.

Sternlicht, M. Issues in counseling and psychotherapy with mentally retarded individuals. In I. Biahler & M. Sternlicht (Eds.), *The psychology of mental retardation: Issues and approaches*. New York: Psychological Dimensions, 1977.

Sternlicht, M. Personality: One view. In J. Wortis (Ed.), *Mental retardation and developmental disabilities* (Vol. 8). New York: Brunner/Mazel, 1976.

Sternlicht, M., & Deutsch, M. *Personality development and social behavior in the mentally retarded*. Lexington, Mass.: Lexington Books, 1972.

Sullivan, H. S. *Conceptions of modern psychiatry*. New York: Norton, 1940.

Thorndike, E. L. *Animal intelligence: Experimental studies*. New York: Macmillan, 1911.

Waisbren, S. E. Parents' reactions after the birth of a developmentally disabled child. *American Journal of Mental Deficiency*, 1980, *84*, 345–351.

Wolpe, J. *Psychotherapy by reciprocal inhibition*. Stanford, Calif.: Stanford University Press, 1958.

four

Anxiety Disorders

Thomas H. Ollendick
Duane G. Ollendick

The purpose of this chapter is to review and evaluate anxiety disorders in the mentally retarded. In pursuing this goal, issues related to diagnosis, incidence, and assessment are examined. Further, etiologic considerations are reviewed, and innovative treatment strategies for reducing anxiety and enhancing constructive social behaviors are considered. Quite obviously, a chapter such as this cannot claim to provide an index to all of the literature or issues in this field. Rather, our goal has been to present a picture of major considerations, trends, and points of view that lead to an understanding and appreciation of the present status of the study of anxiety in the mentally retarded and to suggest future research directions.

The association of mental retardation and psychopathology has a rather long history; in fact, early conceptualizations did not differentiate between these two notions. In an eloquent historical review, Rosen, Clark, and Kivitz (1976) provide a detailed examination of the coexistence and treatment of these two "conditions." In ancient Greece and Rome, for example, mentally dull and deviant children were viewed alike; both were treated as objects of scorn, ridicule, and persecution. In Rome, it is alleged that such children were disposed of in the Tiber by their parents to relieve themselves and society of the burden of support. Such practices were most probably associated with prevailing conceptions of mental retardation and psychopathology: both were viewed as biologic or organic imbalances of "humoral substances." Although notions of psychopathology and mental retardation changed over the following centuries, these conditions continued to be viewed alike. In medieval times, for example, both mentally retarded and emotionally disturbed persons served as fools or court jesters or were regarded as *les enfants du Bon Dieu,* who wandered unmolested about the streets of Europe. Kindness and forebearance, in contrast to scorn and ridicule, characterized treatment at this time. As noted by Rosen et al. (1976) and Zilboorg and Henry (1941), this humane attitude toward the mentally retarded and emotionally disturbed was short-lived, however, and was soon replaced by a view of such persons as demoniacs or possessed. According to this viewpoint, evil spirits inhabited mentally retarded and psychiatrically impaired individuals, and such persons were to be regarded with suspicion and fear. Both John Calvin and Martin Luther denounced such persons as "filled with Satan;" treatment ranged from humiliation, rejection, and imprisonment to burning at the stake.

Despite the lack of distinction between mental retardation and psychopathology in these earlier times, they did eventually become separated in the thinking of observers of human behavior (Beier, 1964; Rosen et al., 1976). In the late 18th and early 19th centuries, prompted by advances in the fields of anatomy, neurology, and physiology, distinctions began to be more clearly drawn between mental retardation as an organically caused intellectual deficit and psychopathology as a functionally determined emotional disorder. As the student of psychopathology and mental retardation undoubtedly knows, such demarcations were observed to be more illusory than real. Several forms of psychopathology were discovered to be organically based, and various types of mental retardation were found to be affected, if not determined by, environmental influences. Nonetheless, an important distinction between mental retardation and psychopathology survived this era: the primary deficit of the mentally retarded was considered to be lowered intellectual ability whereas that of the psychiatrically impaired was considered to be emotional. Thus, the conception of mental retardation and psychopathology as distinct entities was realized.

Unfortunately, this development led to the common view that mentally retarded persons were in some way oblivious to, or refractory to, "emotional" problems. Primary emphasis was placed on intellectual training and habilitation. If emotional or behavioral problems became evident, such persons were immediately institutionalized for the "protection of society from the deviant" (Wolfensberger, 1972). As noted by numerous authors (e.g., Beier, 1964; Benton, 1964, 1980; Bialer, 1970; Heber, 1964), at the beginning of the 20th century the personality of the mentally retarded was largely ignored or viewed as unimportant.

Throughout the current century, however, a resurgence of interest in psychopathology in the mentally retarded has been witnessed. For example, in 1922 Potter elaborated on specific emotional problems of the mentally retarded and described a method for their evaluation. He noted that many mentally retarded persons display problems in nervous energy, sociability, mood, conduct, and other unique pathological traits. Such findings "tend to indicate a neurotic or psychotic state in addition to the initial intellectual defects" (Potter, 1922, p. 492). Similarly, Tredgold (1947) examined mental disturbances among the mentally retarded and specifically observed variants of psychoneuroses, psychoses, and dementia. He regarded hysterical manifestations as the most frequently observed neurotic pattern, followed by anxiety states and obsessive-compulsive reactions. More recent reviews have been provided by Sarason (1953), Benton (1964, 1970), Menolascino (1970), and Balthazar and Stevens (1975).

It is evident from this brief introductory overview that mental retardation and psychopathology are observed to coexist, even though they are viewed as distinct entitites. Despite the emergence of this viewpoint, very little is known about the incidence, assessment, or diagnosis of specific pathological disorders in the mentally retarded, such as anxiety. The primary goal of this chapter is to examine available information and to present an overview of anxiety disorders in the mentally retarded. In addition, a review of etiologic considerations, as well as treatment strategies, is undertaken in order to provide a broader perspective in which to conceptualize the coexistence of these two conditions.

• DIAGNOSTIC ISSUES •

In the group of problematic behaviors subsumed under anxiety disorders, anxiety is viewed as either a predominant disturbance or an attempt to control various symptoms. Disorders in which anxiety is the predominant disturbance involves those classified under anxiety states according to DSM-III (1980): the panic disorder, in which anxiety attacks occur unpredictably; the generalized anxiety disorder, in which anxiety persists for at least one month's duration; and the obsessive compulsive disorder, in which there are recurrent obsessions or compulsions. The second major set of anxiety disorders are phobic disorders. These include agoraphobia with or without panic attacks, in which there is a marked fear of being alone or being in places where escape would be difficult or help unavailable; social phobia, which involves persistent fear of social situations; and simple phobia, which involves fear of situations not covered in the first two categories (sometimes called the "specific" phobias). DSM-III articulates yet another category under the classification of anxiety disorders—the posttraumatic stress disorder, in which anxiety symptoms develop following a psychologically traumatic event. Quite clearly, a variety of anxiety disorders are described in DSM-III.

As can be seen by referring to the DSM-III manual, very specific and careful criteria are delineated for the differential diagnosis of the anxiety disorder subtypes. As will be seen, however, research has yet to be reported which examines subtype prevalence in the mentally retarded, in spite of the fact that several authors have reported higher incidences of anxiety in the retarded than in the general population (Cochran & Cleland, 1963; Feldhusen & Klausmeier, 1962; Malpass, Mark, & Palermo, 1960). In the authors' experience, the subtypes seen under the anxiety states and phobic disorders occur rather frequently, in both institutionalized and outpatient mentally retarded. The posttraumatic stress disorders seem more difficult to diagnosis because of the frequent inaccessability of cognitive information, although we have seen many cases in which there is a sudden, although delayed, occurrence of anxiety symptoms following a traumatic event, such as the death of a care-giving parent. Clearly this is an area in need of investigative research.

The definition that DSM III uses for mental retardation was developed in accordance with terminology and classification schemes of the American Association on Mental Deficiency (AAMD): "mental retardation refers to subaverage general intellectual functioning which originates during the developmental period and is associated with impairment in adaptive behavior" (Heber, 1961, p. 3). Although the two classification systems are similar, DSM-III distinguishes four major subtypes which reflect the degree of intellectual impairment (mild, moderate, severe, profound), and AAMD offers additional medical and behavioral classificatory categories. The medical categories deal primarily with etiological considerations whereas the behavioral categories present a standardized system for measurement of adaptive behavior.

From a purely definitional perspective, the development of anxiety in the mentally retarded is similar to that observed in persons of average or above average intellectual functioning; that is, the same group of problematic behaviors currently defined as anxiety disorders are seen in the mentally retarded as well. In addition to the higher incidence of anxiety disorders in retarded persons previously reported, greater susceptibility to anxiety disorders has been postulated by several authors (e.g., Bialer, 1970, Cochran & Cleland, 1963; Hutt & Gibby, 1965; Knights, 1963; Warren & Collier, 1964) because of their developmental immaturity, institutionalization, educational failures, and limited verbal language skills.

Moreover, difficulties in diagnosing anxiety in the mentally retarded frequently occur because of similarities between anxiety and other behavioral problems commonly seen in the mentally retarded. It is for this reason that Barker (1979) notes that a "comprehensive assessment of the child in the context of his or her family, school . . . is essential first" (p. 178). Although the assessment of anxiety disorders in the mentally retarded will be covered extensively in the following section, an example may help illustrate the difficulty of diagnosis if strict definitional guidelines are not followed. Common problematic behaviors frequently seen in the institutionalized retarded include those which generally fall within the category of atypical stereotyped movement disorder (DSM-III). Such behaviors include repetitive movements which may be either rhythmic and involuntary. These behaviors are in contrast to ritualistic compulsive behaviors seen in the anxiety-based obsessive compulsive disorders and which are "repetitive and seemingly purposeful behaviors that are performed according to certain rules or in stereotypical fashion" (p. 234). These two sets of behaviors, though topographically similar, are distinct and have clear implications for accurate diagnosis. Knowing when a behavior is stereotypic and when it is compulsive can, of course, be difficult to discern. Nonetheless, if diagnostic guidelines are followed, such distinction can be made.

• INCIDENCE •

Surprisingly, the incidence of anxiety in the mentally retarded has received little attention. This inattention is particularly perplexing since it has long been known that anxiety can serve to facilitate performance under certain conditions and to debilitate it under others (Spence, 1958). Given the variety of performance deficits in the mentally retarded, more concerted attention and parametric research was anticipated. This situation prevails even into the present time, despite the current impetus to measure adaptive and maladaptive behavior in the mentally retarded (e.g., Balthazar, 1971, 1973; Nihira, Foster, Shellhaas, & Leland, 1974, a,b), and to devise effective habilitation programs (Balthazar, 1976; Nihira & Shellhaas, 1970).

An early indication of the incidence of generaly anxiety in mentally retarded inpatients was reflected in Penrose's (1938) clinical and genetic study of 1280 cases of mental retardation. In this study, Penrose reported that 132 individuals (10.3%) were "psychoneurotic," marked by nervous energy and anxiety. Neuer (1947) reported similar findings. Of 300 new or readmitted patients in a state institution, he found 39 (13%) classifiable as "neurotic," characterized by restlessness, anxiety, and compulsions. In a more recent study, Craft (1959) examined 324 mentally retarded inpatients and found that 104 (33%) could be diagnosed as "personality disorders," with anxiety prominent. Collectively, these studies suggest that one-tenth to one-third of mentally retarded inpatients may be generally anxious. Of course, these studies are not without their share of methodological flaws. As in early surveys with the intellectually normal, standardized diagnostic criteria were not used and a considerable amount of investigator bias was present. Nonetheless, these surveys are useful in focusing attention on anxiety disorders in the mentally retarded. Comprehensive and sophisticated studies of mentally retarded inpatients, employing criteria of DSM-III, remain to be conducted.

A similar state of affairs exists in determining the incidence of anxiety in outpatient mentally retarded persons. In an early study by Webster (1963), 159 children between three and six years of age were examined. A heterogeneous sample of children was studied with such disorders as Down's syndrome, metabolic disorders, prenatal skull anomalies, organic brain disorders, and familial etiologies. Further, all levels of retardation were represented, although 75 percent were organically impaired and had IQs below 50. Webster reported that "not a single child was simply retarded" (1963, p. 38); in fact, *all* the children were reported to have some level of emotional disturbance: 35 percent were rated as mildly disturbed, 48 percent moderately disturbed, and 17 percent severely disturbed. Of interest to this chapter, excessive fears and inhibitions as well as compulsive traits and nervous mannerisms were described (although exact percentages were not provided). The accuracy and significance of these findings must, of course, be interpreted cautiously. As with inpatient studies, interviewer bias and nonspecific definitions of anxiety were apparent in this study. Further, the fact that 100 percent of the mentally retarded children were found to be emotionally disturbed suggests that the criterion measure of "disturbance" must not have been an exacting or demanding one. For these reasons, these estimates appear to be inflated.

In a more recent study, Richardson, Katz, Koller, McLaren, and Rubinstein (1979) reported the incidence of "neurotic" problems in a lifespan study of 222 mentally retarded children. These children represented all the mentally retarded children born in a British city between 1951 to 1955 and were followed from birth to 22 years of age. Throughout this 22-year span, it was determined that 26 percent of the children displayed neurotic problems (e.g., problems with "nerves" and anxiety), and another 20 percent showed conduct and antisocial problems. The frequency of such problems was highest for those with IQs of less than 50. Sex differences were not observed. This study appears to be one of the more exacting ones, employing unbiased interviewers, behavioral observation procedures, and relying on supplemental reports from school records and hospital records for those in institutional care.

This latter study, though not utilizing criteria of DSM-III and not specifying anxiety disorders, is probably the most informative study available in this area. It represents a longitudinal study and suggests that over one-fourth of mentally retarded children exhibit neurotic problems by early adulthood. Further, it indicates that such problems are observed during childhood and adolescence, that they are equally prevalent in males and females, and that those with lowered IQs are more susceptible. In contrast, prevalence of anxiety for the nonretarded in Great Britain and the United States is estimated at 2 to 5 percent, with typical age of onset in the mid-20s, and with females twice as likely to be diagnosed as males (Clum & Pickett, in press; Marks & Lader, 1973). Clearly, mentally retarded children and adults appear to be more susceptible to anxiety than nonretarded persons.

This pattern of findings was also observed in a series of studies comparing levels of self-reported anxiety in retarded and nonretarded individuals. Although problems exist in the use of self-reporting measures with retarded persons (see next section), Pryer and Cassel (1962) reported that commonly used anxiety scales (e.g., Children's Manifest Anxiety Scale, Test Anxiety Scale for Children) were reliable and useful for the mentally retarded. In general, greater self-reported anxiety was found in institutionalized retarded persons than in either noninstitutionalized retarded or normal controls (e.g., Cochran & Cleland, 1963; Feldhusen & Klausmeier, 1962; Malpass et al., 1960). In these studies, the noninstitutionalized retarded were also more anxious than matched normal controls. An exception to this pattern was reported by Lipman (1960), who found no differences in the anxiety level between groups of retarded and nonretarded persons in approximately equal mental ages.

What can be concluded about the incidence of anxiety disorders in the mentally retarded? First, it must be emphasized that *no* studies employed exacting criteria and that none examined "anxiety" in its various states, as detailed in DSM-III. Further, a majority of the studies are characterized by subjectivity, retrospective report, and interviewer bias. Within these limitations, however, it seems safe to suggest that anxiety— at least in its general pervasive form—is more prevalent in the mentally retarded than in nonretarded persons, is more likely to be observed earlier in more severely retarded persons than in mildly retarded or normal individuals, and is equally prevalent in males and females. Admittedly, these conclusions are tentative and in need of empirical verification.

• ASSESSMENT •

Given the paucity of well-controlled research examining anxiety in the mentally retarded, it is not at all surprising that few studies proscribe detailed assessment strategies for its measurement. In this section, we shall endeavor to show that assessment procedures commonly used with nonretarded persons are applicable, in a majority of instances, to the mentally retarded as well. Historically, researchers and clinicians in this area have seemingly assumed that mentally retarded persons lack sufficient verbal skills or introspective skills, or both, to make assessment feasible. Although these assumptions may be accurate for nonverbal profoundly and severely retarded persons, they appear less true for 95 percent of retarded individuals: the moderately and mildly retarded. From the onset, however, we must admit that research is meager; what follows is our attempt to illustrate the potential utility of comprehensive assessment. We shall examine three specific assessment strategies: the clinical interview, self-report and other-report rating forms, and behavioral observation procedures. Although physiological measures have been used in the assessment of anxiety in nonretarded populations, such measurement has not been conducted to date with retarded persons. Accordingly, the use of this measure is not reviewed here.

• The Clinical Interview •

In general, the clinical interview has two primary goals: (1) to establish a positive relationship between the client and the clinician and (2) to obtain specific information regarding target behaviors. Establishing a relationship maximizes chances that a client will honestly share his or her problems (Truax & Carkhuff, 1967), whereas obtaining specific information ensures that antecedent and consequent conditions associated with target problems are identified and that a treatment program can be formulated. Although these goals are listed separately, we view them both as critical and indispensable to accurate assessment. We have found that basic skills, including empathy, warmth, and genuineness, help put the retarded (as well as the nonretarded) client at ease and make the interview a nonthreatening experience. Under such conditions, rapport is more easily established and the client's concern about self-disclosure is minimized (Lazarus, 1971).

In dealing with retarded clients, special problems with rapport may arise because of limited verbal abilities, frequent fear of strangers, and distrust of their own ability to communicate effectively. Although these problems may exist, all too frequently notions such as "he's too retarded to understand my question" and "there's no use in asking her what she's anxious about, she won't be able to tell me anyway" unnecessarily prevail. It is suggested that such statements reflect the clinician's inability to communicate with the client, not the retarded person's inability to comprehend appropriately phrased questions. When interviewing retarded persons, it becomes necessary to simplify questions and to make them concrete and specific. Such a strategy requires skill and patience: skill in using words the retarded client will understand and patience in clarifying and restating questions until they are understood. The retarded person's awareness of situations which lead to anxiety, how he or she handles those situations, and what he or she might do to alter them are all important areas of examination. Quite obviously, an interview along the lines suggested here is most appropriate for mildly or moderately retarded persons who are verbal.

Whether the individual is verbal or nonverbal, mildly or severely retarded, we recommend a clinical interview to observe first-hand his or her reaction to the interview setting and to determine the presence of more generalized anxiety. In nonverbal clients, physical symptoms of anxiety such as nervousness, sighing, shortness of breath, and palpitations might readily be observed. With verbal clients, these physical symptoms as well as self-statements about feeling uneasy, uncomfortable, and afraid might also be obtained.

Very few studies have examined the reliability, validity, or utility of the clinical interview with retarded persons (Ballinger, Armstrong, Presly, & Reid, 1975; Pilkington, 1972). In one of these studies (Ballinger et al., 1975), the reliability and validity of the Clinical Interview Schedule developed by Goldberg, Cooper, Eastwood, Kedward, and Shepherd (1970) were examined in 13 verbal and 14 nonverbal moderate to profoundly retarded inpatients. The Clinical Interview Schedule consists of a set of questions and observations designed to assess a variety of problems, including depression and anxiety. The first part of the schedule is verbally oriented (and hence used only for verbal clients), but the second part is observational in nature (thus appropriate for both verbal and nonverbal clients). The interview takes about half an hour to complete. In reference to the measurement of anxiety, Ballinger et al. reported acceptable interrater reliability, with interrater agreement higher for persons with verbal ability than for those without. Validity was assessed by comparing raters' observations in the interview with an overall psychiatric rating of anxiety provided by each patient's consultant (therapist). Correspondence between these ratings was also acceptable, thus lending a degree of construct validity to the use of this interview procedure. Quite obviously, such an interview is most appropriate when one is interested in determining the overall level of anxiety. When more specific anxiety states are to be examined, a more detailed and specific strategy will need to be used. Nonetheless, the results of this study as well as those of Pilkington (1972) suggest the potential utility of interview procedures to obtain reliable and valid information with the mentally retarded.

• Rating Forms •

In general, two types of ratings have been used to assess anxiety: (1) self-report of attitude and feelings and (2) other reports of observed behavior. Although both types of ratings have distinct limitations, self-report tests provide specific information about felt anxiety from the retarded persons' perspective and other-report forms provide supplemental information from an external source. For nonverbal and severely or profoundly retarded persons, other-reports may be the primary source of information. An advantage of using both forms is that they provide a means of comparing the individual clients with group norms. Such norms provide chronological and mental age standards of comparison and assist the clinician in determining the intensity and extensiveness of anxiety. A final advantage of these forms is related to their utility as outcome measures of treatment efficacy. Such questionnaires can be administered prior to treatment, following treatment, and at appropriate follow-up intervals to assess both specific and generalized change.

A variety of self-report measures of anxiety and fear have been used with normal children and adults (e.g., Lick & Katkin, 1976; Ollendick, 1979a). With mentally retarded persons, fewer scales have been used; typically, such scales have been standardized on normal children or adolescents and then adapted for use with the mentally retarded. For example, the most frequently used scale is the Children's Manifest Anxiety Scale (Castaneda, McCandless, & Palermo, 1956). This scale has been used in a number of studies, many of which have affirmed an increased incidence of anxiety in the mentally retarded (e.g., Cochran & Cleland, 1963; Malpass et al., 1960). The scale is particularly useful in identifying not only an overall level of anxiety but also specific areas of anxiety or fear. Pryer and Cassel (1962) found sufficiently high test-retest reliability, whereas Balla and Zigler (1979) summarized a number of validity studies with mentally retarded persons to make this questionnaire a useful instrument.

In a somewhat similar vein, we have adapted the Scherer and Nakamura (1968) fear survey schedule for children for use with mentally retarded persons (Ollendick, 1978). This scale consists of 80 items that potentially elicit fear or anxiety; individuals are asked to indicate whether a specific item (e.g., "fire" and "doctor") frightens them "not at all," "some", or "a lot." Although the revised test is still in its experimental form, initial results indicate acceptable test-retest reliability, internal consistency, and construct validity. To date, the schedule has been used only with the moderately and mildly retarded. Further, we have found it useful to present pictures of some of the items to select individuals to assist them in adequately imagining scenes.

In a recent study examining fear of strangers in mentally retarded children, Matson (in press, a) employed an innovative variant of this procedure. Children in a trainable classroom were taken to an empty room in the school where a stranger (a male experimenter) was waiting and told to "go introduce yourself to the nice man." Following their effort, they were shown pieces of paper, numbered 1 to 7, which represented varying degrees of fear (i.e., 1 = none, 7 = great). Each child was asked to rate how "afraid" this encounter had made them. To enhance the accuracy of ratings, bar graphs of varying heights were placed above the numbers to visually depict amounts of fear. Matson (in press, a) reported that these moderately retarded children understood the measurement aspects of the scale, as reflected in a high reliability between the subject's own rating and that of unobtrusive observers. Further, self-report fear of strangers decreased as a result of treatment (participant modeling, see Treatment section) and paralleled changes in observed fear.

Thus, although only a limited number of studies have utilized self-report measures, initial studies appear promising. As with clinical interviews, if rating items are presented in an appropriate format, they can provide potentially reliable, valid, and useful information. Innovative strategies which take into consideration specific cognitive limitations of retarded persons are likely to be more useful.

As with self-report techniques, a host of other-report rating forms have been used with the mentally retarded. In this approach, members of the family or significant others (e.g., teachers, aides) fill out checklists or rating forms that describe situations in which the client experiences anxiety and the degree of observed anxiety. Several useful forms are available, including the Louisville Fear Survey Schedule for Children (Miller, Barrett, Hampe, & Noble, 1972), the AAMD Adaptive Behavior Scale (Nihira et al., 1974 a, b), and the Balthazar Scale of Adaptive Behavior (Balthazar, 1971, 1973). These latter scales measure a variety of other behaviors in addition to those related to fear and anxiety (see Meyers, Nihira, & Zetlin, 1979 for a review).

As with interview and self-report data, issues related to reliability and validity are integrally related to the acceptability and clinical utility of such rating forms. O'Leary and Johnson (1979) have identified three primary factors which increase reliability and validity of such scales: (1) clearly defined reference points on the scale (anchor points), (2) the inclusion of more than two points on the scale, and (3) a rater who has extensive experience with the person being rated. Other issues related to the total number of items, as well as their specificity, are also important (Cronbach, 1960).

Since the reader is undoubtedly familiar with the AAMD and Balthazar Scales, we shall illustrate the use of the Louisville Fear Survey for

Children (Miller et al., 1972) with the mentally retarded. This survey is an 81-item inventory that covers an extensive range of fears and anxieties found in children and adolescents. Each item is rated on a three-point scale: no fear, normal or reasonable fear, or unrealistic fear (excessive). The survey was originally developed and standardized for normal children; it possesses sound test-retest and interjudge reliability and acceptable construct validity. Further, the survey has been factor analyzed and found to possess three primary factors: physical injury, natural events, and psychic stress (Miller et al., 1972). Representative items include "getting lost," "bathrooms," "storms," "having an operation," "snakes," and "being criticized." Unlike self-report scales, other report surveys are filled out by parents or attendants.

In a recent study, Guarnaccia and Weiss (1974) employed this survey with 102 trainable retardates, ranging in age from 6 to 21 and in IQs from 15 to 65. Items were filled out by parents and then factor analyzed. Based on this procedure, Guarnaccia and Weiss reported four primary dimensions of fear in mentally retarded children and young adults: separations, natural events, physical injury, and animals. The first three factors closely paralleled those obtained by Miller et al. (1972) for children and adolescents of average intelligence between 6 and 16 years of age. However, Miller et al. did not find a separate factor for animals, as was found by Guarnaccia and Weiss. This would seem to suggest that fears of animals are more homogeneous, if not more frequent, in mentally retarded persons. This, of course, is consistent with developmental findings, which show that fears of animals are more common in chronologically younger and developmentally delayed children (Ollendick, 1979a).

A major advantage of scales like the Louisville Scale and the AAMD and Balthazar Scales is that they can be filled out by parents or significant others. They do not rely on self-report and can be used whether the individual is verbal or nonverbal, mildly or profoundly retarded. As shown in the Guarnaccia and Weiss (1974) study, identification of a variety of fears and anxieties can be achieved with relative ease with such a procedure. Further, such a scale can be used as an outcome measure to examine both specific and generalized effects following treatment. In the Matson (in press, a) study reviewed earlier, the Louisville Scale was used in such a manner.

In sum, both self-report and other-report questionnaires or surveys can be used to assess perceived fears and anxieties. Though much research remains to be carried out on the reliability and validity of these measures with the mentally retarded, they provide valuable information and appear highly promising.

• Behavioral Observation •

Direct observation of the client's behavior in the presence of anxiety-eliciting stimuli is the hallmark of the behavioral approach to assessment. Within this tradition, assessment has ranged from unobtrusive observation in the naturalistic environment to direct observation in contrived or simulated laboratory settings (Lick & Katkin, 1976). Such observations provide a direct sample of behavior in anxiety-eliciting situations and are the least inferential of data collection methods (Goldfried & Kent, 1972). However, as we have noted elsewhere (Ollendick & Cerny, 1981), data obtained from behavioral observation should not be viewed as "better" than those obtained from clinical interview or rating methods. Rather, such data should be viewed as complementary.

In behavioral observation systems, a behavior or set of behaviors indicative of anxiety are operationally defined, observed, and recorded in a systematic fashion. Depending on the comprehensiveness of the system, the behavior of others in the environment might also be observed and recorded to determine their functional relationship to the anxiety. This information is used to determine antecedent and consequent conditions under which anxiety occurs and to assess behavior change following implementation of appropriate treatment programs. Data from such a "functional analysis" (Bijou & Peterson, 1971; Kanfer & Saslow, 1969; Kazdin & Straw, 1976), when combined with the aforementioned sources of data (clinical interview, rating forms), lead to specific treatment programming and treatment evaluation.

As with other types of assessment, behavioral observation procedures must possess adequate reliability and validity before their routine use can be endorsed. Further, the data obtained must be clinically meaningful and useful. Although early behaviorists tended to accept behavioral observation data based on their deceptively simplistic face validity, more recent investigators have enumerated a variety of problems related to their utility (e.g., Johnson & Bolstad, 1973; Kazdin, 1977). Among these issues are the complexity of the behavioral observation code, observer bias, observer drift, and the reactive nature of the observation process itself. In general, the *number of response categories* scored in an observation system is inversely related to the reliability and accuracy of scoring. These findings suggest that a limited number of behaviors be monitored at any one time. *Observer bias* is present when the observer reports observations that are influenced by sources other than the actual occurrence of anxiety. Such factors as knowledge of expected outcome and awareness that reliability estimates are being obtained are sources of observer bias; these factors can be controlled for by keeping observers "blind" to hypotheses related to treatment and by ensuring that interrater reliability estimates are being obtained without the rater's knowledge. Closely related to observer bias is *observer drift,* the tendency of observers to alter the definition of the observed behavior. Some observers may become more stringent in their criterion, and others may become more lenient. In either case, the basic problem is a deviation from a previously agreed upon operational definition of the target behavior. Observer drift can be rectified by periodically retraining observers and by informing them that reliability checks on adherence to the original definitions will be made periodically.

From our experience, the greatest threat to the validity and utility of observational data appears to come from the reactive nature of being observed. In general, it has been found that individuals alter their behavior when being observed, usually in therapeutic directions. As a result, the validity of the observed behavior (e.g., its frequency or duration) may be questionable. One solution to this problem is to use indigenous observers (i.e., ward personnel, parents) as recorders of behavior in the natural setting. Reactive effects should be less evident with such observers; of course, problems associated with observer bias and observer drift would still be present and need to be controlled. As can be seen from this brief overview of behavioral observation, this method is not without its share of methodological problems. Nonetheless, whenever possible, we highly recommend direct observation of behavior in the natural setting.

When issues of complexity, observer bias, observer drift, and reactivity are appropriately controlled for, naturalistic observation represents one of the most elegant measures of anxiety. Indexes of anxiety can be operationally defined and directly observed. For example, both nonverbal and verbal behaviors can be observed when the anxious and fearful mentally retarded person is escorted to the interview room for a physical examination. Such observations might reveal sighs, shortness of breath, heart palpitations, screams, and statements of worry or panic. As long as such behaviors are operationally defined in advance and are reliably observed, they can be used as valid sources of data for assessment and treatment outcome. In a similar fashion, fears and anxieties associated with any situation or event can be operationally defined, observed, and recorded.

As might be discerned, however, naturalistic observation is likely to be time-consuming and costly. Considerable time, as well as additional personnel, are required for adequate observation. Further, some anxieties and fears are not easily observed in the natural environment or may not occur when the individual is being observed. In such instances, direct observation in contrived or simulated settings has been recommended (e.g., Lick & Katkin, 1976). In the simulated setting, specific stimuli associated with the target behavior (anxiety) are presented so that the target behavior can be observed under controlled, standardized conditions. Simulated observations are especially helpful when anxiety is of low frequency (but nonetheless intense) or when it fails to occur in the natural environment because of reactivity. Recent reviews suggest that the more closely these simulated settings approach the natural environment, and the less intrusive they are in regard to methodological and observer effects, the more reliable and valid they are likely to be (Evans & Nelson, 1977).

Behaviorally oriented studies examining anxiety in mentally retarded persons have routinely used direct observation procedures in addition to clinical interviews and rating forms. As noted previously, these observations have been conducted in either simulated or naturalistic settings. Use of a simulated setting is nicely illustrated in Matson's (in press, a) study investigating fear of strangers in mentally retarded children. In this study, Matson devised a simulated situation in which each child was instructed to approach and speak to four unknown "strange" adults. Approach was defined by distance in feet from the stranger, and speaking was defined as the total number of words exchanged with the adult stranger. In this manner, Matson was able to measure and study fear of strangers in a laboratory setting which closely simulated what might actually occur in the natural environment. Somewhat similarly, Peck (1977) used the Behavior Avoidance test, originally introduced by Lang and Lazovik (1963), to assess fear of heights in mentally retarded adults. Subjects reporting a fear of heights were instructed to climb to the fifth floor of a metal grate fire escape and lean over and look at the ground for 30 seconds at each floor and climb down the fire escape in a graded series of 23 graduated steps. Clearly, assessment was conducted in a simulated setting but was subsequently useful in disensitizing (see Treatment section) previously fearful subjects. Simulated, structured settings have also been used to offset anxiety and to teach social interaction skills to retarded persons who are socially anxious or deficient in social settings. For example, Perry and Cerreto (1977) and Kelly, Furman, Phillips, Hathorn, and Wilson (1979) have employed social interaction simulations to measure the acquisition and maintenance of such skills.

One of the issues related to the use of measurement in simulated settings is the degree of generalization to the natural environment. That is, one might ask how representative is behavior in these simulated settings? Did retarded children in the Matson study and retarded adults in the Peck study "behave" as they would have in the natural environment? A partial answer to this question can be found in another study conducted by Matson (in press, b). In this study, fear of entering a grocery store was examined in mildly and moderately retarded adults. Fear was defined as approach behavior to the feared stimulus (store) and the number of overt statements about unwillingness to enter the store (e.g., "I get scared going into stores," and "All them peoples will laugh at me"). Initially, these behaviors were measured both in the natural environment and in a simulated setting in the workshop. A high degree of correspondence between these two settings was found. Further, following training and treatment (participant modeling, see Treatment section) in the simulated workshop setting, training was extended to the community—the natural environment. In this fashion, Matson was able to ensure the transfer of training and to match performances in simulated and naturalistic settings.

In sum, direct observation of anxious and fearful behaviors in naturalistic and simulated settings represents the hallmark of behavioral assessment. These observations, which are not without their own special set of limitations, are a welcome complement to clinical interviews and self-report and other-reporting rating forms. Although direct observations of the client in naturalistic situations are desired, such measurements are time-consuming, costly, and, at times, impractical. For these reasons, simulated settings which approximate those of the natural setting are likely to be used with continuing frequency. If so, considerably more research regarding their reliability, validity, and utility are needed. Nonetheless, when such observations are combined with other sources of data, a comprehensive assessment of fear or anxiety in the mentally retarded is clearly available. We see no reason to assess the retarded any differently from the nonretarded; however, it must be emphasized that skill and patience are required.

• ETIOLOGICAL CONSIDERATIONS •

The etiological basis for the development of anxiety disorders in the mentally retarded will now be considered. Four major viewpoints are identified and elaborated upon in the following sections.

• Cerebral Defect •

In the medical classification section of the AAMD taxonomy (Heber, 1961), eight major etiological categories for mental retardation are presented in which retardation is regarded "as a manifestation of some underlying disease process or medical condition" (p. 7). The first seven of these categories distinguish those cases in which mental retardation is consistent with a "structural reaction" (Bialer, 1970), that is, physiological or anatomical pathology, or both, and in which both retarded development and the given pathology can reasonably be accounted for by central nervous system dysfunction. The last category of the eight is reserved for cases in which no medical pathology is observed and for which there is "presumptive evidence that psychosocial or psychogenic factors bear some causal relationship to the observed retardation" (Bialer, 1970, p. 611). Robinson and Robinson (1965) discuss other etiological sources, all of which are subsumed under the category of cerebral defect. These include factors of hereditary and genetic endowment, genetic syndromes, development of the central nervous system, syndromes resulting from damage by the physical environment (like congenital hypothyroidism and anomalies of the skull and brain), and a variety of environmental agents (such as maternal nutrition, infections, anoxia, drugs, birth injury) which may lead to cerebral defect. Since the focus of this chapter is on the etiology of anxiety disorders in the mentally retarded, "cerebral defect" factors must be considered in how they either enhance the development of anxiety or prohibit the retarded individual from coping with and reducing anxiety. In order to do so, characteristics of individuals with mental retardation due to cerebral defect will be considered.

As indicated by the AAMD's definition of mental retardation such individuals are characterized by subaverage general intellectual functioning and impairment in adaptive behavior. For purposes of the present discussion, cerebral defect will be considered the major etiological factor causing subaverage general intellectual functioning with the impairment in adaptive behavior resulting from this defect. Subaverage intellectual functioning is frequently seen as impairing development of adaptive behavior in three areas: maturation, learning, and social adjustment (Robinson & Robinson, 1965). Briefly, these are defined as development of self-help skills in infancy and early childhood, development of knowledge acquired as a function of experience, and development of ability to maintain oneself independently. A slower developmental rate, interferences with the ability or inability to learn or profit from experiences beyond a specified level, and difficulties in social adjustment are, of course, common characteristics of the mentally retarded.

Developmental timetables for the maturation of infants and young children are well known, and, generally speaking, parents have set expectations that children will achieve certain milestones on time. As is frequently observed, however, children with mental retardation due to cerebral defect frequently have maturational lags in the development of self-help skills such as crawling, walking, talking, habit training, and interaction with age peers. What happens with the parents' expectations when their child does not perform according to developmental timetables? It has been frequently observed by the authors that this produces heightened and increased anxiety for the *parents*. Often they themselves are filled with self-doubt, failure, and wonderment of what they might be doing wrong or not doing properly. The psychological literature is replete with studies which reveal how personality and emotional characteristics are transmitted from parent to child or, at least, how similar characteristics are observed in both. For example, Ollendick (1977) found a significant relationship between anxiety in parents and in their normal children. From this vantage point, although cerebral defect might not be a direct cause of anxiety in mentally retarded children, it is evident how an external source (parents) may enhance development of anxiety in their children. Incidentally, in the authors' opinion, this attests to the importance for physicians, psychologists, and other health care professionals adequately counseling parents on appropriate expectations for their mentally retarded children. Thus, it is observed how one factor, such as maturational lag, may inadvertently lead to increased anxiety when considered from the cerebral defect viewpoint.

Individuals with mental retardation due to cerebral defect are also observed to have limitations in the learning process. Occasionally these limitations are associated with conditions such as hereditary deafness or blindness. It should be noted, however, that sensory impairments cause mental retardation in only a small number of cases. In these cases, however, the implication is that the mentally retarded individual "has been deprived of appropriate learning experiences as a direct function of his sensory impairment" (Bialer, 1970, p. 619).

Some of the most frequently seen learning limitations in the mentally retarded include distractibility, poor memory, low general capacity to learn, low motivational level, and heightened expectancy for failure; the intent here is neither to offer an all-inclusive list of limitations nor to review this extensive literature. The intent is only to illustrate that individuals with mental retardation due to cerebral defect have learning limitations, some of which are unique to their condition. For example, several authors (e.g., Balla & Zigler, 1979; Beier, 1964; Heber, 1964) have commented on the correspondence between mentally retarded persons' expectance for failure and an inability to learn (see also the Experiential Consideration section). Similarly, in an extensive study of normal children, Coleman, Campbell, Hobson, McPartland, Mood, Weinfeld, and York (1966) found that having a sense of control over one's environment was a major determinant of academic success. If, indeed, the mentally retarded have an increased expectancy for failure and, therefore, less of a sense of control, it could easily be seen why they have greater difficulty in learning situations. Anxiety is frequently seen as a concomitant of both the control and learning variables (Bialer, 1970; Lefcourt, 1976; Ollendick, 1979; Ollendick, LaBerteaux, & Horne, 1978; Phares, 1976).

Difficulties in adjusting to social standards and practices are also seen as precipitating anxiety in the mentally retarded. Of relevance here is research conducted on how mentally retarded persons view themselves in comparison to others and, how they feel about themselves, that is, the level of their self-concept. Heber (1964) reports a paucity of self-concept literature on the mentally retarded and reports that "one can only speculate about the self-concept of the mentally retarded" (p. 147). Perhaps the paucity of research is due to factors such as difficulty of measurement, as previously discussed. Nonetheless, as has been seen (e.g., Matson, in press, a, b), modifications and novel attempts are being made to study this area. Subsequent to Heber's (1964) review, several other authors (Brengelmann, 1967; Merlet, 1964; Perron & Pecheaux, 1964; Ringness, 1961) suggested that the mentally retarded tend to overestimate their self-concept and their performance. Interestingly, although they tended to overrate their own self-concept, VonBracken (1967a, 1967b) reported that they still consistently rated themselves as inferior to nonretarded peers. Of related significance to difficulties of social adjustment are behavioral difficulties of social adjustment noted in the mentally retarded (see extensive review by Beier, 1964) which, in themselves, may be anxiety producing. Difficulties with social adjustment are therefore seen as another anxiety precipitant in mentally retarded individuals where cerebral defect is known to exist.

In sum, although the literature and available research between anxiety disorders and mental retardation due to cerebral defect is only suggestive and, further, frequently only indirectly related, one begins to appreciate how organic conditions are related to psychological disorders. The factors of maturation, learning, and social adjustment were considered by the authors; in the authors' experience these have been related to conditions subsumed under mental retardation due to cerebral defect.

• Psychodynamic Viewpoint •

As summarized by Robinson & Robinson (1965), personality theorists have tended to ignore the development of personality constructs in mentally retarded persons. Although it may be accurate to state that mentally retarded children are basically no different from normal children except in lower intellectual development, this lone difference demands considerable attention. Robinson and Robinson (1965) highlight this point: "They are not able to keep pace intellectually in a world that places ever greater stress on intellectual accomplishments. This fact defines an important dimension of similarity, and it seems reasonable to suppose that this dimension is intricately interwoven with a great variety of other personality dimensions" (p. 276).[1]

The focus of the present section will be on the development of anxi-

---

[1]Reprinted with permission from Robinson, H. B., & Robinson, N. M. The mentally retarded child: A psychological approach. New York: McGraw Hill, 1965.

ety in the mentally retarded from a psychodynamic viewpoint. The core of this discussion stems from early analytic work of Freud and later of his students and followers. It should be noted, however, that the development of personality in the mentally retarded from a psychodynamic viewpoint has not been widely studied; as recently as 1972, Sternlicht and Deutsch pointed out that "our knowledge of the development of the personality of the retarded child consists of little more than educated guesses" (p. 1).

To explore and understand the etiology of anxiety in the retarded, a brief review of basic Freudian concepts will be undertaken. In-depth reviews are available elsewhere and the interested reader is referred to these for additional consideration (e.g., Hutt & Gibby, 1958; Robinson & Robinson, 1965; Sternlicht, 1976). Briefly, Freud (1949) hypothesized that personality consists of three interactive systems—the id, ego, and superego. The *id* was thought to contain everything that is inherited, that which is in contact with bodily processes, and that portion of mental life which includes instincts. As a child grows and comes into contact with the external world, the *ego* develops as an outgrowth from a portion of the id. The ego enables a child to interact with the real world and is concerned with testing reality and bringing id impulses into harmony with reality. The third component of the personality, the *superego*, develops through experiences with parents and other environmental sources and is the formulation of values and social behavior. The superego is seen as an outgrowth of the ego, as the ego was an outgrowth of the id.

Sternlicht (1976) states that, "mental retardation, by definition, would be a deficiency in ego development, since the defective ego is not able to adequately govern both cognitive and intellectual functioning" (p. 190). Previously, Pearson (1942) had surmised that the basic personality defect for the mentally retarded would be in the organization and function of the ego, which would also result in malfunction of the superego. Cobb (1961) hypothesized that because of their slow cognitive development, mentally retarded individuals would have problems in primitive differentiation, integration, and generalization. He felt these problems hampered the ego in effectively dealing with the environment. Robinson and Robinson (1965) stated that, as a result of a defective ego, "the retarded person is seriously handicapped in his inability to handle the demands of the id and the superego in the context of the real world" (p. 238). Sternlicht (1976) indicates that because the superego develops from the ego there is also a functional deficiency in the superego.

Pertinent to the discussion of personality development from the psychodynamic viewpoint is the notion of defense mechanisms, techniques with which the personality defends itself against psychic conflict. Of special interest for the present consideration of the mentally retarded are those defense mechanisms required to deal with anxiety and guilt, both of which result from a defective ego. Quite simply, when the ego fails to deal satisfactorily with the id's demands, it experiences anxiety, a fearful, vague disturbance in emotional organization. And when the superego's dictates are not obeyed, the ego experiences a particular form of anxiety, labeled guilt.

It is hypothesized that mentally retarded persons experience more frequent and more intense difficulties with anxiety as a result of these processes. The greater the severity of mental retardation, the more defective the ego structure would be and, therefore, the greater the anxiety the individual would experience. Robinson and Robinson (1965) illustrate further how the lack of normal growth of the ego prohibits a developing grasp of reality and an inability to comprehend and anticipate the consequences of one's actions. As was previously noted by Cobb (1961), decreased abilities in discrimination, generalization, and other types of learning are present. Hence, for example, a mentally retarded child who does not learn that writing on the walls will be punished regardless of whether the writing is done with pencil, pen, crayon, or paint will experience much greater difficulty and anxiety in the learning process. Similarly, greater anxiety would be expected in the mentally retarded child who has great difficulty in controlling aggressive impulses. The resultant anxiety from the ever-present task of a weakened, defective ego to continually compromise the demands of the id with the dictates of the superego may, indeed, be overwhelming at times.

Certain authors have also written about periods of heightened anxiety in a mentally retarded child's life. Robinson and Robinson state that the order of life stages through which development proceeds from a psychodynamic viewpoint is the same as that for the normal child; however, the ability of the retarded child to resolve the task of each period is reduced. Because the entire organism matures more slowly, greater time is needed in, for example, relinquishing the bottle, establishing voluntary control over eliminative habits, and learning eating behaviors. Depending on the expectations of parents, the care and patience given in the teaching of habits and skills, and the level of retardation, anxiety may surely be resultant. Special problems may also arise during the latency period (end of childhood to beginning of puberty). At least one author (Kiefer, 1949) hypothesized this period to be particularly stressful in that feelings of insecurity were brought about by attempts to work out a delayed "Oedipal complex."

Hirsch (1959) perhaps best delineates the ramifications of psychodynamic theory in terms of the defective ego. He states the following:

> The major difference between the retarded child and his normal peers rests in the retarded child's ego limitation. This limitation seriously interferes both with his capacity to obtain, through his own efforts, optimal needed

satisfaction, as well as with his capacity to meet environmental demands. (p. 369)

In sum, the psychodynamic viewpoint strongly suggests that increased anxiety disorders in the mentally retarded are due to a "deficiency in ego development." With the ego's inability to make a satisfactory compromise between the instincts of the id and the demands of the superego, anxiety occurs. As with other aspects of anxiety in the mentally retarded, however, the psychodynamic viewpoint is in need of additional empirical investigation and verification.

• Learning Viewpoint •

Although theories of personality development differ to a great extent in the role they assign to learning, none of them denies that learning occupies a central position in shaping human behavior. Some, for example, emphasize genetic and hereditary factors as seen in the section on cerebral defect, whereas others emphasize biologic and psychosocial developmental factors as seen in the section on the psychodynamic viewpoint. The learning viewpoint is rooted in the assertion that mentally retarded individuals learn in the same manner that normal, nonretarded individuals do. Robinson and Robinson (1965) have concluded that "when existing research designs have been extended to retarded subjects, the general laws of learning have almost invariably been demonstrated to apply to them as well as to other organisms" (p. 327). Furthermore, extending this viewpoint, Ellis, Barnett, and Pryer (1960) and Orlando and Bijou (1960) suggested that behavior of the mentally retarded follows the same general law as that of other persons. Etiological considerations for development of anxiety disorders in the mentally retarded appear to be like those for normal individuals. From the outset, however, it is noted that there is a paucity of professional writing on this topic. The purpose of the remaining discussion of this section will be to illustrate different models of anxiety development and maintenance from a learning perspective and to provide commentary on special ramifications and problems that mentally retarded individuals have because of their specific limitations.

Lick and Katkin (1976), in their recent review of anxiety assessment, note three models which fall within the behavioral or learning tradition. The most influential model of the three is the stimulus-response model, which evolved from the work of Pavlov (1941), Hull (1943), and Wolpe (1958). This model argues that anxiety is a classically conditioned response that is evoked by environmental, proprioceptive, or cognitive stimuli. The second model has developed from the work of Bandura (1968) and Meichenbaum (1974) and is referred to as social learning or cognitive-mediational model. These models assume that cognitive activity associated with external stimuli plays an important role in developing and maintaining anxiety. Lick and Katkin have labeled the third and final model the response-reinforcement model. According to this model, consequences of a fear (anxiety) reaction have important implications for development and maintenance of fear (anxiety). Lick and Katkin (1976) cite the work of Lazarus (1971) and Fodor (1974) as supportive, and liken the effects of this model to the concept of secondary gain.

Before the direct implications of anxiety development from these three models can be more fully explored, some important limitations of the mentally retarded need to be acknowledged. Generally, these limitations have a direct bearing on the theories of learning proposed (Robinson & Robinson, 1965). The first limitation is related to the learning response itself. Robinson and Robinson note that before learning can occur, elements of the correct response must be present. As the process of learning is occurring, therefore, they see the response being continually shaped and modified. As such, correct responses become increasingly more complex and symbolic. The mentally retarded person has a limited repertoire of responses both in number and complexity. (This has, in fact, been well researched by learning studies on complex tasks with the mentally retarded, e.g., Ellis et al., 1960).

The second major limitation of the mentally retarded concerns the learning of cues. Simply defined, a cue is a signal, or stimulus, which usually occurs in the environment but which also may be internal. If a person is to learn when and where to respond appropriately, he or she must be able to pay attention to both external and internal cues. Again, research has been conducted which indicates that discrimination learning is more difficult for the mentally retarded than for the normal population (e.g., Girardeau, 1959; Rudel, 1959). In addition, evidence was presented earlier which affirms that mentally retarded persons frequently have trouble with hyperactivity and inattention, behavior difficulties that interfere with the learning of cues. In addition, Robinson and Robinson note that mentally retarded individuals who have damaged central nervous systems have difficulty responding to appropriate cues. One possibility, of course, is that the sensory abilities of these individuals are defective to such an extent that they are prohibited from seeing, hearing, or interpreting cues accurately.

As noted earlier in this section, there is a scarcity of research on how anxiety develops and how it is maintained in the mentally retarded. Although learning studies have been carried out, few, if any, have addressed anxiety, per se. Much of the following discussion will, therefore, draw upon general learning studies and be applied to the models of anxiety, although the relationship is speculative at this point.

Perhaps most of what has been gleaned from general learning research with the mentally retarded is most applicable to the stimulus-response model of anxiety attainment. It should be remembered that this model posits that anxiety is a conditioned response evoked by environmental, proprioceptive, or cognitive stimuli. Pertinent to this model, then, is the previous discussion regarding the lower ability at discrimination learning of the retarded. Thus, once anxiety has been conditioned or learned as a response to a certain stimulus, the probability is high that like stimuli will also elicit the anxiety response. This is seen as directly attributable to the retarded person's inability to accurately discriminate one stimulus from another. Other studies (Cromwell, Palk, & Foshee, 1961; Franks & Franks, 1950) have suggested that organically impaired mentally retarded individuals are much slower in extinguishing conditioned responses than normal individuals. An implication from these studies may well be that anxiety is maintained at a greater level once it has developed as a conditioned response in the learning cycle.

The cognitive-mediational model of anxiety assumes that cognitive anxiety associated with external stimuli plays an important role in development of anxiety. Little of the learning research appears related here, although when Robinson and Robinson (1965) commented that general laws of learning are as applicable to the retarded as they are to normals, they noted that this "is particularly true of behaviors which do not call into play the more complex cognitive processes" (p. 327). Other related studies (Berkson & Cantor, 1960; Blue, 1963; Johnson & Blake, 1960) suggest that as a learning task becomes more difficult and verbal mediators become more important, retardates are at an increasingly greater learning disadvantage. Perhaps limitations in "complex cognitive processes" inhibit such learning for the mentally retarded individual. As should be easily evident, there is much room for study and exploration regarding the plausibility of this anxiety model with the retarded.

Probably even fewer learning studies are directly related to the response-reinforcement model of anxiety. From an experimental viewpoint, however, Spradlin (1962) found that extinction was less closely related to the schedule of reinforcement under which a response was originally learned in retarded persons. In another piece of related work, Girardeau (1962) found that it was more difficult to establish secondary reinforcers with retarded subjects. Although these studies do not appear to have a direct bearing on this model, it would appear that they have approached study of its components. Still to be investigated directly is the schedule of reinforcement as it pertains to the consequences of anxiety, and how the consequences may or may not be related to the notion of secondary gain for reinforcement.

In summary, from the learning perspective, anxiety develops similarly in mentally retarded individuals and in the general, nonretarded population. Research has yet to be conducted, however, on how special learning problems of the mentally retarded may affect the maintenance of anxiety disorders. It may well be that the learning perspective, as well as the other etiological perspectives, accounts for only a portion of the increased prevalence of anxiety disorders observed in the mentally retarded population.

• Experiential Viewpoint •

The fourth etiologic viewpoint to be considered is derived from the experiential histories of the mentally retarded. Because of their limited abilities and skills, mentally retarded persons are subject to diverse and extensive failure experiences. The impact of such experiences and their contribution to high levels of pervasive anxiety can best be understood within social learning theory (Rotter, 1954). In social learning theory, two major constructs, expectancy and reinforcement value, are proposed to mediate performance and determine behavior. Stated succinctly by Rotter (1954), "the occurrence of a behavior of a person is determined not only by the nature or importance of goals or reinforcements but also by the person's anticipation or expectancy that these goals will occur" (p. 102). Reinforcement value can be defined as the individual's preference for any given reinforcement, and expectancy refers to one's subjective estimate that reinforcement will occur following specific behavior. Since issues related to reinforcement were examined in an earlier section, we shall focus our efforts here on expectancy and illustrate how excessive failure experiences lead to reduced expectancies and contribute to the ontogenesis of high anxiety in the retarded. Our discussion shall be necessarily brief since this area has not been fully explored or critically examined.

According to social learning theory, expectancy is a function of situational expectancy (developed as a function of success-failure experiences in a specific situation) and generalized expectancy (accrued from success-failure experiences in similar situations and generalized to the present one). In novel situations, generalized expectancy is prepotent since the individual has not yet had opportunity to experience specific success or failure in that situation. As experience is gained in the specific situation, however, situational expectancy is heightened and generalized expectancy is diminished. Thus, both situational and generalized expectancies are learned and determined by success-failure experiences. Phares (1976) summarizes such developments as follows: "Expectancies for the outcomes of behaviors are learned, and they depend upon the degree of success or failure that they have enjoyed in the past" (p. 13). As noted earlier, an inordinate amount of failure is experienced in the mentally retarded. With many failures and few successes, a low generalized expectancy of goal-attainment is developed and subsequently affirmed by additional failure experiences in new situations. Such a situation becomes circular: low expectancy leads to lowered performance which, in turn, leads to lowered specific expectancy and to reduced generalized expectancy for future behaviors (Heber, 1964). This set of failure experiences and reduced expectancies is hypothesized, in turn, to result in increased levels of anxiety (Balla & Zigler, 1979).

Much of the work in this area has been conducted by Zigler and his associates. In an early study, Stevenson and Zigler (1958) reported that retarded children were more anxious and performed more poorly than nonretarded children of the same mental age. They postulated that greater failure experiences in the retarded resulted in low generalized expectancies of success and increased levels of anxiety (inferred from performance decrements). Similar observations have been reported by Gruen and Zigler (1968) and Kier and Zigler (1975). In addition, Ollendick, Balla, and Zigler (1971) demonstrated that if the mentally retarded were provided sufficient "doses" of success experience, their situational expectancy of success was increased and their inferred level of anxiety was decreased. Further, it has been shown that retarded persons placed in environments that provide a high number of successful learning experiences are characterized by enhanced expectancies of success and, consequently, lowered levels of anxiety (Gruen, Ottinger, & Ollendick, 1975). In still other studies, retarded persons undergoing extreme failure experiences have been observed to be more dependent, wary, and outer-directed, and they evince lowered self-concepts (Balla & Zigler, 1979). Clearly, the effects of prolonged failure experiences are profound, potentially leading to anxiety and related behaviors (Ollendick, 1979b).

Although literature on the association between failure experiences and anxiety in the mentally retarded is suggestive, definitive work is yet to be accomplished. Intuitively, it seems obvious that continual failure would contribute to heightened anxiety. Yet, careful study is required to affirm that anxiety covaries directly with increased failure experiences before this view can be fully endorsed. As with other etiologic views, failure experiences might well account for a subset of anxiety behaviors in the mentally retarded, especially those related to more pervasive anxiety.

• TREATMENT CONSIDERATIONS •

As we have indicated in this chapter, the incidence of anxiety and fear in the mentally retarded is high. Whether these emotional states are a direct result of organic limitations, psychodynamic constructs, learning formulations, or experiential histories, anxiety and fear are most evident in the mentally retarded person and lead to escape or avoidance of specific situations. As early as 1966, both Zigler (1966) and Bijou (1966) suggested that the behavior of the mentally retarded was characterized by avoidance patterns triggered by anxiety related to specific aversive events and feared aversive environmental consequences. More recently, Menolascino (1977) suggested that inability to deal with social and environmental stress makes retarded individuals more vulnerable to anxiety and related emotional disturbances. Given these viewpoints and the reported level of anxiety and fear in the retarded, one might well expect a plethora of treatment studies directed at reducing such maladaptive states. Very little research is available, however. As indicated in the opening comments of this chapter, the authors believe this state of affairs developed because professionals were more concerned about "educating" intellectual deficits than "modifying" emotional states and behaviors. More emphasis was placed on intellectual enrichment than emotional and behavioral development.

Within certain limitations, it is maintained that the same therapeutic procedures found to be effective with nonretarded persons are also effective with retarded individuals. Accordingly, this section will briefly illustrate the potential utility of drug treatment and behavior therapy in the reduction of anxiety and fear and the use of skill training procedures in the acquisition of appropriate social and vocational skills for the mentally retarded. The authors are cognizant of the fact that anxiety reduction alone is insufficient; skill enhancement procedures which teach mentally retarded persons appropriate prosocial skills, are also needed. These prosocial skills, in turn, are hypothesized to alter the vicious circle between intellectual and behavioral deficits and increased vulnerability to anxiety and related emotional disturbances.

• Psychopharmacologic Treatment •

Drug treatment has a significant part to play in the treatment of anxiety in the mentally retarded. For many mentally retarded persons, drug treatment may serve to make the individual more amenable to traditional psychotherapy or behavior therapy. Of course, medications need to be administered in therapeutic doses, not simply used to control unwanted or distasteful behaviors (Matson, Ollendick & DiLorenzo, 1980). In the treatment of anxiety, two major types of drugs have been used: benzodiazepines and beta-adrenergic blocking agents. According to Blackwell (1973), benzodiazepines and their derivatives are the most frequently used antianxiety drugs in the United States. Solomon and Hart (1978) more recently noted that "benzodiazepines, of which valium and librium are the best known examples, are probably the most prescribed class of drugs in the world" (p. 823). Although widespread use of these drugs cannot be disputed, well-controlled research is less evident (Clum & Pickett, in press; Solomon & Hart, 1978). Frequently, the utility of these drugs is based on uncontrolled clinical trials which are plagued with methodological difficulties and inconsistent findings. Nonetheless, Solomon and Hart (1978) concluded from a review of 78 double-blind studies (some of which included mildly retarded individuals) that benzodiazepines were more effective in the reduction of anxiety than were placebos. Based on the reported success of these drugs in relieving symptoms of anxiety, their use has become widely accepted, at least with nonretarded and mildly retarded individuals. Of course, documented adverse side effects of the benzodiazepine compounds should be closely monitored with the mentally retarded. Among these side effects are sedation, dizziness, psychomotor retardation, weakness, unsteadiness, and disorientation. Occasionally, these side effects may be more problematic for the retarded individual than the somatic and physiologic correlates of anxiety. Consider, for example, the side effects of sedation and psychomotor retardation on an already sluggish moderately retarded person. Such effects might well compound the individual's ability to function, even though his or her anxiety might be appropriately reduced.

The second class of drugs, the beta-adrenergic blocking agents, have been used less frequently and, consequently, their effects and side effects are less well known. In fact, their general use has not yet been fully approved by the Food and Drug Administration and they have not yet been systematically applied with highly anxious mentally retarded persons. Their use is detailed here, however, to underscore the complexity of the anxiety response and to acknowledge their potentially beneficial effects. Wheatley (1969) and Tanna, Penningroth, and Woolson (1977) have examined the use of such drugs, most notably propranolol, with nonretarded anxiety neurotics. To illustrate their use, brief background information about the physiology of the anxiety response is necessary. In general, pharmacologic techniques have indicated that receptors of the sympathetic nervous system can be divided into two types: alpha and beta. Only the beta-receptors are relevant for our present discussion. Beta-receptors are found in the heart, skeletal, and bronchial muscle, the blood vessels, and the gastrointestinal tract and bladder. As a result of beta-receptor stimulation, increases in heart rate, myocardial contractility, dilation of skeletal arterioles, and bronchodilation result. These very same physiological responses are observed in many anxious individuals. Given these similarities and the accurate identification of beta-receptors, development of beta-adrenergic blocking drugs received considerable impetus (Tanna et al., 1977). Interestingly, in the studies undertaken by Wheatley (1969), and Tanna et al., use of the beta-adrenergic blocking drug propranolol resulted in reduced somatic symptoms (e.g., tremors, tachycardia) but not reduced psychological symptoms (e.g., self-reported feelings of panic or nervousness). Similar findings were reported by Cleghorn, Peterfy, Pinter, and Pattee (1970) and Jefferson (1974). As a result, Cleghorn et al. have concluded that propranolol and other beta-adrenergic blockers are primarily useful in reducing somatic symptoms (especially cardiovascular symptoms) and that they are useful in reducing psychological symptoms of anxiety only when they are secondary to somatic sensations. Such a conclusion remains to be empirically validated, however.

Even though propranolol and other beta-adrenergic drugs have not been systematically examined with the mentally retarded, they would appear to posess considerable promise. It might well be the case that they will be most effective for panic and pervasive anxiety states—conditions characterized by heightened somatic symptoms. Although the possibilities are only speculative at this time, these drugs might also be more effective with severely and profoundly retarded persons (whose anxiety appears to be primarily somatic) and the benzodiazepines more effective with the moderately and mildly retarded. Regardless of these speculations, with the advance of well-controlled clinical trials, both of these classes of drugs might well represent meaningful adjunctive aids in the reduction of anxiety in the mentally retarded.

Of course, drug treatment cannot be expected to reduce all aspects of anxiety. Neither, for that matter, should it be used for all highly anxious retarded persons, nor necessarily be viewed as the treatment of choice. Rather, the decision to use drug treatment should be based on clinical data available. It should not be avoided when called for, nor used as a panacea to reduce all types and degrees of anxiety. In many instances, traditional therapeutic procedures and behavioral procedures are efficacious in the absence of drug treatment. Although both traditional and behavioral procedures have been effective with anxious persons (e.g., Sloane, Staples, Cristol, Yorkston, & Whipple, 1975), we shall limit our discussion here to behavioral procedures. Such procedures have been used with increasing frequency in the mentally retarded.

• Behavioral Treatment •

As noted in our review of learning theory and etiology, anxiety and fear can be learned according to specific principles of respondent, vicarious, and operant conditioning. Once acquired, it is probable that they are maintained by a complex, interactive process that involves all of these principles (Ollendick, 1979a). An example may help clarify this situation.

A retarded individual with generalized, free-floating, and pervasive anxiety may have developed this anxiety through respondent conditioning following numerous exposures to failure experiences, resulting in extreme panic or anxiety when in evaluative situations. Now, the individual avoids social-evaluative situations because she or he is convinced that such failure, and resultant anxiety, will undoubtedly occur once again. Alternately, the person's anxiety may have developed through vicarious conditioning. Although he or she may not have directly experienced excessive failure, the individual may have observed others endure such experiences and the anxiety or fear that followed. Subsequently, those anxious or fearful feelings are avoided by refusal to partake in similar situations. Still, the individuals' anxiety may have been acquired through operant conditioning. The person's parents or ward staff may have taught him or her to be anxious by reinforcing avoidance of actions that risk failure and remaining dependent on them. They may have selectively attended to, and reinforced, anxious and avoidant behaviors.

From this example, it should be evident that anxiety *could* have developed according to any one of these conditioning models. Once acquired, the anxiety could be maintained by a combination of these conditioning events. For example, the retarded person who has been respondently or vicariously conditioned to avoid evaluative situations may then be operantly conditioned to maintain the anxiety through excess attention, reassurance, and affection. Similarly, the person who has been operantly conditioned to avoid evaluative situations may then be vicariously conditioned to maintain it through the modeling of similar behaviors in others. Alternately, his or her operantly conditioned avoidance and resultant anxiety may be maintained through direct experiences of failure, resulting in respondent conditioning. The important conclusion to be drawn from this example is that anxiety, from the behavioral perspective, may be acquired and maintained through an interactive combination of conditioning processes (Ollendick, 1979a). Such a situation has direct implications for treatment, especially learning-based treatments.

A wide variety of behavioral procedures have been used in the treatment of anxiety and fear in both retarded and nonretarded populations. The majority of these procedures have been derived directly from principles of respondent, vicarious, and operant conditioning, as discussed earlier. We shall illustrate two of these behavioral procedures: systematic desensitization and participant modeling. As shall be seen shortly, both of these procedures have relied on operant reinforcement procedures to solidify and amplify their effectiveness when used with the mentally retarded.

Systematic desensitization, developed by Wolpe (1958), is the most frequently used behavioral technique for the treatment of fear and anxiety. Based on principles of respondent conditioning, systematic desensitization can be described as a graduated, deconditioning procedure. Wolpe proposed that the most effective way to reduce anxiety was to inhibit it by super imposing on it an incompatible, alternative response: "If a response antagonistic to anxiety can be made to occur in the presence of anxiety-provoking stimuli so that it is accompanied by a complete or partial suppression of the anxiety responses, the bond between these stimuli and the anxiety responses will be weakened" (p. 71). Relaxation has been the antagonistic response most frequently used, although other responses have also been used (e.g., pharmacological agents, humor, food, sex, and positive imagery). Typically, however, the person is trained in deep muscle relaxation and a graduated hierarchy of anxious or fearful stimuli is generated. While the individual is deeply relaxed, the fear or anxiety-eliciting stimuli are presented in the order of least to most anxiety-producing. This part of treatment is the desensitization proper and leads to suppression of the anxiety response. As noted by Wolpe (1958), it is imperative that the counterconditioning response (i.e., relaxation) be maximal so that anxiety be inhibited at each step of the hierarchy. The anxiety-arousing stimuli can be presented imaginally or in vivo. When presented in vivo, the person uses relaxation skills to proceed along a planned, graduated hierarchy of anxiety-arousing stimuli in real-life settings.

Although the theoretical model underlying systematic desensitization has been questioned (e.g., Leitenberg, 1976; Yates, 1975), there is little doubt that it is a highly effective procedure, at least with nonretarded adults (Rimm & Masters, 1974) and nonretarded children (Ollendick & Cerny, 1981). Fewer systematic investigations have been conducted with mentally retarded children and adults, but the literature available affirms its potential efficacy. Obler and Terwilliger (1970), for example, successfully treated neurologically impaired, mildly retarded children who were afraid to ride the bus or who were fearful of dogs. Imaginal and in vivo desensitization, as well as positive reinforcement, were used. Similarly, Guralnik (1973), Rivenq (1974), Freemen, Roy, and Hemmick (1976), Mansdorf (1976), and Luiselli (1977, 1978) successfully treated anxieties and fears in the mentally retarded, including fear of riding in a car, fear of heights, fear of toilets, anxieties about physical examinations, and fear of people with bodily hair. In these studies, in vivo procedures were combined with imaginal ones, and positive reinforcement procedures for performing the approach response were used. Further, a variety of counterconditioning agents were used, including relaxation training, food, and a positive relationship. All of these variations and modifications of the standard desensitization procedures would seem particularly advisable for mentally retarded persons. Limitations in cognitive abilities may make it difficult for the retarded person to visualize adequately the imaginal stimuli and to fully master the relaxation response (Harvey, 1979). Further, reinforcement to perform the avoided behaviors ensures that appropriate behaviors are indeed practiced in real life. As the discerning reader undoubtedly recognizes, anxiety reduction in these studies is achieved through a combination of respondent and operant techniques. Whether or not both procedures are necessary is unknown and must await further research. Nonetheless, the combination of these procedures would appear to be highly effective, at least with moderately and mildly retarded persons.

Although respondent conditioning has emphasized the role of direct learning experiences in the acquisition and reduction of anxieties and fears, vicarious conditioning has emphasized the role of observational learning (Bandura, 1968, 1976). Bandura states that "research conducted within the broad framework of social learning theory provides considerable evidence that virtually all learning phenomena that result from direct experiences can occur vicariously, as a function of observing other people's behavior and its consequences for them" (Bandura, 1968, p. 201). As with systematic desensitization and its variants, procedures based on vicarious conditioning have also been used frequently to reduce anxiety and fear in retarded and nonretarded populations. Three types of modeling have been used: filmed modeling, live modeling, and participant modeling. Filmed modeling consists of having the person observe a graduated series of films in which a model exhibits progressively more intimate interaction with the feared object or setting, whereas live modeling consists of having the individual observe a *live* model engage in graduated interactions with a *live* feared object or participate in real-life situations which are anxiety producing. Participant modeling, on the other hand, consists of live modeling, physical contact with the therapist, and guided practice in the feared situation. In addition to observing another interact fearlessly, the person is provided physical support and contact while practicing the appropriate behavior. Following appropriate modeling, reinforcement might also be provided to ensure performance of the newly learned behaviors. As is evident, principles of vicarious and operant conditioning are utilized in participant modeling procedures.

Studies with the nonretarded have generally shown that filmed modeling is effective in about 25 to 50 percent of cases, live modeling in about 50 to 67 percent, and participant modeling in 80 to 92 percent of cases (Ollendick, 1979a). However, it is unlikely that such a degree of success would be obtained with the mentally retarded, at least for filmed and live modeling. There is a notable absence of studies that have used filmed or live modeling with the mentally retarded. This is perhaps not surprising, given attentional and cognitive limitations of such persons. In fact, only one study has used filmed modeling (Peck, 1977) and it was found to be largely ineffective. On the other hand, studies that have reported success have used participant modeling procedures (Matson, in press, a, b; Peck, 1977). In these studies, mildly and moderately retarded persons were treated. Procedurally, fearful and avoidant persons first observed the therapist perform the desired behavior; then, the individual was physically and verbally guided to repeatedly practice the appropriate behavior with the therapist's support. Next, the person practiced the appropriate response alone but still in the therapist's presence. Finally, the individual was reinforced for performing the desired response alone. In these studies, nearly all subjects were able to inhibit their fear or anxiety and express more appropriate behavior.

In sum, both modeling and systematic desensitization (and their variants) represent potentially effective strategies, especially with mildly and moderately retarded persons. However, systematic and parametric research has not been conducted and is obviously required before full endorsement of these procedures can be offered. They, along with drug treatment, however, show considerable promise in reducing fear and anxiety.

• Skill Acquisition Procedures •

Although anxieties and fears may be diminished with drug or behavioral treatments, or both, the prosocial skills that take their place are not necessarily learned. As we have noted, many anxieties and fears in the mentally retarded develop and are maintained because of an absence of appropriate interpersonal and vocational skills. A review of these specific deficits as well as others is beyond the scope of this chapter; however, we shall illustrate the importance of such skills as they are related to interpersonal fears and anxieties. It has now been amply demonstrated that mentally retarded persons are deficient in interpersonal skills and that the absence of these skills leads to anxiety and fear (Bijou, 1966; McDaniel, 1960; Weiss & Weinstein, 1967; Zigler, 1966). The importance of such skills is further illustrated in their relationship to sociometric acceptance by others (Kelly et al., 1979) and to successful community adjustment (Schalock & Harper, 1978). To the extent that a retarded person engages in interpersonally inappropriate or deficient behaviors, he or she may become an aversive stimulus whom others seek to avoid. This active avoidance limits opportunities for appropriate interaction and may well lead to rejection, anxiety, and fear.

Several methods have been proposed for teaching appropriate interpersonal skills to the mentally retarded, including operantly based contingency programs (e.g., Brodsky, 1967; Deutsch & Parks, 1978; Luiselli, Colozzi, Donellon, Helfen, & Pemberton, 1978) and vicariously based social learning programs (e.g., Afflect, 1975a, b; Gibson, Lawrence, & Nelson, 1976; Matson & Stephens, 1978; Matson & Zeiss, 1978, 1979; Perry & Cerreto, 1977; Rychtarik & Bornstein, 1979). In these studies, conversation skills, assertion skills, and prosocial skills (e.g., cooperating, sharing) have all been taught. Collectively, these skills have come to be known as "social skills" (Bellack & Hersen, 1977). Although issues in generalization and maintenance remain, these studies indicate that the mentally retarded can acquire social skills and that these skills are useful in offsetting the deleterious effects of interpersonal anxiety and fear. Whether or not these skills might be used in a preventive mode remains to be investigated.

In sum, although numerous methodological and treatment issues remain, we have noted that both drug and behavioral treatments show considerable promise in alleviating anxieties and fears in the mentally retarded. Further, teaching mentally retarded persons appropriate skills seems possible and warranted. When minor alterations or variations are made in anxiety-reduction and skill-acquisition procedures, they appear to be effective with the mentally retarded. Thus, it seems to us that new procedures for the mentally retarded are not required. Clearly, however, more systematic and large-scale research with these procedures is required before their clinical utility can be fully supported.

• SUMMARY AND CONCLUSIONS •

As we have noted, the association between psychopathology and mental retardation has a rather long history. Yet we must conclude our review by noting that our knowledge at this time is limited, rudimentary, and clearly in need of refinement and expansion. Little systematic work has been conducted; rather, investigations in this area, for the most part, have been piecemeal and appear to wax and wane, depending on individual investigator's interest, enthusiasm, and persistence.

Although it would appear that anxiety is more prevalent in the mentally retarded, only one prospective study is available which pursued mentally retarded infants into adulthood (Richardson et al., 1979). Additional studies of this type are needed, as well as studies which "track" the mentally retarded through their daily experiences and demonstrate that anxiety and fear indeed covary with traumatic events and accumulated failure experiences. Similarly, considerably more research is needed to establish reliable and valid assessment devices so that the true incidence of anxiety can be discerned in this population.

Numerous etiologic issues remain. Although we have delineated causal models based on cerebral defect, psychodynamic, learning, and experiential hypotheses, all remain to be more fully supported. It may well be that each of these causal routes accounts for some portion of the mentally retarded who are highly anxious. Since this is most probably the situation, we suggest that clinicians and researchers become more accepting and tolerant of these various approaches. All too frequently, we allow our conceptual "blinders" to disguise and distort what we study and how we study it.

Encouragingly, treatment studies fare somewhat better. Pharmacologic and behavioral treatments seem especially promising. They, too, however, are in need of systematic and parametric attention.

In sum, our review of anxiety disorders in the mentally retarded produces more questions than answers. Much remains to be accomplished. However, for us this represents an exciting challenge; the area appears to be fertile grounds for exploration.

• REFERENCES •

Afflect, G. G. Role-taking ability and interpersonal conflict resolution among retarded young adults. *American Journal of Mental Deficiency*, 1975a, *80*, 233–236.

Afflect, G. G. Role-taking ability and the interpersonal competencies of retarded children. *American Journal of Mental Deficiency*, 1975b, *80*, 312–316.

Balla, D., & Zigler, E. F. Personality development in retarded persons. In N. R. Ellis (Ed.), *Handbook of mental deficiency, psychological theory and research*. Hillsdale, N.J.: Lawrence Erlbaum, 1979.

Ballinger, B. R., Armstrong, J., Presly, A. S., & Reid, A. H. Use of standardized psychiatric interview in mentally handicapped patients. *British Journal of Psychiatry*, 1975, *127*, 540–545.

Balthazar, E. E. *Balthazar scale of adequate behavior I: Scales for functional independence*. Champaign, Ill.: Research Press, 1971.

Balthazar, E. E. *Balthazar scales of adaptive behavior II: Scales of social adaptation*. Palo Alto, Calif.: Consulting Psychologist Press, 1973.

Balthazar, E. E. Developing programmes for decision-making in residential institutions: A systematic approach. *REAP*, 1976, *2*, 77–87.

Balthazar, E. E., & Stevens, H. A. *Emotionally disturbed mentally retarded: A historical and contemporary perspective*. Englewood Cliffs, N.J.: Prentice-Hall, 1975.

Bandura, A. Effecting change through participant modeling. In J. W. Krumboltz and C. E. Thoresen (Eds.), *Counseling methods*. New York: Holt, Rinehart and Winston, 1976.

Bandura, A. Modeling approaches to the modification of phobic disorders. In R. Porter (Ed.), *Ciba Foundation Symposium: The role of learning in psychotherapy*. London: Churchill, 1968.

Barker, P. *Basic child psychiatry.* Baltimore: University Park Press, 1979.

Beier, D. C. Behavioral disturbances in the mentally retarded. In H. A. Stevens and R. Heber (Eds.), *Mental retardation: A review of research.* Chicago: University of Chicago Press, 1964.

Bellack, A. S., & Hersen, M. *Behavior modification: An introductory textbook.* Baltimore: Williams & Wilkins, 1977.

Benton, A. L. Interactive determinants of mental deficiency. In H. C. Haywood (Ed.), *Socio-cultural aspects of mental retardation.* New York: Appleton Century Crofts, 1970.

Benton, A. L. Psychological evaluation and differential diagnosis. In H. A. Stevens and R. Heber (Eds.), *Mental retardation: A review of research.* Chicago: University of Chicago Press, 1964.

Berkson, G., & Cantor, G. N. A study of mediation in mentally retarded and normal school children. *Journal of Educational Psychology,* 1960, *51,* 82–86.

Bialer, I. Relationship of mental retardation to emotional disturbance and physical disability. In H. C. Haywood (Eds.), *Sociocultural aspects of mental retardation.* New York: Appleton Century Crofts, 1970.

Bijou, S. W. A functional analysis of retarded development. In N. R. Ellis (Ed.), *International review of research in mental retardation.* New York: Academic Press, 1966.

Bijou, S. W., & Peterson, R. F. The psychological assessment of children: A functional analysis. In P. McReynolds (Ed.), *Advances in psychological assessment* (Vol. 2). Palo Alto, Calif.: Science and Behavior, 1971.

Blackwell, B. Psychotropic drugs in use today: The role of diazepam in medical practice. *Journal of the American Medical Association,* 1973, *225,* 1637–1641.

Blue, C. M. Performance of normal and retarded subjects on a modified paired-associate task. *American Journal of Mental Deficiency,* 1963, *68,* 228–234.

Brengelmann, J. C. Die Untersuchung der personlichkeit des Retardierten. (Investigating the personality of the retarded). In F. Merz (Ed.), *Reports of the 25th Congress of the German Society for Psychology.* Gottingen, Germany: C. J. Hogrefe, 1967.

Brodsky, G. The relation between verbal and non-verbal behavior change. *Behaviour Research and Therapy,* 1967, *5,* 183–191.

Castaneda, A., McCandless, B. R., & Palermo, D. N. S. The Children's Form of the Manifest Anxiety Scale. *Child Development,* 1956, *27,* 317–326.

Cleghorn, J. M., Peterfy, G., Pinter, E. J., & Pattee, C. J. Verbal anxiety and the beta adrenergic receptors: A facilitating mechanism. *The Journal of Nervous and Mental Disease,* 1970, *151,* 266–272.

Clum, G. A. & Pickett, C. Panic disorder and generalized anxiety disorders. In P. B. Sutker and H. Adams (Eds.), *Comprehensive Handbook of Psychopathology.* New York: Plenum, in press.

Cobb, H. V. Self-concept of the mentally retarded. *Rehabilitation Records,* 1961, *2,* 21–25.

Cochran, I. L., & Cleland, C. C. Manifest anxiety of retardates and normals matched as to academic achievement. *American Journal of Mental Deficiency,* 1963, *67,* 539–542.

Coleman, J. S., Campbell, E. Q., Hobson, C. J., McPartland, J., Mood, A. M., Weinfeld, F. D., & York, R. L. *Equality of educational opportunity.* Washington, D.C.: U.S. Government Printing Office, 1966.

Craft, M. Mental disorder in the defective: A psychiatric survey among inpatients. *American Journal of Mental Deficiency,* 1959, *63,* 829–834.

Cromwell, R. L., Palk, B. E., & Foshee, J. G. Studies in activity level: V. The relationships among eyelid conditioning, intelligence, activity level, and age. *American Journal of Mental Deficiency,* 1961, *65,* 744–748.

Cronbach, L. J. *Essentials of psychological testing.* New York: Harper & Row, 1960.

Deutsch, M., & Parks, L. A. The use of contingent music to increase appropriate conversational speech. *Mental Retardation,* 1978, *16,* 33–36.

Diagnostic and statistical manual of mental disorders (3rd ed.). Washington, D.C.: American Psychiatric Association, 1980.

Ellis, N. R., Barnett, C. D., & Pryer, M. W. Operant behavior in mental defectives: Exploratory studies. *Journal of the Experimental Analysis of Behavior,* 1960, *3,* 63–69.

Evans, I. M., & Nelson, R. O. Assessment of child behavior problems. In A. R. Ciminero, K. S. Calhoun, and H. E. Adams (Eds.), *Handbook of behavioral assessment.* New York: Wiley-Interscience, 1977.

Feldhusen, J. F., & Klausmeier, H. J. Anxiety, intelligence, and achievement in children of low, average, and high intelligence. *Child Development,* 1962, *33,* 403–409.

Fodor, I. G. The phobic syndrome in women: Implications for treatment. In V. Franks and V. Burtle (Eds.), *Women in therapy.* New York: Brunner/Mazel, 1974.

Franks, V., & Franks, C. M. Conditioning in defectives and in normals as related to intelligence and mental deficit: The application of a learning theory model to a study of the learning process in the mental defective. *Proceedings of the London Conference on the Scientific Study of Mental Deficiency,* July 1950.

Freeman, B. J., Roy, R. R., & Hemmick, S. Extinction of a phobia of a physical examination in a seven-year-old mentally retarded boy: A case study. *Behaviour Research and Therapy,* 1976, *14,* 63–64.

Freud, S. *An outline of psychoanalysis.* New York: Norton, 1949.

Gibson, F. W., Lawrence, S. P., & Nelson, R. O. Comparison of three training procedures for teaching social responses to developmentally disabled adults. *American Journal of Mental Deficiency,* 1976, *81,* 379–387.

Girardeau, F. L. The effect of secondary reinforcement on the operant behavior of mental defectives. *American Journal of Mental Deficiency,* 1962, *67,* 441–449.

Girardeau, F. L. The formation of discrimination learning sets in mongoloid and normal children. *Journal of Comparative and Physiological Psychology,* 1959, *52,* 566–570.

Goldberg, D. B., Cooper, B., Eastwood, M. R., Kedward, H. B., & Shepherd, M. A standardized psychiatric interview for use in community surveys. *British Journal of Preventive and Social Medicine,* 1970, *24,* 18–23.

Goldfried, M. R., & Kent, R. N. Traditional versus behavioral personality assessment: A comparison of methodological and theoretical assumptions. *Psychological Bulletin*, 1972, *77*, 409–420.

Gruen, G. E., Ottinger, D. R., & Ollendick, T. H. Probability learning in retarded children with differing histories of success and failure in school. *American Journal of Mental Deficiency*, 1975, *79*, 417–423.

Gruen, G. E., & Zigler, E. F. Expectancy of success and the probability learning of middle-class, lower-class and retarded children. *Journal of Abnormal Psychology*, 1968, *73*, 343–352.

Guarnaccia, V. S., & Weiss, R. L. Factor structure of fears in the mentally retarded. *Journal of Clinical Psychology*, 1974, *30*, 540–544.

Guralnik, M. J. Behavior therapy with an aerophobic mentally retarded young adult. *Journal of Behavior Therapy and Experimental Psychiatry*, 1973, *4*, 263–265.

Harvey, J. R. The potential of relaxation training for the mentally retarded. *Mental Retardation*, 1979, *17*, 71–76.

Heber, R. (Ed.). A manual on terminology and classification in mental retardation. *American Journal of Mental Deficiency*, 1961. (Monograph Supplement)

Heber, R. Personality. In H. A. Stevens and R. Heber (Eds.), *Mental retardation: A review of research*. Chicago: University of Chicago Press, 1964.

Hirsch, E. A. The adaptive significance of commonly described behavior of the mentally retarded. *American Journal of Mental Deficiency*, 1959, *63*, 639–646.

Hull, C. L. *Principles of behavior*. New York: Appleton Century Crofts, 1943.

Hutt, M. L., & Gibby, R. G. *The mentally retarded child*. Boston: Allyn and Bacon, 1958.

Hutt, M. L., & Gibby, R. G. *The mentally retarded child: Development, education, and treatment*. (2nd ed.) Boston: Allyn and Bacon, 1965.

Jefferson, J. W. Beta-adrenergic receptor blocking drugs in psychiatry. *Archives of General Psychiatry*, 1974, *31*, 681–690.

Johnson, G. O., & Blake, K. A. Learning performance of retarded and normal children. *Syracuse University Special Education Rehabilitation Monograph*, 1960, No. 5.

Johnson, S. M., & Bolstad, O. D. Methodological issues in naturalistic observation: Some problems and solutions for field research. In L. A. Hamerlynck, L. C. Handy, and E. J. Mash (Eds.), *Behavior change: Methodology, concepts, and practice*. Champaign, Ill.: Research Press, 1973.

Kanfer, F. H., & Saslow, G. Behavioral diagnosis. In C. M. Franks (Ed.), *Behavior therapy: Appraisal and status*. New York: McGraw-Hill, 1969.

Kazdin, A. E. Artifact, bias, and complexity of assessment: The ABC's of reliability. *Journal of Applied Behavior Analysis*, 1977, *10*, 141–150.

Kazdin, A. E., & Straw, M. K. Assessment of behavior of the mentally retarded. In M. Hersen and A. S. Bellack (Eds.), *Behavioral assessment: A practical handbook*. New York: Pergamon Press, 1976.

Kelly, J. A., Furman, W., Phillips, J., Hathorn, S., & Wilson, T. Teaching conversation skills to retarded adolescents. *Child Behavior Therapy*, 1979, *1*, 85–97.

Kiefer, R. H. Psychiatric approach to mental deficiency. *American Journal of Mental Deficiency*, 1949, *53*, 601–605.

Kier, R. J., & Zigler, E. F. *Success expectancies and the probability learning of children of low and middle socioeconomic class.* Unpublished manuscript, Yale University, 1975.

Knights, R. M. Test anxiety and defensiveness in institutionalized and noninstitutionalized normal and retarded children. *Child Development*, 1963, *34*, 1019–1026.

Lang, P. J., & Lazovik, A. D. Experimental desensitization of a phobia. *Journal of Abnormal and Social Psychology*, 1963, *66*, 519–525.

Lazarus, A. A. *Behavior therapy and beyond.* New York: McGraw-Hill, 1971.

Lefcourt, H. M. *Locus of control.* New York: Wiley, 1976.

Leitenberg, H. (Ed.), *Handbook of behavior modification and behavior therapy.* Englewood Cliffs, N.J.: Prentice-Hall, 1976.

Lick, J. R., & Katkin, E. S. Assessment of anxiety and fear. In M. Hersen and A. S. Bellack (Eds.), *Behavioral assessment: A practical handbook.* New York: Pergamon Press, 1976.

Lipman, R. S. Children's manifest anxiety in retardates and approximately equal MA normals. *American Journal of Mental Deficiency*, 1960, *64*, 1027–1028.

Luiselli, J. K. Case report: An attendant-administered contingency management program for the treatment of a toileting phobia. *Journal of Mental Deficiency Research,* 1977, *21*, 283–288.

Luiselli, J. K. Treatment of an autistic child's fear of riding a school bus through exposure and reinforcement. *Journal of Behavior Therapy and Experimental Psychiatry*, 1978, *9*, 169–172.

Luiselli, J. K., Colozzi, G., Donellon, S., Helfen, C. S., & Pemberton, B. W. Training and generalization of a greeting exchange with a mentally retarded language-deficient child. *Education and Treatment of Children*, 1978, *1*, 23–30.

Malpass, L. F., Mark, S., & Palermo, D. S. Responses of retarded children to the Children's Manifest Anxiety Scale. *Journal of Educational Psychology*, 1960, *51*, 305–308.

Mansdorf, I. J. Eliminating fear in a mentally retarded adult by behavioral hierarchies and operant techniques. *Journal of Behavior Therapy and Experimental Psychiatry*, 1976, *7*, 189–190.

Marks, I., & Lader, M. Anxiety states (anxiety neurosis): A review. *Journal of Nervous and Mental Disease,* 1973, *156*, 3–18.

Matson, J. L. Assessment and treatment of clinical fears in mentally retarded children. *Journal of Applied Behavior Analysis*, in press, a.

Matson, J. L. A controlled outcome study of phobias in mentally retarded adults. *Behaviour Research and Therapy*, in press, b.

Matson, J. L., Ollendick, T. H., & DiLorenzo, T. M. Time-out and the characteristics of mentally retarded institutionalized adults who do or do not receive it. *Mental Retardation*, 1980, *18*, 181–184.

Matson, J. L., & Stephens, R. M. Increasing appropriate behavior of explosive chronic psychiatric patients with a social skills training package. *Behavior Modification*, 1978, *2*, 61–75.

Matson, J. L., & Zeiss, R. A. Group training of social skills in chronically explosive, severely disturbed psychiatric patients. *Behavioral Engineering*, 1978, *5*, 41–50.

Matson, J. L., & Zeiss, R. A. The buddy system: A method for generalized reduction of inappropriate interpersonal behavior of retarded psychiatric patients. *British Journal of Social and Clinical Psychology*, 1979, *18*, 401–405.

McDaniel, J. Group action in the rehabilitation of the mentally retarded. *Group Psychotherapy*, 1960, *13*, 543.

Meichenbaum, D. *Cognitive behavior modification*. Morristown, N.J.: General Learning Press, 1974.

Menolascino, F. J. (Ed.), *Psychiatric approaches to mental retardation*. New York: Basic Books, 1970.

Menolascino, F. J. *Challenges in mental retardation: Progressive ideology and services*. New York: Human Science Press, 1977.

Merlet, L. Perception de soi et status sociometrique chez les adolescents debiles mentaux. (Perception of self and sociometric status in mentally retarded adolescents). In J. Oster (Ed.), *Proceedings of the International Copenhagen Congress on the Scientific Study of Mental Retardation* (Vol. 2). Copenhagen: Det Berlingske Bogtrykkeri, 1964.

Meyers, C. E., Nihira, K., & Zetlin, A. The measurement of adaptive behavior. In N. R. Ellis (Ed.), *Handbook of mental deficiency, psychological theory and research*. Hillsdale, N.J.: Lawrence Erlbaum, 1979.

Miller, L. C., Barrett, C. L., Hampe, E., & Noble, H. Factor structure of childhood fears. *Journal of Consulting and Clinical Psychology*, 1972, *39*, 264–268.

Neuer, H. The relationship between behavior disorders in children and the syndrome of mental deficiency. *American Journal of Mental Deficiency*, 1947, *55*, 143–147.

Nihira, K., Foster, R., Shellhaas, M., & Leland, H. *AAMD Adaptive behavior scale*. Washington, D.C.: American Association on Mental Deficiency, 1974a.

Nihira, K., Foster, R., Shellhaas, M., & Leland, H. *Manual for AAMD adaptive behavior scale*. Washington, D.C.: American Association on Mental Deficiency, 1974b.

Nihira, K., & Shellhaas, M. Study of adaptive behavior: It's rationale, method and implication in rehabilitation programs. *Mental Retardation*, 1970, *8*, 11–16.

Obler, M., & Terwilliger, R. F. Pilot study on the effectiveness of systematic desensitization with neurologically impaired children with phobic disorders. *Journal of Consulting and Clinical Psychology*, 1970, *34*, 314–318.

O'Leary, K. D., & Johnson, S. B. Psychological assessment. In H. C. Quay and J. S. Werry (Eds.), *Psychopathological disorders of children*. New York: Wiley, 1979.

Ollendick, D. G. Parental locus of control and the assessment of children's personality characteristics. *Journal of Personality Assessment*, 1979, *43*, 401–405.

Ollendick, D. G. *The relationships among parental locus of control, children's locus of control, anxiety, achievement, and locus of conflict in fourth grade children.* Unpublished doctoral dissertation, Indiana State University, 1977.

Ollendick, D. G., LaBerteaux, P. J., & Horne, A. M. Relationships among maternal attitudes, perceived family environments, and preschooler's behavior. *Perceptual and Motor Skills*, 1978, *46*, 1092–1094.

Ollendick, T. H. Fear reduction techniques with children. In M. Hersen, R. M. Eisler, and P. M. Miller (Eds.), *Progress in behavior modification* (Vol. 8). New York: Academic Press, 1979a.

Ollendick, T. H. The revised fear survey schedule for children. Unpublished manuscript, Indiana State University, 1978.

Ollendick, T. H. Success and failure: Implications for child psychopathology. In A. J. Finch, Jr., and P. C. Kendall (Eds.), *Clinical treatment and research in child psychopathology.* New York: Spectrum Publications, 1979b.

Ollendick, T. H., Balla, D., & Zigler, E. F. Expectancy of success and the probability learning performance of retarded children. *Journal of Abnormal Psychology*, 1971, *77*, 275–281.

Ollendick, T. H., & Cerny, J. A. *Clinical behavior therapy with children.* New York: Plenum Press, 1981.

Orlando, R., & Bijou, S. W. Single and multiple schedules of reinforcement in developmentally retarded children. *Journal of the Experimental Analysis of Behavior*, 1960, *3*, 339–348.

Pavlov, I. P. *Conditioned reflexes and psychiatry.* New York: International Publishers, 1941.

Pearson, G. H. J. The psychopathology of mental defect. *Nervous Child*, 1942, *2*, 9–20.

Peck, C. L. Desensitization for the treatment of fear in the high level adult retardate. *Behaviour Research and Therapy*, 1977, *15*, 137–148.

Penrose, L. S. *A clinical and genetic study of 1,280 cases of mental defect.* London: Medical Research Council Special Report No. 229, 1938.

Perron, R., & Pecheaux, M. G. Les debiles mentaux percoivent-ils leur handicap? Donnees experimentales sur l'auto-estimation de l'equipment personnel. (Are the mentally retarded aware of their handicap? Experimental data on the self estimation of personal ability). In J. Oster (Ed.), *Proceedings of the International Copenhagen Congress on the Scientific Study of Mental Retardation* (Vol. 2). Copenhagen: Det Berlingske Bogtrykkeri, 1964.

Perry, M. A., & Cerreto, M. C. Structured learning training of social skills for the retarded. *Mental Retardation*, 1977, *15*, 31–34.

Phares, E. J. *Locus of control: A personality determinant of behavior.* Morristown, N.J.: General Learning Press, 1976.

Pilkington, T. L. Psychiatric needs of the subnormal. *British Journal of Mental Subnormality*, 1972, *38*, 66–70.

Potter, H. Personality in the mental defective with a method for its evaluation. *Mental Hygiene*, 1922, *6*, 487–497.

Pryer, M. W., & Cassel, R. H. The Children's Manifest Anxiety Scale: Reliability with aments. *American Journal of Mental Deficiency*, 1962, *66*, 860.

Richardson, S. A., Katz, M., Koller, H., McLaren, L., & Rubinstein, B. Some characteristics of a population of mentally retarded young adults in a British city: A basis for estimating some service needs. *Journal of Mental Deficiency Research*, 1979, *23*, 275–283.

Rimm, D. C., & Masters, J. C. *Behavior therapy: Techniques and empirical findings*. New York: Academic Press, 1974.

Ringness, T. A. Self concept of children of low, average, and high intelligence. *American Journal of Mental Deficiency*, 1961, *65*, 453–461.

Rivenq, B. Behavioral therapy of phobias: A case with gynecomastia and mental retardation. *Mental Retardation*, 1974, *12*, 44–45.

Robinson, H. B., & Robinson, N. M. *The mentally retarded child: A psychological approach*. New York: McGraw-Hill, 1965.

Rosen, M., Clark, G. R., & Kivitz, M. S. (Eds.). *The history of mental retardation: Collected papers* (Vol. 1). Baltimore: University Park Press, 1976.

Rotter, J. B. *Social learning and clinical psychology*. Englewood Cliffs, N.J.: Prentice-Hall, 1954.

Rychtarik, R. G., & Bornstein, P. H. Training conversational skills in mentally retarded adults: A multiple baseline analysis. *Mental Retardation*, 1979, *17*, 289–293.

Rudel, R. G. The absolute response in tests of generalization in normal and retarded children. *American Journal of Psychology*, 1959, *72*, 401–408.

Sarason, S. B. *Psychological problems in mental deficiency* (2nd ed.). New York: Harper & Row, 1953.

Schalock, R. L., & Harper, R. S. Placement from community-based mental retardation programs: How well do clients do? *American Journal of Mental Deficiency*, 1978, *83*, 240–247.

Scherer, M. W., & Nakamura, C. Y. A fear survey schedule for children (FSS-FC): A factor analytic comparison with manifest anxiety (CMAS). *Behaviour Research and Therapy*, 1968, *6*, 173–182.

Sloane, B., Staples, F. R., Cristol, A. H. Yorkston, N.J., & Whipple, K. Short-term analytically oriented psychotherapy versus behavior therapy. *American Journal of Psychiatry*, 1975, *132*, 373–377.

Solomon, K., & Hart, R. Pitfalls and prospects in clinical research on antianxiety drugs: Benzodiazepines and placebo—a research review. *The Journal of Clinical Psychiatry*, 1978, *61*, 823–829.

Spence, K. W. A theory of emotionally-based drive (D) and its relation to performance in simple learning situations. *American Psychologist*, 1958, *13*, 131–141.

Spradlin, J. E. Effects of reinforcement schedules on extinction in severely mentally retarded children. *American Journal of Mental Deficiency*, 1962, *66*, 634–640.

Sternlicht, M. Personality: One view. In J. Wortis (Ed.), *Mental retardation and developmental disabilities*. New York: Brunner/Mazel, 1976.

Sternlicht M., & Deutsch, M. *Personality development and social behavior in the mentally retarded*. Lexington, Mass.: Lexington Books, 1972.

Stevenson, H. W., & Zigler, E. F. Probability learning in children. *Journal of Experimental Psychology*, 1958, *56*, 185–192.

Tanna, V. T., Penningroth, R.P., & Woolson, R. F. Propranolol in the treatment of anxiety neurosis. *Comprehensive Psychiatry*, 1977, *18*, 319–326.

Tredgold, A. F. *A textbook of mental deficiency* (7th ed.). Baltimore: Williams & Wilkins, 1947.

Truax, C. G., & Carkhuff, R. R. *Toward effective counseling and psychotherapy: Training and practice.* Chicago: Aldine, 1967.

VonBracken, H. Attitudes on mentally retarded children. Paper presented at the First Congress of the International Association for the Scientific Study of Mental Deficiency, Montpellier, France, September 1967a.

VonBracken, H. Behinderte Kinder in der Sicht ihrer Mitmenschen. (Retarded children as viewed by the world). In F. Merz (Ed.), *Reports of the 25th Congress of the German Society for Psychology.* Gottingen, Germany: C. J. Hogrefe, 1967b.

Warren, S. A., & Collier, H. L. Children's manifest anxiety scale: Validity and applicability for retarded subjects and comparison to normals. *Training School Bulletin,* 1964, *60*, 192–200.

Webster, T. Problems of emotional development in young retarded children. *American Journal of Psychiatry*, 1963, *120*, 37–43.

Weiss, D., & Weinstein, E. A. Interpersonal tactics among mental retardates. *American Journal of Mental Deficiency*, 1967, *72*, 267–271.

Wheatley, D. Comparative effects of propranolol and chlordiazepoxide in anxiety states. *British Journal of Psychiatry*, 1969, *115*, 1411–1412.

Wolfensberger, W. *Normalization.* Toronto: National Institute on Mental Retardation, 1972.

Wolpe, J. *Psychotherapy by reciprocal inhibition.* Stanford: Stanford University Press, 1958.

Yates, A. J. *Theory and practice in behavior therapy.* New York: Wiley, 1975.

Zilboorg, G., & Henry, G. W. *History of medical psychology.* New York: Norton, 1941.

Zigler, E. Research on personality structure in the retardate. In N. R. Ellis (Ed.), *International review of research in mental retardation.* New York: Academic Press, 1966.

five

Affective Disorders

Johnny L. Matson
Rowland P. Barrett

Affective disorders, particularly the more severe forms, have been reported since the beginning of recorded time. Descriptions of affective disorders are found among the early writings of the Egyptians, Greeks, Hebrews, and Chinese. Furthermore, the report of many depressive disorders were colorfully described by prominent writers including Shakespeare, Poe, Hemingway, and Dostoevsky (Coleman, Butcher, & Carlson, 1980). Recurrent episodes of depression have also been noted in many past world leaders, such as the Roman emperor Tiberius and the French King Louis XI (Pinel, 1962) and, more recently, Abraham Lincoln and Winston Churchill (Bootzin, 1980).

The first reports describing the existence of affective disorders in the mentally retarded appeared in the late 1800s (Clouston, 1883; Hurd, 1888). The diagnosis of the problem has traditionally been made only in the most severe forms of depression (e.g., manic-depressive) and the persons identified have generally been those hospitalized in psychiatric institutions or residential facilities for the mentally retarded (James & Snaith, 1979). In some instances these persons have also been outpatients of various mental health facilities. Therefore, the available data tend to be skewed in the direction of a very specialized and, in some ways, unrepresentative sample of mentally retarded persons.

Identification of mentally retarded persons with an affective disorder has been influenced almost exclusively by trends in differential diagnosis of psychopathology in persons of normal intelligence. These models of depression for persons of normal intelligence have proliferated in the United States and Britain over the past 25 years, and the disorder has typically been identified as the most common form of psychopathology in populations of normal intelligence (Akiskal & McKinney, 1973).

Emil Kraepelin (1889) was the first person to formally classify depression. His earliest conceptualization of this disorder was that persons with affective and psychomotor retardation (termed volitional inhibition) and those who manifested agitation and apprehension as primary symptoms were separate groups. Both Kraepelin's followers and critics (Gillespie, 1926; Lewis, 1934) exclusively emphasized the concept of a single endogenous factor. The influence of this notion, which emphasized a singular manifestation of symptomatology, grew rapidly during the 1920s (Gillespie, 1926), remained popular thereafter, and was reflected in the nomenclature used in identifying depressed mentally retarded persons of the period.

This diagnostic approach prevailed for some time and it has only been in recent years that other methods of conceptualizing the problem have emerged. These systems are binary in nature and are termed bipolar-unipolar and reactive-endogenous. A more detailed description of these systems will follow in the section on definition of affective disorders. More important, these trends indicate that a long precedent exists for diagnosing depression in the mentally retarded based on methods established for persons of normal intelligence.

• DEFINITION AND ASSESSMENT •

The term affect is roughly equivalent to emotion or mood (Coleman et al., 1980). These disorders are dominated by extreme elation or depression, with the latter being the most frequent subcategory of affective problems. (The remainder of this chapter will focus primarily on depression.) By contrast, schizophrenia is largely a disturbance of thought as opposed to mood.

• Diagnostic Systems •

In recent years the bipolar-unipolar and reactive-endogenous classification schemes have been the most dominant. Winokur (1973) presented the former classification model based on research using family constellations of depressed patients. The bipolar disorder is generally considered to be depression with or without mania; but in either case, the patient is also more retarded in psychomotor activity, has a higher genetic loading for affective disorders, and is more likely to have postpartum affective episodes and a large number of previous periods in which symptomatology prevalent in affective disorders was present. Empirical demonstration of these two forms of the disorder are well documented (Akiskal & McKinney, 1973).

Family studies of inpatients by Perris (1966) and studies by Winokur (1973) on both hospitalized patients and outpatients have supported the idea of two genetic subtypes of depression: bipolar (manic-depressive) and unipolar (recurrent depressive). These data are enhanced by studies supporting the belief that the two subtypes fit Kraepelin's original group of volitional inhibition (bipolar) and apprehensive (unipolar) depressives (Detre, Himmelhock, Swartzburg, Anderson, Byck, & Kupfer, 1972; Kupfer, Himmelhock, Swartzburg, Anderson, Byck, & Detre, 1972; Kupfer, Pickar, Himmelhoch, & Detre, 1975). Psychophysiological measures of sleep activity, clinical presentation, treatment responsiveness (Schildkraut, Keeler, Papousek, & Hartman, 1973), and spinal fluid level (3-methoxy-4-hydroxy-phenylalanine) data support this bipolar-unipolar position.

The second binary system, endogenous-reactive, is described by Rosenthal and Klerman (1966) and Mendels and Cochran (1968). They reviewed behavioral characteristics of this classification system established in seven factor analytic studies. The general findings indicated that endogenous depressives could be described as those who tended to be older, with a previous history of depressive episodes, with greater amounts of weight loss, early morning awakening, self-reproach and guilt, and lesser degrees of hysteria and inadequacy than in reactive depressives. The nature of the relationship between psychotic and neurotic depressions, or alternatively between the endogenous and exogenous or reactive depressions, is still unresolved and is unlikely to be resolved in the near future. This situation exists because the argument over this classification scheme has been continuing for over 50 years (Kendell, 1976).

The third and most recent revision of the *Diagnostic and Statistical Manual of Mental Disorders* (DSM-III) published by the American Psychiatric Association (1980) has also established a classification scheme of depressive disorders. This system is the most frequently used means of categorizing psychopathology in the United States and is therefore of great importance. As the reader will note, this system is the primary means of classification and diagnosis emphasized throughout the present text.

The most recent version of DSM-III has been slanted in such a way as to favor the bipolar-unipolar binary system. However, this binary approach was not relied on totally in DSM-III. Other additions were deemed necessary since no system has been able to aptly describe all types of depression in a clear and systematic fashion. The result is an increased number of categories by which to classify depression. Thus, the divisions of affective disorders proposed include *major affective disorders*, in which there is a full affective syndrome; *other specific affective disorders*, in which there exists only a partial affective syndrome of at least two years' duration; and *atypical affective disorders*, a category for affective disorders that cannot be classified in either of the two specific subclasses.

Major affective disorders include bipolar disorders and major depressions, differentiated by the presence (bipolar) or absence of a manic episode. The category of other specific affective disorders, on the other hand, includes cyclothymic and dysthymic disorders. In the cyclothymic disorder, there are symptoms characteristic of both the depressive and the manic syndromes, but they are not of sufficient severity or duration to meet the criteria for major depressive or manic episodes. In dysthymic disorders (or depressive neuroses), the symptoms are not of sufficient severity and duration to meet the criteria for a major depressive episode, and there has been no history of hypomanic episodes.

As alluded to earlier, all of these systems were developed for persons of normal intelligence and have been adopted for use with the mentally retarded. A note of caution is warranted, however. These diagnostic systems are far from adequately refined for use with persons of normal intelligence (Schwartz & Johnson, 1981), and the mentally retarded population provides additional confounding problems. Thus, some diagnostic categories may have little or no utility for this population, particularly for the more seriously impaired mentally retarded (e.g., profoundly retarded). In this latter group, manifestations of depression may be markedly different, whereas in other subpopulations of the mentally retarded few categories or no disorder of this variety may exist. This latter point is particularly true with the profoundly mentally retarded, nonambulatory person (James & Snaith, 1979).

• Behaviors that Categorize the Syndrome •

Considerable controversy has surrounded the definition of behaviors considered representative of depressive features of affective disorders. As previously noted, this constitutes the vast majority of symptoms that constitute affective disorders. The primary difficulty surrounding definition is theoretical. The two primary theoretical camps emphasize either a social learning or biologically based model with observable, measurable, and often operationally defined symptoms. However, the latter group also tends to emphasize a combined psychodynamic-biologic approach in which internal mechanisms and masked symptoms are considered the primary characteristics of the disorder (Cytryn & McKnew, 1974; Freud, 1957; Frommer, 1968; Malmquist, 1975; Todan, 1962). Given the state of methodology with respect to assessment, the former classification system has greater potential for empirical validation of depression with mentally retarded persons.

Only one study (Matson, 1982) has been conducted specifically to identify behaviors characteristic of depression in the mentally retarded. (The numerous noncontrolled descriptive papers that note symptoms of depression are acknowledged but cannot be considered of great utility in establishing a scientifically based system of diagnosis and categorization.) As a result, very little *specific information* on behaviors and the degree to which they are manifested, particularly in the milder forms of depression, can be identified. However, limited data collected on persons of normal intelligence have been obtained and provide a general framework from which to start. Such an approach seems reasonable since there is little question that depression occurs in the mentally retarded (see the section on incidence).

As previously noted, one can base a diagnosis of depression on whether behaviors are observable or inferred. If the latter approach is taken, somatic complaints, enuresis, self-stimulation, and phobias would be among the behaviors *possibly* identified as symptomatic of the disorder. It is the authors' contention that a scientific approach to the problem can only be employed if the former view is taken. Lefkowitz (1980) has succinctly described this situation as follows: "The use of the term possible in a scientific context is problematic because events encompassed by the term are not subject to rules of statistical inference and thus of predictive statistics," (p. 191).

Later research may show high correlations between those operationalized behaviors with face validity and those without. Nevertheless, an objectively identified and measurable group of behaviors must constitute the initial core group of depressive symptoms. This approach was also adopted when attempting to establish assessment methods for identifying depression in children from the existing criteria used with adults of normal intelligence. An additional advantage to this approach is that the more rigorous and systematic the definition, the less frequently the disorder is identified (Carlson & Cantwell, 1980). Therefore, by diagnosing observable behaviors with a high degree of face validity, the practitioner and researcher can obtain not only a more reliable system, but a more conservative one, as well. The present authors have chosen a system proposed by Cytryn, McKnew, and Bunney (1980) as exemplary. Using a core group of symptoms, factor analytic methods were used to establish other behaviors that may be specific to particular subpopulations of mentally retarded persons (e.g., mild versus severely mentally retarded; adults versus children). In the Cytryn et al. study, four of the most prevalent methods of assessing childhood depression were noted (adult depressive disorders were also routinely diagnosed with some of these symptoms). These included the most widely accepted of the diagnostic criteria of the DSM-III of the American Psychiatric Association (1980), Cytryn and McKnew's (1972) criteria, Brumbeck, Dietz-Schmidt, and Weinberg's (1977) system, which had a derivation similar to the DSM-III, and the criteria of Kovacs and Beck (1977), which follows Beck's (1967) cognitive theory of affective disorders. Based on the behaviors proposed as characteristic of depression in each, a point-by-point comparison was made that showed a striking overlap in symptoms.

To establish a rigorous set of behaviors that define the depressive syndrome, Cytryn et al. (1980) established their core set of behaviors by choosing those that were reflected in at least three of the four diagnostic systems noted previously. The behaviors derived from this procedure included dysphoria, sadness, hopelessness, sleep disturbance, psychomotor retardation, loss of pleasure, low self-esteem, decreased concentration, aggression, suicide statements, disturbances in social, familial, or school or workshop behavior, loss of interest, somatic complaints, and loneliness. Durations of time over which each of these behaviors varied were from one week to several months, with one month being the closest to the mean.

Many of the behaviors that characterize depression are complex and difficult to conceptualize. As a result of this difficulty, in addition to the time concepts needed to evaluate such complex responses, a knowledgeable informant would typically need to be used, at least in part, to assess depression. The ability of more cognitively adept persons to give self-reports of symptoms is currently being assessed in the mentally retarded (Kazdin, Matson, & Senatore, in press).

In three studies, operationalized behaviors of mentally retarded adults have been identified as those which are applicable for treatment. In perhaps the most meaningful of these diagnostic studies, Schloss (in press) obtained 18 five-minute observations of nine depressed and nine nondepressed institutionalized mentally retarded adults on verbal and nonverbal social interaction patterns. Experimental groupings were based on diagnostic criteria used in both the DSM-III and the Beck Depression Inventory (Beck, Ward, Mendelson, & Erbaugh, 1961). These data showed that at least five differences in social behavior existed between the depressed and non depressed groups: (1) other individuals were more likely to request action from depressed subjects than to make declarative statements; (2) the depressed subjects were more likely to gain compliance by exhibiting negative affect; (3) the depressed subjects were more likely to resist requests by exhibiting negative affect; (4) other individuals were more likely to exhibit negative affect when interacting with depressed subjects; and (5) staff rather than peers were more likely to interact with depressed mentally retarded adults.

The other two published studies on empirically validated behaviors characteristic of depression in the mentally retarded can also be conceptualized within the same general framework. One of these reports (Matson, Dettling, & Senatore, 1981) involved a 32-year-old male in the low borderline range of intellectual functioning, diagnosed as severely depressed using DSM-III criteria. Target behaviors frequently noted in therapy sessions included statements concerning self-worth, suicidal statements, and statements of past history (e.g., how great life used to be but how terrible it is currently).

In the third study, which used four mentally retarded adults, two of whom were mildly mentally retarded and two of whom were moderately mentally retarded, diagnoses of depression were determined on the Self-Rating Depression Scale (Zung, 1965, 1972), Beck Depression Inventory (Beck et al., 1961), Minnesota Multiphasic Personality Inventory (Hathaway & McKinley, 1967), and operationally defined behaviors characteristic of depression including numbers of words spoken, somatic complaints, irritability, grooming, negative self-statements, flat affect, eye contact, and speech latency. Subjects were matched with nondepressed persons of similar age, intellectual level, and sex who did not display these problems. These pretest data showed major differences between the depressed and nondepressed groups, thus supporting the Schloss (in press) findings (Matson, in press).

At least with the limited data available on such "higher functioning" mentally retarded persons, the behaviors manifested and the fashion in which they were displayed seemed analogous to what has been found in persons of normal intelligence. Therefore, the behaviors previously described as characteristic of depression would seem applicable to at least some subgroups of the mentally retarded population (i.e., mild, moderate).

In terms of behaviorally assessing depression in the mentally retarded, one of three basic systems would seem feasible based on research and clinical practice with normal populations. These include directly interviewing the persons and obtaining ratings of the mentally retarded person's behavior by knowledgeable informants or through direct behavioral observations. All three of these systems are likely to be of some utility under certain conditions with the mild and moderately mentally retarded adult and older children (Shapiro & Barrett, 1982). The situation with severe and profoundly mentally retarded and young children is such that interviews are likely to be of little value, whereas ratings by knowledgeable informants and direct behavioral observations are more likely to be applicable (Shapiro & Barrett, 1982).

Interviews of mentally retarded persons in the hopes of obtaining information on depressive behavior have been conducted in at least two studies to date (Matson, Dettling, & Senatore, 1981; Kazdin, Matson, & Senatore, in press). In the first of these studies, information specific to the patients' past experiences and suicidal ideation were recorded based on their presence during therapy sessions. In the latter study, the Self-Rating Depression Scale (Zung, 1965, 1972), the Beck Depression Inventory (Beck et al., 1961), and the Minnesota Multiphasic Personality Inventory (Hathaway & McKinley, 1967) were read to the patients individually, and a verbal response was then elicited from the patient. These measures have frequently been given to adults of normal intelligence who read and then scored the measure. With the minor modification of orally presenting the items and then obtaining verbal responses, these tests were administered with little difficulty (Kazdin, Matson, & Senatore, in press). Further investigation with persons possessing fewer expressive skills are required to establish the lower limits of this testing format with the mentally retarded. Also, test parameters such as response sets and acquiescence to authority figures need to be investigated, particularly since past research on interviewing has resulted in inaccurate data because of high levels of compliance on the part of the mentally retarded (e.g., Sigelman, Budd, Spankel, & Schoenrock, 1981).

The second means of assessment with the mentally retarded has proven to be perhaps the most popular and is referred to as ratings by significant others or the most knowledgeable informant. This *third-party method* has frequently been used for assessing adaptive and other behaviors with this population (Nihira, Foster, Shellhaas, & Leland, 1974). The Rating Scale for Primary Depressive Illness (Hamilton, 1960) is the most popular of these measures for use with persons of normal intelligence. In previous experimental work, 152 men and 120 women were tested with this instrument and an intercorrelation matrix of the scales' items were factor-analyzed by the method of principal components followed by a Varimax rotation, resulting in factor scores for rotated as well as unrotated factors. Matson, Kazdin, and Senatore (1981) have also applied this measure for assessing depression in mildly and moderately mentally retarded adults. A corresponding scale for assessing depression in severely and profoundly mentally retarded adults and in mentally retarded children is needed but is yet to be developed.

The third type of assessment for depression is to operationally define behaviors that can be directly observed in either analog or naturalistic environments. Schloss (in press) has provided an excellent example of this method which has already been discussed. Further work in this area and both of the previously noted assessment modes seems necessary. However, these initial data would seem to indicate that all three methods of assessing depression can be used with at least some segments of the mentally retarded population.

• INCIDENCE •

In a number of survey studies, most of which were conducted in England, high rates of depression, particularly the more severe forms of depression such as manic-depressive disorders, have been noted in the mentally retarded. In the Colchester survey of 1938 (Penrose, 1962), 24 out of 1280 institutionalized mentally retarded persons were diagnosed as bipolar depressives. Pollack (1945) in a survey of 444 mentally deficient hospitalized patients, found that 39.6 percent had both mental retardation and psychosis, with 1.6 percent of the overall sample presenting as bipolar depressive mentally retarded persons. In a third review, Duncan, Penrose, and Turnbull (1936) reported that 27 percent of 81 depressed patients admitted to the hospital during 1934 also suffered from cognitive impairments. Payne (1968), in a more recent study with 216 mentally retarded persons, found four bipolar depressives. In still another survey, Neustadt (1928) found 14 cases of unipolar depression in 190 mentally retarded persons with emotional disturbance. Herskovitz and Plesset (1941) found a high incidence of bipolar depression also, but none of their cases were with persons with IQs below 50. Similar rates were observed by Weaver (1946) following the assessment of 8000 soldiers discharged from the military following World War II. In all of these cases, IQs were less than 75. Forty-four percent of the males and 38 percent of the females evinced personality problems, with one of the most frequently reported being depression. Thus, from the data obtained across these studies, a clinical picture of frequent and severe depression emerges from within the mentally retarded population.

James and Snaith (1979) reviewed several recent surveys of mentally retarded, hospitalized adults in England, which showed a minimal prevalence of depression at 12 out of 1000 cases. This rate is less than what was reported in the previously noted studies. However, the criterion for evaluating the disorder could have been markedly different in this study, in relation to other reports, and to some degree obscure the issues surrounding specific incidence rates of actual depression in the mentally retarded. Despite this problem, the present authors contend that depression is indeed evident in the mentally retarded, a position strongly supported by other researchers (e.g., Craft & Land, 1959).

Based on the majority of studies reported, depression is probably pervasive in the mentally retarded, although the limited available data lend only indirect support to this contention. In addition, this problem has quite likely been exacerbated for the deinstitutionalized group of mentally retarded persons, since major changes in life events are generally considered to be highly stressful and to enhance the likelihood of emotional disturbance (Bassuk & Gerson, 1978). Additional community stress points include the family of the mentally retarded individual (Robinson & Robinson, 1976). It has been reported, for example, that families with a mentally retarded child have a divorce rate five times greater than that for the general population. Moreover, these persons tend to have less financial security, less job satisfaction, fewer family support systems, and a more chaotic life than persons of normal intelligence (MacMillan, 1977), all of which are factors associated with high rates of psychopathology (Van Hasselt, Hersen, Whitehill, & Bellack, 1979).

Based on the data available from research conducted in England and the United States, the following conclusions appear warranted with respect to affective disorders in this group: (1) clinical symptoms of depression and mania, as described in the DSM-III, do occur in the mentally retarded; (2) affective features become less typical and hence more difficult to diagnose as one moves to increasingly lower classification levels of mental retardation; and (3) the limited data available suggest that prevalence rates of affective disorders in the mentally retarded approach those evident in the nonretarded group (James & Snaith, 1979).

Given the current trends in mental health care and recent evidence as to the prevalence of affective disorders, the need for research into diagnosis, assessment, and treatment seems evident. In the following sections greater elaboration on these and related topics will be made.

• ETIOLOGY •

A large number of postulates relating to the factors that cause depression have been proposed for populations of normal intelligence but largely ignored for the mentally retarded. These have included strictly biological, behavioral-learning based, and psychodynamic models, in addition to those that combine biological approaches with one of the other two.

The only two models of depression that have been applied to the mentally retarded are the learned helplessness approach of Seligman (1975) and Lewinsohn's (1975) social learning theory. An animal analog exists for both of these systems, with the learned helplessness approach having the most empirical support at the infrahuman level. In the prototype experiment of the learned helplessness approach, Seligman and

Maier (1967) employed three groups of dogs restrained in a hammock. One group could turn off (escape) electric shock by depressing a panel with the nose or side of their head. Members of a second yoked group received the same number of shocks in the same duration and pattern, but no contingency for escape was presented. The third group served as a control and did not receive shock. One day later, all of the dogs were subjected to escape-avoidance shock in a shuttlebox. The dogs in all of the groups except the shock-no escape condition learned the escape paradigm, thereby presenting evidence that this group had "learned to be helpless."

Seligman (1975) has proposed that helplessness is a learned operant that is negatively reinforced and results because animals learn during inescapable shock that treatments which terminate the aversive stimulus are independent of their behavior and this learning transfers to the subsequent escape-avoidance training situation. He points out that learned helplessness manifests itself in deficits in motivation, cognition, and emotions. Six aspects of learning in animals are noted to be roughly analogous to human behavior. These include passivity and psychomotor retardation, human feelings of worthlessness and belief in the futility of behavior, the spontaneous dissipation of depression, reductions in aggression, sexuality, and social interest, weight loss, and depletion of brain norepinephrine. It should be noted, however, that many of these characteristics may also be accounted for by theoretical explanations outside of the learned helplessness model (e.g., biologic-psychodynamic model).

A number of recent studies have been conducted which purport to validate this etiological-theoretical approach to the development of depression in the mentally retarded. One failure paradigm that could be interpreted within the learned helplessness framework is described as the interrupted tasks paradigm (Butterfield, 1964). In this experiment, the child is given a series of behaviors to perform. On some tasks the patient is interrupted prior to completion, and on others the patient is allowed to complete the task. After task presentation is completed, the child is asked to choose tasks from among those previously presented that he or she wished to do (interrupted tasks are considered failures and completed tasks successes). Research in this area has consistently shown that brighter children and older mentally retarded children tend to choose to repeat previously interrupted tasks (Bialer & Cromwell, 1960; Butterfield, 1964; MacMillan, 1969a, b), with mental age being a more important variable than chronological age (Bialer, 1961). These data indirectly support the contention that learned helplessness may be correlated with cognitive development, thus having obvious implications for the mentally retarded population.

Two general themes prevail in the data just discussed: success and failure experiences influence the general drive level of children and the histories of mentally retarded children, unlike those of normal intelligence, are characterized primarily by failure experiences (MacMillan, 1977). The proponents of this view maintain that these histories result in differing expectations of success which, in turn, underlie a wide variety of behavioral differences between normal and mentally retarded children (Butterfield & Zigler, 1965). However, these data have not been consistent; in some cases mentally retarded children exposed to failure experiences have performed better than children of normal intelligence (Gardner, 1957).

Floor and Rosen (1975) have described the passivity in these studies on academic behavior of mentally retarded children as helplessness. They have proposed that mentally retarded persons who have been conditioned over a period of years to the rigid patterns of institutional living may exhibit these traits when and if released from institutions. DeVellis (1977) has extended Floor and Rosen's (1975) hypothesis to Seligman's learned helplessness model, and a parallel argument on the failure of mentally retarded children has been proposed by Weise (1979). A major problem with these hypotheses is that none of the studies have been accomplished with persons actually diagnosed as depressed.

As noted earlier, the second model, the social learning approach, incorporates a social isolation hypothesis that has been empirically validated with animals, including dogs (Scott, Stewart, & DeGhett, 1973) and monkeys (Berkson, 1967). By depriving these animals of social contact, the authors of these studies have observed characteristic patterns of behavior analogous to depression in humans. These behaviors included listlessness, apathy, anorexia, and other responses that characterize depression. This approach builds on Harlow's (1958) original work on social deprivation with rhesus monkeys.

Many mentally retarded persons are isolated in institutions, group homes, nursing homes, and other large facilities. Attempts at care and habilitation of this population within these settings has produced behavior that parallels Harlow's (1958) and Suomi and Harlow's (1977) findings closely (Baumeister, 1978). Also, since verbal behavior in humans remains the dominant force in interactions, the isolation interaction paradigm should be viewed on both verbal and nonverbal dimensions. Additionally, since mentally retarded persons are markedly deficient in these verbal behaviors (Keane, 1972; Spreen, 1965), the likelihood of isolation and possible depression would seem to be enhanced. This situation helps explain the high incidence of psychopathology reported in this group (Rutter, Tizard, Yule, Graham, & Whitmore, 1976).

The lack of social skill assets of mentally retarded persons may, in part, account for the problems encountered by many depressed persons and may further exacerbate their problem. This general premise has been espoused by Lewinsohn (1975) and is supported by recent studies conducted by Matson (1982) and Schloss (1982). In these situations, mild and moderately mentally retarded adults diagnosed as depressed, using the multiple criteria viewed as standard protocol in the field for such diagnosis, have shown greater deficits in social behavior than those mentally retarded individuals for whom a diagnosis of depression was not made.

Certainly, more work in these areas is needed. However, these two approaches support, at least in part, models for establishing the etiological factors that result in this disorder. Unfortunately, no biological data on the depressed mentally retarded person is available. This information is greatly needed if a full understanding of this complex problem is to emerge.

• TREATMENT •

Since few studies are available in the existing literature on the treatment of affective disorders with the mentally retarded, this topic can be covered briefly. All of these studies employed a case report or single-case experimental design with three studies employing pharmacological methods and two employing behavior modification (more elaborate descriptions of pharmacological and behavioral treatments are presented in ensuing chapters).

With respect to the pharmacological studies, major tranquilizers were used in two of the reports (trifluoperazine and chlorpromazine) and lithium was used in the third. Rioth (1961) reports on a trifluoperazine trial, in which a 35-year-old Down's syndrome male with an IQ of 45 was treated after imipramine, electroconvulsive shock therapy, and chlorpromazine proved to have little effect on the magnitude of major depressive symptomatology such as delusions, hallucinations, severe withdrawal, and crying. Rioth reported major improvements with the use of trifluoperazine, but no controlled experimental methods of evaluating treatment outcome were used.

Adams, Kirowitz, and Ziskind (1970), in a second uncontrolled case study, used chlorpromazine to successfully treat a psychotic-based depression in an 18-year-old mildly mentally retarded girl. No reports of other treatment attempts prior to the utilization of this medication had been made.

The final drug study reviewed involved the use of lithium to treat a group of five mentally retarded institutionalized persons (Rivinus & Harmatz, 1979). Intellectual level varied from mild (N = 1), moderate (N = 3), to severe (N = 1). Four of the patients were diagnosed as bipolar depressives, and one person had unipolar depression based on DSM-III criteria.

After an initial 90-day baseline, each patient received lithium for one year, followed by a second 90-day baseline, then a second lithium trial of one and a half years. Positive effects occurred only when lithium trials were in effect.

Two behaviorally oriented studies of depression have also been reported. Individuals had not been previously diagnosed as psychotic, as was typically the case among the pharmacological studies, and the behaviors targeted for treatment were more clearly operationally defined. In one study, Matson, Dettling, and Senatore (1981) treated a 32-year-old male in the mild to borderline range of mental retardation for depression initially precipitated by his removal from a state institution for the mentally retarded. Upon discharge, after spending most of his life in an institutional setting, the patient became increasingly reclusive and depressed. An A-B-A experimental design was employed with a daily maintenance dosage of 100 mg of imipramine used throughout. The problematic behaviors targeted for treatment included self-worth, suicide statements, and statements of past history. Each behavior was rapidly modified only when the behavioral contingencies of instructions, modeling, performance feedback, and reinforcement were put into effect. These findings were later replicated with four mild to moderately mentally retarded adults with a broader number of target behaviors (Matson, 1982). An analysis of the changes in the depressive behaviors was made so that they might conform with behaviors of nondepressed mentally retarded persons (see Figs. 5-1 and 5-2.)

These initial empirical studies demonstrate the potential utility of at least two approaches to treating depression in the mentally retarded. The few published studies provide only limited evidence regarding efficacy, however, and much more research is needed. The potential for successful treatment of depressive disorders in the mentally retarded is further supported by the numerous treatment studies conducted with persons of normal intelligence.

Another important area for exploration relative to the development of successful treatments is the establishing of broad-based and effective assessment methods. Little research has been done in this area in the past, which makes it difficult to assess treatment effectiveness adequately. It is hoped that studies in this area will also appear in the not-too-distant future.

Despite the limited data available on effective treatment of depression in the mentally retarded, the outlook for an improved expanded data base looks promising because of the number of effective therapies now available for the treatment of depression in the population with normal intellectual functioning (Liberman, 1981). The likelihood that the effectiveness of these numerous treatments and combinations of treatments can be extended to include certain subgroups of the mentally retarded also appears promising. Such is the case because of the many varied causes of depression that exist, the wide variation in sources maintaining the symptoms (as well as deficits, excesses, assets, interpersonal resources, and environments), and the disparities in age and intellectual ability.

Some examples of the variability in pharmacotherapy approaches to the treatment of depression should provide a viable model for similar treatments with the mentally retarded. Barchas, Berger, Cigramello, and Elliot (1977) note that the empirical evidence in pharmacotherapy of depression seems to indicate that those persons with psychotic symptoms probably should be treated with an antipsychotic, whereas anxious, hostile, irritable, or agitated patients should receive a combination of antipsychotics and tricyclics. In both of these cases, dosages would need to be titrated over time to establish an appropriate level of clinical dose responsiveness.

In an excellent summary of treatments for depression, Liberman (1981) not only noted the possible pharmacotherapy approaches briefly reviewed here but offered a model for the use of behavior therapy procedures. His first suggestion was to employ problem-solving strategies in which the person selects which problems are interfering with functioning, which are maintaining the depression, how to enhance the strengths in the ongoing therapy, and establishes the most practical means that can be used to produce desired individual changes. Should this approach fail, a more structured treatment regimen is proposed. It is suggested that the therapist employ attention and praise as contingent reinforcers for adaptive verbalizations during therapy sessions and for reports of completed homework assignments. It is also noted that the therapist will be able to use the already established positive therapeutic alliance in a contingent manner to strengthen assets and to help the patient accomplish goals selected during the earlier problem-formulating module. Liberman (1981) concludes that the problem-formulation and contingency management modules therefore are quite compatible with one another.

If progress in the two behavior therapy modes described above are not sufficient, a family therapy approach is suggested. The basis for such treatment is Vaughn and Leff's (1976) findings that patients relapsed much more often when they were living with a key relative who made two or

---

Figure 5-1 (following pages). Rate of target behaviors for Ruth and Ted across sessions. Social validation criteria for successful treatment are represented by the horizontal lines with shaded areas to connect them. This constitutes a band one standard deviation above and below the mean for the two nondepressed mentally retarded persons matched with the subjects on age and sex. (Reprinted with permission from Matson, J. L. The treatment of behavioral characteristics of depression in the mentally retarded. *Behavior Therapy*, 1982, *13*, 209–218.)

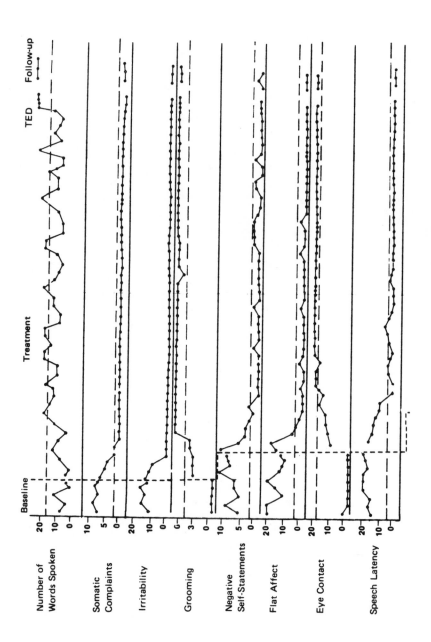

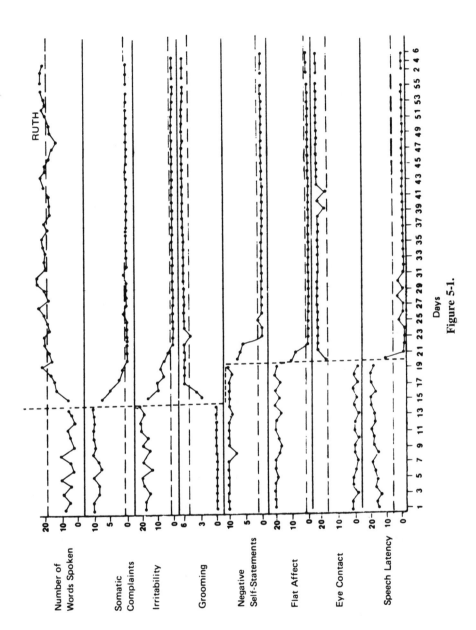

Figure 5-1.

137

more critical remarks about the patient in a 90-minute family interview. This inability to adapt appropriately to criticism would mitigate toward the development of a means to alter family interaction patterns. Treatment techniques considered viable for this approach include instructions, social and recreational activities, communication skills training, and contingency contracting. A more detailed description of this approach is provided elsewhere (Liberman & Roberts, 1976; Liberman, Wheeler, De Visser, Kuehnel, & Kuehnel, 1980; Liberman, Wheeler, & Sanders, 1976).

Liberman (1981) also points out that a number of additional behavioral treatments have been demonstrated to be effective. These include cognitive therapy (Beck, 1970), anxiety management techniques (Meichenbaum, 1977), and social skills training (Lewinsohn, 1975). Additional approaches emphasizing multimodal treatment also exist and have some empirical support (Lazarus, 1974). Unfortunately, there is insufficient empirical evidence as to which treatments are most effective with what type of patients and with particular types of derpessions under varying experimental conditions. Thus, the choice of treatments and order in which they are presented are largely professional preference when addressing persons of normal intelligence. Since the data are so scanty with the mentally retarded, the choice is even more related to individual judgment by the clinician. What these data with persons of normal intelligence do provide, however, are several possible treatment alternatives and a rationale for rank ordering at least some of these interventions. A more empirically based system for treatment selection awaits further research.

• CONCLUSIONS •

Affective disorders, particularly depression, do seem to be present in the mentally retarded (James & Snaith, 1979; Rutter et al., 1976). The disorders identified, however, tend to be of a very serious nature (manic-depressive psychosis). Little information on milder forms of depression are available, and the means of assessing depression have typically been a great deal less than optimal. Additionally, the available data are primarily concerned with adults, and appear to be more valid, reliable, and comprehensive for mildly and moderately mentally retarded than for severely and profoundly mentally retarded.

The treatment literature is even more limited. Very little is known about how these problems can be treated most efficaciously, with only a very limited number of pharmacological and behavior therapy studies reported and no empirically based dynamically oriented treatment studies having been conducted. The likelihood of developing appropriate treatments is quite great, however, given the successful treatment studies reported for those patients of normal intelligence. It may be some time, however, before this problem can be resolved. This is true because little is known about how to differentially diagnose depression in the mentally retarded and much controversy about what constitutes depression in persons of normal intelligence continues to exist and is likely to affect the definition of depression in this latter group for some time. Because of these problems, it is currently impossible to establish acceptable dependent variables for most depression research with the mentally retarded. This state of affairs has led Matson (1982) to define treated behaviors as *characteristic* of the syndrome rather than to claim improvement over the disorder per se. Much research in all of these areas is needed.

The need for more research on the problem areas related to depression in the mentally retarded must also be emphasized. The impetus for this recommendation is the current social and legislative movement to place large numbers of previously institutionalized persons in community living arrangements and the trend toward shorter inpatient stays for those persons who are hospitalized for either acute onset or chronic illness. It is generally concluded by investigators in the field that the major changes inherent in movement from one environment to another, as occurs in de-institutionalization, places great stress on the former patient. Stress leads to higher rates of psychopathology, including depression. A second factor pertains to expectations of those persons in the mentally retarded person's environment. It is certainly likely that higher expectations for normal behavior will be presented by community members than by professional staff, many of whom are exposed to grossly deviant behavior on a daily basis in the institutional setting. Thus, depressive behavior, and quite likely of a relatively severe nature, would be more readily tolerated socially within the institution than in the community setting. Finally, legal and ethical obligations to provide treatment for mentally retarded persons' depression in the same manner as for persons of normal intelligence seems warranted. To provide these needed clinical services, it will be necessary to perform the appropriate research in order to develop effective diagnostic and treatment systems.

Despite the small amount of research on affective disorders with the mentally retarded and the perceived need for considerable additional information in this area, the future could be bright. The massive amounts of

---

Figure 5-2 (following pages). Rate of target behaviors for Crystal and Shelia across sessions. Social validation criteria for successful treatment are represented by the horizontal lines with shaded areas to connect them. This constitutes a band one standard deviation above and below the mean for the two nondepressed mentally retarded persons matched with the subject on age and sex. (Reprinted with permission from Matson, J. L. The treatment of behavioral characteristics of depression in the mentally retarded. *Behavior Therapy,* 1982, *13*, 209–218.)

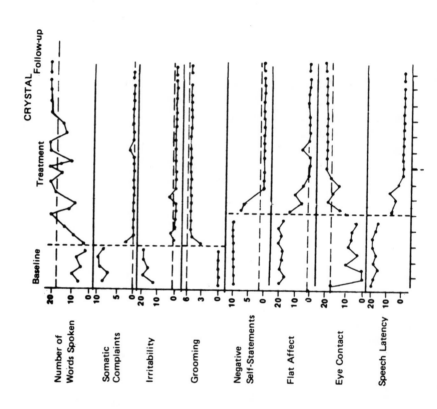

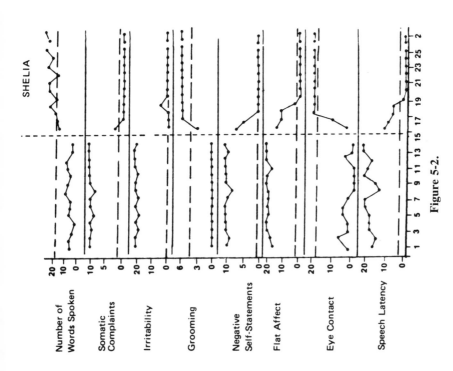

Figure 5-2.

141

research with persons of normal intelligence have proved to be fruitful, and what little has been done with the mentally retarded has resulted in equally positive results. It is hoped that the trend toward improved diagnosis and care of the mentally retarded in this area of psychopathology will continue to accelerate.

• REFERENCES •

Adams, G. L., Kirowitz, J., & Ziskind, E. Manic depressive psychosis, mental retardation, and chromosomal rearrangement. *Archives of General Psychiatry*, 1970, *23*, 305–309.

American Psychiatric Association. *Diagnostic and statistical manual of mental disorders* (3rd ed.). Washington, D.C.: American Psychiatric Association, 1980.

Akiskal, H. S., & McKinney, W. T. Depressive disorders: Toward a unified hypothesis. *Science*, 1973, *182*, 20–29.

Barchas, J. D., Berger, B. A., Cigramello, R. D., & Elliot, G. R. (Eds.). *Psychopharmacology: From theory to practice*. New York: Oxford University Press, 1977.

Bassuk, E. L., & Gerson, S. Deinstitutionalization and mental health services. *Scientific American*, 1978, *2*.

Baumeister, A. A. Origins and control of stereotyped movements. In C. E. Meyers (Eds.), *Quality of life in severely and profoundly mentally retarded people: Research foundations for improvement*. Washington, D.C.: American Association on Mental Deficiency, 1978.

Beck, A. T. Cognitive therapy: Nature and relation to behavior therapy. *Behavior Therapy*, 1970, *1*, 184–200.

Beck, A. T. *Depression: Clinical, experimental, and theoretical perspectives*. New York: Harper & Row, 1967.

Beck, A. T., Ward, L. H., Mendelson, M., & Erbaugh, M. D. An inventory for measuring depression. *Archives of General Psychiatry*, 1961, *4*, 561–571.

Berkson, G. Abnormal stereotyped motor acts. In J. Zubin & H. F. Hunt (Eds.), *Comparative psychopathology: Animal and Human*. New York: Grune & Stratton, 1967.

Bialer, I. Conceptualization of success and failure in mentally retarded and normal children. *Journal of Personality*, 1961, *29*, 303–320.

Bialer, I., & Cromwell, R. Task repetition in mental defectives as a function of chronological age and mental age. *American Journal of Mental Deficiency*, 1960, *65*, 265–268.

Bootzin, R. R. (Ed.), *Abnormal psychology: Current perspectives* (3rd ed.). New York: Random House, 1980.

Brumbeck, R. A., Dietz-Schmidt, S. G., & Weinberg, W. A. Depression in children referred to an educational diagnostic center: Diagnosis and treatment and analysis of criteria and literature review. *Diseases of the Nervous System*, 1977, *38*, 529–535.

Butterfield, E. L. The interruption of tasks. Methodological, factual, theroetical issues. *Psychological Bulletin,* 1964, *62,* 309–322.

Butterfield, E. L., & Zigler, E. The effects of success and failure on the discrimination learning of normal and retarded children. *Journal of Abnormal Psychology,* 1965, *70,* 25–31.

Carlson, G. A., & Cantwell, D. P. A survey of depressive symptoms, syndromes, and disorder in a child psychiatric population. *Journal of Child Psychology and Psychiatry,* 1980, *21* 19–25.

Clouston, T. S. *Clinical lectures on mental diseases.* London: Churchill, 1883.

Coleman, J. C., Butcher, J. N., & Carlson, R. C. *Abnormal psychology and modern life.* Glenview, Ill.: Scott, Foresman, 1980.

Craft, M., & Land, M. *Mental disorder in the defective: A psychiatric survey among inpatients.* Washington, D.C.: American Association on Mental Deficiency, 1959.

Cytryn, L., & McKnew, D. H. Factors influencing the changing clinical expression of the depressive process in children. *American Journal of Psychiatry,* 1974, *131,* 879–881.

Cytryn, L., & McKnew, D. H. Proposed classification of childhood depression. *American Journal of Psychiatry,* 1972, *129,* 149–155.

Cytryn, L., McKnew, D. H., & Bunney, W. Diagnosis of depression in children: A reassessment. *American Journal of Psychiatry,* 1980, *137,* 22–25.

Detre, T. P., Himmelhoch, J. M., Swartzburg, M., Anderson, C. M., Byck, R., & Kupfer, D. J. Hypersomnia and manic-depressive disease. *American Journal of Psychiatry,* 1972, *128,* 1303–1305.

DeVellis, D. F. Learned helplessness in institutions. *Mental Retardation,* 1977, *15,* 10–15.

Duncan, A. C., Penrose, L., & Turnbull, R. Mental deficiency and manic depressive insanity. *Journal of Mental Science,* 1936, *82,* 635–641.

Floor, L, & Rosen, M. Investigating the phenomenon of helplessness in mentally retarded adults. *American Journal of Mental Deficiency,* 1975, *79,* 565–572.

Freud, S. Mourning and melancholia (1917). *Collected papers* (Vol. 4). London: Hogarth Press, 1957.

Frommer, E. Depressive illness in childhood. *British Journal of Psychiatry,* 1968, *2,* 117–123.

Gardner, W. I. *Effects of interpolated success and failure on motor task performance in mental defectives.* Paper presented at the Southeastern Psychological Association, Nashville, Tenn., March 1957.

Gillespie, R. D. Discussion on manic-depressive psychoses. *British Medical Journal,* 1926, *2,* 878–879.

Hamilton, M. A rating scale for depression. *Journal of Neurology, Neurosurgery, and Psychiatry,* 1960, *23,* 56–62.

Harlow, H. F. The nature of love. *American Psychologist,* 1958, *13,* 673–685.

Hathaway, S. R., & McKinley, J. C. *Minnesota Multiphasic Personality Inventory: Manual for Administration and Scoring.* New York: Psychological Corporation, 1967.

Herskovitz, H. H., & Plesset, M. R. Psychoses in adult mental defectives. *Psychiatric Quarterly,* 1941, *15,* 574–588.

Hurd, H. M. Imbecility with insanity. *Journal of Insanity*, 1888, *45*, 263–371.

James, F. E., & Snaith, R. P. *Psychiatric illness and mental handicap.* London: Gaskell, 1979.

Kazdin, A. E., Matson, J. L., & Senatore, V. Assessing depression in borderline, mild, and moderately mentally retarded adults. *American Journal of Psychiatry*, in press.

Keane, V. E. Incidence of speech and language problems in the mentally retarded. *Mental Retardation*, 1972, *10*, 3–8.

Kendell, R. E. The classification of depressions: A review of contemporary confusion. *British Journal of Psychiatry*, 1976, *7*, 15–28.

Kovacs, M., & Beck, A. T. An empirical-clinical approach toward a definition of childhood depression. In J. G. Schulterbrandt & A. Raskin (Eds.), *Depression in childhood: Diagnosis, treatment, and conceptual models.* New York: Raven Press, 1977.

Kraepelin, E. *Psychiatrie: Ein Lehrbuch für Studierende und Aertze* (3rd Ed.). Leipzig, Barth, 1889.

Kupfer, D. J., Himmelhoch, J. M., Swartzburg, M., Anderson, C. M., Byck, R., & Detre, T. P. Hypersomnia in manic depressive disease (a preliminary report). *Diseases of the Nervous System*, 1972, *33*, 720–724.

Kupfer, D. J., Pickar, D., Himmelhoch, J. M., & Detre, T. P. Are there two types of unipolar depression? *Archives of General Psychiatry*, 1975, *32*, 866–871.

Lazarus, A. A. Multimodal behavioral treatment of depression. *Behavior Therapy*, 1974, *5*, 549–554.

Lefkowitz, M. M. Childhood depression: A reply to Costello. *Psychological Bulletin*, 1980, *87*, 191–194.

Lewinsohn, P. M. The behavioral study and treatment of depression. In M. Hersen, R. M. Eisler, and P. M. Miller (Eds.), *Progress in behavior modification* (Vol. 1). New York: Academic Press, 1975.

Lewis, A. J. Melancholia: A clinical survey of depressive states. *Journal of Mental Science*, 1934, *80*, 277–378.

Liberman, R. P. A model for individualized treatment. In L. P. Rehm (Ed.), *Behavior therapy for depression: Present status and future directions.* New York: Academic Press, 1981.

Liberman, R. P. & Roberts, J. Contingency management of neurotic depression and marital disharmony. In H. Eysenck (Ed.), *Case studies in behavior therapy.* London: Routledge & Kegan Paul, 1976.

Liberman, R. P., Wheeler, E., De Visser, L., Kuehnel, J., & Kuehnel, T. *Handbook of marital therapy*, New York: Plenum, 1980.

Liberman, R. P., Wheeler, E., & Sanders, N. Behavioral therapy for marital disharmony. *Journal of Marriage and Family Counseling*, 1976, *2*, 383–390.

MacMillan, D. L. *Mental retardation in school and society.* Boston: Little, Brown, 1977.

MacMillan, D. L. Motivational differences: Cultural-familial retardates vs. normal subjects on expectancy for failure. *American Journal of Mental Deficiency*, 1969a, *74*, 254–258.

MacMillan, D. L. Resumption of interrupted tasks by normal and educable mentally retarded subjects. *American Journal of Mental Deficiency*, 1969b, *73*, 657–661.

Malmquist, C. P. Depression in childhood. In F. F. Flach & S. C. Draghi (Eds.), *The nature and treatment of depression*. New York: Wiley, 1975.

Matson, J. L. The behavioral treatment of depression in the mentally retarded. *Behavior Therapy*, 1982, *13*, 209–218.

Matson, J. L., Dettling, J., & Senatore, V. Treating depression of a mentally retarded adult. *British Journal of Mental Subnormality*, 1981, *16*, 86–88.

Meichenbaum, D. H. *Cognitive-behavior modification*. New York: McGraw-Hill, 1977.

Mendels, J., & Cochran, L. The nosology of depression: The endogenous-reactive concept. *American Journal of Psychiatry*, 1968, *124*, 1–11.

Neustadt, R. *The episodic psychosis of the defective*. Berlin: Karger, 1928.

Nihira, K., Foster, R., Shellhaas, M., & Leland, H. *AAMD Adaptive Behavior Scale*. Washington, D.C.: American Association on Mental Deficiency, 1974.

Payne, R. The psychotic subnormal. *Journal of Mental Subnormality*, 1968, *14*, 25–34.

Penrose, L. S. *The biology of mental defectives*. New York: Grune & Stratton, 1962.

Perris, C. A study of bipolar (manic-depressive) and unipolar recurrent depressive psychoses. *Acta Psychiatrica Scandanavica*, 1966, *42*, 58–67.

Pinel, P. *A treatise on insanity (1801)* (D. D. Davis, trans.). New York: Hafner, 1962.

Pollack, H. M. Mental disease among mental defectives. *American Journal of Mental Deficiency*, 1945, *49*, 477–480.

Rioth, A. I. Psychotic depression in a mongol. *Journal of Mental Subnormality*, 1961, *7*, 45–47.

Rivinus, T. M., & Harmatz, J. S. Diagnosis and lithium treatment of affective disorder in the retarded: Five case studies. *American Journal of Psychiatry*, 1979, *136*, 551–554.

Robinson, N. M. & Robinson, H. B. *The mentally retarded child*. New York: McGraw-Hill, 1976.

Rosenthal, S. H., & Klerman, G. L. Content and consistency in the endogenous depressive pattern. *British Journal of Psychiatry*, 1966, *112*, 471–484.

Rutter, M., Tizard, J., Yule, W., Graham, P., & Whitmore, K. Isle of Wight studies, 1964–1974. *Psychological Medicine*, 1976, *7*, 313–332.

Schildkraut, J. J., Keeler, B. A., Papousek, M., & Hartman, E. MHPG excretion in depressive disorders: Relation to clinical subtypes and desynchronized sleep. *Science*, 1973, *181*, 762–764.

Schloss, P. J. Verbal interaction patterns of depressed and non-depressed institutionalized mentally retarded adults. *Applied Research in Mental Retardation*, 1982, *3*, 1–12.

Schwartz, S., & Johnson, J. H. *Psychopathology of childhood: A clinical experimental approach*. New York: Pergamon Press, 1981.

Scott, J. P., Stewart, J. M., & DeGhett V. J. Separation in infant dogs: Emotional response and motivational consequences. In J. P. Scott & E. C. Senay (Eds.), *Separation and depression: Clinical and research aspects*. Washington, D.C.: American Association for the Advancement of Science, 1973.

Seligman, M. E. P. *Helplessness: On depression, development and death.* San Francisco: Freeman, 1975.

Seligman, M. E. P., & Maier, S. F. Failure to escape traumatic shock. *Journal of Experimental Psychology,* 1967, *74,* 1–9.

Shapiro, E. S. & Barrett, R. P. Behavioral assessment of the mentally retarded. In J. L. Matson & F. Andrasik (Eds.), *Treatment issues and innovations in mental retardation.* New York: Plenum Press, 1982.

Sigelman, C. K., Budd, E. C., Spankel, C. L., & Schoenrock, C. J. When in doubt, say yes: Acquiescence in interviews with mentally retarded persons. *Mental Retardation,* 1981, *19,* 53–58.

Spreen, O. Language functions in mental retardation: A review. I. Language development, types of retardation, and intelligence level. *American Journal of Mental Deficiency,* 1965, *6,* 482–494.

Suomi, S. J., & Harlow, H. F. Production and alleviation of depressive behavior in monkeys. In J. D. Maser & M. E. P. Seligman (Eds.), *Psychopathology: Experimental models.* San Francisco: Freeman, 1977.

Todan, J. M. Depression in children and adolescents. *American Journal of Orthopsychiatry,* 1962, *32,* 404–414.

Van Hasselt, V. B., Hersen, M., Whitehill, M. B., & Bellack, A. S. Social skills assessment and training for children: Evaluative review. *Behavior Research & Therapy,* 1979, *17,* 413–438.

Vaughn, C. E., & Leff, J. P. The measurement of expressed emotion in the families of psychiatric patients. *British Journal of Social and Clinical Psychology,* 1976, *15,* 157–165.

Weaver, S. J. *Effects of motivation-hygiene orientations, and interpersonal reaction tendencies in intellectually subnormal children.* Ann Arbor, Mich.: University Microfilms, 1966.

Weaver, T. R. The incidence of maladjustment among mental defectives in military environment. *American Journal of Mental Deficiency,* 1946, *51,* 238–246.

Weise, J. R. Perceived control and learned helplessness in mentally retarded and non-retarded children: A developmental analysis. *Developmental Psychology,* 1979, *15,* 311–319.

Winokur, G. The types of affective disorders. *Journal of Nervous and Mental Disease,* 1973, *156,* 82–96.

Zung, W. W. K. A cross-cultural survey of depressive symptomatology in normal adults. *Journal of Cross-Cultural Psychology,* 1972, *3,* 177–183.

Zung, W. W. K. A self-rating depression scale. *Archives of General Psychiatry,* 1965, *12,* 63–70.

six

Psychosis and Mental Retardation: Issues of Coexistence

Raymond G. Romanczyk
Janet A. Kistner

Historically, one finds minimal distinction made between subcategories of severe developmental and psychotic disorders. Terms such as *insane, feeble minded,* and *deviants* were all somewhat used interchangeably, and even today it is not uncommon for the lay public to equate retardation with mental illness. Recently there have been significant changes, given the perspective of historical trend (Romanczyk, Kistner, & Crimmins, 1980), but nevertheless important unanswered questions remain regarding appropriate assessment, classification, and service delivery for individuals with severe impairments. It seems that our information concerning the severely disturbed is biased in that the diagnoses of mental retardation and psychosis appear to be used in a mutually exclusive manner. As an example, the population of psychotic and autistic individuals has been underestimated because of the broad use of mental retardation as a diagnostic category.

There are a number of issues that relate to diagnostic differentiation of mental retardation and psychosis:

1. Etiology—it may be assumed that the more precise the diagnostic classification, the more efficient the etiological research will be.

2. Treatment—it is often assumed that accurate and specific diagnosis is important with respect to treatment selection and prognosis.
3. Resources—accurate demographics are needed for the appropriate allocation of resources for service delivery.
4. Clustering—especially in regard to schools and residential facilities, many programs impose grouping by handicapping condition. This may or may not be a valid or effective method, and it presupposes accurate diagnostic practices. This often relates to other placement decisions, such as developmental center versus psychiatric hospital.

The issues raised and the general area of the interface between mental retardation and psychosis are extensive and wide-ranging topics. This chapter will selectively review psychosis (i.e., schizophrenia and autism), diagnostic practices, etiological theories, and treatment strategies, and finally provide a summary and overview of what are considered the most important issues.

• DIAGNOSIS •

• Diagnosis of Mental Retardation •

In the organization of DSM-III, mental retardation is classified in the section entitled "Disorders Usually First Evident in Infancy, Childhood, or Adolescence." Diagnoses of disorders in this section are applicable to adults if the condition was manifested prior to adulthood and has persisted. Further, unless otherwise specified, diagnostic categories may be simultaneously applied.

According to DSM-III, (APA, 1980) the diagnostic criteria for mental retardation are as follows:

A. Significantly subaverage general intellectual functioning: an IQ of 70 or below on an individually administered IQ test (for infants, since available intelligence tests do not yield numerical values, a clinical judgment of significant subaverage intellectual functioning). B. Concurrent deficits or impairments in adaptive behavior, taking the person's age into consideration. C. Onset before the age of 18. (pp. 40–41)[1]

In discussing the application of these criteria, DSM-III points out an element of flexibility and discretion in considering a diagnosis of mental retardation for individuals scoring in the borderline range of intellectual functioning. By placing equal emphasis on an assessment of age-appropri-

---

[1]Reprinted with permission from the American Psychiatric Association. *Diagnostic and statistical manual of mental disorders* (3rd ed.). Washington, D.C.: American Psychiatric Association, 1980.

ate adaptive behavior, an arbitrary IQ cutoff score alone does not dictate the decision to diagnose mental retardation. Adaptive behavior is defined as "the effectiveness with which an individual meets the standards of personal independence and social responsibility expected of his or her age group" (p. 37). Given the lack of standardized measures of adaptive behavior, clinical judgment is necessary for the assessment of general adaptation.

DSM-III also provides for four distinct subtypes of mental retardation, reflecting the degree of intellectual impairment. The subtypes and guidelines for distinguishing between them are subtype of mental retardation (mild, moderate, severe, and profound) and IQ level (50–70, 35–49, 20–34, and below 20). There is also an additional categorical code for "Unspecified Mental Retardation" to be assigned when there is a strong presumption of significant intellectual impairment but the individual is untestable by standardized intelligence tests.

With regard to cases in which the initial onset of the clinical features of retardation occur after the age of 18 years, the syndrome is dementia and is classified as an organic mental disorder. When there is a regression from normal intellectual functioning and adaptive behavior prior to age 18, both mental retardation and dementia are diagnosed. This is consistent with the manual's discussion of differential diagnosis, which states that "the diagnosis of mental retardation should be made whenever present regardless of the presence of another diagnosis." Additionally, in the discussion of associated features of mental retardation, it is stated that "when another mental disorder is present, it should also be coded on Axis I" (p. 37). Clearly, the use of multiple primary (Axis I) diagnosis in conjunction with mental retardation is endorsed and prescribed by DSM-III. Therefore, when an individual exhibits bizarre, maladaptive, or dysfunctional behavior in addition to having deficits in both intellectual functioning and adaptive behavior which occur prior to adulthood, primary diagnoses in addition to mental retardation are justifiable when the symptomatology meets the diagnostic criteria of another distinct disorder. However, it is notable that the manual's examples of multiple diagnoses with mental retardation are drawn from the section on "Infancy, Childhood, or Adolescence Disorders," such as the attention deficit disorders and the pervasive developmental disorders.

• Diagnosis of Pervasive Developmental Disorder •

In addressing the problems with the commonly used, highly unreliable, and often interchangeable diagnoses for individuals with severe developmental and psychological impairment, DSM-III provides a classification of pervasive developmental disorders. In the introduction of this classification, the manual states that these disorders "are characterized by distortions in the development of multiple basic psychological functions that are involved in the development of social skills and language, such as attention, perception, reality testing, and motor movement" (p. 86).

Two major subtypes of these disorders are defined with the primary distinction pertaining to age of onset. The first subtype is infantile autism, which has the following diagnostic criteria (APA, 1980):

1. Onset before 30 months of age.
2. Pervasive lack of responsiveness to other (autism).
3. Gross deficits in language development.
4. If speech is present, peculiar speech patterns such as immediate and delayed echolalia, metaphorical language, pronominal reversal.
5. Bizarre responses to various aspects of the environment, e.g., resistance to change, peculiar interest in or attachments to animate or inanimate objects.
6. Absence of delusions, hallucinations, loosening of associations, and incoherence as in schizophrenia (pp. 89–90).

In the manual's discussion of predisposing factors for infantile autism, known organic impairments (e.g., maternal rubella, phenylketonuria, encephalitis, etc.) are listed as etiological predispositions. With regard to differential diagnosis with mental retardation, DSM-III acknowledges that behavioral abnormalities similar to those in autism are often exhibited in mental retardation, but the full syndrome of infantile autism is rarely present. However, if "both disorders are present, both diagnoses should be made" (p. 89). DSM-III also provides a categorical code for infantile autism, residual state, which is used when the full syndrome had once been present but only residual characteristics of autism are currently manifest.

The second subtype of pervasive developmental disorders is childhood onset pervasive developmental disorder, which has the following diagnostic criteria (APA, 1980):

1. Gross and sustained impairment in social relationships, e.g., lack of appropriate affective responsivity, inappropriate clinging, asociality, lack of empathy.
2. At least three of the following:
    • Sudden excessive anxiety manifested by such symptoms as free-floating anxiety, catastrophic reactions to everyday occurrences, inability to be consoled when upset, unexplained panic attacks
    • Constricted or inappropriate affect, including lack of appropriate fear reactions, unexplained rage reactions, and extreme mood lability

Mental retardation refers to significantly subaverage general intellectual functioning existing concurrently with deficits in adaptive behavior, and manifested during the developmental period.[2]

General intellectual functioning is defined as the results obtained by assessment with one or more of the individually administered general intelligence tests developed for that purpose.

Significantly subaverage is defined as IQ more than two standard deviations below the mean for the test.

Adaptive behavior is defined as the effectiveness or degree with which an individual meets the standards of personal independence and social responsibility expected for age and cultural group.

Developmental period is defined as the period of time between birth and the 18th birthday. (p. 11)[2]

Further, the manual presents a dual classification approach: a biomedical and a behavioral system. The biomedical system, designed to separate groups on the basis of etiology or presumed etiology, has no direct analogy in DSM-III. In the multiaxial diagnostic classification scheme of DSM-III, the listing of etiological or complicating medical factors is regarded on the third axis. The AAMD system includes divisions derived from the *International Classification of Disease* (ICD) and DSM-II. Under this system, a psychiatric disorder may be considered an etiologic agent and would dictate classification under the major category, mental retardation following psychiatric disorder. A psychiatric disorder which is present but not considered etiologic would be coded under additional medical information categories. In this case, the manual refers to DSM-II for appropriate usage of terms such as psychosis and neurosis.

The behavioral system of classification is more directly analogous to the DSM-III criteria. However, no reference is made to psychiatric disorder within this system. The degree of impairment in functioning for both measured intelligence and adaptive behavior is divided into four levels: mild, moderate, severe, and profound. Intellectual functioning must be measured by an individually administered intelligence test with levels defined in Table 6-1 (Grossman, 1977, p. 19).

Adaptive behavior "must be determined on the basis of a series of observations in many places over considerable periods of time" (Grossman, 1977, p. 17). The use of a combination of published scales and clinical judgment is preferred in evaluating adaptive behavior.

According to the manual, a valid diagnosis of mental retardation must satisfy the requirements of subaverage intellectual functioning and deficits in adaptive behavior. Although intelligence tests can satisfy the first

---

[2]Reprinted with permission from Grossman, H. J. (Ed.). *Manual on terminology and classification*. Washington, D.C.: American Association on Mental Deficiency, 1977.

Table 6-1

Measurement of Intellectual Functioning According to Two
Intelligence Scales

	Obtained Intelligence	Quotient
Levels	Stanford, Binet, & Catell (SD 16)	Wechsler Scales (SD 15)
Mild	67–52	69–55
Moderate	51–36	54–40
Severe	35–20	39–25 (extrapolated)
Profound	19 and below	24 and below

Reprinted with permission from Grossman, H. J. (Ed.). *Manual on terminology and classification.* Washington, D.C.: American Association on Mental Deficiency, 1977, p. 19.

requirement, adaptive behavioral scales alone cannot fully satisfy the second. "Therefore, the ultimate determination of mental retardation still rests on clinical judgment" (p. 22).

In summary, the two major diagnostic classification systems indicate that a diagnosis of mental retardation does not preclude an additional diagnosis of other psychopathological disorders. In our experience, the populations that exist in state hospitals and residential developmental centers typically have considerable overlap. However, there appears to be a continuing subtle bias toward considering psychopathological behavior of a mentally retarded individual as qualitatively different, even if the explicit criteria of a specific disorder are met. For instance, the DSM-III *Case Book* (Spitzer, Skodol, Gibbon, & Williams, 1981) provides an example of a 15-year-old boy with Down's syndrome who is exhibiting severely disruptive and physically assaultive behavior leading to a request for hospitalization. With regard to the issue of multiple diagnoses, the authors present the following discussion:

> This child, as is often the case, presents for admission because of destructive and aggressive behavior, not because of impairment in intellectual functioning. Presumably, this aggressive behavior is a persistent pattern. Should one therefore make an additional diagnosis of conduct disorder? We think not. The DSM-III criteria for conduct disorder do not rule out moderate or severe mental retardation, but since most clinicians would regard this boy's aggressive behavior as qualitatively different from the aggressive behavior of a child with conduct disorder, perhaps the criteria for conduct disorder should rule out moderate or severe mental retardation (as severe mental retardation is ruled out in the diagnosis of antisocial personality disorder). (pp. 188–189)[3]

---

[3]Reprinted with permission from Spitzer, R. L., Skodol, A. E., Gibbon, M., & Williams, J. B. *DSM-III Case Book.* Washington, D.C.: American Psychiatric Association, 1981.

The interpretative rationale for differential diagnosis based on quantitative differences in this example case clearly reflects a largely unstated bias in diagnostic practice. The only example in the casebook using multiple diagnosis with mental retardation involves a diagnosis of infantile autism. Earlier, we noted that the widely encompassing criteria for childhood onset pervasive developmental disorder may also mitigate consideration of additional diagnoses other than mental retardation.

This bias in diagnostic practice is central to the issue of creating diagnostic classification systems. Traditionally, a major reason for diagnosis has been the conceptualization of the disorder and the identification of appropriate treatment procedures. By considering the psychopathological disorders of mentally retarded individuals as qualitatively different from intellectually normal individuals, it follows that there may be significant differences in treatment approaches. This issue will be addressed further in later sections, especially as it relates to the behavioral as compared to the traditional assessment/diagnostic process. A critical question is whether or not specific diagnosis, emphasizing either the retardation aspects or the psychotic aspects, actually results in any functional difference in treatment choice and outcome. At this point, two major psychotic disorders, schizophrenia and autism, will be reviewed with respect to their frequency within the retarded population and how the degree of retardation interacts with assessment, treatment, and prognosis. A separate review of pervasive developmental disorder will not be included because of the current paucity of research. Instead, empirical findings for this disorder are provided in the section on schizophrenia.

• ADULT ONSET SCHIZOPHRENIA •

• Incidence •

The first question one must ask if interested in the relationship between adult-onset schizophrenia and mental retardation is "How many (or what percentage of) mentally retarded individuals will warrant a diagnosis of schizophrenia?" Opinions regarding the concomitance of schizophrenia and mental retardation vary widely, from those who consider the disorder to be very rare among retardates to those who believe that retarded individuals have a greater susceptibility to the disorder (Sarason & Goldwyn, 1958; Tredgold, 1952). Numerous studies have undertaken the task of determining the incidence of schizophrenia among retardates, or the incidence of retardation among schizophrenics, and have yielded some discrepancies. In part, these discrepancies probably stem from different methods of collecting data. Some studies based their information on records from psychiatric hospitals or mental retardation institutions. Neuer (1947) examined the records of 300 consecutive admissions to a state school for the retarded and reported that approximately 11 percent were psychotic (unfortunately, specific diagnoses within the broad category of psychosis were not available). Yielding an even higher estimate of incidence, Angus (1948) reviewed 150 admissions to the Devereaux Schools and found that 28 percent of the sample was schizophrenic. However, a much lower estimate of incidence of schizophrenia among retardates is reported by Penrose (1954). In his study, the frequency of schizophrenia (as noted by diagnosis in the patients' records) was examined for a group of institutionalized retardates (N = 1280). Penrose found that 3.7 percent of the retardates in the institution were also diagnosed as schizophrenic. A breakdown of the frequency of schizophrenia by level of retardation was also examined with the following results: IQ 70 to 85, 4.5 percent, 50 to 70, 2.5 percent, 30 to 50, 3.7 percent; and less than 30, 5.9 percent.

Epidemiological surveys of a particular geographic area constitutes another method to determine the concomitance of schizophrenia and mental retardation. Based on the Rhode Island mental deficiency register, Wunsch (1951) provided an estimate of incidence of psychosis among 6000 mentally retarded persons and found slightly more than 1 percent were classified as psychotic (it is not known how many of those labeled psychotic were schizophrenics). Two epidemiological studies conducted in Sweden examined the incidence of retardation among schizophrenics (Hallgren & Sjogren, 1959; Larsson & Sjogren, 1954) and reported a significant association between mental retardation and schizophrenia. The rate of mental retardation within their schizophrenic sample was approximately 10 percent versus an incidence of 3 percent in the general population.

Thus, studies examining the concomitance of the diagnoses of schizophrenia and mental retardation reveal very large differences in estimates. Such differences are probably a function of several factors, such as the unreliability of the diagnosis of schizophrenia, different sampling procedures, and variations in the purposes of the studies (e.g., incidence of mental retardation among schizophrenics versus incidence of schizophrenics among the retarded). Clearly, the highest estimates of concomitance were reported from studies drawing their samples from institutions. The information from studies based on the institutionalized retarded is biased in two ways: (1) the samples have a very large number of severely retarded cases (disproportionate to the total mentally retarded population), and (2) of those cases with moderate retardation, a disproportionate number includes those who are difficult to manage or who engage in antisocial behaviors, or both, because these are the persons most likely to be institutionalized (Saenger, 1960). Data based on institutionalized samples of the retarded thus cannot be generalized to the mentally retarded population as a whole.

Another obstacle to determining the number of mentally retarded individuals who display behaviors that meet the criteria of a schizophrenic diagnosis is the well-established bias among many practitioners that a retarded individual cannot be schizophrenic. Given that almost all studies examining the incidence of schizophrenia in the retarded based their estimates on diagnoses in the patients' records, it is reasonable to suggest that these might be underestimated because of these biases.

There has been a long-standing controversy about the validity of a diagnosis of schizophrenia in patients with low IQ. Hayman (1939) and Herskovitz & Plesset (1941), for example, did not believe that clinicians could obtain the information needed to make a diagnosis of schizophrenia in patients with IQ scores below 50. In contrast, others based their diagnosis of schizophrenia in severely retarded persons on stereotyped and bizarre motor patterns and mannerisms along with other information (Critchley & Earl, 1932; Rollin, 1946). For the most part, any relationship between schizophrenia and mental retardation involves mildly and moderately retarded persons. Those with more severe levels of retardation are usually diagnosed as psychotic at an early age, thus falling into the category of autism or childhood schizophrenia. Generally, there is little controversy over diagnostic procedures with higher functioning retarded who have speech in that typical schizophrenic psychoses do occur in the retarded with IQ scores of approximately 50 or above.

However, the question remains, "Is schizophrenia more prevalent among retarded individuals?" Because of methodological problems in interpreting results of the studies reviewed, an answer to this question still eludes us. The data are suggestive of increased incidence of schizophrenia among the retarded and support a conclusion that schizophrenia does exist among the retarded. Although reliable estimates of the concomitance of schizophrenia and mental retardation are lacking, we can certainly conclude that there are many retarded individuals who display behaviors that meet the criteria for a diagnosis of schizophrenia; thus, an understanding of the manner in which mental retardation influences the prognosis, etiology, and treatment of schizophrenia is needed.

• Prognosis for Retarded Schizophrenics •

There are several studies that examine the extent to which retardation affects prognosis of schizophrenics. Some introductory comments about methodology are needed, however, before the results of the relevant studies are presented. First, most studies that evaluated IQ and prognosis did not specifically examine the influence of mental retardation on prognosis. Their low IQ groups were frequently above the cutoff criterion for a diagnosis of retardation. Nevertheless, the information provided from these studies should shed some light on prognosis of retarded schizophrenics. Second, some of the studies that examined prognoses of high and low IQ groups did not discriminate between adult-onset schizophrenics and those who had been diagnosed schizophrenic as children. Thus, the results of the studies to be presented must be interpreted cautiously.

In general, findings from all studies indicate that low IQ is associated with poor prognosis among schizophrenics. Several studies have shown that schizophrenics with low IQs are hospitalized earlier than schizophrenics of higher IQ (Offord & Cross, 1971; Pollack, 1960). In 1960, Pollack and his colleagues published data which showed a positive, linear relationship between IQ scores and age of hospitalization up until the age of 16 and only a nonsignificant trend in the same direction after this age. Belmont and his colleagues replicated Pollack's finding. Comparing two groups of schizophrenics, those with early and those with late onset of the disorder, he found that their IQ scores were significantly different. The early-onset group scored approximately 10 points lower than the other group.

A well-designed study by Offord and Cross (1971) also examined prognosis, but unlike the other studies, only adult-onset schizophrenics were included in their study. These authors found schizophrenics with IQ scores below 80 were first hospitalized for schizophrenia more than 4 years earlier than those with IQ scores between 80 and 99, and almost 10 years earlier than individuals with IQs of 100 or over. Interestingly, data from Pollack's study did not show a significant relationship between IQ and first hospitalization after the age of 16. Perhaps the significant difference of the Offord and Cross study is a function of a more homogeneous sample.

In addition to the finding relating IQ to age of hospitalization, Offord and Cross also reported a significant relationship between IQ and length of hospitalization. Schizophrenic adults with low IQ (usually in the mildly retarded range) spend more time in psychiatric hospitals than schizophrenics iwht IQs of 90 or above. Thus, low-IQ (below 80) schizophrenics are more likely to exhibit behavioral characteristics of schizophrenia at a younger age, be hospitalized earlier, and spend more time in psychiatric hospitals than are schizophrenics of higher IQs.

Other indexes of outcomes for schizophrenics have also shown a positive relationship between good prognosis and intelligence. Stotsky (1952) examined the backgrounds and characteristics of schizophrenics who were later classified as remitted versus those who remained actively schizophrenic. He found that remitted schizophrenics had higher IQs than nonremitted schizophrenics. Although the nonremitted schizophrenics were not necessarily retarded, these findings suggest that retarded schizophrenics may have a relatively poorer prognosis. Pollack (1960) noted that there was a positive relationship between discharge ratings (much improved, improved, unimproved) and IQ scores. Half of the schizophrenics who were rated "unimproved" had IQ scores below 90. Also, in a later study by Pollack (Pollack, Woerner, & Klein, 1968) it was noted that a low IQ (less than 90) was significantly related to poor posthospital adjustment.

An area of great interest is how retarded schizophrenics respond to specific types of treatment. Unfortunately, studies investigating the relationship of IQ and response to specific treatment techniques have been lacking. Two studies evaluated the effects of insulin coma treatment and concluded that schizophrenic patients with IQ scores of less than 90 responded poorly. The relationship between response to behavioral intervention strategies or to drug therapy and the intelligence of the schizophrenic has not been investigated.

• Etiology •

• *Pseudoretardation* •

Some investigators would argue that it is erroneous to conclude that there is a concomitance of two disorders, mental retardation and schizophrenia; rather, mental retardation (or some amount of intellectual deterioration) is an integral part of schizophrenia. Bleuler's original formulation of schizophrenia was that individuals showed intellectual deterioration, often in the retarded range. Certainly, most would agree that schizophrenia is a thought disorder and that the cognitive deficits which are key criteria for making a diagnosis of schizophrenia are the same deficits that could impair intellectual functioning. Because of these generally accepted ideas about schizophrenia, questions regarding the concomitance of mental retardation and schizophrenia have seldom been addressed. However, several recent studies have challenged the assumption that intellectual deterioration is common to all schizophrenics and that IQ scores of schizophrenics may be below average but still not indicative of "true" mental retardation.

Lane, Albee, and their colleagues conducted a series of studies to test the hypothesis that the IQs of schizophrenics decreases with the onset of this disorder. They suggested that if intellectual deterioration accounts for a preponderance of low IQ scores among schizophrenics, then one would expect that the premorbid IQ scores of shizophrenics would not significantly differ from individuals matched for age and socioeconomic status. Furthermore, one should expect a significant decrement between premorbid IQ and IQ at adulthood. These hypotheses were tested, and the results indicated that there was not a significant decrease in IQ from childhood to adulthood and that IQ among schizophrenics was very stable over the years (Albee, Lane, Corcoran, & Werneke, 1963). Interestingly, these authors' data revealed that schizophrenics had significantly lower IQ scores than their siblings (Lane & Albee, 1964; Lane & Albee, 1965) and their schoolmates (Albee, Lane, & Reuter, 1964) in childhood, long before the characteristics of schizophrenia were exhibited. These findings suggest that low IQ increases the likelihood of developing schizophrenia as an adult. However, it is important to emphasize that the low IQ scores for most of their samples were still within the normal range of intelligence.

• Biological •

A general biological hypothesis to explain the concomitance of mental retardation and schizophrenia might state that both disorders are caused by some hypothesized third process, probably some form of organic brain dysfunction. The types of information that are usually relied upon to support a biological hypothesis are events such as increased findings of neurological abnormalities (e.g., seizure, abnormal EEG records) or a high frequency of concomitance of mental retardation and schizophrenia. Unlike the data on autism and retardation, for which there are findings suggestive of an organic brain dysfunction, there is, as yet, little empirical support for a biological explanation which posits a single cause for both mental retardation and schizophrenia.

Of course, it is possible that preconceived ideas that moderately and severely retarded persons cannot show true signs of schizophrenia and the consequent tendency to exclude from research samples schizophrenics with an accompanying diagnosis of mental retardation have obscured a relationship to a biological cause. There are interesting data from several studies of schizophrenia and inheritability which have shown that mental retardation is much more likely to occur in families of schizophrenics than nonschizophrenics (Heston, 1966). This finding has not received much attention because the focus of these studies has been on increased rates of schizophrenia among relatives. The data might be interpreted as suggestive evidence for joint inheritability of mental retardation and schizophrenia or for the inheritance of some hypothesized variable (e.g., organic brain dysfunction) which leads to the development of both mental retardation and schizophrenia. Clearly, these findings of increased frequency of mental retardation among relations of schizophrenics merit further investigation. However, at present, no explanation of the relationship between mental retardation and schizophrenia based on biological causes can be made.

• Predisposition—Stress •

A popular etiological theory of schizophrenia is that some individuals are born with a biological predisposition to develop schizophrenia. When individuals with this predisposition encounter frequent or traumatic stress, then the behavioral characteristics of schizophrenia become noticeable. Average or above average intelligence may help individuals to cope with life stress and perhaps offers protection to individuals who are predisposed to becoming overtly schizophrenic. However, individuals with low IQ would be expected to encounter more problems of coping in their daily environment. Increased frequency of failure and rejection from peers, and thus increased stress, are much more likely to occur to retarded individuals (Robinson & Robinson, 1976).

This hypothesis best accounts for available data on incidence of mental retardation and schizophrenia as well as the poor prognosis of retarded schizophrenics. Increased incidence of mental retardation in schizophrenics could be accounted for by the fact that persons with a predisposition to schizophrenia and a low IQ are more likely to manifest characteristics of schizophrenia earlier and, once institutionalized, are more likely not to improve and thus remain in the hospital. In contrast, persons with the same inherited vulnerability for schizophrenia with average or above average IQ will, if they become psychotic at all, manifest behaviors characteristic of schizophrenia at a later age.

With respect to etiology of schizophrenia among the retarded, several summary statements can be made. First, retardation can coexist with schizophrenia and is not simply pseudoretardation. Second, the etiological theories of schizophrenia among the retarded are the same as those postulated for schizophrenia of nonretarded populations. Although it is possible that the causes of schizophrenia among the retarded are different (e.g., joint heritability of mental retardation and schizophrenia), there is no empirical support for this position at present.

• INFANTILE AUTISM •

According to Kanner's (1943) original description of infantile autism, the intellectual potentials of these children were assumed to be within the normal range, and their functional retardation (e.g., poor academic performance, failure to engage in socially appropriate behaviors) was reflective of their social aloofness and negativism, not their intelligence. Certainly autistic children, especially those below the age of 5, are very difficult to test because of their frequent tantrums and lack of attention. Kanner and others believed that if one could increase their social awareness and reduce their emotional withdrawal, then autistic children would display age-appropriate cognitive skills. The autistic child's good rote memory, attractive, serious-looking appearance, coordination, and lack of physical stigmata served to reinforce Kanner's assumption of normal intelligence of autistic children.

However, with the accumulation of information about autistic children, especially follow-up studies, many professionals have challenged the assumption of normal intellectual potential, entertaining the idea that many autistic children do not have normal potential but are, in fact, retarded. This change of opinion was derived from numerous studies of the performance of autistic children on standardized intelligence tests. Research has shown that the intelligence of autistic children can be measured reliably (DeMyer, Barton, Alpern, Kimberlin, Allen, Yang, & Steele, 1974; Lockyer & Rutter, 1969), and that IQ scores of autistic children have reasonably good predictive ability with respect to academic performances and adjustment as an adult (Bartak & Rutter, 1971; Mittler, Gillies, & Jukes, 1966; Lockyer & Rutter, 1969; Rutter & Bartak, 1973).

Even those children who were initially untestable on the most common IQ tests were able to perform consistently when presented with very simple test items (Alpern, 1967), and follow-up studies of autistic children have revealed that many children who were initially untestable, performed in a manner similar to severely retarded individuals when observed at an older age (Lockyer & Rutter, 1969). These findings do not support explanations of low IQ which are based on negativism or lack of motivation. Thus, it appears from a series of studies that IQ scores function in a similar manner to the normal population.

The incidence of infantile autism in the mentally retarded population is difficult to estimate, but all researchers would agree that the incidence within a retarded population is many times greater than within the general population which is thought to be somewhere in the range of 0.45 to 0.70 per 10,000 (Lotter, 1966; Treffert, 1970). Based on examinations of 159 preschool children suspected of retardation, Webster (1970) places the number of retarded children with severe emotional disturbance at 17 percent, with approximately 8 percent exhibiting psychotic behavior. Surveying a broader age range, Menolascino (1965b) found that 24 percent of 616 children under 8 years of age who were suspected of being retarded warranted a formal psychiatric diagnosis.

From a review of the literature, Pollack (1967) concluded that one-third to one-half of autistic children have IQ scores below 70. DeMyer et al. (1974) reported a substantially higher percentage (94 percent) of her sample falling within the retarded range. Similar to DeMyer's estimates, Kolvin, Humphrey, and McNay (1971) found that 51 percent of their sample of autistic children were either untestable or obtained IQ scores below 50 and 43 percent scored between 50 and 89. Clearly, characteristics of autism are found in much higher frequency among retarded than among nonretarded children. Furthermore, there seems to be a positive relationship between behavioral indexes of autism and degree of retardation (Wing, 1978).

• Assessment •

The criteria for a diagnosis of autism vary according to the age of the child. Impaired social relationships at the age of 6 months, for example, would probably include such descriptive accounts as does not cuddle, remains stiff in mother's arms, and doesn't reach out to be picked up, whereas the behaviors describing the same diagnostic criterion for a 4-year-old suspected of autism would be much different. Most probably one would note that the 4-year-old allows him- or herself to be held and cuddled but rarely initiates contact and seldom seeks comfort from significant adults. The diagnostic criteria are not operationally defined, so that a variety or continuum of behaviors could fulfill the diagnostic criteria which vary not only with chronological age (CA) but also with mental age (MA). The clinician attempting to make a diagnosis of autism must ask two questions "Does this behavior occur as often with nonpsychotic individuals of a similar IQ?" or "Does a lack of this behavior indicate autism or reflect the behavioral deficits of children with similar levels of intellectual functioning?"

Making a differential diagnosis becomes increasingly more difficult as the degree of retardation increases. Severely and profoundly retarded children display many behaviors that are frequently associated with psychosis, most notably self-stimulation and self-injury. Most professionals would agree that the presence of these behaviors in severely and profoundly retarded children should not be used as diagnostic criteria. Yet the limited behavioral repertoires of children with IQ scores less than 50 makes it very unlikely that the criteria are sufficient for a diagnosis of autism. More information about the interaction of diagnostic criteria and intellectual functioning is needed to facilitate accurate diagnosis of autism and to provide information about the disorder. Two methods for obtaining this information are possible: (1) comparative studies of autistic and nonpsychotic children matched for MA and (2) comparisons of subgroups of autistic children based on IQ scores. The importance of studying the relationship between behavioral indexes of autism and degree of retardation has only recently been emphasized. In the past, there was a tendency toward viewing mental retardation and autism as two distinct disorders rather than as coexisting conditions, and attempts were made to determine the primacy of one over the other rather than to observe the interaction of the two. Recent research which has addressed changes in behavioral indexes of autism as a function of IQ are reviewed for the three major diagnostic criteria of autism.

• Impaired Social Relationships •

A number of studies have attempted to delineate the behavioral differences between autistic and nonautistic individuals in their frequency and quality of social contact. The most popular dependent measure of social interactions has been eye contact. Much has been written about the autistic child's gaze avoidance, suggesting negativism and physical avoidance of social contact. However, data comparing autistic and nonautistic individuals matched for MA do not support these descriptions. Hutt and Ounsted (1966) found that the autistic person rarely initiated social contacts but did not physically withdraw from the approach of others. In fact, the autistic child tolerated closer physical contact than children in the control group. Also, although the autistic children made fewer and briefer visual contacts with familiar adults, they were similar to the nonautistic in proximity and approach (Castell, 1970).

Hermelin and O'Connor (1970) found that autistic children displayed less visual orientation to people and objects, but their responses to people or images of people were not significantly different from their responses to objects. Churchill & Bryson (1972) compared autistic and nonautistic children matched for MA and found no significant differences in amount of visual fixation or physical avoidance between the two groups.

These studies seem to argue against an active avoidance of social contact. Differences between autistic and nonautistic matched on MA are best reflected in frequency of initiation of social contact and quality of social interactions. Even the measure of initiation seems to discriminate less between mentally retarded and autistic children as they approach adolescence. Older autistic children seem motivated to make social contact but seem to lack the skills (Clark & Rutter, 1977; Dewey & Everard, 1974; Ricks & Wing, 1975; Rutter, 1970).

Measures of the quality of social interactions have been especially difficult to develop, and most research has concentrated on eye contact with, physical approach to, and avoidance of adults. A very important study was conducted by Wing in which a more detailed assessment of social interactions was provided. Wing and her colleagues (Wing, 1978; Wing, Yeates, Brierly, & Gould, 1976; Wing & Gould, 1978) studied the relationship between social aloofness and level of cognitive development of psychotic and nonpsychotic retarded children. Using an epidemiological approach, Wing and Gould identified all the children in a particular geographical area who might show some or all of the characteristics of autism. Children whose records included a diagnosis of autism, psychosis, or schizophrenia, or with descriptive labels of severe language impairment, were included in their sample. Also included were all children who attended special schools, classes, or clinics for any kind of physical or mental handicap. A total of 167 children were identified and detailed information was collected for these children. Structured interviews with each child's mother, teacher, or nurse, behavioral ratings of the child in school, and several tests of language comprehension and nonverbal skills provided the data base.

Ratings of sociability were based on the children's response to physical contact, engaging in social play, recognition of and differentiation between familiar people and strangers, and pointing things out for adults to look at. A score on a 5-point scale ranging from 1 (no interest in social contact) to 5 (enjoys and initiates social contact) was assigned to each child. Presence or absence of appropriate eye contact was rated separately.

Based on two criteria (social withdrawal and maintenance of sameness) 84 of the 167 children in the sample were labeled psychotic. This group was divided into three subgroups based on level of cognitive development. At each of three intellectual levels there was a psychotic and a nonpsychotic group. Thus, this study made it possible to compare autistic children of one intellectual level with those of another level as well as to compare autistic and nonautistic children of comparable mental age.

The results of this study showed major differences between the psychotic and nonpsychotic children at each level of cognitive development as well as significant differences among the subgroups of psychotic children. For both psychotic and nonpsychotic children, sociability scores were related to estimated levels of cognitive development. Social avoidance was most obvious in the more severely handicapped group.

Although lower sociability scores were more frequent for the low functioning psychotic and nonpsychotic children, differences between these groups were still apparent. The lowest functioning nonpsychotic children differed from the psychotic children of comparable intellectual level in that they responded to social approaches with appropriate smiling and they also used gestures such as pointing, facial expression, and vocalizations to communicate to others. As the level of cognitive development increased, the psychotic and nonpsychotic children's social withdrawal decreased. However, there were still noticeable differences between the psychotic and nonpsychotic children in the groups with the highest level of intellectual functioning. These differences were reflected most in initiation of social contact and in inappropriate eye contact. Rather than gaze-avoidance, frequent staring at others and generally making eye contact at unusual times were reported among the psychotic children of the highest functioning group. Inappropriate eye contact was seldom a noticeable problem for the nonpsychotic group regardless of intellectual level whereas, in the psychotic group, lack of appropriate eye contact was associated with poor cognitive skills.

• Insistence on Sameness •

One of the major diagnostic criteria set forth by Kanner (1949) was "insistence on sameness." This description involves by far the most inferences and has proven most difficult to agree on in terms of behavioral referents. Through Kanner's case descriptions it seems that he used this description to refer to the extreme emotional upset triggered by imposing change in some aspect of the child's life, especially through the interruption of repetitive routines in which the autistic child frequently engages. "Insistence on sameness," then, refers to the exhibition of a variety of stereotyped, repetitive behaviors and emotional upset when interrupted or prevented from engaging in these behaviors. Rutter (1978) delineated five types of behaviors which he believed constituted Kanner's criteria of insistence on sameness. These are (1) rigid and limited play patterns, such as endlessly lining up objects; (2) strong attachments to a particular object or objects; (3) unusual preoccupations; (4) rituals (e.g., touching compulsions); and (5) marked resistance to change (e.g., child becomes distressed if the furniture is moved or there is a change in the daily schedule). Rutter suggests that there are age-related changes in the expression of insistence on sameness, with rituals and preoccupations being more likely among older, verbal autistic children. Unfortunately, there have been very few systematic investigations of this behavioral index of autism.

The most detailed information of the relationship between mental age and repetitive, stereotyped activities is provided by the epidemiological study by Wing described in the previous section. In addition to collecting data on social interactions, ratings of the frequency and complexity of repetitive stereotyped behavior and play skills were also made. Simple stereotypies included behaviors such as tapping, arm flapping, and flicking of paper and were rated as present if they were observed in very high frequency. Repetitive routines were described as elaborate if they "involved manual dexterity and organization of materials and the environment." Criteria for inclusion in the autistic group were social aloofness and elaborate rituals. Both had to be present from before the age of two-and-a-half. The simple stereotypies were much more frequently observed in the lower functioning groups, with no differences between the psychotic and nonpsychotic groups. Elaborate routines, however, occurred only in the psychotic children, and within the psychotic group there was a much greater frequency of elaborate rituals among the higher functioning group who displayed a level of manual dexterity that was not often present in the psychotic group of lowest cognitive development.

Wing (1978) also collected information about play skills which she divided into three groups: (1) "No symbolic play—child does not use toys or materials to represent real objects or situations," (2) "stereotyped symbolic play—child uses toys or other materials to represent real objects but repeats the same narrow range of activities over and over again," and (3) "true symbolic play—representational play that can change in theme" (p. 33).[4]

Only 1 of 84 psychotic children engaged in symbolic play, whereas 57 percent of the nonpsychotic group did. For both groups true symbolic play was observed only in the groups with the highest cognitive development (language and nonverbal MA > 20 months). Stereotyped symbolic play did not occur in the nonpsychotic group but was observed in 35 of the 84 psychotic children. Within the psychotic group there was a strong association between MA and play patterns, with stereotyped play occurring most frequently in the highest MA group. Absence of symbolic play was more frequent for the psychotic group, but within each group there was a negative correlation with MA.

It is much more difficult to discriminate among psychotic and nonpsychotic children with a verbal and nonverbal MA of less than 20 months when considering the diagnostic criteria of insistence on sameness. One reason for the difficulty is the controversy over inclusion of simple stereotypies or self-stimulation as a criterion. Because self-stimulation is frequently observed in severely and profoundly retarded individuals, it is not considered to be sufficient for a diagnosis of autism.

• Language Abnormalities •

Although it is not one of the major diagnostic criteria specified by Kanner (1949), language abnormalities are used, in part, as a basis for diagnostic decisions by many professionals. Case descriptions of autistic children are rich with examples of peculiar language usage, which include (1) echolalia, (2) pronoun reversal, (3) neologisms, and (4) literal use of language. In addition to abnormal language is delayed onset of speech and failure to use speech to communicate with others. It is estimated that less than half of all autistic children will develop speech, and the best predictor of language development is IQ. Nonretarded and mildly retarded autistic children are much more likely to have speech than autistic children

---

[4]Reprinted with permission from Wing, L. Social, behavioral and cognitive characteristics: An epidemiological approach. In M. Rutter & E. Schopler (Eds.), *Autism*. New York: Plenum Press, 1978.

of lower intellectual functioning. Comparisons of autistic and nonautistic children matched for MA indicate that the greatest differences between the mildly retarded autistic and the nonautistic are in the presence of unusual language characteristics (echolalia, pronoun reversals, etc.) and spontaneous use of language (Cunningham, 1968; Ricks & Wing, 1975). For children of lower IQ, the differences between autistic and nonautistic children of similar MA is the higher frequency of muteness and lack of nonverbal communication, such as pointing and making gestures, among autistics (Bartak & Rutter, 1976; Bartak, Rutter, & Cox, 1975; Ricks & Wing, 1975).

There are differences not only in expressive language but in receptive language and language-related cognitive skills as well. At each level of retardation, the receptive language deficits of autistic children are more severe than those of their nonautistic counterparts (DeMyer et al., 1974). There are also significant differences in skills such as sequencing and semantic-based memory performance which cannot be accounted for only by degree of retardation (Hermelin, 1978).

Presence of language abnormalities such as echolalia and pronoun reversal are fairly reliable behavioral indexes of autism and are frequently used in making a diagnosis. However, language characteristics are not very helpful in making a diagnosis of autism when the child is moderately or severely retarded since it is much more probable that the child will not have speech. At lower intellectual levels, information about the child's ability to understand language and attempts to communicate nonverbally will be most useful in determining a diagnosis.

• Prognosis and IQ of the Autistic Child •

Level of intelligence, as indexed by IQ test scores, is associated with major differences in biological as well as social outcome. In general, prognosis is worse for retarded than for nonretarded autistic children, and among retarded autistic children, those with lower IQ scores have a poorer prognosis. With respect to biological variables, the Maudsley Hospital study reported that 36 percent of their autistic sample with IQ scores below 70 exhibited epileptic seizures in late childhood or adolescence, whereas none of the nonretarded autistic children developed epileptic seizures (Bartak & Rutter, 1976). Other investigators have revealed similar findings of increased evidence for a neurological disorder in cases of autism with moderate, severe, or profound retardation (Chess, Korn, & Fernandez, 1971; Goldfarb, 1961; Rutter, 1970; Rutter, Bartak, & Newman, 1971). In addition to predicting outcome based on biological variables, IQ test scores are also the best predictors of autistic children's educational and social progress. Approximately half of nonretarded autistic persons hold regularly paid employment or go on for higher education, whereas few autistic persons with IQ scores below 70 and virtually none with IQ scores below 50 are able to hold jobs. In relation to their unemployability, retarded autistic individuals are much less likely to achieve any degree of social independence and are more likely than nonretarded autistic individuals to be placed in institutions (Rutter, 1970). Finally, the retarded autistic are less likely to acquire academic skills than those who are nonretarded. About three-fourths of the nonretarded autistic acquired competence in basic math skills whereas only one-fifth of the autistic with IQ scores below 70 reached this level of competence (Bartak & Rutter, 1976).

An important and somewhat pessimistic finding is that IQ measures predict outcome not only in groups of autistic children given little active treatment but for autistic children who have been given skilled help over many years (Rutter & Bartak, 1973). Regardless of the type or intensity of treatment, retarded autistic children show little improvement in intellectual functioning or in the cognitive deficits characteristic of autism. However, gains due to treatment interventions have been reported for retarded autistic children in the areas of reducing excessive, inappropriate behavior, increasing communication skills, and improving social relationships (Rutter, 1978; Lovaas, Schreibman, & Koegel, 1976).

Thus, retarded autistic children, especially those with IQ scores below 50) are less likely to hold jobs or be socially independent. They are more likely to be placed in residential institutions and more likely to exhibit seizures or other evidence of neurological disturbance. Finally, they will show less progress in specific treatment programs than nonretarded autistic children but usually do benefit from educational and behavioral interventions.

• Etiology •

• *Psychogenic* •

In his original description of the syndrome of infantile autism, Kanner (1943) noted that the parents of these children tended to be very intelligent, cold, and unemotional. His comments drew attention to parental characteristics and the possibility that abnormal parent–infant interactions or psychopathology of the parents was the cause of autism. Many of the early etiological theories suggested that psychogenic factors caused autism, and other theories proposed that autism results from the child being biologically predisposed to the disorder and the parents providing inadequate child-rearing. The range of negative characteristics attributed to parents of autistic children is wide, and investigators have devised many ways of studying the parents, including data from psychometric tests, structured interviews, systematic observation, questionnaires, and checklists.

Early studies tended to compare groups of parents, those of autistic and of normal children. The results supported the hypothesis that there was increased psychopathology and negative characteristics among the parents of autistic children (Kanner, 1949; Eisenberg & Kanner, 1956; Esman, Kohn, & Nyman, 1959; Kaufman, Frank, Heims, Herrick, Rusir, & Willer, 1960; Block, 1969; Goldfarb, 1961; Meyers & Goldfarb, 1962). These investigators concluded from their findings that the parents of the autistic group have abnormalities that could account for their children's problems. However, as Bell (1968) points out, comparisons of autistic children with normal or even physically ill children is invalid for assessing parental effects because it entirely ignores child effects. An alternative interpretation of the increased pathology among parents of autistic children is that the deviancy develops as a response to the child's abnormalities. If the goal of a study is to assess differences in parental behavior which are not simply responses to their children's pathology, then comparisons need to be made with families of children who have a developmental handicap but are not autistic (Cantwell, Baker, & Rutter, 1978). Interestingly, when appropriate comparison groups are used, there is no evidence to support a psychogenic hypothesis (Klebanoff, 1959; Pitfield & Oppenheim, 1964). The parents of the autistic children differ from the parents of normal children, but there is a similarity among the parents of various groups of disturbed children. These findings imply that the child's behavior has resulted in an increase in parental distress and maladjustment.

Thus, there is a lack of empirical evidence for a psychogenic cause of autism. Although signs of psychopathology among the parents of autistic children have been obtained, these signs are not greater than the pathology observed with parents of children who are not autistic but are developmentally handicapped. Furthermore, the parents of autistic children do not show signs of severe psychopathology which seems to be required in order to produce a disorder as profound as autism. The parental characteristics would have to be so debilitating as to cause all the features of autism as well as mild to profound levels of mental retardation. Even those children who have been raised in the most physically and emotionally deprived environments have not yielded children whose problems are similar to or as severe as those of autistic children.

• *Biological Causes* •

Recent studies suggest that there is a strong association between retardation due to organic brain dysfunction and the presence of autism (Ornitz, 1978; Robinson & Robinson, 1976). Perhaps the strongest evidence for such an association is the long list of organic brain syndromes which have been reported to occur in association with autism. These include Addison's disease (Money, Borrow & Clarke, 1971), cerebral lipoidosis (Creak, 1963a), infantile spasms (Creak, 1963b; Kolvin, Ounsted, Humphrey, McNay, Richardson, Garside, Kidd, & Roth, 1971; Menolascino, 1965a; Schain & Yannet, 1960; Taft & Cohen, 1971), phenylketonuria (Anthony, 1962) and congenital rubella (Chess, 1971; Chess, Korn, & Fernandez, 1971).

Ornitz, Guthrie and Farley (1977) studied a group of 74 autistic children and reported that 23 percent of this group exhibited evidence of organic brain disorder and 17.6 percent were judged to have some minor condition. Of the 23 percent with strong evidence for organic brain disorder there were four cases of neonatal respiratory distress, three cases of congenital rubella, one case of infantile spasms, two cases of cerebral palsy, one case of microencaphaly, and several cases of rare syndromes. The evidence from these numerous studies indicates that autism is often a manifestation of organic brain pathology. However, the exact nature of brain damage which results in autism is still being debated. Rimland (1964) has argued for many years that defects in the reticular formation underlie the autistic syndrome. His hypothesis is that autistic children are underaroused, whereas others suggest that these children are overaroused (Hutt & Hutt, 1969) or that they have rapidly alternating levels of arousal (Ornitz & Ritvo, 1968). DeLong (1978) has hypothesized that the autistic have a unique impairment of the function of the left hemisphere. However, the occurrence of autism with so many different types of organic brain syndromes leads one to the conclusion that a single etiology of autism is unlikely. Ornitz (1978) reviewed the literature on hypothesized biological causes of autism and offers an interesting conceptualization. He postulates that genetic damage (pathologic changes in genetic structure) involving the left temporal lobe might underlie a particular type of language impairment in some retarded children and that a small percentage of these children also show all the signs of infantile autism. He suggests that the mechanism for the genetic damages could occur through a number of different medical conditions such as those mentioned earlier in this section. Depending on when during or prior to pregnancy the genetic damage occurs, the central nervous system (CNS) pathology will vary. Thus, Ornitz suggests that autism may not have a single etiology but perhaps a single pathologic mechanism involving particular functional brain systems which are affected by different diseases but result in the same behavioral manifestations of autism.

One way of learning more about the pathologic mechanisms involved in the development of autism is to intensively study the concomitance of autism with one type of organic brain syndrome. Clearly, the work of Chess and her extensive investigations of congenital rubella is the best example of this approach. The prevalence rate of autism in her sample of rubella children was 412 per 10,000 with an additional 329 per 1000 exhibiting most, but not all, of the criteria for autism. Chess noted that the type of sensory impairment the rubella child had was related to the presence of autism. Autism was only observed in children with some hearing loss and was most frequently observed in children who had both hearing loss and mental retardation. However, Chess points out that there were many nonautistic children with sensory deficits. Differences among the autistic and nonautistic rubella children with sensory deficits included the following: (1) remediational aid (cataract removal, hearing aids) resulted in appropriate use and signs of improvement for the nonautistic children but little change and lack of use of the aids by autistic children; (2) nonautistic children with hearing loss were very visually alert to their surroundings and exhibited appropriate responsiveness, whereas, the autistic rubella children did not seem to be visually alert or responsive; (3) the autistic children lacked gestures which the nonautistic sensory impaired and retarded rubella children displayed.

Chess's work has provided very useful information about the link between a congenital disorder, sensory impairments, retardation, and autism. However, the exact mechanism by which organic damage manifests itself behaviorally as autism remains to be determined.

• TREATMENT APPROACHES •

Historically the treatment of psychoses and other severe disturbances has evolved from simple institutional placement, with custodial care as the focus, to attempts at curing the disorder through psychological and medical approaches to treatment. There were concerted attempts in in the mid-1800s by proponents of the educational model to change the emphasis from custodial care to education. However, this approach, fueled by the proponents' somewhat overzealous faith in the possibilities of the educational technology of the day, was doomed to failure. By the latter half of the 19th century institutions were well established as custodial facilities for the purpose of segregation and containment of the disturbed and retarded.

The discovery of the major and minor tranquilizers in the mid-1900s led to a surge in employment of traditional therapy with previously restrained and isolated residents. Although there was a subsequent trend toward using medication as treatment rather than in conjunction with treatment, the possibilities of treating the severely disturbed began to be established (Romanczyk, Kistner, & Crimmins, 1980). The general approaches to therapy that have been utilized, psychotherapy and behavior therapy, are considered here.

Psychotherapy is based on the assumption that human behavior is understandable and alterable. Changes in behavior are brought about primarily through the interactive process between client and therapist. According to Weiner (1975), "the capacity of a patient to express and reflect on his experience is perhaps the most obvious of the patient characteristics associated with improvement in psychotherapy" (p. 17). Weiner also outlined three patient characteristics which have been found to be most related to improvement in psychotherapy: "(a) whether the patient is motivated for psychotherapy, (b) whether he is able to reflect and talk about himself, and (c) whether despite his difficulties he has retained a generally well-integrated level of personality functioning" (p. 61).[5]

It is apparent from these criteria that those individuals who display impairments in intellectual and adaptive functioning or lack of responsiveness to others and show gross deficits in language development and bizarre responses to the environment are least likely to show improvement in psychotherapy. Further, reviews of the efficacy of psychotherapy approaches, including Virginia Axline's play therapy and Bruno Bettelheim's child-centered therapy, indicate limited utility for severely disturbed populations (Clarizio & McCoy, 1976; Nathan & Harris, 1975).

In summary, there are several factors that preclude the selection of psychotherapy as the treatment of choice for severely disturbed individuals. First, these approaches tend to require extensive training of the primary service provider. Second, at least for severely disturbed children, there is disagreement among psychotherapists regarding the appropriateness of psychotherapy as a treatment choice. Finally, there is limited empirical evidence supporting the efficacy of psychotherapy with severely disturbed populations (Romanczyk et al., 1980).

In contrast to psychotherapeutic approaches, behavioral approaches have been extensively applied and evaluated for a wide range of problematic behaviors, in a variety of diagnostic populations (e.g., Leitenberg, 1976; Ross, 1981). Following is a brief review of several of these areas.

• Toilet Training •

Behavioral approaches have been employed in toilet training and treatment of incontinence or enuresis and encopresis, with the primary focus being contingent reinforcement of appropriate toileting behaviors (Seigel & Richards, 1978).

Approximately 20 percent of children fail to gain nocturnal bladder control by age 5, and 50 percent of these children remain enuretic at age 10. A frequently used treatment method for nocturnal enuresis is the bell-

---

and-pad method which is based on conditioning principles. The pad is designed so that urination causes a bell or buzzer to sound, thus in principle pairing the sound with cues for bladder fullness and the need to urinate. The child is awakened by the bell and is instructed to turn it off and to finish urinating in the toilet. Typically, praise or tangible reinforcers are employed to reward the child for dry nights. Most enuretic children require four to eight weeks with the pad before 14 consecutive dry nights are attained. This method has been found to be more effective than traditional psychotherapy and drug therapy for treatment of childhood enuresis (Seigel & Richards, 1978).

Ayllon, Simon, and Wildman (1975) reported effective treatment of a seven-year-old boy using positive reinforcement. A star chart was employed with stars awarded for soiling-free days. Seven consecutive soiling-free days were rewarded by an outing. There had been no remission at an 11-month follow-up. Reinforcement techniques have also been found to be very effective when used in combination with procedures labeled overcorrection (Ross, 1981). One variation of this technique is "positive practice," a technique outlined for the general public in a book by Azrin and Foxx (1974). The technique, which has been used extensively for normal children, involves a day of intensive training in toileting, ensuring high rates of urination by frequent fluid intake. Appropriate urination results in positive reinforcement whereas "accidents" are followed by 10 practice trials of steps of appropriate toileting (Foxx & Azrin, 1973).

Toilet training with the retarded, as well as the psychotic, in some cases, has been problematic for significant numbers of such individuals. Indeed, the lack of self-toileting skills has often been a focus of criticisms of certain institutions. However, drawing on the literature on normals and behavioral technology, significant changes have occurred.

The alarm pad device has been extended for daytime use in underpants and has been utilized successfully in combination with positive reinforcement and overcorrection for severely retarded individuals (Azrin & Foxx, 1971). The device can detect moisture from urination or defecation and thereby facilitates immediate delivery of consequences. Foxx and Azrin (1973) provide a manual for application of this technique to toilet training the severely retarded.

Another overcorrection procedure was employed successfully by Matson (1977) to treat encopresis in a 16-year-old autistic boy. The procedure required the boy to attempt voiding in the toilet for two minutes, change, clean himself, and place dirtied items in the laundry following each incidence of soiled pants.

In summary, both straightforward use of positive reinforcement and combinations of methods such as reinforcement plus overcorrection, or positive practice have been found to be effective in teaching toileting skills (Ross, 1981). As Birnbrauer (1976) has noted, we now have techniques for toilet training many of even the most profoundly retarded individuals.

• Self-Help and Language Skills •

Teaching tasks such as self-feeding, shoe-tying, and complex discriminations can be achieved through a combination of verbal instructions, prompts, and physical guidance. Backward chaining and manual guidance of responses with gradual fading of the guidance has been effectively used in teaching self-feeding and dressing (Birnbauer, 1976; Touchette, 1978). Touchette (1978) discusses application of these procedures to teaching various skills to mentally retarded individuals. He also suggests using a sequence of tasks which gradually increases in difficulty such that the learner is less likely to make an error. Errorless instruction results in consistent success for the learner. This may be an important factor in decreasing frustration for the retarded child. Touchette sees the value of behavior therapy in remediating behavior insuficiencies in the retarded not only for simple self-help skills but for more complex behaviors as well.

Schreibman & Koegel (1981) prescribe a similar approach to behavior modification programs for autistic children. They provide a general format for a training trial:

1. The teacher (parent) presents a clear stimulus (command or question) to the child who is quietly attending to the task.
2. The stimulus may optionally be followed by a prompting cue designed to evoke the desired response.
3. The child responds correctly or incorrectly.
4. The teacher responds (with a reward or punishment). (p. 506)

They also discuss teaching gradual approximations through shaping and chaining procedures such as backward chaining for teaching dressing.

Early behavioral studies clearly established that it was possible to teach complex behaviors such as verbal skills by applying basic learning principles (Lovaas & Newsom, 1976). The approach applied to behavior deficit typically involves application of differential reinforcement. A plethora of research investigations of the effectiveness of errorless learning and discrimination learning for language training has led to development of a number of systematic language training programs.

Lovaas (1977) outlines a language training program designed for utilization with autistic children. The approach can also be applied with other language-impaired individuals. The technique, which is based on learning theory principles, involves prompting, shaping, and discrimination learning. Lovaas provides a training sequence which evolves through shaping initial verbal imitation to verbal discriminations and finally generalization to spontaneous speech. In a similar vein, Kent (1974) employs principles of reinforcement theory in a language acquisition program for use with severely retarded or multiply impaired individuals.

The program stresses recording all verbal responses and reinforcing appropriate responses or approximations. Guess, Sailor, and Baer (1978) also utilize learning principles in a program which clearly delineates trainer stimulus presentations and expected responses from the student. The program involves a sequence of steps that may be presented in order or deviated from on the basis of failure to acquire a given skill.

Common to all of these techniques is emphasis on a systematic approach to teaching language in small progressive steps. Reinforcement is employed to increase frequency of vocalizations and to shape correct verbalizations. The programs provide a systematic approach to language training appropriate to even the most severely disturbed and retarded populations.

An advantage of behavioral approaches is that behavioral interventions of the type described can be enhanced through their application by parents. Improvements in areas of behavior deficit such as language, self-help, and social skills have been documented for parent-operated contingency management (Wahler, 1976). Further, application of these techniques by parents has led to improved generalization of treatment at follow-up (Lovaas et al., 1973).

• Aggression •

Aggression is frequently a major factor in the expulsion of individuals from nonrestrictive settings and subsequent placement in more restrictive settings. Although aggression may lend itself to a variety of causal interpretations, considerable documentation exists for the effectiveness of behavioral interventions for aggressive behavior. Forehand and Baumeister (1976) and Birnbrauer (1976) provide reviews of the literature on the behavioral treatment of aggression, as well as other anti social and aberrant behaviors, in retarded individuals. Although there are no reported successes of treatment by differential reinforcement of other, more adaptive behaviors (DRO) alone for seriously aggressive behavior, a number of studies demonstrate the effectiveness of DRO in combination with continent time-out. However, it should be noted that time-out has been used to encompass a broad range of procedures in these studies, for example, up to 120 minutes in a restraint chair (Vukelich and Hake, 1971), 2 minutes in a seclusion room (Bostow and Bailey, 1969), and 20 seconds of restraint (held by teacher) (Repp & Deitz, 1974). The results of a study investigating the parameters of seclusion time-out by White, Nielsen, and Johnson (1972) suggest that brief periods of time-out may be as effective as longer periods if the individual has not had prior experience with the longer durations of time-out. The reader is referred to Hobbs and Forehand (1977) for further review of the parameters of time-out.

Another example of the importance of a thorough functional analysis of behavior and environmental events is the case in which aggressive or disruptive behavior functions as an escape response. Two studies demonstrated the failure of time-out procedures in that increases in the rate of problematic behavior were observed in two autistic children (Plummer, Baer, & LeBlanc, 1977; Solnick, Rincover, & Peterson, 1977). Solnick et al. (1977) subsequently suppressed tantrum behavior by a brief (10-sec) restraint of the child's hands in order to prevent finger-flicking self-stimulation. The investigators concluded that this self-stimulation was the functional reinforcer for tantrums. Plummer et al. (1977) demonstrated subsequent suppression of their autistic subject's disruptive behavior by employing paced instructions without procedural time-out, that is, teacher instructions were delivered at a set pace regardless of the child's behavior. Carr, Newsom, and Binkoff (1980) conducted a more thorough analysis of the escape-from-demand function of aggressive behavior in two retarded children. They demonstrated that escape-motivated aggression could be substantially reduced by introducing strongly preferred reinforcers for appropriate response to demands (which may be conceptualized as a type of DRO). These authors also provide data indicating that aggression may be reduced by providing an alternative, nonaggressive escape response. Last, they demonstrated suppression of aggression by an extinction procedure in which one subject was restrained in a chair with a seat belt during one-hour sessions which were not terminated until five minutes had passed without aggression. Subsequently, they were able to remove the seat belt while maintaining suppression of aggression and continuing instructional demands.

A variety of punishment procedures have also been employed for the treatment of aggressive behavior in retarded and severely disturbed populations. Employing variations of overcorrection, Foxx and Azrin (1972) implemented a "restitutional overcorrection" procedure for the suppression of severely disruptive and aggressive behavior in profoundly retarded institutionalized adults, and Webster and Azrin (1973) utilized a "required relaxation" procedure for similar clients. Colletti, Kaplan, Brutvan, and Romanczyk (1981) utilized an "enforced relaxation" procedure to suppress serious aggressive behavior in a severely retarded, emotionally disturbed youth. Enforced relaxation involved holding the child in a prone position on a cushioned mat for 10 minutes of nonstruggling.

Luce, Delquardi, and Hall (1980) suppressed aggressive behavior in two severely disturbed children with a "contingent exercise" procedure which required the children to engage in sitting down on the floor and then standing up 10 times. In a variation on this theme, Romanczyk, Colletti, Plienis, Meinhold, Bauer, and Cooper (1981) employed a "contingent effort" procedure which required the child to maintain a push-up position for an eight-minute period. This procedure was successful in the rapid and enduring suppression of aggressive and disruptive behaviors of five disturbed children in classroom settings. In addition, the effectiveness was generalized from the initial implementation by supervisory staff to the implementation by the classroom teachers.

• Self-Injurious Behavior •

Self-injurious behavior is an extremely problematic behavior pattern that is often assumed to be associated with serious psychopathology. Although it has a rather low prevalance of less than 5 percent in psychiatric populations (Bachman, 1972; Lester, 1972), the incidence may be as high as 40 percent for institutionalized schizophrenic children and 15 percent for institutionalized retarded children (see Schroeder, Schroeder, Smith, & Dalldorf, 1978). The typical traditional treatment for severe cases of self-injury has been the use of long-term restraint or sedation, or both. Both of these treatments have considerable potential for severe iatrogenic effects. Furthermore, these treatments do not serve to alleviate the problem but only to prevent its expression, and in some cases they may actually aggravate the condition (Romanczyk, Kistner, & Plienis, 1982).

Evidence suggests that genetic and organic factors in the motivation of self-injurious behavior in some specific medical conditions, such as Lesch-Nyhan and Cornelia de Lange syndromes, and otitis media (see Carr, 1977; Russo, Carr, & Lovaas, 1980). Lovaas and Newsom (1976), Carr (1977), Russo et al. (1980), and Romanczyk, Kistner, and Plienis (1982) provide contemporary reviews of the evidence supporting a behavioral conceptualization of the etiology and treatment of self-injurious behavior as an operant that may be a function of social consequences or specific eliciting stimulus conditions, or both. These authors review investigations employing single case design methodology demonstrating the effectiveness of a variety of behavioral interventions, including differential reinforcement, extinction, time-out/seclusion, overcorrection, and contingent punishment. Given the ethical issues, situational constraints, and serious ramifications of self-injurious behavior, a variety of methodological problems exist in the published reports of behavioral treatments for self-injury (see Romanczyk, Kistner, & Plienis, 1982). Although the evidence supporting a learning-based etiology is inconclusive, the number of reported successes in the literature strongly supports a behavioral conceptualization of the treatment of self-injury for most cases. The importance of conducting a thorough behavior analysis is clear in that a variety of functional relationships between self-injurious behavior and environmental events has been demonstrated. For example, Carr et al. (1976) demonstrated that self-injury is an eight-year-old schizophrenic boy served to function as an escape response from teacher demands. In other words, when the teacher made task demands, the rate of self-injurious behavior increased; when the teacher ceased making demands, the rate decreased. On the other hand, Bucher and Lovaas (1968) conducted an analysis of self-injury in a seven-year-old retarded boy who had been maintained in restraints for 24 hours a day because of high levels of self-injury. An extinction procedure was employed wherein the child was isolated in his bed for an hour and a half each day, unrestrained. After initial high rates, the self-injurious behavior decreased dramatically, indicating that social attention may have been a factor in maintaining the behavior.

Romanczyk, Kistner, and Plienis (1982) have also proposed a two-component, operant-respondent conceptualization of self-injurious behavior in which the initial occurrences may be an elicited response to a high-arousal-producing event. Subsequently, the behavior is shaped and maintained by environmental consequences. In an innovative approach to the assessment and treatment of a severely self-injurious institutionalized young woman who was mildly retarded and psychotic, Romanczyk, Plienis, Flachs, and Spettell (1981) employed this conceptualization by continuously monitoring measures of physiological arousal in the assessment and initial stages of treatment. Episodes of self-injury in the assessment phase were elicited by restraint removal and were correlated with increased arousal. Reapplication of restraints reduced attempts at self-injury and appeared correlated with reduction in arousal. These data provide support for the respondent-operant model in that antecedent stimuli to self-injury appeared to have multiple stimulus functions as both conditioned and discriminative stimuli. Initial treatment sessions incorporated this form of feedback to the therapist on a continuous basis, and virtually complete suppression of self-injury was achieved. Subsequently, the treatment was extended so that the client was unrestrained during all waking hours and engaged in a full schedule of habilitative activities. In the fifth month of follow-up, only one occasion of self-injury had been recorded, and substantial improvements in the client's social, affective, self-help, and task-oriented behavior have been noted by staff.

Romanczyk, Colletti, Reynolds, Kitz, and Kraemer (1981) conducted a quantitative review of 69 reports published between 1964 and 1979 concerning the behavioral treatment of self-injurious behavior. The subjects in 72 percent of these reports were diagnosed as retarded whereas 28 percent received other primary diagnoses, such as psychotic or schizophrenic. About 90 percent of these studies reported elimination or substantial suppression of self-injury, and over 80 percent reported maintenance of treatment gains at follow-up. Clearly, behavioral intervention for self-injurious behavior has documented efficacy as a viable treatment alternative.

• Self-Stimulatory Behavior •

As is the case with self-injurious behavior, there is no consensus or conclusive evidence to support any one position for conceptualizing the etiology, functional significance, and maintenance of self-stimulatory behavior. However, there is general agreement that high rates of self-stimulatory behavior (e.g., rocking, head weaving, mouthing, finger play) occupy a disproportionate status in the behavioral repertoires of severely disturbed individuals and reduce their opportunities to engage in more adaptive, goal-directed behaviors (see Baumeister & Forehand, 1973; Forehand & Baumeister, 1976; Lovaas & Newsom, 1976; Romanczyk, Kistner, & Plienis, 1982; Ross, 1981). Aberrant self-stimulatory behavior has been observed in approximately 65 percent of the institutionalized retarded population (see Forehand & Baumeister, 1976). Similarly, Lovaas and Newsom (1976) and Romanczyk, Kistner, and Plienis (1982) have noted that problematic self-stimulatory behavior is a major characteristic of autistic, psychotic, and other severely disturbed child populations.

Lovaas, Litrownik, and Mann (1971) provide data indicating that the extent of self-stimulation displayed by autistic children varied inversely with the reinforcement obtained for other behavior. Koegel and Covert (1972) provided further support for these findings by demonstrating that three autistic children were unable to acquire and perform a simple discrimination until self-stimulatory behavior was suppressed. However, Klier and Harris (1977) did not find a consistent inverse relationship between self-stimulation and learning in four autistic children. Their analysis indicated the importance of considering the nature of the self-stimulatory behavior, the requirements of the task, and the functional level of the child. These findings demonstrate the importance of assessing functional relationships between behaviors rather than assuming the need to suppress maladaptive behavior in order to teach adaptive skills.

Reports of behavioral treatment strategies for the suppression of self-stimulation indicate that these behaviors can be controlled by the contingent presentation of certain positive and aversive events. Diverse methods for reducing self-stimulation have been reviewed by Baumeister and Forehand (1973), Forehand and Baumeister (1976), and Romanczyk, Kistner, and Plienis (1982). The type of interventions that have been attempted may be categorized as follows: differential reinforcement, extinction, time-out, overcorrection, and punishment.

A minimally intrusive treatment strategy for suppression of self-stimulatory behavior is DRO. The results of the study by Lovaas, Litrownik, and Mann (1971) suggest that as the child is trained and reinforced for performing an alternative response, rates of self-stimulatory behaviors decreased. In support of this finding, Baumeister and Forehand (1973) found that high rates of reinforcement for performing an operant task resulted in suppression of self-stimulation in severely retarded subjects. Another method of DRO is to reinforce the individual for the absence of self-stimulatory behavior for specified intervals of time. Repp, Deitz, and Speir (1974) reinforced institutionalized retarded subjects for the absence of self-stimulation for intervals of 30 to 60 seconds. Rates of self-stimulation rapidly decreased and remained low for all treatment sessions.

However, documented results of DRO procedures for suppressing self-stimulation are mixed. Attempts to replicate success and to assess relative efficacy in comparison to other procedures have produced negative results (Azrin, Kaplan, & Fox, 1973; Harris & Wolchik, 1979). Unfavorable results with DRO may be partly a function of the reward value of the manipulated reinforcer in relation to the value of the reinforcement derived from self-stimulation. Several studies have demonstrated that sensory events, such as vestibular, auditory, and visual stimuli, can be effective reinforcers for children who exhibit self-stimulatory behavior (Freeman, Frankel, & Ritvo, 1976; Hung, 1978; Rincover, Newsom, Lovaas, & Koegel, 1977). Enhancing the efficacy of the contingent reinforcers so that they are competitive with the stimulation that the individuals provide themselves may increase the therapeutic potential of DRO procedures. However, our current state of knowledge suggests that although DRO alone may not be generally effective in suppressing self-stimulation, it is desirable to use DRO in combination with other decelerative procedures.

Time-out and extinction are seldom utilized for the reduction of self-stimulatory behavior, for the same reason—both allow the uninhibited occurrence of the behavior. Given the apparent reinforcing properties of self-stimulatory behavior, the application of a time-out or extinction contingency typically has no effect. Their use is therefore most often contraindicated for suppressing self-stimulation. An exception to this rule is the sensory extinction procedure described by Rincover (1978). Extinction procedures in behavioral treatments generally refer to the withholding of attention on the occurrence of the target behavior, presuming that social attention is a functional reinforcer for the behavior. Rincover (1978) states that the procedure for sensory extinction of self-stimulatory behavior involves masking or removing various types of sensory stimulation that reinforce a child's stereotyped, repetitive behavior procedures. For example, he presents data demonstrating the suppression of plate-spinning behavior in a psychotic child by covering the table surface with a rug which eliminated auditory feedback for spinning. He also presents data on the reduction of hand-flapping by using a blindfold and masking the proprioceptive feedback by attaching a small vibrating mechanism to the back of the child's hand. However, these variations are less demonstrative of the sensory extinction conceptualization in that punishment and response cost may have been functional elements of these procedures (see Ross, 1981).

Overcorrection is a form of punishment that has frequently been used to suppress self-stimulation (see Ollendick & Matson, 1978). The rationale and description of overcorrection procedures are provided in Foxx and Azrin (1973). The effectiveness of overcorrection procedures in suppressing self-stimulatory behavior has been demonstrated with mentally retarded (Azrin et al., 1973; Wells, Forehand, & Hickey, 1977), autistic (Harris and Wolchik, 1979), schizophrenic (Epstein, Doke, Sajwaj, Sorrell, Rimmer, 1974), and emotionally disturbed children (Wells, Forehand, Hickey, & Green, 1977). However, some reports show that overcorrection is not always successful, may not produce desirable generalizability, and may produce negative side effects (Azrin et al., 1973; Rollings, Baumeister, & Baumeister, 1977). Rather than a single clearly definable procedure, overcorrection is a set of procedures with a broad range of topographic and temporal parameters. In an analysis of two major components, restitution and positive practice, Ollendick and Matson (1976) showed both to be effective in suppressing inappropriate behavior. Further, in their review of the published studies investigating overcorrection, Ollendick and Matson (1978) conclude that overcorrection is generally effective in suppressing self-stimulatory behavior and that maximum effectiveness is attained by adhering to the original procedural guidelines proposed by Foxx and Azrin (1972, 1973).

Along with the problems of generalizability and potential side effects, a major concern with the use of punishment is that legal and ethical standards demand that intrusive procedures be used as seldom as possible and only when other treatment methods have failed. Given that self-stimulatory behaviors do not produce physical harm to the child or others in the environment, it is difficult to reach a consensus concerning to use of aversive procedures for the treatment of self-stimulation.

• SUMMARY •

There are several conclusions that are appropriate. First, there does not appear to be clear agreement on the appropriate categorization of an individual who is retarded and displays psychotic behavior. Indeed, even the manner in which one describes the individual appears to influence the process, such as speaking of a psychotic individual who is mentally retarded rather than a retarded person displaying psychotic behavior. Perhaps the most parsimonious system would be a descriptive diagnostic process rather than a class diagnostic process. As was pointed out in the section on etiology, particular characteristics appear to have prognostic significance but not simply the classification of retarded or psychotic. Even within comparatively well-delineated disorders, such as autism, extensive disagreement is found. Lovaas (1971), in the context of a panel discussion concerning autism and its diagnosis, stated that

> I often think we haven't reached a place yet where we can define autism. The kind of definitional search you people are engaged in may lead us to make premature decisions about what it is we are studying. It seems that what you're trying to do is just not possible. You attempt to give autism a functional definition but you do not have the data. All the discussion seems arbitrary to me, how much to include or not to include. The definition of autism will not be settled by debate.
>
> Let me make the point this way. What I'm struck with in studying autistic children is that they present a whole set of behaviors and these different behaviors have different properties. The problem behaviors don't hang together. For example, the laws that govern autoerotic behavior are different from the laws that govern self-destructive behavior. Furthermore, the variables that control autoerotic behavior are different from the variables that control speech. Therefore, I say we don't work with autistic children but with different kinds of behaviors which functionally can be grouped according to the laws that regulate them. (pp. 108–109)[6]

The point being made here is that the behavioral characteristics are of paramount importance, and the placement of an individual into a particular category is much less useful. This stance is certainly not limited to the current topic and could easily be extended to many other diagnostic categories. It may clearly be subsumed under the approach known as behavioral assessment. Although this topic is too broad to cover here, its utility and systematization are very strong points in its favor. This is especially true when one examines what is perhaps the most important assumption concerned with diagnosis: that is, that it assists in determining the appropriate treatment procedures. It is clear from our brief overview of treatment effectiveness, and is well substantiated in the behavioral literature as a whole, that assignment to a particular class does not significantly predict the outcome of intervention, nor does it predict the treatment procedures utilized.

However, it is true that the simultaneous classification of retardation and psychosis does provide actuarial prognostic information, as was illus-

---

[6]Reprinted with permission from Lovaas, O. I. General discussion. In D. W. Churchill, G. D. Alpern, & M. K. DeMyer (Eds.), *Infantile autism: Proceedings of the Indiana University Colloquium.* Springfield, Illinois: Charles C. Thomas, 1971.

trated in the section on schizophrenia. Similarly, a recent report by the New York State Office of Mental Retardation (September 1981—Technical Monograph 81-02) indicated an important series of findings based upon their survey of 25,000 developmentally disabled individuals in New York State. The report states in part that

> *Summary of Findings.* In brief, these analyses suggest that: (1) a small majority of the DD [developmental disability] population sample surveyed display some type of problem behavior, but only 12.5 percent display antisocial behavior, (2) behavior problems are more frequent and severe among PDD [psychiatric and developmental disability] than among DD individuals, regardless of intellectual level or living situation, (3) less marked mental retardation is association with lower frequency and severity of problem behaviors, though this relationship is mediated by age, (4) persons with severe, rather than profound, mental retardation evidence the most serious and frequent problem behaviors, (5) persons residing in more restrictive settings have more frequent and severe problem behaviors, and (6) the probability that an individual will be diagnosed as PDD rather than DD varies as a function of problem behavior severity, level of intellectual functioning, and living situation. (p. 111)[7]

It is also of interest to note that the report did mention the fact that "it can be argued that this figure [the diagnostic classification of PDD] could be deflated by failure of developmental disabilities personnel to recognize psychiatric involvement" (p. 109), although the report continues by stating that it is believed this was compensated for in their analysis. The findings of the report also underscore the problems in this type of analysis of separating diagnostic groups from behavior categorizations; that is, is association of a greater proportion of behavior problems with a psychiatric diagnosis and developmental disability a function of some causal relationship or simply an artifact in that the presence of severe behavior problems is criterion for the psychiatric diagnosis?

In conclusion, this chapter can be summarized by saying that appropriate concurrent diagnosis, to the extent that it reliably identifies subgroups within the general categories of retardation and psychosis, is a useful source of information for research and administrative purposes. If advances are to be made in the area of etiology, greater refinement of the diagnostic process is a necessity. However, with respect to providing treatment services to a given individual, the utility of concurrent diagnosis has yet to be demonstrated. We remain pessimistic in this regard, given the complexity of the treatment decision process and the complexity of each individual. A behavioral assessment approach to treatment

---

[7]Reprinted from New York State Office of Mental Retardation, Technical Monograph 81-02, September 1981.

decisions is the most appropriate method, both programmatically and conceptually.

• REFERENCES •

Albee, G. W., Lane, E. A., Corcoran, C., & Werneke, A. Childhood and intercurrent intellectual performance of adult schizophrenics. *Journal of Consulting Psychology*, 1963, *27*(4), 364–366.

Albee, G. W., Lane, E. A., & Reuter, J. M. Childhood intelligence of future schizophrenics and neighborhood peers. *Journal of Psychology*, 1964, *58*, 141–144.

Alpern, G. D. Measurement of "untestable" autistic children. *Journal of Abnormal Psychology*, 1967, *72*, 478–496.

American Psychiatric Association. *Diagnostic and statistical manual of mental disorders* Washington, D.C.: American Psychiatric Association, 1980. (3rd ed.).

Angus, L. R. Schizophrenia and schizoid conditions in students in a special school. *American Journal of Mental Deficiency*, 1948, *53*, 227–238.

Anthony, E. J. Low-grade psychosis in childhood. In B. W. Richards (Ed.), *Proceedings of the London Conference on the Scientific Study of Mental Deficiency*, 1962, *2*, 398–410.

Ayllon, T., Simon, S., & Wildman, R. W. Instructions and reinforcement in the elimination of encopresis: A case study. *Journal of Behavior Therapy and Experimental Psychiatry*, 1975, *6*, 235–238.

Azrin, N. H. and Foxx, R. M. A rapid method of toilet training the institutionalized retarded. *Journal of Applied Behavior Analysis*, 1971, *4*, 88–99.

Azrin, N. H. & Foxx, R. M. *Toilet training in less than a day*. New York: Simon & Schuster, 1974.

Azrin, N. H., Kaplan, S. J., & Foxx, R. M. Autism reversal: Eliminating stereotyped self-stimulation of retarded individuals. *American Journal of Mental Deficiency*, 1973, *78*, 241–248.

Bachman, J. A. Self-injurious behavior: A behavioral analysis. *Journal of Abnormal Psychology*, 1972, *80*, 211–224.

Bartak, L., & Rutter, M. Differences between mentally retarded and normally intelligent autistic children. *Journal of Autism and Childhood Schizophrenia*, 1976, *6*, 109–120.

Bartak, L., & Rutter, M. Educational treatment of autistic children. In M. Rutter (Ed.), *Infantile autism: Concepts, characteristics and treatment*. London: Churchill-Livingstone, 1971.

Bartak, L., Rutter, M., & Cox, A. A comparative study of infantile autism and specific developmental receptive language disorder. *British Journal of Psychiatry*, 1975, *126*, 127–145.

Baumeister, A. A., & Forehand, R. Stereotyped acts. In N. R. Ellis (Ed.), *International review of research in mental retardation* (Vol. 6). New York: Academic Press, 1973.

Bell, R. Q. A reinterpretation of the direction of effects in studies of socialization. *Psychological Review*, 1968, *75*, 81–95.

Birnbrauer, J. S. Mental retardation. In H. Leitenberg (Ed.), *Handbook of Behavior modification and behavior therapy*. Englewood Cliffs, N.J.: Prentice-Hall, 1976.

Block, J. Parents of schizophrenic, neurotic, asthmatic, and congenitally ill children: A comparative study. *Archives of General Psychiatry*, 1969, *20*, 656–674.

Bostow, D. E., & Bailey, J. B. Modifications of severe disruptive and aggressive behavior using brief time-out and reinforcement procedures. *Journal of Applied Behavior Analysis*, 1969, *2*, 31–37.

Cantwell, D. P., Baker, L., & Rutter, M. Family factors. In M. Rutter & E. Schopler (Eds.), *Autism—A reappraisal of concepts and treatment*. New York: Plenum Press, 1978.

Carr, E. G. The motivation of self-injurious behavior: A review of some hypotheses. *Psychological Bulletin,* 1977, *84*, 800–816.

Carr, E. G., Newsom, C. D., & Binkoff, J. A. Escape as a factor in the aggressive behavior of two retarded children. *Journal of Applied Behavior Analysis*, 1980, *13*, 101–118.

Carr, E. G., Newsom, C. D., & Binkoff, J. A. Stimulus control of self-destructive behavior in a psychotic child. *Journal of Abnormal Child Psychology*, 1976, *4*, 139–153.

Castell, R. Physical distance and visual attention as measures of social interaction between child and adult. In S. J. Hutt & C. Hutt (Eds.), *Behavior studies in psychiatry*. Oxford: Pergamon, 1970.

Chess, S. Autism in children with congenital rubella. *Journal of Autism and Childhood Schizophrenia*, 1971, *1*, 33–47.

Chess, S., Korn, S. J., & Fernandez, P. B. *Psychiatric disorders of children with rubella*. New York: Brunner/Mazel, 1971.

Churchill, D. W., & Bryson, C. Looking and approach behavior of psychotic and normal children as a function of adult attention or preoccupation. *Comprehensive Psychiatry*, 1972, *13*, 171–177.

Clarizio H. F. & McCoy, G. F. *Behavior disorders in children* (2nd ed.). New York: Crowell, 1976.

Clark, P., & Rutter, M. Compliance and resistance in autistic children. *Journal of Autism & Childhood Schizophrenia*, 1977, *7*, 33–48.

Colletti, G., Kaplan, J. Brutvan, L., & Romanczyk, R. G. *Enforced relaxation: Application to severe aggression and acting out behavior*. Presented at Association for Behavior Analysis Eighth Annual Convention, Milwaukee, Wisc., May 1981.

Creak, E. M. Childhood psychosis: A review of 100 cases. *British Journal of Psychiatry*, 1963a, *19*, 84–89.

Creak, E. M. Schizophrenic syndrome in childhood: Progress report of a working party. *Cerebral Palsy Bulletin*, 1963b, *3*, 501–503.

Critchley, M., & Earl, D. J. Tuberose sclerosis and allied conditions. *Brain*, 1932, *55*, 311–346.

Cunningham, M. A. A comparison of the language of psychotic and non-psychotic children who are mentally retarded. *Journal of Child Psychology and Psychiatry*, 1968, *9*, 229–244.

Delong, G. R. A neuropsychologic interpretation of infantile autism. In M. Rutter, & E. Schopler (Eds.), *Autism: A reappraisal of concepts and treatment*. New York: Plenum Press, 1978.

DeMyer, M. K., Barton, S., Alpern, G. D., Kimberlin, C., Allen, J., Yang, E., & Steele, R. The measured intelligence of autistic children. *Journal of Autism and Childhood Schizoprenia*, 1974, *4*, 42–60.

Dewey, M. A. & Everard, M. P. The near-normal autistic adolescent. *Journal of Autism and Chilahood Schizophrenia*, 1974, *4*, 348–356.

Eisenberg, L., & Kanner, L. Early infantile autism 1943–55. *American Journal of Orthopsychiatry*, 1956, *26*, 556–566.

Epstein, L. H., Doke, L. A., Sajwaj, T., Sorrell, S., & Rimmer, B. Generality and side effects of overcorrection. *Journal of Applied Behavior Analysis*, 1974, *7*, 385–390.

Esman, A. H., Kohn, M., & Nyman, L. The family of the "schizophrenic" child. *American Journal of Orthopsychiatry*, 1959, *29*, 455–459.

Forehand, R., & Baumeister, A. A. Deceleration of aberrant behavior among retarded individuals. In M. Hersen, R. M. Eisler, & P. M. Miller (Ed.), *Progress in Behavior Modification* (Vol. 2). New York: Academic Press, 1976.

Foxx, R. M. & Azrin, N. A method of eliminating aggressive-disruptive behavior of retarded and brain damaged patients. *Behavior Research and Therapy*, 1972, *10*, 15–27.

Foxx, R. M. & Azrin, N. H. The elimination of autistic self-stimulatory behavior by overcorrection. *Journal of Applied Behavior Analysis*, 1973a, *6*, 1–14.

Foxx, R. M., & Azrin, N. H. *Toilet training the retarded*. Champaign, Ill.: Research Press, 1973b.

Freeman, B. J., Frankel, F., & Ritvo, E. R. The effects of response contingent vestibular stimulation on the behavior of autistic and retarded children. *Journal of Autism and Childhood Schizophrenia*, 1976, *6*, 353–358.

Goldfarb, W. *Childhood schizophrenia*. Cambridge: Harvard University Press, 1961.

Grossman, H. J. (Ed.). *Manual on terminology and classification*. Washington, D.C.: American Association on Mental Deficiency, 1977.

Guess, D., Sailor, W., & Baer, D. M. *Functional speech and language training for the severely handicapped*. Lawrence, Kan.: H & H Enterprises, 1978.

Hallgren, B., & Sjogren, T. A clinical and genetic statistical study of schizophrenia and low grade mental deficiency in a large Swedish rural population. *Acta Psychiatrica et Neurologica Scandinavia*, 1959, *35*, 7–65.

Harris, S. L., & Wolchik, J. A. Suppression of self-stimulation: Three alternative strategies. *Journal of Applied Behavior Analysis*, 1979, *12*, 185–199.

Hayman, M. The inter-relations of mental defect and mental disorder. *Journal of Mental Science*, 1939, *85*, 1183–1193.

Hermelin, B. Images and Language. In M. Rutter & E. Schopler (Eds.), *Autism—A reappraisal of concepts and treatment*. New York: Plenum Press, 1978.

Hermelin, B., & O'Connor, N. *Psychological experiments with autistic children*. Oxford: Pergamon Press, 1970.

Herskovitz, H. H., & Plesset, M. R. Psychoses in adult mental defectives. *Psychiatric Quarterly*, 1941, *15*, 574–588.

Heston, L. Psychiatric disorders in foster home reared children of schizophrenic mothers. *British Journal of Psychiatry*, 1966, *112*, 819–825.

Hobbs, S. A., & Forehand, R. Important parameters in the use of timeout with children: A re-examination. *Journal of Behavior Therapy and Experimental Psychiatry*, 1977, *8*, 365–370.

Hung, D. W. Using self-stimulation as reinforcement for autistic children. *Journal of Autism and Childhood Schizophrenia*, 1978, *8*, 355–366.

Hutt, C., & Hutt, S. J. Biological studies of autism. *Journal of Special Education*, 1969, *3*, 3–11.

Hutt, C., & Ounsted, C. The biological significance of gaze aversion with particular reference to the syndrome of infantile autism. *Behavioural Science*, 1966, *11*, 346–356.

Kanner, L. Autistic disturbances of affective contact. *Nervous child*, 1943, *2*, 217–250.

Kanner, L. Problems of nosology and psychodynamics of early infantile autism. *American Journal of Orthopsychiatry*, 1949, *19*, 416–426.

Kaufman, I., Frank, T., Heims, L., Herrick, J., Rusir, D., & Willer, L. Treatment implications of a new classification of parents of schizophrenic children. *American Journal of Psychiatry*, 1960, *116*, 920–924.

Kent, L. R. *Language acquisition program for the retarded or multiply impaired.* Champaign, Ill.: Research Press, 1974.

Klebanoff, L. B. I. Parental attitudes of mothers of schizophrenic, brain-injured & retarded and normal children. *American Journal of Orthopsychiatry*, 1959, *29*, 445–454.

Klier, J., & Harris, S. L., Self-stimulation and learning in autistic children: Physical or functional incompatibility? *Journal of Applied Behavior Analysis*, 1977, *10*, 311.

Koegel, R. L., & Covert, A. The relationship of self-stimulation to learning in autistic children. *Journal of Applied Behavior Analysis*, 1972, *5*, 381–387.

Kolvin, I., Humphrey, M., & McNay, A. Cognitive factors in childhood psychoses. *British Journal of Psychiatry*, 1971, *118*, 415–419.

Kolvin, I., Ounsted, C., Humphrey, M., McNay, A., Richardson, L. M., Garside, R. F., Kidd, J. S. H., & Roth, M. Six studies in the childhood psychoses. *British Journal of Psychiatry*, 1971, *118*, 381–419.

Lane, E., & Albee, G. W. Childhood intelligence of schizophrenics and siblings. *American Journal of Orthopsychiatry*. 1965, *35*, 747–753.

Lane, E., & Albee, G. W. Early childhood intellectual differences between schizophrenic adults and their siblings. *Journal of Abnormal and Social Psychology*, 1964, *68*, 193–195.

Larsson, T., & Sjogren, T. A methodological psychiatric and statistical study of a large Swedish rural population. *Acta Psychiatrica et Neurologica Scandinavia*. 1954.

Leitenberg, H. (Ed.). *Handbook of Behavior Modification and Behavior Therapy.* Englewood Cliffs, N.J.: Prentice-Hall, 1976.

Lester, D. Self-mutilating behavior. *Psychological Bulletin*, 1972, *78*, 119–128.

Lockyer, L., & Rutter, M. A five to fifteen year follow-up study of infantile psychosis. III. Psychological aspects. *British Journal of Psychiatry*, 1969, *115*, 865–882.

Lotter, W. Services for a group of autistic children in Middlesex. In J. K. Wing (Ed.), *Early childhood autism*. Oxford: Pergamon Press, 1966.

Lovaas, O. I. General discussion. In D. W. Churchill, G. D. Alpern, & M. K. DeMyer (Eds.), *Infantile autism: Proceedings of the Indiana University Colloquium*, Springfield, Ill.: Charles C. Thomas, 1971.

Lovaas, O. I. *The autistic child-language development through behavior modification*. New York: Irvington, 1977.

Lovaas, O. I., Koegel, R., Simmons, J. Q., & Long, J. S. Some generalization and follow-up measures on autistic children in behavior therapy. *Journal of Applied Behavior Analysis*, 1973, *6*, 131–166.

Lovaas, O. I., Litrownik, A., & Mann, R. Response latencies to auditory stimuli in autistic children engaged in self-stimulatory behavior. *Behavior Research and Therapy*, 1971, *9*, 34–49.

Lovaas, O. I., Schreibman, L., & Koegel, R. A behavior modification approach to the treatment of autistic children. In E. Schopler & R. Reichler (Eds.), *Psychopathology and child development*. New York: Plenum Press, 1976.

Lovaas, O. I., & Newsom, C. D. Behavior modification with psychotic children. In H. Leitenberg (Ed.), *Handbook of behavior modification and behavior therapy*. Englewood Cliffs, N.J.: Prentice-Hall, 1976.

Luce, S. C., Delquardi, J., & Hall, R. V. Contingent exercise: A mild but powerful procedure for suppressing inappropriate verbal and aggressive behavior. *Journal of Applied Behavior Analysis*, 1980, *13*, 583–594.

Matson, J. L. Simple correction for treating an autistic boy's encopresis. *Psychological Reports*, 1977, *41*, 802.

Menolascino, F. J. Autistic reactions in early childhood—Differential diagnosis consideration. *Journal of Child Psychology and Psychiatry*, 1965a, *6*, 203–218.

Menolascino, F. J. Emotional disturbance and mental retardation. *American Journal of Mental Deficiency*. 1965b, *70*, 248–256.

Menolascino, F. J. Psychiatric aspects of mongolism. *American Journal of Mental Deficiency*. 1965c, *69*, 653–660.

Meyers, D. I., & Goldfarb, W. Psychiatric appraisal of parents and siblings of schizophrenic children. *American Journal of Psychiatry*, 1962, *118*, 902–915.

Mittler, P., Gillies, S., & Jukes, E. Prognosis in psychotic children. Report of follow-up study. *Journal of Mental Deficiency Research*, 1966, *10*, 73–83.

Money, J., Borrow, N. A., & Clarke, F. C. Autism and autoimmune disease—A family study. *Journal of Autism and Childhood Schizophrenia*, 1971, *1*, 146–160.

Nathan, P. E., & Harris, S. L. *Psychopathology and Society*. New York: McGraw-Hill, 1975.

Neuer, H. The relationship between behavior disorders in children and the syndrome of mental deficiency. *American Journal of Mental Deficiency*, 1947, *52*, 143–147.

New York State Office of Mental Retardation. Technical Monograph 81-02, September 1981.

Offord, D. R., & Cross, L. A. Adult schizophrenia with scholastic failure or low I.Q. in childhood. *Archives of General Psychiatry*, 1971, *24*, 431–436.

Ollendick, T. H., & Matson, J. L. An initial investigation into the parameters of overcorrection. *Psychological Reports*, 1976, *39*, 1139–1142.

Ollendick, T. H., & Matson, J. L. Overcorrection: An overview. *Behavior Therapy*, 1978, *9*, 830–842.

Ornitz, E. N. M. Biological homogeneity or heterogeneity? In M. Rutter & E. Schopler (Eds.), *Autism*. New York: Plenum Press, 1978.

Ornitz, E. M., Guthrie, D., & Farley, A. J. The early development of autistic children. *Journal of Autism and Childhood Schizophrenia*, 1977, *7*, 207–229.

Ornitz, E. M., & Ritvo, E. R. Perceptual inconstancy in early infantile autism. *Archives of General Psychiatry*, 1968, *2*, 389–399.

Penrose, L. S. Observations on the aetiology of mongolism. *Lancet*, 1954, *1*, 505–509.

Pitfield, M., & Oppenheim, A. Childrearing attitudes of mothers of psychotic children. *Journal of Child Psychology and Psychiatry*, 1964, *5*, 51–57.

Plummer, S., Baer, D. M., & LeBlanc, J. Functional considerations in the use of procedural timeout and an effective alternative. *Journal of Applied Behavior Analysis*, 1977, *10*, 687–705.

Pollack, M. Comparison of childhood, adolescent, and adult schizophrenias. Etiologic significance of intellectual functioning. *Archives of General Psychiatry*, 1960, *2*, 652–660.

Pollack, M. Mental subnormality and childhood schizophrenia. In J. Zubin & G. A. Jerris (Eds.), *Psychopathology in mental development*. New York: Grune & Stratton, 1967.

Pollack, M., Woerner, M. G., & Klein, D. F. I.Q. differences between hospitalized schizophrenic and personality disorder patients and their normal subjects. *Proceedings of the 76th Annual Convention of the American Psychological Association*, 1968, *57*, 491–492.

Repp, A. C., & Deitz, S. M. Reducing aggressive and self-injurious behavior of institutionalized retarded children through reinforcement of other behaviors. *Journal of Applied Behavior Analysis*, 1974, *7*, 313–325.

Repp, A. C., Deitz, S. M., & Speir, N. C. Reducing stereotypic responding of retarded persons by the differential reinforcement of other behavior. *Journal of Mental Deficiency*, 1974, *79*, 279–284.

Ricks, D. M., & Wing, L. Language communication and the use of symbols in normal and autistic children. *Journal of Autism and Childhood Schizophrenia*, 1975, *5*, 191–220.

Rimland, B. *Infantile autism*. New York: Appleton Century Crofts, 1964.

Rincover, A. Sensory extinction: A procedure for eliminating self-stimulatory behavior in developmentally disabled children. *Journal of Abnormal Child Psychology*, 1978, *6*, 299–310.

Rincover, A., Newsom, C. D., Lovaas, O. I., & Koegel, R. L. Some motivational properties of sensory reinforcement with psychotic children. *Journal of Experimental Child Psychology*, 1977, *24*, 312–323.

Robinson, N. M., & Robinson, H. B. *The mentally retarded child* (2nd ed.). New York: McGraw-Hill, 1976.

Rollin, H. R. Personality in mongolism, with special reference to catatonic psychosis. *American Journal of Mental Deficiency*, 1946, *51*, 219–237.

Rollings, J. P., Baumeister, A. A., & Baumeister, A. A. The use of overcorrection procedures to eliminate the stereotyped behaviors of retarded individuals. *Behavior Modification*, 1977, *1*, 29–46.

Romanczyk, R. G., Colletti, G., Plienis, A., Meinhold, P., Bauer, T., & Cooper, E. *Contingent physical effort: Analysis of effectiveness with five aggressive and disruptive children.* Presented at Association for Behavior Analysis Eighth Annual Convention, Milwaukee, Wisc., May 1981.

Romanczyk, R. G., Colletti, G., Reynolds, R., Kitz, D., & Kraemer, D. *The treatment of self-injury: An analysis of subject characteristics, response topography, treatment type, and outcome.* Presented at Association for Behavior Analysis Eighth Annual Convention, Milwaukee, Wisc., May 1981.

Romanczyk, R. G., Kistner, J. A. & Crimmins, D. B. Institutional treatment of severely disturbed children: Fact, possibility, or non-sequitur? In B. Lahey & A. Kazdin (Eds.), *Advances in child clinical psychology.* New York: Plenum Press, 1980.

Romanczyk, R. G., Kistner, J. A., & Plienis, A. Self-stimulatory and self-injurious behavior: Etiology and treatment. In J. Steffen & P. Karoly (Eds.), *Advances in Child Behavior Analysis and Therapy.* Lexington, Mass., Lexington Books, 1982.

Romanczyk, R. G., Plienis, A. J., Flachs, L., & Spettell, J. *The treatment of severe, chronic, self-injurious behavior: Utilization of physiological indices in behavioral assessment and treatment.* Berkshire Conference, Amherst, Mass., October 1981.

Ross, A. O. *Child behavior therapy.* New York: Wiley, 1981.

Russo, D. C., Carr, E. G., & Lovaas, O. I. Self-injury in pediatric populations. In J. Ferguson and C. B. Taylor (Eds.), *Advances in behavioral medicine* (Vol. 3). Holliswood, N.Y.: Spectrum Publications, 1980.

Rutter, M. Diagnosis and definition. In M. Rutter & E. Schopler (Eds.), *Autism—A reappraisal of concepts and treatment.* New York: Plenum Press, 1978.

Rutter, M. L. Psychiatry. In J. Wortis (Ed.), *Mental retardation: An annual review* (Vol. 3). New York: Grune & Stratton, 1971.

Rutter, M. Psychological development—Predictions from infancy. *Journal of Child Psychology and Psychiatry*, 1970, *11*, 49–62.

Rutter, M., & Bartak, L. Special educational treatment of autistic children: A comparative study. II. Follow-up findings and implications for services. *Journal of Child Psychology and Psychiatry*, 1973, *14*, 241–270.

Rutter, M., Bartak, L., & Newman, S. Autism—A central disorder of cognition and language? In M. Rutter (Ed.), *Infantile autism: Concepts, characteristics and treatment.* London: Churchill-Livingstone, 1971.

Saenger, G. *Factors influencing the institutionalization of mentally retarded individuals in New York City.* Albany: Interdepartmental Health Resources Board, 1960.

Sarason, S. B., & Goldwyn, T. Psychological and cultural problems in mental subnormality: A review of research. *Genetic Psychology Monographs*, 1958, *57*, 3–289.

Schain, R. J., & Yannet, H. Infantile autism. *Journal of Pediatrics*, 1960, *57*, 560–567.

Schreibman, L., & Koegel, R. L. A guideline for planning behavior modification programs for autistic children. In S. M. Turner, K. S. Calhoun, & H. E. Adams (Eds.), *Handbook of clinical behavior therapy*. New York: Wiley, 1981.

Schroeder, S. R., Schroeder, C. S., Smith, B., & Dalldorf, J. Prevalence of self-injurious behaviors in a large state facility for the retarded: A three year follow-up study. *Journal of Autism and Childhood Schizophrenia*, 1978, *8*, 261–270.

Seigel, L., & Richards, C. S. Behavioral intervention with somatic disorders in children. In D. Marholin (Ed.), *Child behavior therapy*. New York: Gardner Press, 1978.

Solnick, J. V., Rincover, A., & Peterson, C. R. Some determinants of the reinforcing and punishing effects of timeout. *Journal of Applied Behavior Analysis*, 1977, *10*, 415–424.

Spitzer, R. L., Skodol, A. E., Gibbon, M., & Williams, J. B. *DSM-III Case Book*. Washington, D.C.: American Psychiatric Association, 1981.

Stotsky, B. H. A comparison of remitting and nonremitting schizophrenics on psychological tests. *Journal of Abnormal and Social Psychology*, 1952, *47*, 489–496.

Taft, L. T., & Cohen, H. J. Hypsarrhythmia and childhood autism. A clinical report. *Journal of Autism and Childhood Schizophrenia*, 1971, *1*, 327–336.

Touchette, P. E. Mental retardation: An introduction to the analysis and remediation of behavioral deficiency. In D. Marholin (Ed.), *Child behavior therapy*. New York: Gardner Press, 1978.

Tredgold, A. F. *A textbook of mental deficiency*. Baltimore: Williams & Wilkins, 1952.

Treffert, D. A. Epidemiology of infantile autism. *Archives of General Psychiatry*, 1970, *22*, 431–438.

Vukelich, R., & Hake, D. F. Reduction of dangerously aggressive behavior in a severely retarded resident through a combination of positive reinforcement. *Journal of Applied Behavior Analysis*, 1971, *4*, 215–225.

Wahler, R. G. Child behavior within the family: developmental speculations and behavior change strategies. In M. Leitenberg, (Ed.), *Handbook of behavior modification and behavior therapy*. Englewood Cliffs, N.J.: Prentice-Hall, 1976.

Webster, D. R., & Azrin, N. H. Required relaxation: A method of inhibiting agitative-disruptive behaviors of retardates. *Behavior Research and Therapy*, 1973, *11*, 67–68.

Webster, T. G. Unique aspects of emotional development in mentally retarded children. In F. J. Menolascino (Ed.), *Psychiatric approaches to mental retardation*. New York: Basic Books, 1970.

Weiner, J. B. *Principles of Psychotherapy*. New York: Wiley, 1975.

Wells, K. C., Forehand, R., & Hickey, K. Effects of a verbal warning and overcorrection on stereotyped and appropriate behaviors. *Journal of Abnormal Child Psychology*, 1977, *5*, 387–404.

Wells, K. C., Forehand, R., Hickey, K., and Green, K. D. Efforts of a procedure derived from the overcorrection principle on manipulated and non-manipulated behaviors. *Journal of Applied Behavior Analysis*, 1977, *10*, 679–688.

White, G. D., Nielsen, G., & Johnson, S. M. Timeout duration and the suppression of deviant behavior in children. *Journal of Applied Behavior Analysis*, 1972, *5*, 111–120.

Wing, L. Social, behavioral and cognitive characteristics: An epidemiological approach. In M. Rutter & E. Schopler (Eds.), *Autism*. New York: Plenum Press, 1978.

Wing, L., & Gould, J. Systematic recording of behaviors and skills of retarded and psychotic children. *Journal of Autism and Childhood Schizophrenia*, 1978, *8*, 79–97.

Wing, L., Yeates, S. R., Brierly, L. M., & Gould, J. The prevalence of early childhood autism: A comparison of administrative and epidemiological studies. *Psychological Medicine*, 1976, *6*, 89–100.

Wunsch, W. L. The first complete tabulation of the Rhode Island mental deficiency register. *American Journal of Mental Deficiency*, 1951, *55*, 293–312.

seven

Pharmacotherapy

●●

Stephen E. Breuning
Alan D. Poling

Drugs are commonly prescribed for the mentally retarded with an avowed therapeutic intent—typically the suppression of undesired behaviors and occasionally the facilitation of desired behaviors. The wisdom and success of this practice is essentially unknown, for pharmacotherapy with the mentally retarded has only rarely been appropriately evaluated. It is apparent that in some instances alleged pharmacotherapy involves little more than the use of excessive medication as a chemical straightjacket, a restrictive "treatment" usually devoid of any therapeutic benefit and incompatible with patient habilitation. Such practices have been justly criticized, and recent judicial pronouncements have specifically forbidden carte blanche drug administration. For example, Standard 22 of the "Minimal Constitutional Standards for the Adequate Habilitation of the Mentally Retarded," which arose from the *Wyatt* v. *Stickney* court case adjudicated in Alabama nine years ago, specifies that "*residents shall have the right to be free from unnecessary medication . . . medication shall not*

Preparation of this chapter was partially supported by Grant MH32206 from the National Institute of Mental Health and a Faculty Research Fellowship from Western Michigan University. This chapter is an expanded and updated version of an article appearing in *Clinical Psychology Review*, March 1982.

be used in quantities that interfere with a resident's habilitative program"
(1972a,b, p. 400) (italics added by author).

Although inappropriate drug regimens can be abolished de jure readily enough, providing de facto insurance that medications are used appropriately is quite another matter. In some instances, drugs prescribed for behavior control with the mentally retarded undoubtedly have a therapeutic effect; wholesale condemnation of all pharmacotherapy with the mentally retarded is as foolish as unquestioning acceptance. Appropriate evaluations of specific drug therapies demand empirical comparisons of the efficacy, and the side effects, of drug versus alternative treatments. At present, it cannot be demonstrated that the current prevalence of pharmacotherapy with the mentally retarded is warranted, but this is not to say that specific treatments never lead to improvement in individual patients. Successes certainly have been reported. However, even when conditions have appeared similar, the effectiveness of a given drug in improving a particular target behavior often has differed across studies. Further, most published reports have failed to meet basic criteria for scientific acceptability. It is not clear how, or even if, the results of such studies can be evaluated. Despite this, some replicable data are emerging concerning drug effects in the mentally retarded, and it is hoped that interest in the area will continue to grow. Our purpose in the present chapter is to provide an overview of pharmacotherapy with the mentally retarded.

• BACKGROUND •

The history of drug use with the mentally retarded has rarely been specifically addressed in a published work, perhaps because pharmacotherapy has become popular only within the past 25 years. Sedatives such as bromide and chloral hydrate however, appear to have been used occasionally to acutely manage agitation and aggression in the institutionalized mentally retarded since the turn of the century, while antiepileptics have been used in an attempt to control seizures and sometimes behaviors unrelated to seizures for over 50 years. There are few available data relating to the early use of behaviorally active drugs with the mentally retarded, and the scant information that is available refers primarily to the neuroleptic drugs.

Bair and Herold (1955) conducted one of the first drug studies with the mentally retarded. Ten individuals were administered chlorpromazine in an attempt to control a variety of behavior problems. The results were reported as indicating that 90 percent of the drug-treated subjects showed beneficial response. Subsequent studies by Rettig (1955), Esen and Durling (1956, 1957), MacColl (1956), Craft (1957a,b, 1958), Horenstein (1957), Johnston and Martin (1957), Segal and Tansley (1957), Sprogis, Lezdins,

White, Ming, Lanning, Drake, and Wyckoff (1957), Tarjan, Lowrey, and Wright (1957), Wolfson (1957), Adamson, Nellis, Runge, Cleland, and Killian (1958), Heaton-Ward and Jancar (1958), and Rudy, Himwich, and Rinaldi (1958) are representative of the 1950s. The results were generally favorable to pharmacotherapy, but methodological errors were abundant.

During the 1960s, the use of neuroleptic drugs with the mentally retarded proliferated and dozens of studies were published each year. Incidence data, discussed subsequently, indicated that by 1967 upwards of 55 percent of the mentally retarded individuals in institutions were receiving these drugs.

It is apparent that pharmacotherapy with the mentally retarded gained its impetus with the growing number of reports clearly indicating that neuroleptic drugs were effective, at least to some extent, in treating the symptomatology evinced by adults with psychiatric disorders. The number of patients housed in American public mental institutions, for example, has decreased progressively since 1956, when chlorpromazine was first generally adopted into psychiatry. The positive results reported for neuroleptics with the mentally ill seem to have been inappropriately generalized to the mentally retarded and provided the rationale for exposing mentally retarded patients to neuroleptics and other drugs as well. This rationale and practice was not seriously questioned for many years.

Nonetheless, general concern for the mentally retarded grew throughout the 1960s and 1970s (see Maloney & Ward, 1979; Poling & Breuning, 1982). Institutionalization, and the treatment of the institutionalized mentally retarded, was called into question, in both popular essays such as Blatt and Kaplan's *Christmas in Purgatory* (1966), and more empirical, if equally distressing, articles such as Klaber's (1969) report that severely retarded patients spend nearly half of their time doing nothing. Further, during and after President Kennedy's term in office, national policy concerning the mentally retarded shifted away from custodial care toward habilitation and the guarantee that the constitutional rights of the mentally retarded would be upheld. This change in policy, an increased allocation of funds, and the growing political strength of advocate groups such as the National Association for Retarded Citizens, fostered a dramatic upsurge of scientific interest in how the mentally retarded were being treated, as opposed to how they ought to be treated.

Freeman (1970) and Sprague and Werry (1971) were the first to seriously question the data base and rationale underlying pharmacotherapy with the mentally retarded. Sprague and Werry (1971) conducted an exhaustive review of the methodologies used in the drug studies of the 1950s and 1960s. It was concluded that, with few exceptions, these studies were methodologically inadequate to the point where the results were uninterpretable. Subsequent reviews have drawn the same conclusions

(Aman, in press; Aman & Singh, 1980; Ferguson & Breuning, 1982; Sprague & Baxley, 1978; Sulzbacher, 1973).

Also in the early 1970s, it became evident that certain treatments, such as behavior modification, were effective in improving the repertoire of the mentally retarded. These treatments did not rely on, and were in fact incompatible with, the medical model which portrayed mental retardation as an internalized condition (disease) appropriately treated through internal medicine (drugs). It was also growing obvious that the effectiveness of drugs with the mentally ill was not as clear-cut as it had once seemed. Methodological errors (discussed later) in most published studies made allegedly beneficial effects hard to evaluate, and the discovery of side effects once unknown (e.g., tardive dyskinesias with the neuroleptics) raised important questions concerning the costs versus benefits of pharmacotherapy. Beyond this, several authors specifically emphasized that drug effects in the mentally retarded were essentially unknown (e.g., Freeman, 1970; Lipman, 1970; Spraque & Werry, 1971), and others (e.g., Breuning, O'Neill, & Ferguson, 1980; McConahey, Thompson, & Zimmerman, 1977) reported that drugs did not enhance, and might actually diminish, the effectiveness of behavioral treatments. The offshoot of these developments was a general skepticism concerning pharmacotherapy with the mentally retarded that is continuing to grow. Scientists have begun to call for appropriate evaluations of pharmacotherapy, citizens groups have begun to demand accountability of those who treat the mentally retarded, and court decisions (discussed at the end of this chapter) have supported both positions.

In the following pages the six classes of drugs regularly prescribed to modify the behavior of mentally retarded clients are discussed: neuroleptics, anxiolytics, antidepressants, antimanics, stimulants, and antiepileptics. The conditions for which these drugs are prescribed, their prevalance of use, pharmacologic properties, side effects, and effectiveness are considered, along with availability of alternative behavioral treatments. Beyond this, the methodological issues involved in assessing drug effects and current litigation and legislation with the mentally retarded are summarized. Given the number and complexity of the topics to be addressed, much of this chapter will be an overview rather than a detailed exposition (further coverage of these topics is provided by Breuning & Poling, 1982, in *Drugs and Mental Retardation*).

• CLASSIFICATION OF DRUGS •

Many chemicals are prescribed in the hope of improving the behavior of mentally retarded clients. These drugs can be classified in several ways: according to their chemical structure, mechanism of action, behav-

Table 7-1
Classification of Drugs

Neuroleptic	Anxiolytic	Antidepressant	Antimanic	Stimulant	Antiepileptic
Phenothiazines	*Benzodiazepines*	*Tricyclics*	Lithium Carbonate	Amphetamine	*Barbiturates*
Chlorpromazine	Chlordiazepoxide	Amitriptyline		(Benzedrine)	Phenobarbital
(Thorazine)	(Librium)	(Elavil)		Dextroamphetamine	(Luminal)
Fluphenazine	Diazepam	Desipramine		(Dexedrine)	Primidone
(Prolixin)	(Valium)	(Norpramin)		Methylphenidate	(Mysoline)
Mesoridazine	Oxazepam (Serax)	Imipramine		(Ritalin)	*Benzodiazepines*
(Serentil)	*Diphenylmethane*	(Tofranil)		Magnesium	(see Anxio-
Thioridazine	*Derivatives*	Nortriptyline		Pemoline (Cylert)	lytics)
(Mellaril)	Diphenhydramine	(Aventyl)			*Carbamazepine*
Trifluoprazine	(Benaydral)	*MAO Inhibitors*			(Tegretol)
(Stelazine)	Hydroxyzine	Nialamide			*Hydantoins*
Butyrophenone	(Atarax,	(Niamid)			Ethotoin
Haloperidol	Vistaril)	Phenelzine			(Peganone)
(Haldol)	*Glycerol Derivatives*	(Nardil)			Mephenytoin
Thioxantenes	Meprobamate	Tranylcypromine			(Mesantoin)
Chlorprothixene	(Equanil,	(Parnate)			Phenytoin
(Taractan)	Miltown)				(Dilantin)
Thiothixene					*Succinimides*
(Navane)					Ethosuximide
					(Zarontin)
					Methsuximide
					(Celontin)
					Phensuximide
					(Milontin)
					Sodium Valproate
					Valproic Acid
					(Depakene)

ioral effects, or therapeutic usage. Problems are associated with each mode of classification. Drugs classified according to chemical structures may differ vastly in their behavioral and biochemical actions. Classification according to behavioral action is currently impossible, since data have been collected concerning the behavioral effects of relatively few drugs. Further, most drugs have multiple and complex behavioral actions that are dose-dependent. Classification according to mechanism of action encounters similar difficulties in that most drugs have multiple physiological (and biochemical) effects, which are unknown in many cases.

The most common classification of behaviorally active drugs is according to therapeutic usage with the nonretarded "mentally ill." Here, drugs are grouped together if they are prescribed to treat a given clinical state, for example, depression. The major problem with such a classification is the difficulties inevitably associated with clinical diagnosis; assignment to a diagnostic category typically does not reflect behavioral problems that are homogeneous across clients. Nonetheless, classification of drugs according to the therapeutic application is commonly accepted and of some practical utility. In this chapter, therefore, drugs will be considered according to this format.

Drugs are classified as neuroleptics, anxiolytics, antidepressants, antimanics, and stimulants. In addition to these groups, antiepileptic drugs will be discussed. Antiepileptic medications are regularly prescribed for the mentally retarded (primarily to regulate seizure disorders), are behaviorally active, and are occasionally given specifically for behavior control. For this reason they have been included here. A number of commonly used drugs are presented in Table 7-1 according to their usual therapeutic application.

• RATIONALE FOR PHARMACOTHERAPY •

• Neuroleptics •

The neuroleptics (also known as antipsychotics and major tranquilizers), which include phenothiazines, thioxanthenes, and butyrophenones, when effective "produce a specific improvement in the mood and behavior of psychotic patients without excessive sedation and without causing addiction" (Goth, 1974, p. 221). The first neuroleptic to be systematically evaluated was chlorpromazine (Thorazine), a phenothiazine initially tested for sedative effects. The drug was soon found to possess gangliolytic, adrenolytic, antifibrillatory, antipyretic, anticonvulsant, and antiemetic properties and to potentiate the actions of various analgesic and sedative compounds (Jarvik, 1965). In 1952, the French scientists Delay, Deniker, and Harl reported that chlorpromazine was of value in reducing a variety of psychotic symptoms, including agitation and confusion (Jarvik, 1965). Two years later, Lehmann and Hannahan (1954) published the first study documenting the pharmacotherapeutic use of chlorpromazine in the Western hemisphere, a reportedly successful attempt to manage psychomotor excitation and mania. Following these seminal studies, the use of chlorpromazine became remarkably widespread, and a search was initiated for compounds with similar actions.

One such substance, reserpine, an alkaloid synthesized from the Indian climbing shrub *Rauwolfia serpentina*, briefly competed with chlorpromazine as the neuroleptic of choice in the 1950s. In 1954, Kline found reserpine to be useful in treating psychotic patients, particularly those evincing marked anxiety, restlessness, and hypermobility (Kline, 1954). Subsequent investigations partially confirmed these findings but also disclosed that reserpine produces a range of dangerous side effects, of which severe depression is the most troublesome. The use of rauwolfia alkaloids in psychiatry is relatively rare today, although such drugs continue to be valuable as antihypertensives.

In addition to the phenothiazines, the butyrophenones and thioxanthines are currently used as neuroleptics. Haloperidol (Haldol), first synthesized in Belgium in 1956, is the most commonly prescribed butyrophenone; the drug has a relatively long history of use in Europe, but only recently has been adopted into American psychiatry. The thioxanthenes are very similar to the phenothiazines in chemical structure and pharmacologic activity. In recent years, the thioxanthines chlorprothixene (Taractan) and thiothixene (Navane) have enjoyed some popularity as neuroleptics. However, on the whole, the phenothiazines, butyrophenones, and thioxanthines produce remarkably similar effects (discussed subsequently), and there are no overwhelming data to support any one drug as the neuroleptic of choice.

The primary group of patients for whom neuroleptics are prescribed are nonretarded schizophrenics. Schizophrenia is by no means a precise diagnostic category; schizophrenics are characterized by altered motor behavior, perceptual disturbances (hallucinations), disturbed thinking, altered mood (often flat affect), and unusual interpersonal behavior (Berger, 1978). Specific behavioral correlates of these general disturbances are not easily operationalized, nor are they homogeneous across patients. There are, for example, no unique patterns of motor behavior characteristic of all alleged schizophrenics—some are totally immobile, others engage in frantic and seemingly purposeless stereotypes. At present, the diagnosis of schizophrenia is typically based on clinical impression, not specific empirical signs, and is problematic at best.

The prescription of neuroleptics, like the diagnosis of schizophrenia, involves as much art as science. For example, the *Physicians' Desk Reference* (1980, p. 1639) lists the following conditions as indications for the prescription of chlorpromazine (Thorazine):

> Effective: For the management of psychotic disorders. . . . For control of the manifestations of manic-depressive illness (manic phase). . . .
>
> Probably effective: For the control of moderate to severe agitation, hyperactivity or aggressiveness in disturbed children. . . .
>
> Possibly effective: For control of excessive anxiety, tension, and agitation as seen in neuroses.

At no point in the *Physicians' Desk Reference* are specific behavioral indications for chlorpromazine treatment discussed, nor is there any mention of the use of the drug with the mentally retarded. This latter oversight is of some interest, since it has been speculated for years that neuroleptics may be less useful in anergic, mentally retarded individuals than in excited, nonretarded patients (e.g., National Institute of Mental Health, 1964).

Apparently, prescription of neuroleptics for the mentally retarded rests on a superficial similarity between the behavior of the mentally retarded and that of the mentally ill (schizophrenic or otherwise psychotic). The mentally ill, for example, often engage in stereotypic self-stimulation, speak in largely nonsensical phrases, avoid contact with others, and fail to maintain accepted standards of self-care. Similar behaviors are sometimes seen in the mentally retarded, especially those in institutions. However, despite occasional similarities between the actions of the mentally ill and those of the mentally retarded, there typically are marked differences. In schizophrenic (and other psychotic) patients, the behavioral repertoire usually degenerates with the onset of the condition; no such degeneration is evident in most cases of mental retardation. Thus, the diagnosis of psychosis in this group is open to question. Further, perceptual disturbances (hallucinations) are commonly reported by the mentally ill, but not the mentally retarded.

Even when there is a topographical resemblance between the responses of the mentally ill and the mentally retarded, this does not necessarily imply a similar etiology or that the same treatment will be effective with both groups. A reasonable biochemical explanation of the beneficial actions of these drugs in the mentally ill has been advanced; the applicability of this model to the mentally retarded is unclear. This model is presented in the next section.

With the mentally retarded, the primary value of the neuroleptics seems to be their ability to produce a relatively nonselective sedation. A sedated person may be less likely to engage in undesired actions, but this hardly provides a compelling logical or empirical rationale for pharmaco-therapy. At present, there are only a few specific target behaviors in the mentally retarded that have been found to be selectively improved by any neuroleptic, and no known neuroleptic generally improves the deport-ment of the mentally retarded. The continued use of such drugs with this population seems to rest largely on positive findings with the mentally ill and a paucity of data concerning drug effects in the mentally retarded, coupled with a perhaps unfounded faith in the medical model and a prag-matic need to provide some form of treatment.

• Anxiolytics •

The anxiolytics (minor tranquilizers, antianxiety agents) are pre-scribed for nonretarded patients to treat a number of vaguely defined chronic conditions such as daytime anxiety, insomnia, night terrors, the tension associated with mild depression, and various neuroses. These drugs may also be used on a short-term basis to relieve stress associated with traumatic environmental events (e.g., divorce), and to decrease ad-verse reactions during withdrawal from alcohol and other central nervous system depressants. There are three primary groups of anxiolytics, classi-fied according to chemical structure. These are (1) the benzodiazepines, which include chlordiazepoxide (Librium), diazepam (Valium), and ox-azepam (Serex, Serepax); (2) the diphenylmethane derivatives, such as azacyclonol (Frenquel), diphenhydramine (Benadryl), and hydroxyzine (Atarax, Vistaril), and (3) the glycerol derivatives, of which meprobamate (Equanil, Miltown, Trelman) is the most common and important. Many drugs, such as alcohol and barbiturates, are not formally considered as anxiolytics even though they have similar behavioral effects and are occa-sionally prescribed for the same sorts of problems.

The barbiturates were the first drugs used as antianxiety agents. Ini-tially synthesized in 1903 (barbital), they fell out of favor by the 1950s, because of a marked propensity for inducing tolerance, physical and psy-chological dependence, and occasional lethal reactions. In the early 1950s, the glycerol derivative meprobamate was discovered to have mus-cle relaxant and sedative properties. However, it had many of the same undesirable side effects as the barbiturates. In 1956, Sternbach developed chlordiazepoxide, a drug as therapeutically effective as the barbiturates but with fewer side effects (Jarvik, 1965). The development of the numer-ous other benzodiazepine derivatives followed. Today, the benzodiaze-pines are the most commonly used drugs with chlordiazepoxide and diazepam accounting for about 70 percent of all drug prescriptions (Ray, 1978).

As noted earlier, the antianxiety agents are used to treat a wide variety of patient-reported distresses. Most of these are not grossly debilitating; a usual measure of the success of treatment with anxiolytic agents is the patient's evaluation alone. Overt behavioral measures are rarely employed, either in prescribing anxiolytics for nonretarded patients or in evaluating their effectiveness, which is apparently debatable (e.g., Garattini, Mussini, & Randall, 1973; Greenblatt & Shader, 1974).

For mentally retarded individuals the anxiolytics are less commonly prescribed than the neuroleptics. These drugs are, apparently, used most often to produce chronic sedation, although it is likely that anxiolytics occasionally are employed to reduce withdrawal symptoms in alcoholics and to reduce anxiety during acute stress and disease states. Presumably, these latter usages would be confined to less severely retarded clients who could ask for stress-relieving drugs or develop an alcohol-abuse problem. As will be seen in the subsequent review, there is no reason to believe that antianxiety agents are of general value for improving the behavioral repertoire of the mentally retarded, although some patient-reported problems (i.e., states of anxiety) might be temporarily alleviated.

• Antidepressants and Antimanics •

Like the anxiolytics, the antidepressants are used to treat a wide and ill-defined range of disorders in the nonretarded. In general, depression involves self-reports of sadness, guilt, and incompetency, coupled with observed and reported anhedonia. Weight loss and insomnia are common, as are disturbances in motor behavior, usually involving a general decrease in activity. Depressed people often report minor physical ailments, including constipation, dry mouths, headaches, and backaches; depressed women may stop menstruating. Severely depressed individuals often fail to maintain vocational and professional commitments; suicide becomes a real concern. Depression traditionally has been classified as exogenous (produced by obvious environmental changes, such as the death of a loved one) or endogenous (without obvious cause). Mild depression of the former, and probably also the latter, sort is common and usually does not require treatment. Severe and chronic depression is a very different matter and demands attention. There are no conclusive data on the prevalence of depression in the mentally retarded.

Pharmacologic management of depression involves two major drug classes, (1) the tricyclic antidepressants, which include imipramine (Tofranil), desipramine (Norpramin), amitriptyline (Elavil), and nortriptyline (Aventyl); and (2) the monoamine oxidase (MAO) inhibitors, the most used being nialamide (Niamid), phenelzine (Nardil), and tranylcypromine (Parnate). Both groups of drugs were introduced in 1957, but MAO inhibitors are used less frequently than tricyclics today because they are generally considered less effective and more toxic.

In nonretarded individuals, antidepressants are effective in managing most cases of depression, although the conditions under which antidepressants are beneficial remain open to question. Berger (1978) provides a careful review of antidepressant therapies. Antidepressants rarely are prescribed for the mentally retarded; when they are prescribed, the rationale is unclear. The mentally retarded presumably suffer from depression (see Gardener, 1967), even though severely handicapped individuals may be unable to manage the self-reports indicative of the condition, and might well benefit from antidepressants. However, in a recent review of antidepressant drug use with the mentally retarded, Gualtieri and Hawk (1982) noted that "the only unequivocal indication for the use of tricyclic antidepressants in the mentally retarded is unipolar depression. . . . They are effective for enuresis, but in most cases not necessary. Their use for the treatment of behavior disorders and/or hyperactivity cannot be recommended" (p. 231).

Most, perhaps 80 percent, of depressive illness is unipolar. However, bipolar manic-depressive disorders are not uncommon, and unipolar mania has occasionally been observed. During mania, patients are overly talkative, eat little, exhibit increased motor activity and brittle affect (rapid swings from elation to irritability), express seemingly divergent ideas as units in what is labeled "flight of ideas," and often engage in irresponsible social behavior. Hypomania may serve a person well in our society, but full blown manic episodes wreak havoc with jobs, friends, and family.

Lithium carbonate is the only known antimanic drug. In 1949, the Australian John Cade discovered that lithium salts are effective antimanic agents; this discovery has been heralded as the birth of modern psychopharmacology (Berger, 1978). Lithium was first used clinically in the United States in 1969, and several controlled studies attest to its effectiveness (Berger, 1978). However, acceptance of lithium as an antimanic is by no means unanimous. Gualteri and Hawk (1982), for example, provide the following caution:

Lithium may be considered as a treatment measure for retarded patients in the following categories, but only when other, more conventional treatment approaches have failed and the situation is sufficiently grave to warrant a drug trial.

1. Mentally retarded patients with nonspecific behavior disorders who have a strong family pedigree for bipolar affective disorder and/or lithium response.

2. Patients with severe behavior disorders that are characterized by cyclicity or a strong "affective flavor."

3. Patients with explosive aggressive behavior. (pp. 231–232)[1]

• Stimulants •

The primary use of stimulants is in the treatment of nonretarded, hyperactive children, with whom they have some reported value (see Walker, 1982). Hyperkinesis (also known as hyperactivity, minimal brain dysfunction, and attention deficit disorder) involves a short attention span, aggression typically directed toward peers, impulsivity, and restlessness (Waldrup, Bell, McLaughlin, & Halverson, 1978; Walker, 1982). The etiology of the disorder is unknown. Several hypotheses have been advanced, but none clearly confirmed (Robinson & Robinson, 1976). Hyperkinesis is now generally not regarded as a distinct clinical entity but rather as the upper end of a normally distributed behavioral dimension. Consequently, its assessment is problematic. Clinical evaluation and diffuse ratings by parents and teachers often enter into the diagnosis, although specific empirical criteria are occasionally employed. As Sulzbacher (1973, p. 44) contends:

> the most valid way to evaluate the treatment is to specify exactly what the child did to earn the diagnosis (e.g., left his seat often at school . . .) and then measure those . . . behaviors, under treatment versus no treatment conditions.

Unfortunately, such operational definitions of treated conditions are rare. At present, the stimulants are prescribed for a variety of behavioral problems, such as behavior that is disruptive in the opinion of parents and teachers, generally interfering in some manner with normal classroom or home activities. It should be noted that many of the behaviors exhibited by nonretarded children treated as hyperkinetic are commonly observed in mentally retarded children and adults. It is apparently on this basis that stimulants are used with the mentally retarded even though this use is infrequent. There is, by the way, no accepted biochemical explanation for the beneficial effects of stimulants in any population, although the mechanism of action of these drugs is rather well understood.

---

[1]Reprinted with permission from Gualtieri, C. T., & Hawk, B. Antidepressant and antimanic drugs. In S. E. Breuning & A. D. Poling (Eds.), *Drugs and mental retardation.* Springfield, Ill.: Thomas, 1982.

Specific stimulants used to treat hyperkinesis (and similar problems in the mentally retarded) include amphetamine (Benzedrine), dextroamphetamine (Dexedrine, *d*-amphetamine), methylphenidate hydrochloride (Ritalin), and magnesium pemoline (Cylert). Deanol (Deaner) is also sometimes prescribed as a stimulant and has been used to treat hyperkinesis. However, its clinical efficacy has not been documented, and its mechanism of action is thought to differ from that of the other stimulants. Thus, deanol will not be considered further.

• Antiepileptics •

Unlike the drug classes discussed previously, the antiepileptics are not typically used for behavior control per se but rather to manage a variety of convulsive disorders known collectively as epilepsy. In general, epilepsy involves brief episodes (seizures) in which consciousness is lost or disturbed and the electroencephalograph (EEG) discharge becomes abnormal and excessive. The body may move repetitively in a characteristic pattern (convulsions), and autonomic activity may increase markedly. There are more than a dozen distinguishable forms of epilepsy, based on seizure type and EEG pattern (Toman, 1965). Three of the most common forms of seizure are grand mal (generalized tonic-clonic), petit mal (generalized absence), and psychomotor (complex partial focal) epilepsy. Grand mal epilepsy usually involves tonic spasms of all skeletal muscles followed by clonic jerking and generally depressed central nervous system (CNS) activity. Consciousness is, of course, lost during the episode. Petit mal epilepsy involves brief losses of consciousness during which a characteristic high voltage, bilaterally syncronous, 3-per-second spike-and-wave pattern is evident in the EEG. Petit mal epilepsy may involve clonic jerks, complete relaxation of muscles, or no observable change in muscle tone. Psychomotor epilepsy consists of "attacks of confused behavior with a wide variety of clinical manifestations, associated with bizarre generalized EEG activity during the seizure but with evidence of anterior temporal focal abnormalities even in the interseizure period in many cases" (Toman, 1965, p. 215).

A wide variety of drugs have been and are used as antiepileptics. The first drug to be so used was bromide, whose anticonvulsant properties were accidentally discovered. In 1938, Merritt and Putnam uncovered the anticonvulsant actions of phenytoin (diphenylhydantoin, Dilantin) as part of a systematic investigation of organic chemicals' effects on electrically induced convulsions in rats. Phenytoin soon replaced bromide as the antiepileptic of choice, because the former drug produced less sedation and better seizure management. Since the discovery of phenytoin, many other antiepileptics have been synthesized and adopted in clinical practice.

Pharmacotherapy is the primary treatment of epilepsy. Fortunately, such treatment usually is effective (see Eadie & Tyrer, 1974; Gibbs, Gibbs, Gibbs, Gibbs, Dickman, & Hermann, 1982; Woodbury, Penry, & Schmidt, 1972). Seizure activity is relatively common among the mentally retarded, and in those instances in which epilepsy is clearly evident, antiepileptics may prove invaluable. However, antiepileptics are sometimes used in an attempt to manage nonepileptic behavior and, more frequently, are prescribed to prevent seizures in mentally retarded persons who have never been observed to have seizures or for whom the treatment is of no documented value. As discussed later, there is no logical or empirical reason for attempting to use antiepilepsy drugs in pharmacotherapy. Further, it is becoming clear that antiepileptics may produce undesirable side effects, so that their use should be limited to situations where pharmacological management of epilepsy is both necessary and effective. Our coverage of the antiepileptics will focus on their behavioral effects and use as behavior change agents. For a more complete coverage see Gibbs et al. (1982).

• PREVALENCE OF DRUG USE •

• Neuroleptics •

Surveys spanning the past 10 years have consistently shown that 40–50 percent of the institutionalized mentally retarded are receiving neuroleptic drugs. In the first survey, Lipman (1970) found that 51 percent of the institutionalized mentally retarded were receiving a neuroleptic drug. Chlorpromazine, thioridazine, and haloperidol accounted for over 60 percent of this drug use. Sprague (1977) reported similar prevalence figures as 51 percent of the individuals in his survey received thioridazine or chlorpromazine. Analogous prevalence figures have also been reported by DiMascio (1975), Pullman, Pook, and Singh (1979), Sewell and Werry (1976), and Tu and Smith (1979). Most recently, Craig and Behar (1980) have reported that psychotropic drug use may still be increasing as only 14.1 percent of the sample they surveyed was medication free. Common to all of these surveys is the finding that neuroleptic drugs are often used for extended periods of time and in doses exceeding those recommended by the drug's manufacturer. Comparable prevalence estimates and patterns of antipsychotic drug use have recently been reported with noninstitutionalized mentally retarded individuals. Davis, Cullari, and Breuning (1982) surveyed the prevalence and pattern of drug use with a random sample of 3500 mentally retarded individuals in community foster and group homes. It was found that 58 percent were receiving thioridazine, chlorpromazine, or haloperidol, or a combination of these drugs.

• Anxiolytics •

Anxiolytic drugs are not used nearly as frequently as the neuroleptic drugs with the mentally retarded. In his 1970 survey, Lipman reported that chlordiazepoxide and diazepam were used with about 8 percent of the institutionalized mentally retarded. Cohen and Sprague (1977) reported a slightly lower figure of 5 percent. Hughes (1977) found that as many as 23 percent of his sample received diazepam, primarily for seizure control. With noninstitutionalized mentally retarded individuals the use of these drugs appears to be even lower (Davis et al., 1982).

• Antidepressants and Antimanics •

In Lipman's survey, fewer than 4 percent of the mentally retarded individuals were treated with tricyclics, and no mention was made of lithium treatment (Lipman, 1970). Sprague (1977) reported similar findings. Rimland (1977) reported use of only one tricyclic (nortriptyline) in 71 (3.5%) of over 2000 autistic children, whereas neuroleptics had been used in almost half of the children. Use of MAO inhibitors or lithium were not reported. In a survey of 184 studies of psychoactive drug treatment of the mentally retarded by Lipman, DiMascio, Reatig, and Kirson (1978), only 12 (6.9%) were concerned with tricyclics, none with MAO inhibitors or lithium. Virtually no use of these drugs was found in the survey of noninstitutionalized individuals by Davis et al. (1982).

• Stimulants •

Stimulants have not been used frequently with the mentally retarded. Lipman (1970) reported that less than 3 percent of his sample were receiving drugs of this class. Cohen and Sprague (1977) found a similar prevalence with 2–3 percent of the sample receiving stimulant pharmacotherapy. In community foster and group homes, Davis et al. (1982) found that approximately 2.4 percent of the noninstitutionalized individuals were receiving a stimulant drug. It is interesting to note that stimulant use was almost totally determined (about 95%) by males aged 5–16 having *no* history of institutionalization.

• Antiepileptics •

The use of antiepilepsy drugs with the mentally retarded is second only to that of neuroleptics. This is because epilepsy is a predominant disorder with this population. For example, Corbett, Harris, and Robinson (1975) presented survey data suggesting that about 23 percent of the mildly to moderately retarded, 28 percent of the severely retarded, and 50 percent of the profoundly retarded are likely to experience epilepsy. Phenytoin and phenobarbital are the most frequently used of the antiepilepsy drugs with both institutionalized and noninstitutionalized mentally retarded persons. Sprague (1977) reported that 39.7 percent of 1100 residents of a large state institution were receiving phenytoin and 38.4 percent were receiving phenobarbital. In a smaller institution he found phenytoin use to be 32.6 percent and phenobarbital use to be 28.3 percent. DiMascio (1975) found extremely large prevalence figures of 68 percent for phenytoin and 85 percent for phenobarbital. These figures appear to be extremes. Davis et al. (1982) reported that 34.7 percent of 3496 subjects were receiving phenytoin, 19.4 percent phenobarbital, and 6.9 percent diazepam. A combination of phenytoin and phenobarbital accounted for 53.9 percent of antiepilepsy drug use. The use of other antiepilepsy drugs in the Davis et al. survey included primidone (1.3%), carbomazepine (1.1%), and ethosuximide (0.9%).

• PHARMACOLOGY OF PHARMACOTHERAPEUTIC • AGENTS

• Monoamines and Mental Illness •

Drugs used in pharmacotherapy have many diverse actions. However, the neuroleptics, antidepressants, and antimanics are known to affect brain monoamines (dopamine, norepinephrine, and serotonin), and a tenable model of the therapeutic actions of these drugs in the mentally ill, but not necessarily the mentally retarded, has been developed based on their neurochemical actions. It is beyond our purposes to review this model in detail, or the data supporting it or bringing it into question. Many comprehensive reviews of these topics have appeared (e.g., Berger, 1978; Bernard, 1975; Barchas, Berger, Ciaranello, & Elliott, 1977; Schildkraut, 1970). However, the model asserts in essence that activity in dopaminergic neuronal systems, particularly the mesolimbic–mesocortical pathway, is deficient in schizophrenics. Neuroleptics are known to occupy dopamine receptors without activating them (Berger, 1978) and are assumed to exert their beneficial clinical effects, as well as certain undesired side effects, through this mechanism. The beneficial effects seem to involve receptor blockade (and consequent decreases in activity) in the mesolimbic–mesocortical system; nigrostriatal blockade results in extrapyramidal side effects, whereas endocrine changes are produced by receptor blockade in the tuberoinfundibular pathway.

Depression, unlike schizophrenia, is assumed to be due to a functional underactivity in pathways involving serotonin or norepinephrine, or both, as neurotransmitters, and mania reflects a surfeit of activity in these same pathways. By interfering with an enzyme, MAO, which metabolically inactivates these neurotransmitters, the MAO inhibitors increase functional activity in noradrenergic and serotonergic pathways. Tricyclic antidepressants produce a similar effect by preventing the reuptake of norepinephrine and serotonin into the presynaptic neurons from which they were released. This is a second important mechanism for limiting the actions of the monoamines.

If it is assumed that mania results from excessive activity in noradrenergic or serotonergic neurons, an antimanic should decrease such activity. Some data suggest that lithium does so, insofar as the drug decreases the electrically stimulated release of norepinephrine and seems to enhance its reuptake into the presynaptic neuron. However, it must be emphasized that biochemical explanations of the actions of antidepressants, neuroleptics, and antimanics are by no means universally accepted, nor is it by any means clear that the problem behaviors of the mentally retarded receiving these drugs result from neurotransmitter imbalances of any sort. Berger (1978) makes an appropriate cautionary statement concerning biochemical models of pharmacotherapeutics:

> Neither the biochemical basis of depression nor the mechanisms of action of antidepressants are known with certainty. . . . Recent hypotheses . . . suggest an altered balance between the functional activities of . . . neurotransmitters . . . and . . . that depression and the action of tricyclics are the result of alterations in neurotransmitter receptors rather than in the receptors themselves. (p. 980)

The clinical actions of the anxiolytics have not been related to changes in monoaminergic activity. At present, the site and mode of action of such drugs is unknown, although some research has indicated that the benzodiazepines increase the effectiveness of the (inhibitory) neurotransmitter gamma-aminobutyric acid (GABA).

The amphetamines, prototypic stimulants, appear to facilitate release and block reuptake of both dopamine and norepinephrine, whereas the stimulant methylphenidate appears to be a potent dopamine agonist. The ability of amphetamines to facilitate activity in noradrenergic pathways suggests that the drugs should possess antidepressant activity. However, such effects if observed are weak and short lived. It should be noted that the neurochemical actions of the stimulants are complex and may involve serotonergic and cholinergic as well as dopaminergic and noradrenergic fibers. At present, the relation of the biochemical actions of these drugs to the beneficial changes they can produce in hyperkinetic children are unclear, although several hypotheses have been advanced. Walker (1982) discusses these hypotheses and the neuropharmacological actions of stimulants in detail.

Much work has been done concerning the biochemical actions of antiepileptics (e.g., Woodbury et al., 1972), but uncertainty persists concerning the mechanism of action of these drugs. Some data do suggest that diphenylhydantoin, the most popular antiepileptic, and similar compounds facilitate the active extrusion of sodium from brain cells, and this action has been suggested as accounting for their therapeutic effects. No biochemical rationale exists for using antiepileptics to deal with behavioral problems.

Beyond their effects on putative neurotransmission in the central nervous system, pharmacotherapeutic agents have a variety of other actions, described in the following sections.

• THERAPEUTIC USE AND SIDE EFFECTS •

• Neuroleptics •

Neuroleptics are usually given orally, in a single daily dose. When administered in this fashion, plasma levels usually peak in 1–4 hours. These drugs are lipid soluble and bind with plasma proteins, thus they are broadly distributed throughout the body. The half-life of common neuroleptics is about 24 hours. Their metabolism is poorly understood but seems to involve the oxidative enzyme system of the liver. Certain metabolites are biologically active. Excretion is through the urine and feces, with some drug being eliminated unchanged following discontinuation. It is generally accepted that at least four weeks must pass before most of the drug has been eliminated from the system. This length of time varies with dose.

The neuroleptics differ widely in potency and consequently in doses administered. Trifluoperazine (Stelazine) is, for example, approximately 20 times as potent as chlorpromazine (Thorazine). Regardless of the drug chosen, a low to moderate dose should be prescribed initially, the behavior of interest measured for three to four weeks, and then dose adjustments made as necessary. In some patients, maintenance doses appreciably less than those initially required to manage behavior may be effective.

In general, there are few data to recommend one neuroleptic over another, since their effects are remarkably similar. Dose ranges of the three most used neuroleptics are thioridazine, 50–800 mg/day; chlorpromazine, 30–1000 mg/day; and haloperidol, 1–16 mg/day (some report a haloperidol range of 1–100 mg/day). Many people recommend that more standardized methods of dose determinations be adopted with the mentally retarded (e.g., Aman, in press; Ferguson & Breuning, 1982). At present, milligrams per kilograms body weight determinations are most relevant with the neuroleptics. Ferguson and Breuning (1982), for example, state that "a 400 mg/day dose with a 195 pound man results in a mg/kg dose of 4.5 mg/kg while the same dose with a 106 pound boy is 8.3 mg/kg" (p. 175). As can be seen in Figure 7-2, which appears later, neuroleptics can be shown to have varying effects when assessed on an milligram per kilogram basis. Blood level determinations, the amount of drug measured in the plasma, is an effective method of standardization with some drugs (notably antiepileptics) but is not refined to the point of routine use with neuroleptics. A comprehensive discussion of doses and dose ranges of neuroleptic drugs is provided by Ferguson and Breuning (1982).

Among the common short-term side effects of neuroleptics are mild drowsiness accompanied by apathy and lethargy; autonomic effects such as dry mouth, blurring of vision, and constipation; abdominal pain; orthostatic hypotension; agranulocytosis; tachycardia; jaundice; photosensitivity; and skin rashes. These effects do not occur with all or even most patients; their likelihood increases with dose. Tolerance develops to some of the short-term side effects of neuroleptics, drowsiness in particular.

The most important short-term side effects of the neuroleptics involve the extrapyramidal motor system and include akathisia (constant motor activity), dystonic reactions (spasms of the head, neck, and back muscles), and parkinsonian reactions (body rigidity, masklike facial expression, shuffling gait). These reactions often can be lessened by anticholinergic drugs used to treat Parkinson's disease (e.g., trihexyphenidyl [Artane]) but cannot be dismissed on this basis. Dose reductions or drug changes are often effective in reducing these effects. Dystonic reactions are reportedly more likely to appear when the low dose/high potency neuroleptics (e.g., haloperidol) are prescribed.

Withdrawal dyskinesias, involuntary movements of body parts (usually consisting of dartings and tremors of the tongue, smacking and sucking motions of the lips, and purposeless movements of the hands) following termination of drug treatment, occur in as many as 55–60 percent of mentally retarded individuals receiving neuroleptic drug discontinuation and may last up to 16 weeks (see, e.g., Breuning, 1981; Gualtieri, Breuning, Schroeder, & Quade, 1982). These dyskinesias can be extremely troublesome and are usually not improved by antiparkinsonian drugs. Baldessarini (1980) and Ferguson and Breuning (1982) review these and other side effects of neuroleptics in detail.

Long-term side effects include weight gain, corneal edema, and persistent tardive dyskinesias. Weight gain is common, especially with thioridazine (Mellaril) use. For example, McAndrew, Case, and Treffert (1972) found that 29 of 30 patients gained a median of 10.5 pounds across three months of thioridazine treatment. Coroneal edema is rarely seen and can usually be controlled by dose reduction.

Persistent, or tardive, dyskinesias are topographically identical to withdrawal dyskinesias. Persistent dyskinesias may appear when the individual is on a maintenance drug dose or when the drug is terminated. Recent data suggest the prevalence of tardive dyskinesias with the mentally retarded to be about 17 percent following gradual drug reduction and 23 percent following abrupt termination (Breuning, 1981; Ferguson & Breuning, 1982; Gualtieri et al., 1982). Persistent dyskinesias may be irreversible; no effective treatment is presently available (Baldessarini & Tarsy, 1978; Ferguson & Breuning, 1982). Thus, this disorder is in all likelihood a major danger associated with neuroleptic drug treatment.

As the foregoing indicates, neuroleptics have a wide range of actions. They also interact with other drugs, enhancing the effectiveness of CNS depressants (e.g., barbiturates, anxiolytics, ethanol), and elevating the plasma levels of antiepileptics such as phenytoin (Dilantin). When combined with MAO inhibitors, hypertensive crisis may result. Finally, an additional serious long-term side effect has been identified. It is termed "supersensitivity psychosis" or "acute behavior deterioration" (see Gualtieri & Guimond, 1981). Simply put, following neuroleptic drug discontinuation the individual emits inappropriate behaviors qualitatively different from the initial presenting problem. For example, a client is placed on a drug for hyperactive behavior and develops apparent drug-induced aggressive behavior following drug withdrawal. This is a potentially frightening possibility and research is just beginning to explore this area.

• Anxiolytics •

Like the neuroleptics, the anxiolytics differ primarily in potency. These drugs are orally effective, have rapid onsets of action (peak plasma levels are reached within 15 minutes to one hour), and short half-lives (two to six hours), thus they are commonly administered in three or four daily doses. Initial doses should be low and gradually titrated as required. Three of the more frequently used anxiolytics, chlordiazepoxide, diazepam, and hydroxyzine, have dose ranges of 10–200 mg/day, 2–40 mg/day, and 50–400 mg/day, respectively. Ferguson and Breuning (1982) discuss dose ranges of these drugs. Once behavior is controlled, it is often possible for dose reductions to be made. In part, this reflects the fact that the half-lives of anxiolytics often lengthen with repeated administration. Anxiolytics are lipid soluble and bind with plasma proteins, and they are found in all areas of the body where blood flow is good. These drugs are metabolized by means of the hepatic microsomal system; excretion is primarily in urine. Many metabolites of the benzodiazepines are biologically active.

The actions of the anxiolytics are many. They produce relaxation of the skeletal muscles and generally decrease CNS activity. This latter action is evident in EEG slowing and decreased responsiveness to external stimuli (Baldessarini, 1980). Autonomic effects of blurred vision, urinary incontinence, tachycardia, constipation, and hypotension are sometimes seen. Ataxia and syncopes have occasionally been reported. The latter probably is due to hypotension and the decreased cardiovascular function associated with certain anxiolytics (Baldessarini, 1980).

The most frequent short-term side effects of anxiolytic agents involve the sedative actions of the drugs. Beyond these effects, aggressiveness and irritability have been associated with the benzodiazepines, even at low doses. Increased activity, psychoticlike behavior, and suicidal actions have been reported with higher doses. Other short-term effects include failure to ovulate, headaches, nausea, skin rashes, and impaired sexual performance. Dose reductions, changes in the drug used, or termination of medication usually is effective in dealing with these problems.

The anxiolytics induce physical dependence with chronic use. Withdrawal symptoms involve CNS activation and are similar to those associated with chronic exposure to ethyl alcohol. Gradual termination of medication can, however, reduce the severity of these symptoms. The anxiolytics are reinforcing and have been associated with drug abuse problems in nonretarded patients.

Long-term side effects of anxiolytics are physical and psychological dependence and continuation of the short-term effects discussed previously. There are few significant interactions between anxiolytics and other therapeutic drugs. They interact additively with CNS depressants, and heavy cigarette smoking may reduce their effectiveness at usual therapeutic doses.

• Antidepressants and Antimanics •

Tricyclic antidepressants usually are administered orally. They bind to plasma proteins and are broadly distributed. At therapeutic doses, peak plasma levels occur within 4–9 hours. The half-life of most tricyclics is

10–18 hours; biotransformation is accomplished through the hepatic oxidative drug metabolizing system. Excretion is primarily through the urine.

The tricyclics may produce a prolonged decrease in rapid eye movement (REM) sleep; lowered blood pressure; decreased motor activity; autonomic effects of blurred vision, dry mouth, and urinary incontinence; and central nervous system effects that include insomnia, euphoria, and occasionally seizure induction. Agranulocytosis sometimes occurs in adults. Cardiotoxicity, which has resulted in sudden death, is a real but infrequent problem. Dose reductions or changes in the drug administered may alleviate these effects. Doxepin, for instance, apparently possesses less cardiotoxicity than the other tricyclics. No unique long-term side effects have been associated with these drugs. Short-term side effects may persist, and, given the chemical similarity between tricyclics and phenothiazines, dyskinesias would not appear unlikely, but have not been reported.

Treatment of depressed patients with tricyclics usually begins with low doses that are gradually increased across time. Blood level determinations are usually made, although their clinical value is debatable (Gualtieri & Hawk, 1982). Two to three weeks of drug treatment typically is required for improvement to be manifested in depressed patients. Long-term antidepressant therapy is not usually required to manage depression; drugs often can be successfully withdrawn soon after symptoms clear. Tricyclics usually range in dose from 50 to 300 mg/day.

The MAO inhibitors are rarely used in North America today because of their potential toxicity, especially when combined with other drugs or tyramine-containing foods. Currently, these drugs are used only in severe and intractable cases of depression, preferably only in inpatient facilities where careful monitoring is possible. The pharmacology of MAO inhibitors is poorly understood. These drugs are orally effective and are rapidly excreted in the urine. However, they produce irreversible inactivation of MAO, thus the effects of the drugs are terminated only after a period of several weeks in which new supplies of the enzyme are produced.

The MAO inhibitors inhibit REM sleep. They also produce CNS activation, acute hypotension, and changes in the permeability of erythrocyte membranes in children. Common short-term side effects are irritability, agitation, convulsions, and both hypo- and hypertension. Convulsions, hypertension, hypomania, and hallucinations are common long-term effects.

The MAO inhibitors interfere with the metabolic degradation of many therapeutic drugs (e.g., barbiturates) and increase the effects of many centrally active compounds (e.g., alcohol, tricyclics, amphetamines). The consumption of foods rich in tyramine, such as aged wines and cheeses, may precipitate an acute hypertensive crisis in patients receiving MAO inhibitors. This and other potential side effects demand that MAO inhibitors be used only under strict supervision, when tricyclic antidepressants have proven ineffective.

As Gualtieri and Hawk (1982) note, "starting doses of the MAO inhibitors is idiosyncratic as is the length of time required for a therapeutic effect to become noticeable" (p. 220). Combinations of MAO inhibitors and tricyclic antidepressants are dangerous and should be used only as a last resort. MAO inhibitors have less of a dose range than the tricyclics, 10–75 mg/day depending on the drug.

Lithium carbonate, the only known antimanic, is orally effective. Peak blood levels occur within 2 to 4 hours. The drug's half-life is 24 hours; as an ion, lithium is not metabolized, but rather excreted unchanged in the urine. Lithium does not bind to blood proteins, and enters the CNS with difficulty (brain levels of lithium are usually about 40 percent of plasma levels). Lithium at therapeutic levels is associated with cardiovascular effects including pulse irregularities and hypotension; gastrointeric effects of constipation, diarrhea, nausea, and vomiting; neuromuscular tremors, ataxia, and dyskinesias; endocrine effects that include goiter, hypothyroidism, polydipsia, polyuria, and diabetes insipidus; and leukocytosis (a blood disorder). Other short-term side effects are anoxia, muscular weakness, and drowsiness. At acutely toxic levels, confusion, vomiting, hyperreflexivity, diarrhea, ataxia, coma, and convulsions are observed. These and other side effects dissipate as the dose is decreased. Common long-term side effects are diabetes insipidus, goiter, and hypothyroidism. These disorders typically disappear when treatment is terminated.

Lithium is unique in that blood levels correlate highly with therapeutic effects. Treatment is begun at a low dose (e.g., 300 mg/day) and, after three or four days, a blood sample is taken. Dosage is then changed (usually upward) until a therapeutic level (0.7–1.5 mEq/liter) is reached. In adults, this may require a dose of 900–1500 mg/day. During early states of treatment, blood levels continue to be taken at three-to-four-day intervals; during maintenance, monthly checks may be sufficient. Care must be taken throughout treatment to recognize and deal with developing side effects. Gualtieri and Hawk (1982) discuss antimanics and antidepressants in further detail.

• Stimulants •

The stimulants are orally effective, are rapidly absorbed, and readily enter the CNS. Half-lives differ for methylphenidate (3–4 hours), *d*-amphetamine (about 18 hours in adults, and 5 hours in children), and pemoline (10 hours). Methylphenidate is largely metabolized in the liver; inactive metabolites pass from the body in the urine. Amphetamines and pemoline are partially metabolized, but perhaps 50 percent of these drugs are excreted unchanged in the urine.

Stimulants produce CNS effects of increased heart rate and respiration, increased alertness, and anorexia; small increases in systolic and diastolic blood pressure; increased acid and pepsin secretion; and increased metabolic rate and secretion of growth-stimulating hormone. The most common short-term side effects of stimulant therapy are weight loss, insomnia, abdominal pain, tachycardia, and cardiac arrhythmias. These effects usually subside with dose reduction. Other, uncommon side effects include dizziness, inappropriate increases in verbal behavior, psychosis, and behavioral stereotypy. Impaired growth in children is often posited as a major long-term side effect of stimulants. At present, there is little reason to believe that one stimulant produces fewer or milder side effects than the others.

Stimulants inhibit the metabolism of anticoagulants, anticonvulsants, and tricyclic antidepressants. Stimulants in combination with MAO inhibitors may induce an adrenergic (hypertensive) crisis.

The stimulants differ appreciably in potency, and therefore in dose used at the onset of treatment. Because of their short half-lives, however, all of the stimulants are usually administered in two or three daily doses. Two 5-mg doses of methylphenidate would be a typical initial regimen in children; this would be increased in weekly 5-mg increments until behavior was controlled or a maximum dosage of 40 mg/day was reached. Similar practices would be followed with other stimulants. To avoid gastroenteric distress, these drugs are usually given prior to meals. They are also preferably not administered after 6 P.M. to prevent the possibility of insomnia. With all stimulants, drug use should be discontinued after one month if an effective dose is not found. When medication is effective, drug holidays of one to two weeks should be arranged every two or three months to determine if continued drug use is warranted.

• Antiepileptics •

Many detailed reviews of the pharmacology of the antiepileptics have appeared (e.g., Eadie & Tyrer, 1974; Woodbury et al., 1972). The following is a summary of the pharmacology of phenytoin (Dilantin), the most commonly prescribed antiepileptic. In general, other antiepileptics are qualitatively similar to this prototypic compound.

Phenytoin is orally effective. In humans, its half-life is about 22 hours. The drug is biotransformed in the liver; metabolites are excreted in the urine. Many short- and long-term side effects have been attributed to diphenylhydantoin at therapeutic levels. Among them are hyperglycemia; central nervous system reactions such as nystagmus, ataxia, and confusion; gastroenteric effects such as nausea and constipation; a range of dermatological disorders; hemopoietic complications (e.g, agranulocytosis, leukopenia); and gingival hyperplasia. These effects may be imperfectly managed by dose reductions and supportive therapy. At toxic doses, ataxia, coma, and hypotension ensue; death may result from respiratory depression and apnea.

Appropriate techniques for prescribing antiepileptics to control seizures are based on drug-plasma concentrations and are discussed elsewhere (e.g., Gibbs et al., 1982); however, the suggested optimum therapeutic ranges for phenytoin and phenobarbital are 10–20 μg/ml and 15–40 μg/ml, respectively. There are no published protocols for the use of such medications to control nonseizure behaviors.

METHODOLOGICAL ISSUES IN ASSESSING DRUG EFFECTS

Many studies have attempted to evaluate drug effects in the mentally ill; far fewer have examined drug effects in the mentally retarded. With both subject populations, methodological problems have characterized the vast majority of studies. For example, Klein and Davis (1969) found only 11 of over 12,000 published evaluations of chlorpromazine to be methodologically sound. Marholin and Phillips (1976) subsequently found even these 11 to involve serious methodological flaws, especially with respect to the definition and evaluation of therapeutic change. In a similar vein, Sulzbacher (1973) found that 72.5 percent of published pharmacological studies with children were uncontrolled in that they lacked either double blind conditions or a placebo control. Other reviews have also found methodological errors to be ubiquitous (Aman & Singh, 1980; Freeman, 1970; Lipman, 1970; Lipman et al., 1978; Sprague & Werry, 1971; Wysocki & Fuqua, 1982).

Beyond rendering findings uninterpretable in a scientific sense, methodological errors seem to increase the likelihood that a drug will reportedly produce beneficial effects in a given study (Sulzbacher, 1973). In a real sense, poor research is worse than no research at all. Uncontrolled investigations may indicate a particular drug to be effective (or ineffective), and subsequent clinical judgments may rest on this report, even though the findings are actually artifactual. The purpose of the present section is to outline some methodological issues in evaluating drug effects in the mentally retarded and to suggest strategies for dealing with common problems. These topics are addressed at length in the reviews listed previously, but their importance cannot be overstated. Today, despite literally thousands of published studies, we can safely say little concerning the efficacy of pharmacotherapeutic drugs, especially with the mentally retarded. This distressing state of affairs will change if, and only if, future investigators attend closely to the dictates of scientific investigation.

• Target Behaviors •

The sole objective of drug evaluation is to determine whether the independent variable, drug administration, significantly improves some targeted aspect of the client's behavior, the dependent variable. Deficits in the target behavior (with respect to rate, latency, magnitude, or stimulus control) constitute the problems that drugs are prescribed to treat; improvements in behavior that can be unambiguously ascribed to the drug are the only meaningful demonstration of clinical efficacy. Thus, it is crucial that target behaviors be measured in ways that are clearly defined, empirical, accurate, quantifiable, public, repeatable over time, and valid indexes of the condition ostensibly being treated. Beyond this, target behaviors must be sensitive—able to improve or worsen as a function of treatment.

Evaluations of psychotherapeutic drugs have assessed target behaviors in several ways. Global clinical impression is perhaps the most common. It is also generally unsatisfactory, for it is never apparent what aspects of a patient's repertoire a clinician is evaluating (or even if she or he is responding to the patient's actions), or if the clinician's assessment is accurate and unbiased. Further, the replicability of clinical impression across time or clinicians is rarely high. Because of these factors, it has been recommended (e.g., Wysocki & Fuqua, 1982) that global clinical impressions as an index of drug effects can no longer be justified. At minimum, whenever human observers are used to quantify a drug effect, it must be clearly demonstrated that independent observers can agree in their evaluations (Marholin & Phillips, 1976). However, measure of interobserver agreement is infrequently calculated in psychopharmacological research (e.g., Poling, Cleary, & Monaghan, 1980).

Self-reports to date are particularly troublesome indexes of change, because they rarely involve public events and are quite sensitive to non-drug factors. Previously the authors stated that although patient reports of discomfort may be the sine qua non for initiating or terminating pharmacotherapy, especially when anxiolytics are considered, self-reports are from a methodological perspective relatively weak data and should be considered as secondary to other, more objective measures. At present this statement is tempered slightly. Recent research has shown the use of self-report information with mildly retarded individuals may be of value as an adjunct in assessing neuroleptic-induced behavior impairments as well as the magnitude of drug-induced dyskinesias and supersensitivity psychosis (Breuning, 1982a).

Standardized tests, such as personality inventories and intelligence tests, are objective and repeatable. Such tests, however, are indirect measurements of the conditions of interest, and under standard testing conditions are usually of limited sensitivity (e.g., Breuning & Davidson, 1981). Further, their relationship to the condition drugs are intended to better is rarely apparent. For these reasons, the use of most standardized tests to assess drug effects in the mentally retarded cannot be recommended unless procedural modifications, as identified by Breuning and Davidson (1981), are incorporated.

Direct measurement of specific responses is the best means of assessing drug effects. In some instances, automated equipment may be used to index the target behavior. For example, a child may be given methylphenidate to increase the time he or she spends seated in the classroom. Time spent in seat could be monitored easily and accurately by affixing a microswitch to the seat and operating a timer when the microswitch was depressed. Although such applications are feasible, to date automated equipment has rarely been used to assess behaviors of direct clinical relevance but has proven most valuable in laboratory studies where analogs of clinically significant responses are investigated.

Although studies in this area are relatively rare, Davis, Poling, Wysocki, and Breuning (1981), Hollis and St. Omer (1972), Sprague, Barnes, and Werry (1970), Wysocki, Fuqua, Davis, and Breuning (1981), Walker (1982), and others have shown that laboratory studies may provide sensitive and seemingly valid measures of drug effects in the mentally retarded. Among the laboratory assays that have proven useful are performance under operant schedules of reinforcement, delayed and nondelayed matching to sample, and repeated acquisitions of response sequences. These procedures enable the experimenter to produce stable and enduring baseline patterns of learning and performance against which drug effects may be evaluated. It is unfortunately beyond the scope of this chapter to discuss these procedures in detail; their usefulness in drug evaluation is considered at length in several chapters of a recent text (Breuning & Poling, 1982).

Direct and repeated measurements of behavior, which do not include post hoc evaluations by means of behavior rating scales, are probably the best way to evaluate drug effects. Here, some specific target behavior is repeatedly measured across time in the presence and absence of drug. Some aspect of the target behavior is the problem pharmacotherapy attempts to alleviate, not a measure of some posited underlying state. Direct measurement of target behaviors typically requires the use of human observers. This is expensive and requires due caution, as Poling et al. (1980, p. 243) have emphasized:

> As transducers, humans are invariably suspect. Folklore suggests that lay observations are an imperfect reflection of actual happenings, and a large and growing body of data indicates that allegedly scientific observations sometimes provide an inaccurate index of the variables being considered. Among the factors demonstrated to influence reported observations are the observer's motivation and expectations, the specifics of the observational situation, the observational and data recording techniques that are being used, and the characteristics of the behavior being monitored.
>
> In view of these considerations, researchers in applied behavior analysis have gone to great lengths to ensure the believability of their observations. Beyond defining in detail the behavior(s) under consideration and carefully describing the observational procedures, these investigators nearly always provide some measure of interobserver agreement, which specifies the correspondence obtained between the data recorded by each of two (or more) independent observers. Where feasible, "blind" observers—individuals not aware of the experimental conditions in effect—are employed, and video tapes of the subject's behavior are made and subsequently used to check the accuracy of reported data.[2]

It is beyond our purposes to further discuss observational techniques; several texts in the area of behavioral assessment provide detailed coverage (e.g., Bailey, 1977; Cone & Hawkins, 1977; Haynes, 1978). However, the quantification of dependent variables in drug research is by no means a trivial issue. Sulzbacher (1973) found that the type of response measurement was related to a high degree to the probability of a beneficial drug effect being reported in studies with children. In his study, the probability of a beneficial effect across measures was as follows: global clinical impression (.88), rating scales (.57), direct measurement of behavior (.41), and psychological test (.17). Given this confounding of response measurement and reported outcome, clear interpretation of drug efficacy is simply impossible.

• Assessment Designs •

All experimental evaluations of pharmacotherapies involve a comparison of performance under conditions that are assumed to differ only in whether or not the drug is administered. This comparison can be made either within or between subjects and according to various logical configurations or research designs.

---

[2]Reprinted with permission from Poling, A., Cleary, J., & Monaghan, M. The use of human observers in psychopharmacological research. *Pharmacology, Biology and Behavior*, 1980, *13*, 243–246.

In between-subjects (group) comparisons, considered at length in many texts (e.g., Keppel, 1972; Kirk, 1968), groups of subjects considered to be equal in pertinent characteristics are used. At a given point in time, one group receives the drug and the other does not. Their performance is then compared, usually by means of inferential statistics. If a statistically significant difference is obtained, it is attributed to the drug. It must, however, be emphasized that a statistically significant difference may be of little clinical importance; that is, small but real (statistically significant) changes in a target behavior may not actually improve the patient's lot. Assessment of clinically significant change, regardless of experimental design, usually involves (1) evaluation by the person or persons who initially defined the problem or (2) comparison with a peer group not considered to manifest the problem being treated.

A common between-subjects design is the crossover design, in which one group begins with a placebo and subsequently is switched to the drug, and the order of conditions is reversed for the other group. This design can be extended to multiple conditions in which individuals in groups receive each of several conditions in a different order, for example, two drug treatments, a behavioral treatment, and a placebo control; in this case, it is known as a counterbalanced design. If a given condition produces an effect, the group receiving the condition, regardless of the order, should be affected similarly.

Both of these designs are frequently used because all subjects receive all conditions, thus minimizing ethical considerations, each is sensitive to drug effects, and fewer subjects are required than in most other group designs. However, these designs require that the effects of a given treatment are reversible so that they will not interact with subsequent treatments. If the proper response measures are used (nonpermanent products), this problem can be avoided in most drug investigations by allowing a sufficient "washout" period between treatments (e.g., stimulants usually require a minimum of 24 hours whereas many neuroleptics require at least four weeks).

Between-subjects designs can yield meaningful evaluations of drug effects. However, it is often difficult or impossible to find large and homogeneous subject populations from which to select experimental and control groups. Also, some between-subjects designs require an untreated control group, which may be hard to justify ethically. Finally, in a typical group study, some subjects improve during treatment, some worsen, and some remain unchanged. These differences, important to the clinician, are obscured in between-subjects analyses. An example of this is reported by Breuning, Davis, Matson, and Ferguson (in press). Because of these problems, within-subjects comparisons have been strongly advocated for drug evaluation (e.g., Wysocki & Fuqua, 1982).

In within-subjects designs, each subject serves as his or her own control; that is, the individual's performance is tested in the presence and absence of the drug. There are many variations of such designs. Probably the most common is the withdrawal (sometimes misleadingly termed the reversal, see Hersen & Barlow, 1976) design, in which the subject alternately receives the drug and the placebo. In general, behavior is repeatedly measured in each condition under the empirically substantiated assumption that the more continuously behavior is sampled, the better the measurement reflects the subject's usual behavior (see Wysocki & Fuqua, 1982). This design is powerful, but the termination of effective medication may raise ethical and practical objections. Further, treatment (drug) effects may be irreversible, which precludes evaluation by means of the withdrawal design. Finally, such designs typically require extended periods of time for completion. This, of course, may be hard to arrange.

An alternative to the withdrawal design is the multiple baseline design. In drug research, this design typically involves multiple (three or four) subjects, although it can be implemented across behaviors or settings in an individual subject. In one example of a multiple baseline across subjects, the target behavior is first measured in a nondrug baseline condition. One subject then receives the drug while performance continues to be measured for the remaining subjects in the baseline condition. This temporally staggered sequence of treatment introduction is continued until all subjects are receiving the drug. Drug effects are evidenced by individual subjects showing a change in behavior after, and only after, treatment (drug) is introduced. In naturalistic settings, this design is very useful in evaluating the drug effects as drug treatment is slowly removed. Statistical evaluations are rarely employed with this or other within-subjects designs. Instead, data are simply graphed and "optically analyzed." This decreases the likelihood of statistical and clinical significance being confused but increases the probability that small treatment effects will go unnoticed. Recently, single-subject statistical procedures have begun to emerge. These procedures are reviewed by Kazdin (1976).

The multiple baseline across subjects design is effective in dealing with irreversible treatment effects and eventually provides treatment for all subjects. Thus, it should prove extremely valuable for pharmacotherapeutic research, and recent investigations have documented the usefulness of the design (e.g., Breuning, O'Neill, & Ferguson, 1980; Davis et al., 1981; Wysocki et al., 1981). Figure 7-1, from Breuning, O'Neill, and Ferguson (1980), is a pictorial example.

Other within-subjects designs (e.g., alternating treatments, multielement, multiple probe, changing criterion) have been developed, but their applicability to pharmacological research remains to be demonstrated. One recent report, however, shows that the alternating treatments design can provide great versatility in evaluating the effects of various behav-

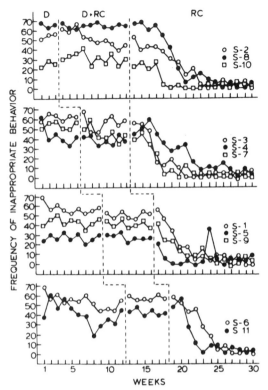

Figure 7-1. Weekly frequency of inappropriate behaviors as a function of psychotropic drug (D), response cost (RC), and combined (D + RC) procedures. (Reprinted with permission from Breuning, S. E., O'Neill, M. J., & Ferguson, D. G. Comparison of psychotropic drug, response cost, and psychotropic drug plus response cost procedures for controlling institutionalized retarded persons. *Applied Research in Mental Retardation,* 1980, *1*, 253–268. Copyright by Pergamon Press, Ltd.)

ioral procedures alone and in combination with neuroleptic and stimulant medications (Breuning & Barrett, 1982). The reader interested in within-subjects experimental designs should consult any of a wealth of recent texts (e.g., Bailey, 1977; Hersen & Barlow, 1976; Johnston & Pennypacker, 1981; Wysocki & Fuqua, 1982).

Both within-subjects and between-subjects designs, used appropriately, allow for meaningful, and theoretically generalizable, evaluations of treatment efficacy, although generalizability is ultimately an empirical, not a theoretical, issue. Within-subjects designs are flexible, since they do not entail adherance to a fixed statistical model and often allow for more intensive evaluations of drug effects, require fewer subjects, and may be more tenable with respect to practical issues. Between-groups comparisons, however, are required to answer actuarial questions (e.g., what percentage of subjects improve when exposed to a particular drug?), and in some instances for the comparison of drug and nondrug treatments.

Our recommendation concerning experimental designs in drug evaluation is for researchers to avoid dogma, become familiar with both between-subjects and within-subjects analyses, and then tailor their studies in consideration of the experimental questions being asked and the realities of their research setting. No one design best serves the clinical psychopharmacologist, and no clinical psychopharmacologist is best served by rigidly adhering to a single design.

• General Considerations •

Regardless of the design used, several general methodological criteria must be met by a scientifically sound drug study. Sprague and Werry (1971) have specified six such criteria that have been rather widely accepted. These criteria are cited in the following sections.

• *Placebo Control* •

To prevent nonspecific factors such as subject or staff expectations and observer bias from confounding the drug effect, an inactive substance similar to the drug being evaluated in size, shape, color, and taste should be administered during nondrug sessions. Inclusion of a no-drug condition as well as a placebo phase allows for an evaluation of possible placebo effects that appear in both placebo and drug conditions. The importance of using a placebo has been empirically demonstrated with mentally retarded individuals—even the severely to profoundly retarded (Breuning, Ferguson, & Cullari, 1980).

• *Double Blind* •

To further prevent bias and expectancy from confounding treatment effects, neither the subject nor the observers should be able to discriminate experimental conditions (for an intentional example of such confounds see Breuning, Ferguson, & Cullari, 1980). In some instances, however, discriminable effects of the drug itself may break the double blind. Subjects, for instance, can probably readily ascertain whether they have received amphetamine or an inert placebo.

• *Standardized Doses* •

Doses should be clearly specified, preferably in units of drug per unit of body weight (mg/kg/day), and results reported separately for each dose. Each dose should be given for a sufficient period of time to allow for adequate evaluation. Different doses should be separated by nondrug periods (no-drug or placebo) long enough to allow the effects of prior doses to disappear. When possible, other medications should be withheld during the period of evaluation. If this cannot be arranged, all drugs taken by a subject should be specified.

• *Standardized Evaluations* •

The effects of treatment must be assessed by procedures of demonstrated sensitivity, reliability, and validity, as discussed previously. Marholin and Phillips (1976) have argued that adequate assessment must include an evaluation of the medication's effects on appropriate as well as inappropriate target behaviors. Simple demonstration of a decrease in some undesired response does not satisfactorily demonstrate clinical efficacy; a drug could produce such an effect through generalized sedation, with a concomitant decrease in appropriate behaviors. For example, Breuning (1982b) has shown that regardless of whether or not an individual is showing a decrease in the targeted behavior, there will also likely be decreases in workshop performance and response to general reinforcement contingencies. The magnitude of these effects vary with dose (see Fig. 7-2).

• *Appropriate Statistical Analyses* •

When inferential statistics are used, the assumptions underlying a particular test must not be violated. Further, statistical significance must not be advanced as being synonomous with clinical significance.

• *Random Assignment of Subjects* •

This criterion relates to the preceding requirement. If, in between-subjects designs, the subjects are not assigned to control and experimental groups in truly random fashion, a fundamental assumption of all inferential statistics (and basic research design) is being badly violated.

At the time Sprague and Werry published these criteria, one or more of them had not been met in the vast majority of studies; this has not changed with time. Recently, in view of the potentially restrictive nature of pharmacotherapies, Sprague and Baxley (1978) have added a seventh criterion to the foregoing. This criterion specifies that drug treatment be compared with some alternative treatment, preferably the best alternative available.

Recently an additional criterion has been espoused by Breuning, O'Neill, and Ferguson (1980) and Breuning, Davis, Matson, and Ferguson (in press). They have argued that the assessment of neuroleptic drug effects following drug discontinuation should be ongoing for at least 12–16 weeks. The arguement stems from their data indicating that the results of shorter evaluations can be confounded by various withdrawal effects such as the dyskinesias previously discussed.

It should be apparent that studies capable of generating believable conclusions concerning the effectiveness of pharmacotherapy with the mentally retarded are by no means easy to conduct. Nonetheless, such studies are possible and have appeared occasionally. It is our hope that with a growing call for methodological sophistication they will proliferate in the near future.

However, several recent reports lead us to wonder if many investigators fail to read, comprehend, or utilize the dictates of scientific rigor. For example, Craft and Schaiff (1980) with fluphenazine, Dale (1980) with lithium, Elie, Langlois, Cooper, Gravel, and Albert (1980), with thioridazine and SCH-12679, and Haegeman and Duyck (1978), with pipamperone, all failed to meet more than three of the seven minimum criteria just summarized. Also, not one of these studies systematically evaluated for adaptive behavior impairments. Perhaps Craft and Schaiff (1980) summarize the results of these studies best as they state, "our results confirm the generally favorable impression of previous studies" (p. 254). The problem here is that the findings are no more than *impressions,* and the methodological sophistication of these current studies reflect minimal advancement from that of the 1950s.

Another recent study, Vaisanen, Viukari, Riman, and Raisanen (1981), compared haloperidol, thioridazine, and a placebo. The primary purpose of this study was to evaluate the relationship between serum levels and clinical responses. There are several positive features to this study such as the use of placebo/double-blind conditions, attempts to partition responders from nonresponders, numerous medical and laboratory assessments, and the monitoring of side effects. However, the behaviors and symptoms were assessed by means of global impression and ratings using a scale of no established validity. Also, a large percentage of the subjects received intermittent treatment with other medications and the doses of thioridazine and haloperidol were not equivalent (for the record, the correlation between serum level and clinical response was poor).

• EFFICACY OF USE, BEHAVIORAL ALTERNATIVE, AND • BEHAVIORAL EFFECTS

As stated earlier, several comprehensive reviews have shown that the vast majority of drug studies with the mentally retarded are inadequate. Lack of placebo controls and double-blind conditions and inappropriate behavioral definitions and methods of data analysis are the most common shortcomings. It is also relatively uncommon to find comparisons of drug treatments with other treatments or evaluations of the drug's effects on measurements of learning, performance, and general adaptive behaviors. A complete review of all the studies examining the efficacy, treatment comparisons, and effects on other positive behaviors is beyond the scope of this chapter; however, results from the methodologically stronger studies will be summarized. The reader is referred to Breuning and Poling (1982) for more comprehensive coverage.

• Neuroleptics •

Drugs in this class are far and away the best studied with the mentally retarded. But few of the studies are methodologically adequate. As reported by Ferguson and Breuning (1982),

> Taken in their best light, the results of studies reviewed above suggest that compared to placebo, a few of the antipsychotic drugs . . . may be useful in reducing certain inappropriate behaviors such as aggression, motor activity, and self-stimulation. (pp. 195–196)

The strongest basis for this conclusion comes from two recent studies (Breuning, 1982b; Singh & Aman, 1981). Singh and Aman reported that a 2.5 mg/kg dose of thioridazine was effective in reducing self-stimulatory behaviors of severely retarded individuals. A greater suppression of self-stimulation did not occur at higher doses. Breuning (1982b) provides a dose-response curve for thioridazine with mentally retarded subjects divided on the basis of being responders (evidence of therapeutic effect) and non-responders. For the responders, 5.9 mg/kg was the optimal dose for reducing aggressive behaviors and 2.5 mg/kg was optimal for reducing self-stimulatory behaviors. Higher doses had little additional effect except for a loss of behavioral control (increased frequencies of inappropriate behaviors). For the nonresponders, the frequency of inappropriate behaviors increased with thioridazine dose. The left two panels of Figure 7-2 summarize these data.

In a recent series of studies with adults and children (Breuning, 1982c) the findings of Breuning (1982b) have been replicated and expanded. Similar methods were used and similar results were obtained with chlorpromazine and haloperidol. Seven doses were assessed in adults with each of these drugs. The seven doses were selected on the basis of chlorpromazine-thioridazine-haloperidol equivalences provided by Davis (1976). The results showed that haloperidol was more effective than chlorpromazine and thioridazine. An optimum haloperidol dose of 0.09 mg/kg/day (4.5 mg/kg/day chlorpromazine-CPZ-equivalent) was found for treating aggressive behavior (with responders) and a dose of 0.05 mg/kg/day (CPZ equivalent of 2.5 mg/kg/day) for self-stimulatory behavior. Ha-

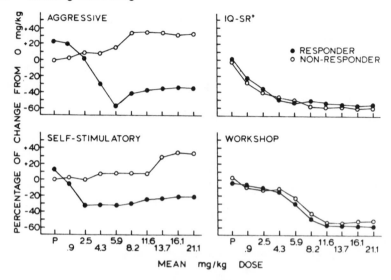

Figure 7-2. Mean percentage of change from 0 mg/kg for responders and nonresponders on measures of aggressive, self-stimulatory intellectual (IQ − SR⁺), and workshop behaviors. P stands for placebo. (Rep…ted with permission from Breuning, S. E. An applied dose response curve of thioridazine with the mentally retarded: Aggressive, self-stimulatory, intellectual, and workshop behaviors—A preliminary report. *Psychopharmacology Bulletin*, 1982, *18*, 57–59. Copyright by U.S. Government.)

loperidol impaired adaptive behavior slightly *less* than thioridazine and chlorpromazine with responders but impaired adaptive behavior *more* with nonresponders.

   With children a thioridazine dose of 3.0 mg/kg/day was optimal for reducing aggressive behaviors and a dose of 2.0 mg/kg/day was optimal for reducing self-stimulatory behavior with responders. Higher doses had little additional effect except for a loss of behavioral control, that is, increased frequency of target behavior. For the nonresponders, frequencies of aggressive and self-stimulatory behavior showed no substantial changes at the lower doses but began to worsen as thioridazine doses increased. For both responders and nonresponders there were significant decreases in intellectual and workshop behaviors at even the low doses, and behaviors worsened as the doses increased.

   With chlorpromazine and haloperidol, four doses were assessed. The four doses were selected on the basis of Part 1 findings in conjunction with chlorpromazine-haloperidol-thioridazine equivalences provided by Davis (1976). Haloperidol was again more effective than the other two medications, with the optimum doses for treating aggressive and self-stimulatory behaviors being 0.05 and 0.03 mg/kg/day, respectively (CPZ equivalences of 2.5 and 1.5 mg/kg/day). With the children there were no differences across the drugs in terms of degree of impaired adaptive behavior and behavioral toxicity. These effects paralleled those found with adults.

The results of the Singh and Aman (1981) and Breuning (1982b,c) studies identify three critical variables in need of careful attention. First, it is clear that some mentally retarded individuals will show positive responses to neuroleptic drug treatment. However, several recent reports show that these individuals represent a percentage drastically lower than the current 60 percent receiving these drugs (e.g., recent findings, currently unpublished, from our investigations suggest that as few as 15 percent of the mentally retarded receiving a neuroleptic actually show decreases in targeted symptoms). Second, when an individual does show a positive response, it is likely to occur at a moderate dose, at least with thioridazine, with little additional effect occurring at higher doses. Third, not only may nonresponders fail to improve with neuroleptic drug treatment, but their behavior may worsen (behavioral toxicity).

Given the questionable efficacy but high prevalence of neuroleptic drug use with the mentally retarded, it would be reasonable to expect to find numerous studies directly comparing the effectiveness of behavior management procedures with neuroleptic drugs. However, only two published studies could be found that made such comparisons.

McConahey et al. (1977) used a placebo-controlled double-blind, crossover design to compare chlorpromazine and a token reinforcement procedure with mentally retarded adult women from one ward (mean IQ of 31, range of 13–59). The dosages were relatively low (0.81 to 3.22 mg/kg) and group analyses were used. It was concluded that the token reinforcement procedure was more effective (clinically and statistically) than chlorpromazine in controlling the inappropriate behaviors and facilitating the development of adaptive behaviors. Behavioral changes were more rapid and consistent with the token reinforcement program.

Breuning, Regan, and Davis (reported in Ferguson & Breuning, 1982) extended the findings of McConahey et al. (1977) by comparing three behavior-management procedures with use of several neuroleptic drugs including thioridazine, chlorpromazine, haloperidol, and mesoridazine. The behavior-management procedures were differential reinforcement of other behavior (DRO), token reinforcement (TE), and token reinforcement–response cost (RC). Four male and five female mentally retarded individuals (mean IQ of 27, range of 8–60) were the subjects, and each received all of the behavior-management procedures in a placebo-controlled, double-blind, randomly counterbalanced sequence with a four-week drug treatment preceding each 16-week behavioral procedure (e.g., drug, DRO, drug, RC, drug, TE). The dosages were moderate to high (3.3–15.4 mg/kg), and the frequencies of inappropriate ward behaviors and percentages of time spent on a task and task completion with tabletop activities were recorded and analyzed on an individual basis. The results showed that in all nine subjects, both the token reinforcement and token-reinforcement/response-cost procedures were substantially more effective than the psychotropic drugs in increasing time on task and percentage of task completion, as well as in reducing the inappropriate target behaviors. The token reinforcement/response cost procedure was more effective than the token reinforcement procedure. There was little evidence of a difference between the drug and DRO conditions.

An important extension of these two studies involved the interactive effects of neuroleptic drug and behavior management procedures. Only two published studies have examined this issue. The previously mentioned McConahey et al. study (1977) involved conditions in which a token-reinforcement procedure was used in combination with chlorpromazine or a placebo. Although comprehensive analyses of the interactive effects were not provided, these authors reported that chlorpromazine decreased the effectiveness of the token reinforcement procedure.

Similar findings were reported in a recent study by Breuning, O'Neill, and Ferguson (1980). This study compared the effectiveness of psychotropic drug (D), response cost (RC), and psychotropic drug plus response cost (D + RC) procedures in controlling the inappropriate behaviors of 18 institutionalized mentally retarded persons (mean IQ of 47, range of 19–64). Both male and female mentally retarded participants from several living units (wards) were included. The drug dosages were moderate to high (6.12–15.06 mg/kg); the target behaviors were recorded by means of a 24-hour event recording with stringent reliability checks, rather than by rating scale, and the results were analyzed on an individual rather than a group basis.

Subjects were randomly assigned to one of two sequences. Sequence I, utilizing 11 subjects, was drug, drug plus response cost, and then response cost. Sequence II, utilizing 7 subjects, was drug, placebo (P), and then response cost. Subjects and staff were blind to conditions and sequences. The results showed that the frequencies of inappropriate behaviors were lowest during the response cost condition. The drug, drug plus response cost, and placebo conditions resulted in similar frequencies of inappropriate behaviors. These frequencies were approximately 45 percent higher than those obtained during the response cost above conditions. Parts of these data appear in Figure 7-1.

Most recently (Breuning & Barrett, 1982), a series of studies provided a comparison of DRO, token reinforcement plus RC, time out (TO), and sensory extinction (SE) procedures alone and in combination with thioridazine, haloperidol, and methylphenidate (each medicine separately).

Medication trials were all double-blind, placebo-controlled, and across several dose values. Several mentally retarded adults and children receiving a given medication were assigned pairs of the behavioral procedures to be treated with. Analyses of treatment effectiveness were across measurements of response suppression and academic–habilitative gains under the placebo and each medication dose using an alternating treatments design.

The results showed that with responders each behavioral procedure showed some evidence of therapeutic effectiveness alone and in combination with methylphenidate at low (0.3 mg/kg) but not higher (0.7+ mg/kg) doses. However, with thioridazine and haloperidol, the RC and DRO were effective during the placebo condition but of limited or no effect as doses were increased. The SE and TO procedures were effective during the placebo phase and interacted beneficially with the neuroleptics at low doses but became less and less effective as the doses increased.

Regardless of the intended effect, pharmacotherapists must be aware of possible neuroleptic drug contratherapeutic behavioral effects. Intelligence test performance, operant paradigms, and changes in adaptive behaviors have been the primary measures of these behavioral effects. Performance on intelligence tests administered under standard testing conditions are very insensitive to drug effects (see Breuning & Davidson, 1981). However, when these same tests are administered under conditions where there is reinforcement for correct responding to test item, performance becomes highly sensitive to drug effects (Breuning, 1982b,c; Breuning & Davidson, 1981; Breuning, Ferguson, Davidson, & Poling, in press). For both responders and nonresponders, thioridazine impairs response to test items when the reinforcement contingency is included. Dolorously, such impaired performance begins to occur at very low doses (see Fig. 7-2, upper right panel).

Four studies have examined the effects of neuroleptic drugs on schedule-controlled or discriminated operant performance of mentally retarded persons. Davis (1971) used a paradigm in which rocking was reinforced in the presence of one stimulus and lever pressing reinforced in the presence of a second stimulus. The reinforcement schedule was a fixed-ratio 15 (FR 15). No consistent differences between thioridazine and the placebo were found. Hollis (1968), using an FR 100 schedule with ball pulling and rocking as responses, found that chlorpramazine had little effect on the rate of ball pulling but decreased the rocking. Hollis and St. Omer (1972) failed to replicate the findings of Hollis (1968). In a more elaborate design, dose-related decreases in both lever pressing and rocking were found. Dose-dependent decrements in operant behavior were also reported by Wysocki et al. (1981). A titrating delayed matching to sample procedure was used. Increased accuracy at longer delay intervals occurred at each dose reduction, with the greatest delay values being achieved after, and only after, a 0-mg level was reached.

There have also been few attempts to assess the effects of neuroleptic drugs on adaptive behaviors. Allen, Shannon, and Rose (1963) reported no differences between thioridazine and the placebo on rating scale measurements of bathing, feeding, socialization, and toileting. Heisted and Zimmerman (1979), found that rating scale measurements of numerous adaptive behaviors showed a worsening of these behaviors during a four-week period following discontinuation of the neuroleptic drug. There are several serious methodological problems with this study (see Ferguson & Breuning, 1982), the most serious being that the four-week postdrug assessment period was inadequate. Breuning (1981) and Breuning, Davis, Matson, and Ferguson (in press) have shown that deterioration in adaptive behavior following drug discontinuation is a likely event and may persist as long as 16 weeks before subsiding. The primary response measure was objective workshop performance assessed by means of the rate of assembling a bicycle brake. Following thioridazine discontinuation there were group performance decreases (decreased rate of assembly) that lasted up to 6 weeks following gradual discontinuation and up to 11 weeks following abrupt discontinuation. After these periods, the rate of assembly began to increase drastically. These effects were attributed to withdrawal dyskinesias and symptoms because subjects not experiencing withdrawal effects showed rapid postdrug performance increases. Marholin, Touchette, and Stewart (1979) showed evidence of increases in workshop performance following chlorpromazine discontinuation.

• Anxiolytics •

The amount of research done on anxiolytics and mentally retarded individuals has been incredibly limited. In fact, there has been a total of only 16 studies, with only one since 1966. Of eight studies examining the effects of the benzodiazepines, only four showed no beneficial effects. The two best controlled of these studies (LaVeck & Buckley, 1961; Walters, Singh, & Beale, 1977) found that the *benzodiazepines* are very likely to result in dramatic *increases in hyperactive behavior.* Five studies examined the effects of the diphenylmethane derivatives, and four were fairly well controlled. With the exception of a study by Segal and Tansley (1957), no study found evidence of positive or negative effects. Segal and Tansley reported clinical impressions of hydroxyzine effectiveness, but it appears that their placebo controls and double-blind conditions were inadequate. Three studies examined the effects of meprobamate (Craft, 1958; Heaton-Ward & Jancar, 1958; Rudy et al., 1958). All were reasonably well controlled and reported no evidence of effectiveness. Ferguson and Breuning (1982) review these 16 studies in detail.

There have been no studies comparing the anxiolytics with other methods of treatment, and there have been no systematic examinations of the effects of anxiolytic drugs on learning, performance, and adaptive behaviors of the mentally retarded.

• Antidepressants and Antimanics •

As with the anxiolytics, minimal research involving the antidepressants and antimanics has been performed with mentally retarded subjects. Also, virtually all of the studies that have occurred are methodologically inadequate. Amitriptiline has been reported effective in controlling disruptive behaviors by Kraft, Ardali, Duffy, Hart, and Pearce (1966) and Keegan, Pettigrew, and Parker (1974). The effectiveness of imiprimine was reported by Bender and Faretra (1961) but not substantiated by Campbell, Fish, Shapiro, and Floyd (1971). Uncontrolled studies with MAO inhibitors have shown conflicting results (Carter, 1960; Soblen & Saunders, 1961; Heaton-Ward, 1962). Several methodologically poor studies have examined the efficacy of lithium treatment with the mentally retarded. These are reviewed by Gaultieri and Hawk (1982). The two most methodologically sound studies were those by Naylor, Donald, LePoidevin, and Reid (1974) and Rivinus and Harmatz (1979). The subjects in both studies appeared to have clear affective symptoms, and the effects were not large but were sufficiently clinically relevant to indicate the value of continued studies of lithium use with the mentally retarded.

There have been no studies comparing the use of antidepressants/ antimanics with other methods of treatment and there have been no systematic examinations of the effects of these drugs on learning, performance, and adaptive behaviors of the mentally retarded.

• Stimulants •

Stimulant drugs are among the least used and researched drugs with the mentally retarded. This is surprising because of their popularity with nonretarded hyperkinetic individuals. Ten fairly well controlled studies have examined use of stimulant drugs with the mentally retarded (reviewed in detail by Walker, 1982). The general concensus of these studies is that, unlike with nonretarded hyperkinetic individuals, stimulant drugs are likely to have no effect or result in a worsening of behavior with the

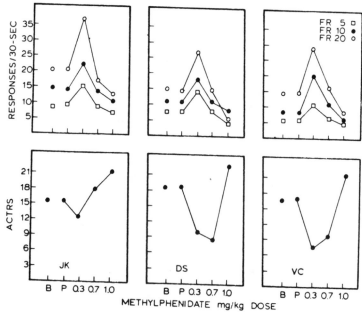

Figure 7-3. Responses per 30-second period on three FR schedules of reinforcement and Abbreviated Conner's Teachers Rating Scale (ACTRS) score on the last day of treatment under baseline (B), placebo (P), and three-dose levels. Upper and lower panels refer to same individual (i.e., JK, DS, or VC).

mentally retarded. McConnell, Cromwell, Bialer, and Son (1964); Alexandris and Lundell (1968); Davis, Sprague, and Werry (1969); and Davis (1971) found minimal to negative effects, whereas Sprague, Werry, and Scott (1967) and Sprague et al. (1970) reported decreased levels of hyperactive behaviors.

A review of the methylphenidate–mental retardation literature shows that virtually every study has used a dosage between 0.25 and 1.0 and, as stated earlier, typically examined only one dosage. This information, coupled with the findings of Sprague and Sleator (1977) and Walker (1982), suggests that a comparison of 0.3, 0.7, and 1.0 mg/kg methylphenidate is reasonable. To test this out a pilot investigation was conducted with these three dosages and six mentally retarded hyperactive individuals.

Four of the individuals were prepubescent children (age 11–13 years) and two were adolescents (ages 15 and 18 years). Four were male and two were female (equally divided amongst children and adolescents), and none had any other psychiatric disorders. All were moderately retarded with the retardation being of unknown etiology (i.e., no other neurological disorders). Hyperactivity was assessed on a daily basis using the Abbreviated Conner's Teacher Rating Scale (ACTRS, Conner, 1973), and each

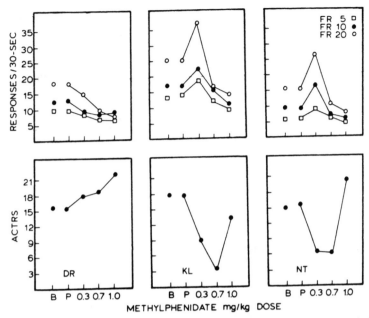

Figure 7-4. Responses per 30-second period on three FR schedules of reinforcement and Abbreviated Conner's Teachers Rating Scale (ACTRS) score on the last day of treatment under baseline (B), placebo (P), and three-dose levels. Upper and lower panels refer to same individual (i.e., DR, KL, or NT).

individual had an initial score above 15. Laboratory performance was assessed using three schedules of reinforcement (FR 5, 10, and 20). Each individual received each schedule in ascending order for each condition (i.e., FR 5, FR 10, and then FR 20), and stable response was obtained in all cases. There were three randomly counterbalanced dosage sequences with two individuals per sequence. Each sequence lasted seven days with seven days of placebo (double-blind) before and after. Figures 7-3 and 7-4 show the results.

Although a complete discussion of the results is beyond the scope of this section, it can be briefly stated that (1) four of the six individuals had substantially reduced ACTRS scores at 0.3 or 0.7 mg/kg methylphenidate, (2) one showed a very slight reduction in ACTRS scores at 0.3, (3) one showed progressive increases in ACTRS scores across dosage, and (4) for five of six individuals ACTRS scores were highest (above baseline and placebo) at the 1.0 mg/kg dosage. With regard to FR performance, five of six individuals showed optimum performance at 0.3 mg/kg, and performance worsened across increasing dosages. The one individual who showed the progressive increases in ACTRS scores (DR) showed no performance enhancement.

The findings clearly show that methylphenidate can be of therapeutic value with some mentally retarded individuals (even adolescents exhibiting hyperactivity) and that the dose-response curve properties of methylphenidate with this population are similar but likely shifted toward lower dosages, to those found with nonmentally retarded children. The *exacerbation* of symptoms by mentally retarded individuals at 1.0 mg/kg is consistent with speculation provided in previous reviews (e.g., Walker, 1982) and suggests that the use of higher dosages of methylphenidate are unlikely to yield therapeutic results. This is particularly important in that some investigators/clinicians recommend 2.0 mg/kg as the optimum dose (e.g., Millichap, 1968). Also, our findings are consistent with those showing no substantial effects of methylphenidate in the treatment of stereotypic behaviors.

There have been only two comparisons of stimulant drug treatment with alternative treatments. Christensen (1975) examined methylphenidate against and in combination with a token reinforcement procedure with mentally retarded hyperactive individuals. The two treatments were not found to interact. This was probably because of the overwhelming success of the token program alone, which resulted in a ceiling effect. Also, the previously referenced series of studies by Breuning and Barrett (1982) found several behavioral procedures to interact positively with low doses of methylphenidate.

Many of the studies examining stimulant efficacy incorporated measures of learning and performance. Bell and Zubek (1961) and Alexandris and Lundell (1968) found decrements in intelligence test performance and no changes in intelligence test performance, respectively, following amphetamine administration. Sprague et al. (1967) reported that dextroamphetamine reduced response latency in a two-choice discrimination task. Less evidence of reduced response latency was found by Sprague et al. (1970). Lobb (1968) reported that a low dose of amphetamine interfered with mentally retarded subjects' ability to learn a conditioned behavioral response. The data in Figures 7-3 and 7-4 clearly show that hyperactive mentally retarded responders can undergo enhanced performances with low dosages of methylphenidate.

• Antiepileptics •

As discussed by Gibbs et al. (1982), there is little question of the efficacy of antiepileptic drugs in the regulation of seizure disorders experienced by the mentally retarded. However, drugs in this class are often used in an attempt to modify a variety of inappropriate behaviors. Phenytoin and phenobarbital are most likely to be used for this purpose. There is no evidence to support this practice, as only one poorly controlled study has examined the efficacy of phenytoin in controlling aberrant behavior with the mentally retarded and there have been no phenobarbitol studies. Goldberg and Kurland (1970) found that with 13 dependent measures, phenytoin resulted in a positive change with only one rating scale dimension—"distractibility." With regard to phenobarbital, it appears that its use to control inappropriate behaviors is more likely to result in increased hyperactivity (see Gibbs et al., 1982). One recent study by Davis et al. (1981) has shown that phenytoin, at doses below the suggested optimum therapeutic levels, can significantly impair matching-to-sample and workshop (bicycle brake assembly) performance of mentally retarded adolescents. Although only these two studies have examined behavioral effects of antiepileptics with the mentally retarded, numerous findings with nonretarded individuals show behavioral impairment similar to that reported by Davis et al. with the use of most antiepileptic drugs (see Gibbs et al., 1982).

Several studies have examined a variety of "psychological" therapies, mostly behavioral, in conjunction with antiepilepsy drugs. These have included reinforcement, punishment, relaxation/desensitization, psychotherapy, and habituation/extinction (Gibbs et al., 1982; Mostofsky and Balaschak, 1977). Many of these procedures have proven effective as adjuncts to pharmacotherapy in that following their initiation there were decreased seizure frequencies or decreased drug dosages, or both, without increased seizure frequency. However, as Gibbs et al. (1982) point out, there is little reason to believe that behavioral procedures offer an alternative to pharmacotherapy for treating seizure disorders. Also, the interested reader is referred to Gibbs et al. for a discussion of methodological and possible ethical problems in the use of behavioral procedures as adjuncts and alternatives to pharmacotherapy.

• LITIGATION AND LEGISLATION •

In the past decade there have been more than 25 legal suits involving pharmacotherapy with mentally retarded individuals. These are reviewed comprehensively by Sprague (1982).

The first major case was that of *Wyatt* v. *Stickney* (1972a,b). The case appeared before Federal District Court Judge Frank M. Johnson and concerned deplorable conditions at a state institution in Tuscaloosa, Alabama. From this case came the often-cited *"Minimum Constitutional Standards for Adequate Habilitation of the Mentally Retarded."* Standard 22 dealt with medication and is briefly summarized in the following:

1. There must be written prescriptions on orders.
2. Prescriptions are to have a 30-day termination or review date.
3. Individual's have the right to be free from unnecessary or excessive medications.

4. There must be documentation on medication changes and effects.
5. Medication is not to be used as punishment, for staff convenience, or as a substitute for habilitative programs or in quantities that interfere with habilitative programs.
6. The drug regimen is to be reviewed for adverse effects and contraindications.
7. There are to be interdisciplinary evaluations (when appropriate) of drug effects.
8. Drugs will be administered only by properly trained staff.

This case established the groundwork for most of the subsequent cases. In 1974 this case became *Wyatt* v. *Aderholdt* and in 1979 became *Wyatt* v. *Ireland*. These changes in defendants reflect changes in the administration of the Alabama institution.

The rulings from the *Wyatt* case were upheld and extended in *Welsch* v. *Likens* (1974, 1977), which took place in Minnesota. Judge Larson was very concerned that the indiscriminant use of pharmacotherapeutic agents was cruel and unusual punishment. Following is a brief summary of the judge's orders:

1. That the behaviors indicating pharmacotherapy be described based upon direct staff observation and in terms of the frequency of occurrence.
2. Neuroleptics are to be used only to prevent injury to self or others or when the behavior is found to impede the implementation of habilitative programs.
3. There shall be neuroleptic drug-free periods of at least 20 days (over what time period was not specified).

This case continued as *Welsch* v. *Dirkswager* in 1977 and *Welsch* v. *Noot* in 1980. Also in 1980 the order was updated and applied to several Minnesota facilities for the mentally retarded.

The same issues raised in the *Wyatt* and *Welsch* cases occurred in *New York ARC* v. *Rockefeller* (1973; *New York ARC* v. *Carey*, 1975). This case resulted in a consent decree which repeated most of the previous orders on medication regulations and added a few new ones. In brief, these included the following:

1. There are to be weekly reviews of the drug regimen by a physician.
2. Written medication policies are to be developed to govern safe administration and handling of all drugs.
3. Medication errors and drug reactions shall be recorded and reported to the prescribing practitioner.

The orders of the *Wyatt, Welsch,* and *New York ARC* cases were upheld in *Gary W.* v. *State of Louisiana* (1976) and *Doe* v. *Hudspeth* (1977). The *Doe* case, in Mississippi, added three new orders: (1) a single daily dose is to be used with neuroleptic maintenance pharmacotherapy, (2) polypharmacy is largely forbidden, and (3) institutions are to have seminars on pharmacotherapy.

Perhaps the most comprehensive and extensive regulations on pharmacotherapy were put forth by Judge Gigonux in a 1978 consent decree in Maine (*Wouri* v. *Zitnay*, 1978). In addition to standards already mentioned, the following was ordered:

1. There will be monthly reviews of the number of residents receiving tranquilizers, phenothiazines, and antiepileptics.
2. Pharmacotherapeutic agents shall only be used as part of an individualized habilitation plan.
3. There will be a statement explaining reasons for the choice of a given medication, including a balancing of expected therapeutic effects and potential adverse effects.
4. There will be a statement of why nonpharmacotherapeutic treatments are inappropriate or inadequate.
5. There will be an explanation to the residents and advocate, in lay terms, giving the reasons for pharmacotherapy, its possible benefits, and its possible adverse consequences.
6. There will be careful monitoring of progress and side effects.
7. There will be evaluations of pharmacotherapeutic effects on educational and habilitative performance.

In an interesting ruling in Kentucky (*Kentucky ARC* v. *Conn.*, 1980), Judge Allen dismissed the complaint, refused to endorse a right to treatment argument, and stated that minimum standards of care had been met even though there may have been excessive use of "chemical restraints" (p. 21).

Most recently, Judge Martin in Iowa awarded a mentally retarded individual $760,165 in damages (*Clites* v. *Iowa,* 1980). Inappropriate use and monitoring of pharmacotherapy were major issues, and it was argued that due to negligence on behalf of Iowa State employees, Timothy Clites developed tardive dyskinesia. Judge Martin concluded that *"major tranquilizers were given for the convenience of staff and not as part of a therapeutic program. . . . Tim did not receive the standard of medical care that was acceptable as reasonable medical practice . . . the Court finds that Tim has T.D. (tardive dyskinesia), the drugs caused it, and it is permanent"*(italics added by author). This is one of the rare cases where a resident of a mental retardation facility was actually awarded damages.

The most pertinent legislation concerning pharmacotherapy is The Developmental Disabled Assistance Bill of Rights (P.L. 95-187, 1975).

This is also referred to as the Developmentally Disabled Bill of Rights. The standards previously outlined are generally encompassed in this document. Also, similar standards are found in several sets of federal regulations such as the Intermediate Care Facilities for the Mentally Retarded (ICFMR). Accreditation Council for Services for Mentally Retarded and Other Developmentally Disabled (ACMRDD), and Joint Commission on the Accreditation of Hospitals (JCAH). These regulations are discussed in detail by Sprague (1982).

• CONCLUSION •

The neuroleptics, particularly thioridazine, are the most widely used pharmacotherapeutic agents with the mentally retarded. It is quite apparent that they are greatly overused. This is unfortunate given the recurring evidence that use of these drugs is most likely to result in decreased learning and performance. These data, coupled with growing evidence that nonresponders, the greatest percentage of the mentally retarded receiving neuroleptics, are very likely to show contratherapeutic changes in target behaviors, and recent estimates of a 20 percent incidence of permanent dyskinesia, show that the risk-to-benefit ratio is incredibly poor. Thus, indiscriminant use of neuroleptics cannot be tolerated.

The anxiolytics, antidepressants, antimanic, and stimulants are used sparingly with the mentally retarded. At present it is virtually impossible to adequately discuss the efficacy of these drugs as pharmacotherapeutic agents with the mentally retarded. Clinical trials have been few and, with rare exception, methodologically inadequate. Systematic investigations of the therapeutic and contratherpeutic effects of drugs in these classes must be critically assessed. Somewhat skeptically, we do not believe that the underutilization of these drugs with the mentally retarded is related to any existing data base, but rather to the fact that their use has not come into vogue. Methodologically rigorous investigations with these medications and the mentally retarded are sorely needed.

Antiepilepsy drugs, when used appropriately, are clearly a valuable therapeutic tool in the regulation of seizure disorders. However, there is a risk of decreased behavioral functioning with their use, most notably in the area of short-term recall. Again, there is no evidence that antiepileptics are effective in the treatment of aggressive, psychotic, self-stimulatory, or other inappropriate behaviors of mentally retarded individuals.

One would like to suppose that inappropriate drug use with the mentally retarded will soon be a thing of the past, and pharmacotherapy will come to be based on sound, empirical principles. Yet, sadly, this is not a foregone conclusion, as evinced by the current prevalence and pattern of drug use, as well as by the quality (i.e., lack of) of many recent research investigations. Many of the persons involved in the decision to initiate or continue pharmacotherapy with the mentally retarded are not abreast of current developments in clinical pharmacology or trained in empirical evaluation, and may well continue to support drug treatments out of an unsubstantiated belief in their value. Further, treatment of the mentally retarded historically has been related to economic factors. Simply put, when the economy is depressed, little time or money is devoted to the handicapped; when the economy improves, concern for the disenfranchised grows. As we enter 1983, the American economy is hardly booming. How this will affect the mentally retarded and other minorities is unknown. However, drug treatment is relatively inexpensive, easy, and capable of making some patients easier to manage with limited staff, even if the ease of management reflects nonspecific sedation incompatible with patient habilitation. Fortunately, recent court decisions require that the value of such therapy be documented. If this requirement is met, pharmacotherapy may indeed prove remarkably valuable with certain mentally retarded individuals, and the remainder will be spared the administration of useless and potentially harmful medications. If not, one may have cause to remember Martin Luther's pronouncement concerning a retarded child: "If I were the Prince, I should take this child to the Moldau River which flows near Dessau and drown him" (in Kanner, 1964, p. 7), and to ask *have drugs replaced the Moldau?*

• REFERENCES •

Adamson, W. C., Nellis, B. P., Runge, G., Cleland, C., & Killian, E. Use of tranquilizers for mentally deficient patients. *AMA Journal of Diseases of Children*, 1958, *96*, 159–164.

Alexandris, A., & Lundell, F. W. Effect of thioridazine, amphetamine, and placebo on the hyperkinetic syndrome and cognitive area in mentally deficient children. *Canadian Medical Association Journal*, 1968, *98*, 92–96.

Allen, M., Shannon, G., & Rose, D. Thioridazine hydrochloride in the behavior disturbances of retarded children. *American Journal of Mental Deficiency*, 1963, *68*, 63–68.

Aman, M. G. Psychoactive drugs in mental retardation. In J. L. Matson & F. Andrasik (Eds.), *Treatment issues and innnovations in mental retardation*. New York: Plenum Press, in press.

Aman, M. G., & Singh, N. N. The usefulness of thioridazine in childhood disorders—Fact or folklore? *American Journal of Mental Deficiency*, 1980, *84*, 331–338.

Bailey, J. S. *Research methods in applied behavior analysis*. Talahassee, Fla.: Copy Grafix, 1977.

Bair, H. V., & Herold, W. Efficacy of chlorpromazine in hyperactive mentally retarded children. *Archives of Neurology and Psychiatry*, 1955, *74*, 363–364.

Baldessarini, R. J. Drugs and the treatment of psychiatric disorders. In A. G. Gilman, L. S. Goodman, & A. Gilman (Eds.), *The pharmacological basis of therapeutics*. New York: Macmillian, 1980.

Baldessarini, R. J., & Tarsy, D. Tardive dyskinesia. In M. A. Lipton, A. DiMascio, & K. F. Killiam (Eds.), *Phychopharmacology—A generation of progress*. New York: Raven Press, 1978.

Barchas, J. D., Berger, P. A., Ciaranello, R. D., & Elliott, G. R. (Eds.). *Psychopharmacology: From theory to practice*. New York: Oxford, 1977.

Barrett, R. P. *An alternating treatments comparison of four behavioral treatments alone and in combination with three psychotropic medications*. Paper presented at the American Psychological Association Conference, Washington, D.C., August 1982.

Bell, A., & Zubek, J. P. Effects of deanol on the intellectual performance of mental defectives. *Canadian Journal of Psychology*, 1961, *15*, 172–175.

Bender, L., & Faretra, G. Organic therapy in pediatric psychiatry. *Diseases of the Nervous System* (supplement 4) 1961, *22*, 110–111.

Berger, P. A. Medical treatment of mental illness. *Science*, 1978, *200*, 974–981.

Bernard, B. K. (Ed.). *Aminergic hypotheses of behavior: Reality or cliche?* Rockville, Md.: National Institute on Drug Abuse, 1975.

Blatt, B., & Kaplan, F. *Christmas in purgatory: A photographic essay on mental retardation*. Boston: Allyon and Bacon, 1966.

Breuning, S. E. An applied dose-response curve of thioridazine with the mentally retarded: Aggressive, self-stimulatory, intellectual, and workshop behaviors—A preliminary report. *Psychopharmacology Bulletin*, 1982b, *18*, 57–59.

Breuning, S. E. *Drug use with the mentally retarded: Efficacy, behavioral effects, side effects, and alternative treatments*. Paper presented at the American Association on Mental Deficiency Conference, Detroit, May 1981.

Breuning, S. E. *The mentally retarded and the right to refuse: Pharmacotherapy and the law from a clinical perspective*. Paper presented at the American Association on Mental Deficiency Conference, Boston, May 1982a.

Breuning, S. E. *Multidimensional dose-response curves of four psychotropic medications with mentally retarded children and adults*. Paper presented at the American Psychological Association Conference, Washington, D.C., August 1982c.

Breuning, S. E., & Barrett, R. P. *Effects of combined pharmacological and behavioral treatments with mentally retarded children: Relationship between different drugs and different behavioral procedures*. Paper presented at the American Association on Mental Deficiency Conference, Boston, May 1982.

Breuning, S. E., & Davidson, N. A. Effects of psychotropic drugs on the intelligence test performance of mentally retarded adults. *American Journal of Mental Deficiency*, 1981, *85*, 575–579.

Breuning, S. E., Davis, V. J., Matson, J. L., & Ferguson, D. G. Effects of thioridazine and withdrawal dyskinesias on workshop performance of mentally retarded young adults. *American Journal of Psychiatry*, in press.

Breuning, S. E., Ferguson, D. G., & Cullari, S. Analysis of single-double blind procedures, maintenance of placebo effects, and drug induced dyskinesia with mentally retarded persons. *Applied Research in Mental Retardation*, 1980, *1*, 237–252.

Breuning, S. E., Ferguson, D. G., Davidson, N. A., & Poling, A. D. Effects of thioridazine on the intelligence test performance of mentally retarded drug responders and non-responders. *Archives of General Psychiatry*, in press.

Breuning, S. E., O'Neill, M. J., & Ferguson, D. G. Comparison of psychotropic drug, response cost, and psychotropic drug plus response cost procedures for controlling institutionalized retarded persons. *Applied Research in Mental Retardation*, 1980, *1*, 253–268.

Breuning, S. E., & Poling, A. D. (Eds.). *Drugs and mental retardation.* Springfield, Ill.: Thomas, 1982.

Campbell, M., Fish, B., Shapiro, T., & Floyd, A. Imipramine in preschool autistic and schizophrenic children. *Journal of Autism and Childhood Schizophrenia*, 1971, *1*, 267–282.

Carter, C. Isocarboxazid in the institutionalized mentally retarded. *Diseases of the Nervous System*, 1960, *21*, 568–570.

Christensen, D. E. Effects of combining methylphenidate and a classroom token system in modifying hyperactive behavior. *American Journal of Mental Deficiency*, 1975, *80*, 266–276.

Clites v. *Iowa.* No. 46274 (Pottawattamie County, Iowa, filed Aug. 7, 1980).

Cohen, M. N., & Sprague, R. L. *Survey of drug use in two midwestern institutions for the retarded.* Paper presented at the Gatlinburg Conference on Mental Retardation, Gatlinburg, Tenn., March 1977.

Cone, J. D., & Hawkins, R. P. (Eds.). *Behavioral assessment: New directions in clinical psychology.* New York: Brunner/Mazel, 1977.

Connerss, C. K. Rating scales for use in drug studies with children. *Pharmacotherapy of children. Special Issue of Psychopharmacology Bulletin*, 1973, 24–84.

Corbett, J. A., Harris, R., & Robinson, R. G., Epilepsy. In J. Wortis (Ed.), *Mental Retardation* (Vol. 3). New York: Brunner/Mazel, 1975.

Craft, M. Tranquilizers in mental deficiency: Chlorpromazine. *Journal of Mental Deficiency Research*, 1957a, *1*, 91–95.

Craft, M. Tranquilizers in mental deficiency: Hydroxyzine. *Journal of Mental Science*, 1957b, *103*, 855–857.

Craft, M. Tranquilizers in mental deficiency: Meprobamate. *Journal of Mental Deficiency Research*, 1958, *2*, 17–20.

Craft, M. J., & Schaiff, A. A. Psychiatric disturbance in mentally handicapped patients. *British Journal of Psychiatry*, 1980, *137*, 250–255.

Craig, T. J., & Behar, R. Trends in prescription of psychotropic drugs (1970–1977) in a state hospital. *Comprehensive Psychiatry*, 1980, *21*, 336–345.

Dale, P. G. Lithium treatment in aggressive mentally subnormal patients. *British Journal of Psychiatry*, 1980, *137*, 469–474.

Davis, K. V. The effect of drugs on stereotyped and non-stereotyped operant behaviors in retardates. *Psychopharmacologia*, 1971, *22*, 195–213.

Davis, K. V., Sprague, R. L., & Werry, J. S. Stereotyped behavior and activity level in severe retardates: The effect on drugs. *American Journal of Mental Deficiency*, 1969, *73*, 721–727.

Davis, J. M. Comparative doses and costs of antipsychotic medication. *Archives of General Psychiatry*, 1976, *33*, 858–861.

Davis, V. J., Cullari, S., & Breuning, S. E. Drug use in community foster-group homes. In S. E. Breuning & A. D. Poling (Eds.), *Drugs and Mental Retardation*. Springfield, Ill.: Thomas, 1982.

Davis, V. J., Poling, A. D., Wysocki, T., & Breuning, S. E. Effects of phenytoin withdrawal on matching to sample and workshop performance of mentally retarded persons. *Journal of Nervous and Mental Disease*, 1981, *169*, 718–725.

Developmentally Disabled Bill of Rights. 42, U.S.C. 6010, 1975.

DiMascio, A. *An examination of actual medication usage in retardation institutions*. Paper presented at the American Association on Mental Deficiency Conference, Portland, Ore., May 1975.

Doe v. *Hudspeth*. Civil No. J75-36 (S.D. Miss., filed Feb. 17, 1977).

Eadie, M. J., & Tyrer, J. H. *Anticonvulsant therapy*. London: Churchill-Livingston, 1974.

Elie, R., Langlois, Y., Cooper, S. F., Gravel, G., & Albert, J. M. Comparison of SCH-12679 and thioridazine in aggressive mental retardates. *Canadian Journal of Psychiatry*, 1980, *25*, 484–491.

Esen, F. M., & Durling, D. Thorazine in the treatment of mentally retarded children. *Archives of Pediatrics*, 1956, *73*, 168–173.

Esen, F. M., & Durling, D. The treatment of fourteen mentally retarded boys with Sparine. *Archives of Pediatrics*, 1957, *74*, 471–474.

Ferguson, D. G., & Breuning, S. E. Antipsychotic and antianxiety drugs. In S. E. Breuning & A. D. Poling (Eds.), *Drugs and mental retardation*. Springfield, Ill.: Thomas, 1982.

Freeman, R. Psychopharmacology and the retarded child. In F. Menolascino (Ed.), *Psychiatric Approaches to Mental Retardation*. New York: Basic Books, 1970.

Garattini, S., Mussini, M., & Randall, L. O. (Eds.). *The benzodiazepines*. New York: Raven Press, 1973.

Gardener, W. I. Social and emotional adjustment of mildly retarded children and adolescents. *Exceptional Children*, 1967, *33*, 106.

Gary, W. v. *State of Louisiana*. 437 F. Supp. 1209 (1976).

Gibbs, E. L., Gibbs, T. J., Gibbs, F. A., Gibbs, E. A., Dickman, S., & Hermann, B. P. Antiepilepsy drugs. In S. E. Breuning & A. D. Poling (Eds.), *Drugs and mental retardation*. Springfield, Ill.: Thomas, 1982.

Goldberg, J. B., & Kurland, A. A. Dilantin treatment in hospitalized cultural-familial retardates. *Journal of Nervous and Mental Disease*, 1970, *150*, 133–137.

Goth, A. *Medical pharmacology*. St. Louis: Mosby, 1974.

Greenblatt, D. J. & Shader, R. J. *Benzodiazepines in clinical practice*. New York: Raven Press, 1974.

Gualtieri, C. T., Breuning, S. E., Schroeder, S. R., & Quade, D. Tardive dyskinesia in mentally retarded children, adolescents, and young adults. *Psychopharmacology Bulletin*, 1982, *18*, 62–65.

Gualtieri, C. T., & Guimond, M. Tardive dyskinesia and the behavioral consequences of chronic neuroleptic treatment. *Developmental Medicine and Child Neurology*, 1981, *23*, 255–259.

Gualtieri, C. T., & Hawk, B. Antidepressant and antimanic drugs. In S. E. Breuning & A. D. Poling (Eds.), *Drugs and mental retardation*. Springfield, Ill.: Thomas, 1982.

Haegeman, J., & Duyck, F. A retrospective evaluation of pipamerone (Dipiperon) in the treatment of behavioral deviations in severely mentally handicapped. *Acta Psychiatrica Belgica*, 1978, *78*, 392–398.

Haynes, S. N. *Principles of behavioral assessment*. New York: Gardner, 1978.

Heaton-Ward, W. A. Inference and suggestion in a clinical trial (Niamid in mongolism). *Journal of Mental Science*, 1962, *107*, 115–118.

Heaton-Ward, W. A., & Jancar, J. A. A controlled clinical trial of meprobamate in the management of difficult and destructive female mental defectives. *Journal of Mental Science*, 1958, *104*, 454–456.

Heisted, G. T., & Zimmerman, R. L. Double-blind assessment of Mellaril in a mentally retarded population using detailed evaluations. *Psychopharmacology Bulletin*, 1979, *15*, 86–88.

Hersen, M., & Barlow, D. H. *Single-case experimental designs: Strategies for studying behavior change*. New York: Pergamon Press, 1976.

Hollis, J. H. Chlorpromazine: Direct measurement of differential behavioral effect. *Science*, 1968, *159*, 1487–1489.

Hollis, J. H., & St. Omer, V. V. Direct measurement of psychopharmacologic response: Effects of chloropromazine on motor behavior of retarded children. *American Journal of Mental Deficiency*, 1972, *76*, 397–407.

Horenstein, S. Reserpine and chlorpromazine in hyperactive mental defectives. *American Journal of Mental Deficiency*, 1957, *61*, 525–529.

Hughes, P. S. Survey of medication in a subnormality hospital. *British Journal of Mental Subnormality*, 1977, *33*, 88–94.

Jarvik, M. E. Drugs used in the treatment of psychiatric disorders. In L. S. Goodman & A. Gilman (Eds.), *The Pharmacological Basis of Therapeutics* (3rd ed.). New York: Macmillan, 1965.

Johnston, A. H., & Martin, C. H. The clinical use of reserpine and chlorpromazine in the care of the mentally deficient. *American Journal of Mental Deficiency*, 1957, *62*, 292–294.

Johnston, J. M., & Pennypacker, H. S. Strategies and tactics of human behavioral research. New York: Lawrence Erlbaum, 1981.

Kanner, L. *A history of the care and the study of the mentally retarded*. Springfield, Ill.: Charles C. Thomas, 1964.

Kazdin, A. E. Statistical analyses for single-case experimental designs. In M. Hersen & D. H. Barlow, *Single case experimental designs*. New York: Pergamon Press, 1976.

Keegan, D. L., Pettigrew, A., & Parker, Z. Psychosis in Down's syndrome treated with amitriptyline. *Canadian Medical Association Journal,* 1974, *110,* 1128–1129.

Kentucky ARC v. *Conn.* Civil No. C78-0157 (W.D. KY., filed March 21, 1980).

Keppel, G. *Design and analysis: A researcher's handbook.* Englewood Cliffs, N.J.: Prentice-Hall, 1972.

Kirk, R. E. *Experimental design: Procedures for the behavioral sciences.* Belmont, Calif: Brooks/Cole, 1968.

Klaber, M. M. The retarded and institutions for the retarded—A preliminary report. In S. B. Sarason & J. Doris (Eds.), *Psychological problems in mental deficiency.* New York: Harper & Row, 1969.

Klein, D., & Davis, J. *Diagnosis and drug treatment of psychiatric disorders.* Baltimore: Williams & Wilkins, 1969.

Kline, N. S. Use of Rauwolfia serpentina in neuropsychiatric conditions. *Annals New York Academy of Sciences,* 1954, *59,* 107–123.

Kraft, I. A., Ardali, C., Duffy, J., Hart, J., & Pearce, P. R. Use of amitryptiline in childhood behavior disturbances. *International Journal of Neuropsychiatry,* 1966, *2,* 611–614.

LaVeck, G. D., & Buckley, P. The use of psychopharmacological agents in retarded children with behavior disorders. *Journal of Chronic Diseases,* 1961, *13,* 174–183.

Lehmann, H. E., & Hannahan, G. E. Chlorpromazine, a new inhibiting agent for psychomotor excitement and manic states. *AMA Archives Neurological Psychiatry,* 1954, *71,* 227–237.

Lipman, R. S., DiMascio, A., Reatig, N., & Kirson, T. Psychotropic drugs and mentally retarded children. In M. A. Lipton, A. DiMascio, & K. F. Killian, (Eds.), *Psychopharmacology: A generation of progress.* New York: Raven Press, 1978.

Lipman, R. S. The use of pharmacological agents in residential facilities for the retarded. In F. Menolascino (Ed.), *Psychiatric Approaches to Mental Retardation.* New York: Basic Books, 1970.

Lobb, H. Trace GSR conditioning with Benzedrine in mentally defective and normal adults. *American Journal of Mental Deficiency,* 1968, *73,* 239–246.

MacColl, K. Chlorpromazine hydrochloride (Targactil) in the treatment of the disturbed mental defective. *American Journal of Mental Deficiency,* 1964, *68,* 647–651.

Maloney, P. M., & Ward, M. P. *Mental retardation and modern society.* New York: Oxford, 1979.

Marholin, D., & Phillips, D. Methodological issues in psychopharmacological research. *American Journal of Orthopsychiatry,* 1976, *46,* 477–495.

Marholin, D., Touchett, P. E., & Stewart, R. M. Withdrawal of chronic chlorpromazine medication: An experimental analysis. *Journal of Applied Behavior Analysis,* 1979, *12,* 159–171.

McAndrew, J. B., Case, Q., & Treffert, D. Effects of prolonged phenothiazine intake on psychotic and other hospitalized children. *Journal of Autism and Childhood Schizophrenia,* 1972, *2,* 75–91.

McConahey, O. L., Thompson, T., & Zimmerman R. A token system for retarded women: Behavior therapy, drug administration and their combination. In J. Thompson & J. Grabowski (Eds.), *Behavior modification of the mentally retarded* (2nd Ed.). New York: Oxford, 1977.

McConnell, T. R., Cromwell, R. L., Bialer, I., & Son, C. D. Studies in activity level: VII. Effects of amphetamine drug administration on the activity level of retarded children. *American Journal of Mental Deficiency*, 1964, *68*, 647–651.

Merritt, H. H., & Putnam, T. J. Sodium diphenyl hydantoinate in treatment of convulsive disorders. *Journal of the American Medical Association*, 1938, *111*, 1068–1073.

Millichap, J. G. Drugs in management of hyperkinetic and perceptually handicapped children. *Journal of the American Medical Association*, 1968, *206*, 1527–1530.

Mostofsky, D. I., & Balaschak, B. A. Psychobiological control of seizures. *Psychological Bulletin*, 1977, *84*, 723–750.

National Institute of Mental Health, Psychopharmacology Service Center Collaborative Study Group. Phenathiazine treatment in acute schizophrenia. *Archives of General Psychiatry*, 1964, *10*, 246–262.

Naylor, G. J., Donald, J. M., LePoidevin, D., & Reid, A. H. A double-blind trial of long-term lithium therapy in mental defectives. *British Journal of Psychiatry*, 1974, *128*, 169–180.

New York ARC v. *Carey.* 393 F. Supp. 715 (1975).

New York ARC v. *Rockefeller.* 357 F. Supp. 752 (1973).

Physicians' Desk Reference (34th ed.). Oradell, N.J.: Medical Economics Co., 1980.

Poling, A. D., & Breuning, S. E. Overview of mental retardation. In S. E. Breuning & A. D. Poling (Eds.), *Drugs and mental retardation*. Springfield, Ill.: Thomas, 1982.

Poling, A. D., Cleary, J., & Monaghan, M. The use of human observers in psychopharmacological research. *Pharmacology, Biology and Behavior*, 1980, *13*, 243–246.

Pullman, R. M., Pook, R. B., & Singh, N. Prevalence of drug therapy for institutionalized mentally retarded children. *Australian Journal of Mental Retardation*, 1979, *5*, 212–214.

Ray, O. *Drugs, society, and human behavior* (2nd Ed.). St. Louis: C. V. Mosby Co., 1978.

Rettig, J. H. Chlorpromazine for the control of psychomotor excitement in the mentally deficient. *Journal of Nervous and Mental Disease*, 1955, *122*, 190–194.

Rivinus, T. M., & Harmatz, J. S. Diagnosis and lithium treatment of affective disorder in the retarded: Five case studies. *American Journal of Psychiatry*, 1979, *136*, 551–554.

Robinson, N. M., & Robinson, H. B. *The mentally retarded child*. New York: McGraw-Hill, 1976.

Rudy, L. H., Himwich, H. E., & Rinaldi, F. A clinical evaluation of psychopharmacological agents in the management of disturbed mentally defective patients. *American Journal of Mental Deficiency*, 1958, *62*, 855–860.

Schildkraut, J. J. *Neuropsychopharmocology and the affective disorders*. Boston: Little, Brown, 1970.

Segal, L. J., & Tansley, A. E. A clinical trial with hydroxyzine (Atarox) on a group of maladjusted educationally subnormal children. *Journal of Mental Science*, 1957, *103*, 677–682.

Sewell, J., & Werry, J. S. Some studies in an institution for the mentally retarded. *New Zealand Medical Journal*, 1976, *84*, 317–319.

Singh, N. N., & Aman, M. G. Effects of thioridazine dosage on the behavior of severely mentally retarded persons. *American Journal of Mental Deficiency*, 1981, *85*, 580–587.

Soblen, R. A., & Saunders, J. C. Monoamine oxidase inhibitor therapy in adolescent psychiatry. *Diseases of the Nervous System*, 1961, *22*, 96–100.

Sprague, R. L. Litigation, legislation, and regulations. In S. E. Breuning & A. D. Poling (Eds.), *Drugs and mental retardation*. Springfield, Ill.: Thomas, 1982.

Sprague, R. L. Overview of psychopharmacology for the retarded in the United States. In P. Mittler (Ed.), *Research to practice in mental retardation—Biomedical aspects* (Vol. 3). Baltimore: University Park Press, 1977.

Sprague, R. L., Barnes, K. R., & Werry, J. S. Methylphenidate and thioridazine: Learning, reaction time, activity, and classroom behavior in emotionally disturbed children. *American Journal of Orthopsychiatry*, 1970, *40*, 615–628.

Sprague, R. L., & Baxley, G. B. Drugs for behavior management with comment on some legal aspects. In J. Wortis (Ed.), *Mental retardation* (Vol. 10), New York: Brunner/Mazel, 1978.

Sprague, R. L., & Sleator, E. K. Methylphenidate in hyperkinetic syndrome: Differences in dose effects on learning and social behavior. *Science*, 1977, *198*, 1274–1276.

Sprague, R. L., & Werry, J. S. Methodology of psychopharmacological studies with the retarded. In N. R. Ellis (Ed.), *International review of research on mental retardation* (Vol. 5). New York: Academic Press, 1971.

Sprague, R. L., Werry, J. S., & Scott, K. G. *Effects of dextroamphetamine on activity level and learning in retarded children*. Paper presented at the Midwestern Psychological Association Conference, Chicago, May 1967.

Sprogis, G. R., Lezdins, V., White, S. D., Ming, C., Lanning, M., Drake, M. E., & Wyckoff, G. Comparative study of Thorazine and Serpasil in the mentally defective. *American Journal of Mental Deficiency*, 1957, *61*, 737–742.

Sulzbacher, S. I. Psychotropic medication with children: An evaluation of procedural bias in results of reported studies. *Pediatrics*, 1973, *51*, 513–517.

Tarjan, G., Lowery, V. E., & Wright W. W. Use of chlorpromazine in two hundred seventy-eight mentally deficient patients. *American Journal of Diseases of Children*, 1957, *94*, 294–300.

Toman, J. E. P. Drugs effective in convulsive disorders. In L. S. Goodman & A. Gilman (Eds.), *The pharmacological basis of therapeutics* (3rd Ed.). New York: Macmillan, 1965.

Tu, J., & Smith, J. T. Factors associated with psychotropic medication in mental retardation facilities. *Comprehensive Psychiatry*, 1979, *20*, 289–295.

Vaisanen, K., Viukari, M., Riman, R., & Raisanen, P. Haloperidol, thioridazine, and placebo in mentally subnormal patients—Serum levels and clinical effects. *Acta Psychiatrica Scandinavica*, 1981, *63*, 262–271.

Waldrop, M. F., Bell, R. Q., McLaughlin, B., & Halverson, C. F. Newborn minor physical anomalies predict short attention span, peer aggression and impulsivity at age 3. *Science*, 1978, *199*, 563–564.

Walker, M. K. Stimulant drugs. In S. E. Breuning & A. D. Poling (Eds.), *Drugs and mental retardation*. Springfield, Ill.: Thomas, 1982.

Walters, A., Singh, N., & Beale, I. L. Effects of lorazepam on hyperactivity in retarded children. *New Zealand Medical Journal*, 1977, *86*, 473–475.

Welsch v. *Dirkswager*. Civil No. 4-72-451 (D. Minn., 1977 Cambridge Consent Decree).

Welsch v. *Likins*. 373 F. Supp. 487 (1974).

Welsch v. *Likins*. 550 F. 2d 1122 (1977).

Welsch v. *Noot*. Civil No. 451 (D. Minn., 1980 System-wide Consent Decree).

Wolfson, I. N. Clinical experience with Serpasil and Thioridazine in the treatment of disturbed behavior of mentally retarded. *American Journal of Mental Deficiency*, 1957, *62*, 276–283.

Woodbury, D. M., Penry, J. K., & Schmidt, R. P. *Antiepileptic drugs*. New York: Raven Press, 1972.

Wouri v. *Zitnay*. No. 75-80-SD (Maine, 1978).

Wyatt v. *Anderholt*. 503 F. 2d 1305 (1974).

Wyatt v. *Ireland*. No. 3195-N (M.D. Ala., filed Oct. 25, 1979).

Wyatt v. *Stickney*. 344 F. Supp. 373 (1972) (a).

Wyatt v. *Stickney*. 344 F. Supp. 387 (1972) (b).

Wysocki, T., Fuqua, R. W. Methodological issues in the evaluation of drug effects. In S. E. Breuning & A. D. Poling (Eds.), *Drugs and mental retardation*. Springfield, Ill.: Thomas, 1982.

Wysocki, T., Fuqua, R. W., Davis, V. J., & Breuning, S. E. Effects of thioridazine (Mellaril) on titrating delayed matching-to-sample performance of mentally retarded adults. *American Journal of Mental Deficiency*, 1981, *85*, 539–547.

eight

Behavioral Treatment of Psychopathological Disorders

Philip H. Bornstein
Paul J. Bach
Basil Anton

This text, and therefore this concluding chapter, is designed to be useful with a wide range of professionals engaged in the delivery of services to mentally retarded persons. As a consequence, many potential readers will not be intimately familiar with research or practice in behavior therapy. Thus, to reach the widest possible audience, this chapter will attempt to present an *overview* of behavioral methods utilized in the treatment process. Those wishing a more technical review of the empirical literature are referred to Matson and Andrasik (in press). In addition, although practical details related to treatment intervention may be discussed from time to time, this chapter's intention is not to provide a "how-to" manual. Before any therapeutic procedures are attempted, therefore, the reader should refer to the original research and obtain the appropriate instruction and supervision required for effective implementation.

Behavioral treatment of psychopathology in mentally retarded indi-

Portions of this chapter were completed while the senior author was on sabbatical leave at Rampton Hospital, Retford, Notts, England.

viduals focuses on those manifestations of pathology or retardation that are behaviorally apparent. As such, it is a direct, noninferential approach to treatment. The focal concern in designing behavior modification programs is thus the alteration of antecedent or consequent events, or both, which will lead to significant, socially demonstrable changes in the behaviors under study. To accomplish this goal, a number of basic strategies and tactical alternatives are at the disposal of the behavior therapist. These basic strategies may be conceptualized as interventions aimed at decreasing maladaptive behaviors or increasing adaptive behaviors. Clearly, these two processes are not separate or unrelated but applied in the current context for organizational purposes. The next two sections of the present chapter will deal with these matters specifically. The fourth and final section offers some suggestions regarding future empirical investigation. All of these subjects will be presented with one very simple goal in mind: to facilitate the development of reliable and clinically significant treatment methods which can be applied in work with mentally retarded and emotionally disturbed individuals.

• DECREASE OF MALADAPTIVE BEHAVIOR •

• Stereotypical Behaviors •

The behavioral repertoire of retarded persons frequently includes recurrent, repetitive touching of various parts of the body with the hands or with some other object (self-stimulatory), often with some force (self-injurious) (Baumeister & Forehand, 1973). These behavior patterns have been referred to alternately as "inappropriate," "self-stimulatory," or "stereotypical." The domain of these behavioral patterns often includes headbanging and head-rolling, self-biting and self-slapping, body rocking, and complex hand movements. In this section, we will attempt briefly to review the formidable literature that has developed attesting to the effectiveness of operant procedures in reducing these stereotypic behaviors (Forehand & Baumeister, 1976; Matson, DiLorenzo & Andrasik, in press; Murphy, 1978; Smolev, 1971).

Repetitious motoric movement, or stereotyped behavior, is a regularly occurring phenomenon in populations of mentally retarded persons. Kaufman and Levitt (1965) estimated the frequency of three common stereotypical behaviors—body-rocking, head-rolling, and complex hand movement—and found that rocking behavior alone occurred in 69 percent of their sample of severely and profoundly mentally retarded persons. Although the etiology and development of stereotypical behavior is not certain, a model that would be representative of current empirical investigations would include the following factors: the behavior arises in the presence of a minimally stimulating environment; this may occur during early life and is then maintained by low levels of extrinsic stimulation; the rate rises with any increase in the organism's level of arousal and decreases, at least momentarily, as a result of conditions of novel stimulation (Berkson, 1967); the behavior can come under the control of environmental stimulation (Hollis, 1978).

• *Punishment-Oriented Procedures* •

One regularly used method to decrease the rate of stereotypical behavior is contingently applied aversive stimulation. Although several aversive stimuli have been used, shock is perhaps the most frequently utilized. The advantages of shock are several. It is mobile, easily delivered on a contingent schedule, flexibly administered with regard to intensity, and rarely habituated to by humans. However, there are several factors mitigating strongly against its use. There are notable moral and legal sanctions on its use in treatment (Parlour & Goldsmith, 1979). Also, shock tends to decrease the rate of all behavior, not just the targeted behavior. Finally, it does not, in and of itself, promote adaptive or prosocial behavior. In part because of these considerations, particularly the administrative (Repp & Deitz, 1978) and moral (Repp & Deitz, 1978a) constraints in the therapeutic use of contingent shock, it should not be considered the treatment of choice except when there is severe and acute medical risk due to life-threatening self-injurious behavior (Corbett, 1975; Muttan, Peck, Whitlow, & Fraser, 1975).

Baumeister and Forehand (1972) reduced various stereotypical behaviors in three institutionalized mentally retarded persons. Rocking was reduced from around 31 instances per minute before treatment to about 2.3 per minute after. However, this decrease was obtained only in the training environment. Although it continued at a low rate for up to 10 months, it did not generalize beyond the specific training setting. Pairing the aversive shock with the loud command, "no," however, rendered the command sufficiently aversive to decrease several self-stimulatory behaviors across settings. Once face-slapping and head-banging came under the control of the verbal command in several settings, other changes in behavior not directly addressed by treatment occurred. Specifically, the children appeared to whine less frequently and attend to adults more regularly. Lovaas and Simmons (1969) also obtained similar results from three persons who chronically exhibited head-banging and face-slapping. They found the response to be setting and trainer specific. Most of the treatment literature confirms the points made by these early investigations:

contingent shock does decrease quickly even high-rate self-injurious behavior, albeit in a fashion which does not generalize well from the initial training situation.

Aversive events other than shock have also been used successfully in the control of stereotypic behaviors. These have included loud commands (Baumeister & Forehand, 1972; Risley, 1968), moderate physical striking (Foxx & Azrin, 1973), and water mist spray (Dorsey, Iwata, Ong, & McSween, 1980).

Risley (1968) demonstrated that shouting "Stop that!," seizing the patient by the arm, and shaking her at the onset of rocking behavior reduced that target from 25 to 1 percent of the total observed time. Similarly, Baumeister and Forehand (1972) found that the command "Stop rocking!," when delivered contingently, reduced the incidences of rocking behavior from 17.0 a minute during the initial baseline to 0.2 a minute following the second series of treatment phases in a reversal design. More recently, Dorsey et al. (1980) suppressed mouthing, hand-biting, skin-tearing, and head-banging in seven profoundly mentally retarded subjects aged 5 to 26 years. The command "no" and the spraying of a water mist generalized both to a second environment and to the single command "no."

Overcorrection is a behavior modification procedure composed of positive practice and restitution components. Positive practice involves the repetitious practice of behaviors that are incompatible to stereotypy while theoretically utilizing muscle groups topographically similar to those involved in the production of the maladaptive behavior. Restitution requires the individual to undo the damage brought about by the maladaptive behavior and to improve on the condition of whatever was harmed. The two treatment techniques are compatible and sometimes used simultaneously (Foxx & Azrin, 1973), but they appear equally effective when used individually (Matson, Horne, Ollendick, & Ollendick, 1979).

Azrin and Foxx and their associates (Azrin, Kaplan, & Foxx, 1973; Foxx & Azrin, 1973) have compared the effects of overcorrection with those of other treatment strategies and judged it to be superior in numerous experimental reports. In fact, other investigators have successfully used overcorrection to suppress stereotypic behavior in a number of different contexts (Marholin & Townsend, 1978; Ollendick, Matson & Martin, 1978). Harris & Wolchik (1979) compared the use of overcorrection with time-out and differential reinforcement of other behaviors as methods of suppressing stereotypy in four mentally retarded males, aged five to seven years. They found overcorrection to be the most successful treatment technique insofar as it was most rapid in its effects, affected all four subjects successfully, and appeared to facilitate appropriate play in the subject population. The treatment did not automatically generalize to other settings, however.

One recent study (Shapiro, Barrett, & Ollendick, 1980) compared the relative effectiveness of restraint and positive practice in the reduction of stereotypic mouthing and face-patting in three mentally retarded girls, ages six to eight years. A concurrent-schedule design was used which alternately administered each treatment so as to assess the effects of each treatment on self-stimulatory and appropriate (visual-motor play) behavior. The authors found no difference between restraint and positive practice in either decreasing self-stimulation or increasing appropriate behavior.

Thus, in sum, it appears that overcorrection procedures are effective in suppressing stereotypy with mentally retarded children, producing rapid and durable effects. However, with adults the results appear to be less uniform (Rollings, Baumeister, & Baumeister, 1977) and less durable (Matson, Ollendick, & Martin, 1979). Additionally, the case has been made (Murphy, 1978; Ollendick & Matson, 1978) that in the instance of self-injurious stereotypy, the treatment is not consistent in its effectiveness across all patients. Moreover, although the data are contradictory (Coleman, Whitman, & Johnson, 1979; Epstein, Doke, Sajwaj, Sorrell, & Rimmer, 1974; Shapiro et al., 1980; Wells, Forehand, Hickey, & Green, 1977), it currently does not appear that overcorrection in and of itself promotes learning of more adaptive behavior. Thus, although numerous problems exist with the use of the overcorrection techniques (Forehand & Baumeister, 1976) and there are some constraints with regard to its known usefulness (Murphy, 1978), it does seem sufficiently promising to warrant continued investigation.

• *Withdrawal of Positive Reinforcement* •

In contrast to punishment, another treatment approach to decreasing the rate of stereotypic behavior has been the withdrawal or withholding of positive reinforcement contingent upon the onset of the target behavior. Such strategies as physical restraint, isolation, or withholding tokens tend to fall within this category.

Lovaas and Simmons (1969) attempted to treat two severely mentally retarded and psychotic children by placing them noncontingently in a room for an hour and a half daily, where they were isolated from interpersonal contact but allowed to engage in stereotypic behavior. The stereotypic behavior did extinguish after 10 to 20 days, however, the length of time required suggests that simple isolation is inadequate to suppress stereotypy. Another procedure utilized in the control of stereotypic behavior has been time-out (Hamilton, Stephens, & Allen, 1967; Lucero,

Frieman, Spoering, & Fehrenbacher, 1976; Pendergrass, 1972). Using time-out, whenever the behavior begins, the individual is placed in an isolation room for a specified period of time. Although this therapeutic tactic does appear to decrease stereotypical behavior and produce a more permanent effect than noncontingent isolation, it also may be a relatively slow process. Physical restraint, as the name implies, reduces stereotypy by briefly preventing the motoric movement, and it, too, has been demonstrated efficacious in controlled investigations (Marholin & Townsend, 1978; Saposnek & Watson, 1974). Finally, response costs, or the withdrawal of some previous positive reinforcement, has also been used to decrease stereotypical behavior. Withdrawal of previously earned tokens (Myers, 1975), withdrawal of hand-holding by staff (Tate & Baroff, 1966), and adding white noise to recorded music (Greene, Hoats, & Hornick, 1970) have each decreased the rate of stereotypic behavior. The difficulty here, however, may sometimes entail an inability to find positively reinforcing events that can be withdrawn upon the occurrence of the target behavior.

In sum, though effective and to some extent durable, the effects produced by withdrawal of positive reinforcement procedures are variable in the amount of time required to produce change. They may simply take too long to act for life-threatening stereotypical behaviors.

• *Reinforcement of Alternative Behavior* •

The third, and final, group of techniques for controlling self-stimulatory behavior involves the reinforcement of alternative, often incompatible, behaviors. The guiding rationale here is that the more regularly reinforced behavior will eventually occur more frequently and take the place of the stereotypical behavior in the patient's repertoire.

Weisberg, Passman, and Russell (1973) used food, social praise, and an imitative learning paradigm to produce a modeled response incompatible with the patient's stereotypic hand movements. Several arm and hand gestures were imitated for the subject by the experimenter with the verbal instruction to "Do this." Successful completion by the subject of the response pattern (with manual guidance) was then rewarded with food and praise. After the manual guidance was phased out of the instruction and the alternative behavior continued to be emitted with verbal instruction and reinforcement alone, the experimenter imitated the stereotypic response with the instruction, "Don't do this." Eventually the two verbal stimuli came to completely control the behavior under study.

Repp, Deitz, and Speir (1974) treated three stereotyped behaviors—hand movements, body rocking, and lip smacking (up and down movement of the lips with fingers—by reinforcing periods of abstinence with verbal praise and a hug. As scheduled increases in the length of time without stereotyped behavior were required for reinforcement, the frequency of the target behaviors decreased to negligible rates. A reversal design was used to demonstrate functional control over the stereotypy. Barmann (1980) also eliminated hand-mouthing in a six-year-old profoundly mentally retarded female with contingent vibration for progressively longer periods of "dry hand." The suppression generalized over trainers and environments and was maintained at a one-year follow-up.

In another study, Azrin, et al. (1973) reduced rocking and head-weaving in severely and profoundly mentally retarded adults by contingently insisting on and manually prompting manual rehearsal of incompatible behaviors. The technique, along with positive reinforcement of alternative, incompatible, behavior reduced the rate of stereotypy to almost zero. Mulhern and Baumeister (1969) decreased stereotypical rocking behavior in two severely mentally retarded women by positively reinforcing periods of nonrocking. Both studies, however, left uncontrolled a number of sources of variation and did not ascertain extended follow-up information with regard to treatment effectiveness. Similarly, one mildly mentally retarded, institutionalized woman, who had for over 40 years engaged in running circles, compulsive back and forth stepping on sidewalks, and other nondirectional locomotor activities was treated by positive reinforcement for direct and prompt movement to a knitting class (Cuvo, 1976). A decrease in walking time to the class was demonstrated as functionally related to the treatment, however, generalized reduction in stereotyped locomotion was not indicated and the author failed to collect target behavior follow-up data.

Although this literature shows a considerable degree of success, there are numerous methodological problems which limit our ability to draw valid treatment conclusions (Johnson & Baumeister, 1978). What must be said, however, is that when faced with life-threatening stereotypic behaviors, the clinician must consider the possibility of punishment-oriented procedures (perhaps used in combination with reinforcement for more appropriate behavior). Under other less serious circumstances, the treatment of choice is apt to be dictated by the exigencies of the more immediate clinical situation.

• Aggressive Behavior •

Some chronic behavior patterns of mentally retarded individuals threaten or, in fact, do harm to other persons or property. Included in this category are physical assault, damaging property, excessive shouting, crying, and general explosive physical or emotional outbursts which might conveniently be called "tantrums."

Much of this behavior occurs in the context of institutionalization. As such, there is a relationship between these behaviors and those discussed in the previous section, for both may be responses to an understimulating environment (Dayan, 1970; Ross 1972). Aggressive behavior is not absent in noninstitutionalized mentally retarded individuals, however, (Calhoun & Matherne, 1975). Consequently, in either group, the suppression of aggressive behavior oftentimes serves as a prerequisite to the training of more appropriate prosocial responses (to be discussed later in this chapter).

• *Punishment-Oriented Procedures* •

The notion of punishing antisocial behavior is an old and intuitively appealing one. Thus, it should not be surprising that such a method of behavioral control has received a good deal of attention. Risley (1968) controlled destructive climbing behavior in a brain-damaged child with contingently applied shock. Three sessions with two shocks per session suppressed the behavior in the laboratory. Another four days of contingent shock at home were required, however, to reduce the frequency of the behavior in that environment from a baseline of 29 a day to 2 a day, with subsequent total suppression. Bucher and King (1971) developed 16 training situations in which an institutionalized retarded individual with a history of destructiveness was contingently shocked for destructive behavior. Shock, in each setting, did not generalize, although suppression occurred more rapidly in progressive settings. These two studies thus suggest that shock does not automatically suppress aggressive behavior across environments. When it is systemtically applied, however, generalization to different settings can apparently be achieved.

Luce, Delguardi, and Hall (1980) treated two severely emotionally disturbed children with exercise (standing and lying, in succession, 5–10 times) contingent upon the occurrence of verbally and physically aggressive behavior. Their results indicated a near zero frequency within 20 days of the initiation of the program. Similar positive results were obtained by Henricksen and Doughty (1967) in the treatment of four profoundly mentally retarded males for fighting, throwing eating utensils, and stealing food. Using a loud verbal reprimand paired with physical restraint decreased such behaviors from 220 occurrences per patient each week to approximately 25 such incidents per patient each week.

Behavioral clinicians have investigated overcorrection in the control of aggressiveness as well as stereotypy. Foxx and Azrin (1972) initially used various overcorrection procedures with three profoundly mentally retarded persons. The first, who habitually overturned furniture, was required to engage in 30 minutes of the following behaviors each time she exhibited the targ et behavior: return the overturned furniture to its correct position, straighten and clean the furniture of other residents on the ward, and apologize to all whose furniture she had disrupted. The second subject habitually bit and grabbed others. Each time these behaviors occurred, she was required (for 30 minutes) to brush her teeth, thoroughly bandage and apply medicine to the area bitten on the other person, and nod her head as the incident report was read to her. The final subject would frequently throw objects and scream. For these behaviors she would have to replace the thrown objects and apologize to the person to whom they belonged or remain quietly in her bed for 15 minutes. These overcorrection procedures resulted in total suppression of the target behaviors in approximately 11 weeks. In addition, beneficial side effects were observed in that subjects interacted more regularly with other residents.

Positive practice overcorrection in the form of compulsory relaxation exercises has been used successfully to suppress inappropriately agitated (i.e., screaming and crying) behavior with mentally retarded persons (Webster & Azrin, 1973). A similar restitutional overcorrection strategy has been used to modify stealing (Azrin & Wesolowski, 1975b) and paper tearing as well (Shapiro, 1979). Thus, it seems that overcorrection has been successfully employed to reduce aggressiveness among institutionalized mentally retarded individuals in a variety of settings and with variant forms of antisocial behaviors (Ollendick & Matson, 1978).

• Withdrawal of Positive Reinforcement •

In addition to punishing aggressive behavior, a second approach includes the withholding of positive reinforcers. Martin and Iagolli (1974) found that simply ignoring the disruptive behavior had no positive effects in treating a severely retarded female who screamed at night. Wolf, Risley, Johnston, Harris, and Allen (1967) obtained similar results in working with an autistic, retarded child who pinched her classmates. However, a moderately mentally retarded aggressive female was able to decrease the incidence of such behavior by means of experimenter-delivered noncontingent, nonresponsiveness (Martin & Foxx, 1973). Barman, Croyle-Barmann, and McLain (1980) also drastically reduced disruptive behavior on a school bus with a music interruption contingency.

Time-out or isolation procedures have also been used to withhold positive reinforcement for aggressive behaviors. Clark, Rowbury, Baer, and Baer (1973) suppressed hitting and choking of other persons in a child with Down's syndrome by making three minutes time-out in an isolation booth contingent upon such behavior. Moreover, isolation has proved successful in suppressing temper tantrums (Wolf, Risley & Mees, 1964), pinching (Wolf et al., 1967), hitting, kicking, and spitting (Calhoun & Matherne, 1975), and both verbal and physical aggression (Peniston, 1975). However, it is unclear what parameters render time-out most effective with mentally retarded populations (Burchard & Barrera, 1972; MacDonough & Forehand, 1973; Pendergrass, 1972). Though it is effective, little evidence exists to suggest how well the treatment generalizes to other environments. In addition, its potential for abuse (*Wyatt* v. *Stickney*, 1972) may well render it inappropriate as a treatment of choice.

• *Reinforcement of Alternative Behavior* •

A third alternative involves the training of other behaviors incompatible with aggression. Vukelich and Hake (1971) treated dangerous aggressive behavior (including choking, tearing clothes, and pulling objects from tables) in an 18-year-old institutionalized female by differential reinforcement. The treatment began with occasional time-out of physical restraints. If, during periods out of restraint no aggressive behavior occurred, the subject was reinforced with desirable food (candy and coke) and focused attention (verbal encouragement and smiling). However, aggressive behavior was negatively reinforced immediately by withdrawal of desirable food and return to physical restraint. Over time this procedure reduced the incidence of aggressive behavior to a negligible rate.

It is important to note that in this and other studies (Bostow & Bailey, 1969; Wiesen & Watson, 1967) positive reinforcement of incompatible responses was combined with contingent removal of all reinforcers in order to successfully suppress the target behavior under study. Other research (Martin, MacDonald, & Omichinski, 1971; Risley, 1968) indicates that rewarding incompatible responses is not a sufficiently powerful intervention to reduce aggressive behavior. Thus, it may be that it is first essential to decrease the high frequency of antisocial behaviors before other, more adaptive, low frequency behaviors can be developed.

One moderately mentally retarded female was treated for temper outbursts with relaxation training, cue conditioning, and cognitive therapeutic procedures designed to establish self-control (Harvey, Karan, Bhargava, & Morehouse, 1978). The combined treatment procedures decreased the incidence of temper outbursts from an average of three a week to less than one a month. This low rate was maintained for up to one year following treatment and generalized to both sheltered workshop and nursing home environments.

Social skills procedures have also been used to train appropriate prosocial behaviors in aggressive, disruptive individuals. Matson and Stephens (1978) treated arguing and fighting among hospitalized patients with mixed diagnoses of mental retardation and psychosis. Individualized component behaviors were targeted for elimination by training appropriate responses to each of six potentially conflictual problem situations. Each patient received a combination of coaching, feedback, rehearsal, modeling, and verbal reinforcement for improvement. Results indicated decreases in inappropriate behavior with generalization to the ward environment. However, three months following the termination of treatment, trained skills showed marked deterioration.

In a second investigation, social skills procedures were used in a group treatment setting to decrease aggressive behavior in four groups of three psychotic-retarded inpatients (Matson & Zeiss, 1978). Two groups received training through a traditional group format and the remaining subject groups were conducted on the ward. Findings revealed that target behaviors were affected by treatment, although more rapidly in the on-ward training groups. In addition, ancillary changes included improvement of physical appearance with treatment gains maintained over a 10-week retraining period.

What, then, is the treatment of choice for aggressive or antisocial behavior among mentally retarded individuals? In part, the answer depends on the level of the patient's retardation. Social skills training programs discussed earlier certainly appear promising but are likely most appropriate for the mildly and moderately retarded individual. For the severely and profoundly retarded person, aversive procedures and, to a lesser extent, time-out may be the treatment of choice. In both instances, however, ethical considerations may mitigate against their use. In any case, treatment options including positive reinforcement of incompatible behaviors need not confront the moral questions associated with the application of punishment-based techniques.

• Idiosyncratic Verbal Behavior •

Although the acquisition of verbal behavior has historically been a controversial aspect of behavioral theory (see Chomsky, 1965; Skinner, 1957), behavior modifiers have not felt it unduly reductionistic to attempt clinical remediation of patients' verbalizations. For example, Barton (1975), using a reinforcement-based program, increased the vocalization of voiced sounds (i.e., vowel or consonant-vowel combinations which were not the product of sneezing or crying) from a baseline rate of five to ten per 15-minute session to more than 50 vocalizations per period. The subject was a nonambulatory eight-year old female with an obtained developmental age of three months. Reinforcement consisted of 10-second bursts of vibration emitted from a vibratory pad placed under the girl. A modified reversal design employing noncontingent reinforcement strongly suggested that voiced sound vocalizations did, in fact, come under the control of vibratory reinforcement. Unfortunately, follow-up data were not presented.

Hamilton and Standhal (1969) treated a 24-year-old profoundly mentally retarded institutionalized female who exhibited no intelligible vocalizations, but characteristically "growled" during the course of the day. By administering shock contingent upon growling behavior for increasing daily intervals, positive treatment effects were obtained. Specifically, growling was reduced to a negligible rate during three months of treatment and maintained at one year's follow-up. In another single case study, an eight-year-old mentally retarded boy, who regularly failed to include articles and some verbs in his normal speech, was operantly trained, using token reinforcement, to construct appropriate sentences when describing pictures (Wheeler & Sulzer, 1970). The employment of these parts of speech generalized to other, nonreinforced pictures, but no data were offered to suggest that changes generalized over time or to nonexperimental environments.

Barton (1975) also increased the rate at which a profoundly retarded 15-year-old female correctly identified pictures of objects she had regularly misidentified on the ward. Correct identifications were rewarded with candy and incorrect identifications were prompted until the correct response was obtained. However, no information was provided regarding generalization of verbal behavior to on-ward situations. In yet another study dealing with verbal behavior, Jackson and Wallace (1974) reinforced loudness in a mentally retarded girl who spoke too softly to be audible. Tokens, delivered automatically when the volume of her speech into a microphone matched a predesignated criterion, served as reinforcers. Volume was gradually increased to an acceptable level as the criterion for receiving tokens was raised. Similarly, Ford and Veltri-Ford (1980) decreased inappropriate vocal behavior in three different environments, for a nine-year-old severely mentally retarded boy, by reinforcing appropriate or quiet verbalizations and punishing inappropriate ones with white noise. Deutsch and Parks (1978) also increased appropriate speech in a 14-year-old moderately retarded male with music reinforcement.

When psychosis accompanies mental retardation, a frequently occurring characteristic is delusional speech, or speech that is only marginally related to events occurring in the person's environment. Kazdin (1971) used a response-cost paradigm to eliminate the blurting out of socially inappropriate phrases in a sheltered workshop environment. The client, a 29-year-old moderately mentally retarded female, who was also diagnosed as psychotic, was required to relinquish a token earned on the job each time she blurted out an inappropriate phrase. The daily verbal reminder and response-cost program resulted in a substantial decrease of inappropriate speech in six weeks and was maintained at a four-week follow-up. Unfortunately, the experimental design did not allow for the establishment of causal relations between the treatment employed and changes obtained.

Finally, modification of inappropriate verbal–delusional behavior in a mentally retarded and psychotic population was undertaken by Stephens, Matson, Westmoreland and Kulpal (1981). Social skills training, involving instruction, rehearsal, modeling, and corrective feedback, was used to increase appropriate social speech and decrease inappropriate psychotic speech. Each of three subjects, all on antipsychotic medication, modified their verbal behavior markedly. Moreover, two of the subjects maintained improvements over the course of a four-month follow-up.

As these examples suggest, the modification of idiosyncratic verbal behavior is neither a cohesive nor an exhaustive field of empirical investigation. Perhaps it is the absence of compelling behavioral theory regarding the acquisition of aberrant verbal behaviors that accounts for this state of affairs. However, the intransigent nature of psychotic verbalizations clearly may be of some influence here as well. Whatever the reason, further research is definitely warranted in the area.

• Bizarre and Disruptive Behaviors •

This last category of maladaptive behaviors lacks the theoretic or topographic unity of previous response categories. Still, after stereotypical, aggressive, and idiosyncratic verbal behaviors have been addressed, there remains a group of behaviors that occur with some regularity in mixed psychotic and mentally retarded populations. Regardless of the specific form the behaviors may take, they all are easily identified as aberrant and interfere with the acquisition of other, more adaptive behaviors.

To begin with, overcorrection procedures have been used successfully to suppress various bizarre and disruptive behaviors found in some severely or profoundly mentally retarded persons. Ingesting excrement and garbage (Foxx & Martin, 1975), exhibitionism (Lutzker, 1974), and sprawling on the floor (Azrin & Weslowski, 1975b) have each been substantially decreased with overcorrection. For example, Foxx and Martin (1975) treated four profoundly retarded adults who ingested trash and excrement by utilizing an overcorrection procedure. Whenever the patients ingested cigarette butts or feces, they were required to spit out the material, brush their teeth and wash very thoroughly, and aid in cleaning either ashtrays or the toilet. Scavenging was reduced to nearly zero within two weeks, and patients who had previously been infected with intestinal parasites were found to be free of them following treatment.

Using a combined treatment approach of positive reinforcement for dryness and overcorrection for wetness, Drabman, Cordua Y Cruz, Ross, and Lynd (1979) treated five profoundly to mildly retarded subjects for chronic drooling. Positive reinforcement consisted of verbal praise delivered at regular intervlas contingent upon dryness. Overcorrection consisted of directions to swallow and 50 repeated wipes with a tissue. Treatment dramatically reduced or eliminated drooling in a period of 4 to 20 weeks. Treatment effects were maintained at a six-month follow-up for four of the five subjects. Additionally, several anecdotal observations render plausible the conclusion that subjects were more attractive and hence received more attention from teachers and parents as a result of their diminished drooling.

Favell, McGimsey, and Jones (1980) treated four profoundly mentally retarded adolescents for rapid eating of meals with verbal praise, food reinforcement, and physical prompts. Using a multiple baseline across subjects design, bites were reduced from a $10^{11}/_{30}$-second period to a $2\ ^3/_{30}$-second period. No follow-up was reported.

Vomiting and rumination have been treated with a number of different techniques. Lemon juice squirted into the mouth of a profoundly retarded three-year old substantially reduced rumination in about two weeks with progress maintained at a six-month follow-up (Becker, Turner, & Sajwaj, 1978). Similar results were obtained in a 16-year-old profoundly mentally retarded male (Marholin, Luiselli, Robinson, & Lott, 1980). A second 17-year-old profoundly retarded male patient did not respond to lemon juice. However, contingent application of tabasco sauce readily brought the behavior under control. Contingent vibration has been used to eliminate rumination in a six-year-old blind and mentally retarded child, with the effects being maintained at one-year follow-up (Barmann, 1980). Contingent playing of music has also decreased the rate of rumination (Davis, Wieseler, & Hunzel, 1980).

White and Taylor (1967) have reported decreases in rumination and vomiting by the contingent application of shock in two profoundly mentally retarded adults. Luckey, Wilson, and Musick (1968), also using contingent shock, decreased rumination and vomiting from slightly over 10 times a day to only twice in two months. Both studies reported beneficial side effects: a decrease of inappropriate eating and increased interaction with others. Kohlenberg (1970) also decreased vomiting in a severely retarded female by applying shock contingent to stomach muscle tensing (a behavior which regularly preceded vomiting). A relapse did occur after one year, however.

Although Azrin and Wesolowski used overcorrection to control vomiting (1975a) (essentially requiring the person to clean up very extensively every time the target behavior occurred), another approach was taken by Wolf, Birnbrauer, Williams, and Lawler (1965). They treated a nine-year-old nonverbal mentally retarded female who was excused from a special education class every time she vomited. Suspecting that absence from class served to reinforce the ruminative behavior, the experimenters required her to remain in class and not return to her dormitory room after she had vomited. Consequently, vomiting was virtually eliminated.

tainer). The collection of baseline data, revealing a low frequency of target behaviors within both major categories, was followed by the implementation of the instructions condition. Instructions, consisting mainly of providing subjects with information or demonstrations regarding the observational items, or both, had little or no effect. This finding was interpreted by the authors as an indication that the low frequency of behaviors noted at baseline was attributable to motivational problems rather than lack of necessary knowledge. The experimenter-scheduling plus self-recording condition, evaluated by means of a multiple baseline design across behaviors, proved much more efficacious, resulting in substantial increases in both behavioral categories. These increases were maintained during the subsequently administered conditions which faded experimenter control. This latter finding was particularly encouraging because it indicated that such behaviors could be maintained in the absence of strong external contingencies.

Another set of skills required for increased independence are those related to increased mobility. Page, Iwata, and Neef (1976) utilized a classroom procedure to train five mentally retarded males (aged 16 to 25) in pedestrian skills. Street-crossing behavior was subjected to a task analysis, yielding five separate sets of skills: (1) intersection recognition skills, (2) pedestrian light skills, (3) skills used at intersections having tricolored lights, (4) skills used at intersections at which a stop sign faced cars traveling across the pedestrian's path, and (5) skills used at intersections at which a stop sign faced cars traveling in the same direction as the pedestrian, or intersections at which there was no traffic control device. An elaborate model, simulating four square city blocks, was used to sequentially teach the five skill sets in the preceding order noted. Training consisted of instructions, reinforcement (praise), feedback, and remediation and was evaluated by means of a multiple baseline design across both subjects and behaviors. Probes, taken both on the classroom model and under actual city traffic conditions, demonstrated increased performance only after the initiation of training, with some facilitation of performance in skill sets not yet trained. Moreover, follow-up probes showed maintenance of appropriate street-crossing behavior two to six weeks post termination of training.

The use of money involves yet another set of skills required for increased independence. Trace, Cuvo, and Criswell (1977) developed an instructional procedure utilizing modeling, shaping, chaining, and fading, to teach coin equivalence to retarded adolescents. Fourteen institutionalized mentally retarded adolescents. Fourteen institutionalized mentally retarded adolescents (seven males; seven females) were matched on a variety of variables (e.g., coin equivalence pretest scores, mental ages [MAs], chronological ages [CAs], and IQs) and then randomly distributed from matched pairs to either an experimental or a no-treatment control group. Experimental subjects underwent six instructional stages, each designed to teach a specific method of combining coins to add up to 10 target values (ranging from 5 to 50¢). A three-component response chain was utilized for each monetary amount, requiring (1) naming, (2) selecting and counting, and (3) depositing the target values into a coin machine. A correct response resulted in both informational feedback and reinforcement (praise, M & M candy, and a happy face); an incorrect response resulted in corrective feedback. Experimental subjects demonstrated significant improvement over the pretest and the controls in their coin equivalence performance on posttest and follow-up one week and one month) assessments. Generalization across training stages, however, was not found to occur.

In an ambitious study looking at a broader set of skills, Marholin, O'Toole, Touchette, Berger, and Doyle (1979) taught four institutionalized mentally retarded adult males to ride a bus to a specific destination, purchase an item, and order and pay for a meal. The three separate behavior sequences were subjected to a task analysis which yielded a total of 77 target behaviors (20 bus-riding, 28 purchasing, and 29 restaurant behaviors). Training consisted of graduated prompting, modeling, corrective feedback, social reinforcement, behavioral rehearsal, and occasional brief time-outs. As evaluated by means of a multiple-baseline design across subjects, treatment proved effective in increasing the correct performance of each behavioral sequence. Moreover, trained skills were found to transfer to a novel environment. A leveling off at a certain performance (60 to 70 percent correct) was found for several subjects, which the authors attributed in part to the prerequisite skills required for target response performance being absent from the subjects' repertoires.

One of the terminal goals in habilitation of the mentally retarded individuals is employment (Cuvo, Leaf, & Borakove, 1978). Perhaps most basic among job-finding skills are those enabling one to fill out a job application form accurately. Clark, Boyd, and Macrae (1975) investigated the efficacy of a classroom procedure in teaching mentally retarded youths to complete job application forms. Training consisted of instructions, modeling of correct performance, practice and verbal feedback, along with praise and tokens contingent upon correct performance. These procedures proved efficacious in teaching subjects to fill out items in new application forms accurately.

Another group of skills related to finding employment are those required in a job interview. Griswell and Lieberman (1977) found that mentally retarded subjects who received videotape reviews of their performance on practice trial interviews or reinforcement (social and monetary) for correct interview performance, or both, displayed significantly higher levels of appropriate body posture and eye contact than control subjects. An investigation aimed at teaching a broader set of job interview skills was conducted recently by Hall, Sheldon-Wildgen, and Sherman (1980). Six mentally retarded adults were trained in three sets of job interviewing skills: (1) office skills (e.g., introducing oneself to a receptionist, stating one's purpose for being there, following directions), (2) application skills (filling out standard job application forms), and (3) interview skills (e.g., good posture, appropriate voice tone and rate of speech, asking and answering questions appropriately). Training included the use of instructions, modeling, role playing, and constructive feedback, coupled with a point economy system. As evaluated by means of a multiple-baseline design, subjects demonstrated substantial improvement over the baseline for each of the three behavior categories. Moreover, trained skills appeared to generalize to a similar but different job interview situation.

Skills required for increased independence (such as those discussed here) are among the more obvious sets of abilities necessary for successful placement in the community. There exists some empirical support for the claim that social skills are also related to successful community placement (Heal et al., 1978; Krisheft, Reynolds, & Stunkard, 1959). In the following section, the social responses of mentally retarded persons are explored.

• Socially Skilled Behavior •

Social skills are all-pervasive, encompassing nearly every aspect of our daily lives. In fact, they are so taken for granted that they seem to elude scientific analysis and operational definition. Phillips (1978) has stated that a person will be considered skilled and competent

> to the extent to which he or she can communicate with others in a manner that fulfills one's rights, requirements, satisfactions, or obligations to a reasonable degree without damaging the other person's similar rights, requirements, satisfactions, or obligations, and hopefully shares these rights, etc., with others in free and open exchange. (p. 13)[2]

This definition, although not intended to suffice under all conditions, does appear to be appropriate across a variety of situations and is thus useful for our present purposes.

That social inadequacy is one of the defining characteristics of mental retardation is generally accepted (Doll, 1941; Grossman, 1973; Heber, 1959; Tredgold, 1952). The American Association on Mental Deficiency

---

[2]Reprinted with permission from Phillips, E. L. *The social skills basis of psychopathology; Alternatives to abnormal psychology.* New York: Grune & Stratton, 1978.

includes impaired social skills as a major component in their definition of mental retardation (Grossman, 1973). Moreover, such impairment has profound influence on the emotional adjustment of mentally retarded individuals. Evidence accumulating over the past 20 years has clearly implicated social competence in the etiology and remediation of psychiatric disorder (Phillips & Zigler, 1961; Frank, 1973). Stable, effective interpersonal ability thus, appears to be a critical factor in promoting sound adjustment and positive, adaptive living skills.

Given the interpersonal deficits characteristic of retarded persons, findings such as these point to the critical need for the development and application of appropriate treatment interventions for this population. Further, and as indicated in our previous section, adequate social skills may be a determining factor in successful community placement. Krisheft et al. (1959) compared subjects successfully placed in the community with those unsuccessfully placed. These subject groups were found to differ significantly on the dimension of social skills, with 81 percent of those successfully placed rated as possessing adequate social skills as compared to 31 percent so-rated in the unsuccessful placement group. Subsequent studies have found significant correlations between social adequacy and successful community placement (Charles & McGrath, 1962; Schalock & Harper, 1978; Skaarbrevik, 1971).

Few attempts have been made to study the nature of the mentally retarded person's interpersonal deficits, let alone develop and evaluate treatment programs to remediate them. A representative, though not exhaustive, sample of studies conducted in this area is reviewed here (although programs designed for the elimination of aggressive behaviors are sometimes considered under the rubric of social skills training, they are not included in this section because they have already been addressed).

One approach that has been taken is the application of operant conditioning techniques to increase and improve the retarded person's interpersonal interactions. Those studies that have investigated the efficacy of this treatment strategy have largely employed positive reinforcers (i.e., tokens, praise, food) to increase desired behavior. Conversation among mildly and moderately retarded persons with basic verbal skills has been one such targeted behavior. Kazdin and Polster (1973) increased the frequency with which two withdrawn, mildly retarded adult males talked to their peers by providing tokens (exchangeable for consumable items and special privileges) as a reinforcer. Music has also been employed successfully as contingent reinforcement to increase appropriate conversational speech in a 14-year-old, moderately retarded male (Deutsch & Parks, 1978).

Play is another social behavior that has been increased successfully by the use of positive reinforcement. Knapczyk and Yoppi (1975) administered token points to five institutionalized mentally retarded children for initiating either cooperative or competitive play. The token points, redeemable for activities, games, or special events, proved effective as reinforcers to increase play behavior. Numerous other investigators have also successfully employed primary token and social reinforcement to increase appropriate social interactions among mentally retarded individuals (Barton, 1973; Luiselli, Colozzi, Donellon, Helfen, & Pemberton, 1978; Paloutzian, Hasazi, Streifel, & Edgar, 1971; Wehman, Karan, & Rettie, 1976).

A second approach that has been utilized for the remediation of retarded persons' interpersonal deficits has been the use of various combinations of instructions, modeling, and reinforcement. This approach has often been used to train isolated social behaviors, such as rule-generated language (Clark, 1972), short conversational units (Garcia, 1972), asking of questions about subjects (Twardosz & Baer, 1973), response to questions about television news (Keilitz, Tucker, & Horner, 1973), eye contact (Stolz & Wolf, 1969), and hand waving (Stokes, Baer, & Jackson, 1974).

Despite agreement as to the importance of adequate interpersonal functioning in the successful adjustment and rehabilitation of the mentally retarded person (McDaniel, 1960; Stephens, 1964), relatively few attempts have been made to train more integrated social responses in this population. However, with the recent emphasis on response acquisition models of intervention, increased opportunity now exists for broader applications of such skills training approaches with mentally retarded populations (see Rychtarik & Bornstein, 1979). Moreover, social skills training methodology appears especially suited to mentally retarded populations for a variety of reasons (see Turner, Hersen, & Bellack, 1978). Most notably, these procedures provide for the shaping of small component behaviors rather than the establishment of broad, global interpersonal responses, thereby reducing the amount of stimuli to which clients must attend.

A recent trend in extending these procedures to mentally retarded subjects has been toward the development of specific assertive behaviors. Zisfein and Rosen (1974), for example, incorporated heterosexual and assertion skills training within a group counseling format for institutionalized mentally retarded patients. Despite clinical impressions and anecdotal reports of therapeutic gains, objective indexes (self-report and behavioral ratings) did not reveal any posttreatment improvement related to a no-treatment control condition.

Findings contrary to these above were recently reported by Turner et al. (1978) using behavioral rehearsal, modeling, instructions, feedback, and reinforcement to train positive and negative assertion in an organically impaired and mentally retarded inpatient. A multiple baseline design was employed to evaluate sequential and cumulative treatment application across component target behaviors (including eye contact, response latency, loudness of speech, number of words spoken, smiles, physical gestures, and overall assertiveness). Positive treatment effects were observed across all component behaviors for both trained and untrained (generalization) scenes. Although there were decrements in several of the target behaviors at a six-month follow-up, subsequent administration of booster sessions resulted in rapid improvement in these areas.

Positive results were also obtained by Wortmann and Paluck (1979) in their application of a social skills treatment package (including modeling, role playing, instructions, behavioral rehearsal, feedback, and reinforcement) to teach assertive responses to five institutionalized, severely retarded women. Treatment was successful in facilitating assertive responses, with generalization observed to untrained situations in the real-life institutional setting. Follow-up assessment at six months revealed some decrement in trained responses, which the authors interpreted as an indication of the need for follow-up treatment to maintain treatment gains.

Social skills training programs have also attempted to establish general social responsiveness and improved communicative abilities among mentally retarded subjects. In a study by Gibson, Lawrence, and Nelson (1976), specific component behaviors of verbalization, recreation, and cooperation were developed in order to improve the peer interaction of three mentally retarded adults. Each of the target behaviors for all subjects were trained under three different conditions: (1) modeling, (2) instructions and feedback, and (3) modeling, instructions, and feedback. A multiple-baseline analysis of the results indicated that all three conditions enhanced target behaviors across subjects. However, the combined procedure of modeling, instructions, and feedback produced more dramatic effects than either of the remaining conditions, whereas instructions and feedback were found to be superior to modeling alone. Unfortunately, assessments of subjects' behavior on alternate days between treatment sessions revealed that all target responses returned to baseline levels of performance, suggesting the ephemeral nature of the treatment effects.

In a recent investigation, Rychtarik and Bornstein (1979) engaged three mentally retarded adults in a conversational skills training program designed to sequentially increase target behaviors of (1) eye contact, (2) conversational questions, and (3) positive conversational feedback. These component behaviors were individually trained by a comprehensive procedure incorporating instructions, modeling, coaching, behavioral rehearsal, video feedback, corrective feedback, and social reinforcement. The effectiveness of the treatment intervention was assessed in subsequent conversations with several unknown, nonretarded adults. A multiple-baseline analysis of the results revealed substantial increases in target behaviors with sequential introduction of the treatment strategy. However, minimal improvement was evinced in independent ratings of overall conversational ability.

In an even more recent investigation, Bornstein, Bach, McFall, Friman, and Lyons (1980) equally divided six mild to moderately retarded adults into two treatment groups differing only in the time of administration of a social skills training program. Treatment (consisting of instruction, modeling, rehearsal, feedback, and reinforcement) evaluated by means of a multiple-baseline design strategy was sequentially and cumulatively applied across target behaviors over a four-week intervention period. The primary dependent measure consisted of laboratory-based behavioral observation probes of training and generalization scenes conducted during baseline, treatment, and follow-up sessions. In addition, social validation measures were also derived as a means of assessing overall interpersonal effectiveness. Results indicated that (1) treatment was effective for virtually all behaviors across all subjects, (2) improvements occurred for both training and generalization scenes, and (3) behavioral performance was maintained one month following the termination of treatment. Although social validity evaluations revealed a substantial increase from pre- to posttreatment, final ratings indicated only "average" interpersonal effectiveness. The authors concluded that although behavioral improvement was more than amply demonstrated in the laboratory, ecological validity (Brofenbrenner, 1977) and preventive aspects of these findings necessitated further assessment in the naturalistic environment.

In another study, Matson, Zeiss, and Bowman (1980) compared a skills training package (including instructions, feedback, modeling, and role playing) with contingent attention for appropriate behavior on a number of targeted social skills (e.g., appearance, compliance, mannerisms, affect, and speech). Twelve male chronic psychiatric patients participated in the study, eight of whom had been diagnosed as mentally retarded (degree not noted). Treatment was administered across groups in a multiple-baseline design. Although both procedures effected some improvement in targeted skills, the social skills treatment produced the more dramatic and sustained gains. Generalization to untreatd behaviors was minimal for both treatment conditions; however, generalization to behaviors on the ward was observed.

A group-administered skills training program has been investigated by Kelly, Wildman, Urey, and Thurman (1979) for its effectiveness in remediating conversational skill deficits in 10 retarded adolescents. Treatment (including instructions, modeling, group discussion, and rehearsal) was introduced in a multiple-baseline fashion across selected target behaviors. As in the study by Rychtarik and Bornstein (1979), generalization was assessed through subjects' interactions with unfamiliar, nonretarded adults. Positive effects were observed during both training and generalization probes, with treatment gains maintained at one-month follow-up.

In a recent study, Matson, Kazdin, and Esveldt-Dawson (1980) explored the effectiveness of a social skills training program applied to mentally retarded children. Two moderately retarded and emotionally disturbed boys (ages 11 and 12 years) were treated for numerous social skills deficits, with instructions, performance feedback, social reinforcement, modeling, and role playing included in the training package. The specific behaviors targeted for intervention included physical gestures, facial mannerisms, eye contact, spoken words, intonation, and content of speech. Separate multiple-baseline designs across behaviors for each child were employed to assess the program's effectiveness. The boys' performance on the target behaviors improved from treatment, with generalization observed to both overall social performance and appropriate motor behavior. Follow-up over four to six weeks demonstrated that these improvements were maintained.

A final treatment approach recently applied for the remediation of social skills deficits in mentally retarded persons is self-monitoring. Matson (1979) empoloyed this procedure for the reduction of negative statements in a 28-year-old, moderately retarded female. The subject was taught how to record negative statements made in an unstructured living area accurately, with instructions, feedback, and modeling by staff included as components of treatment. Functional control of target behavior was demonstrated, with negative statements decreasing under treatment conditions but rapidly returning to baseline levels when treatment was discontinued. The results of this study are encouraging; however, definite conclusions regarding the efficacy of self-monitoring in the area of social skills must await the findings of future research (Matson, DiLorenzo, & Andrasik, in press).

The studies reviewed here attest to the efficacy of the social skills training approach with mentally retarded populations. A limited number of studies have compared this treatment modality with other interventions traditionally applied in the enhancement of social effectiveness. Perry and Cerreto (1977) compared social skills training with discussion and no-treatment controls in the teaching of appropriate mealtime behavior and peer conversational skills to 30 mentally retarded adults. The social skills training package, consisting of modeling, role playing, and social reinforcement, proved the most effective in producing desired behavioral change. Finally, Matson and Senatore (1981) compared a social skills training program with traditional psychotherapy and a no-treatment control condition. Relative efficacy was assessed with regard to a wide range of social skill excesses and deficits in 35 mild to moderately mentally retarded outpatients. Social skills training (consisting of instructions, feedback, statements related to practicing behaviors, and questions related to the targets' behavior performance) proved significantly more effective than either traditional psychotherapy or no-treatment control as assessed by three of the four dependent measures employed. A three-month follow-up revealed some relapse with the social skills training group, though not a significant reduction. The authors interpreted this finding as an indication that maintenance treatment of some form may be required to sustain therapeutic gains.

• Vocational Habilitation •

The development of productive work skills in mentally retarded populations is a normalizing goal (Schipp, Baker, & Cuvo, 1980). Although vocational training of mentally retarded individuals has existed for quite some time, a number of recurrent criticisms tend to be voiced. It has been noted that the tasks given to the retarded are often so menial that they require little training, skill, or attention (Gold, 1973). Sheltered workshops, the setting for a major part of this vocational "training," have often operated by finding work to match the existing skills of their employees rather than by teaching new skills that will make clients more employable (Crosson, 1969). Gold (1973) makes the observation that what is often purported to be training of the mentally retarded is really "exposure," that is, exposing clients to a work situation in hopes that training will somehow occur. He also observes, however, an emerging trend away from an exposure model toward real training.

The application of behavioral interventions to the vocational training of mentally retarded persons has focused on two main areas: (1) increasing productivity and (2) developing new skills. Regarding the former, the goal of increased productivity is not only important because it makes the retarded more employable but also because the existence of sheltered workshops is often dependent on job contracts requiring productive work.

The approach most often taken to stimulate the work productivity of retarded individuals is the application of reinforcement contingencies— most typically utilizing money as the reinforcer. Huddle (1967) examined the effects of monetary reward on the production rate of 48 trainable retarded males. Also examined were the effects of competitive and cooperative work situations. Subjects were equally divided into a reward and no-reward group and then further divided into the following subgroups: (1) working individually, (2) working competitively, and (3) working cooperatively. Reward group subjects received 1 cent for each successfully completed task (assembling a television rectifier unit); the remaining subjects received no compensation. Monetary reward was found to significantly increase production rates, whereas neither competition nor cooperation had a significant effect.

Other researchers have looked more specifically at the effects of having the amount of monetary reward received contingent upon the amount of work produced. Evans and Spradlin (1966) compared productivity rates of mildly retarded institutionalized males under two payment conditions: (1) a salary plan in which pay was provided on a regular basis, independent of production amount, and (2) an incentive plan in which subjects were paid for each unit of work produced. The behavioral task investigated was pulling a knob. Subjects, who were exposed to both payment conditions, produced significantly more under the incentive plan; however, absolute productivity rose only approximately 10 percent.

Another study addressing the issue of production-contingent reward was conducted by Hunt and Zimmerman (1969), investigating the effects of a bonus pay procedure on the productivity of exit ward patients (mean IQ = 75) in a simulated workshop setting. Production was measured by the number of telephone scratch pads correctly counted in an hour. The investigation involved three conditions: (1) baseline, (2) experimental, and (3) return to baseline (ABA design). In the experimental condition, the subjects performed the target work task for two-hour periods, one of which was designated a bonus period during which they could earn one 5-cent coupon (redeemable for canteen items) for each pad correctly counted above their baseline average. The group productivity increased significantly over the baseline under experimental conditions and was also significantly higher during bonus periods than during temporarily adjacent nonbonus periods. Moreover, the increased productivity was maintained during the two-week return-to-baseline condition. The authors concluded, however, that verbal instructions given to subjects may have significantly contributed to their results.

These studies support the effectiveness of reinforcing work with monetary reward, particularly when the amount of compensation is production-contingent. Additional support for this finding is available in the literature (Cohen & Close, 1975; Steinman, 1971). A recent study by Martin and Morris (1980) demonstrates the importance of administering production-contingent reward systems in a manner that clearly teaches the mentally retarded worker the relationship between production and pay. In the sheltered workshop which served as the setting for this study, a production-contingent reward system (5¢ per unit produced) had been in effect for a period of two years. Nonetheless, there were some indications that the employees did not understand the control they had over their earnings. Five severely retarded adults (two male, three female) were selected for participation in this study on the basis of three factors: (1) low production, (2) obvious potential for higher production, and (3) lack of understanding of the relationship between work output and pay. An ABA designed was employed, wherein the training phase included direct visual feedback of production and earnings, along with a ratio scheduling of pay. The visual feedback was provided by placing earned nickels in clear Plexiglas tubes. Production increased significantly over the baseline during the training phase, and the increase was maintained and even heightened after the termination of training. The authors interpreted the results as indicating that the relationship between work and pay had been taught.

Research addressing the issue of productivity has not been limited to the application of monetary reinforcement. Taking a different approach, Zimmerman, Overpeck, Eisenberg, and Garlick (1969) investigated the effectiveness of isolation-avoidance procedures and production-contingent work reinforcement in stimulating productivity. The isolation-avoidance procedure involved removing a subject from other trainees for failure to meet a preestablished production goal. Thus, if a subject met his or her expected goal on a given day, he or she could avoid being isolated from the group on the following day. The production-contingent work reinforcement involved reinforcing subjects for meeting production goals with choice of work (or preferred work). Data were reported on six subjects who received the isolation-avoidance procedure and two who received the production-contingent work reinforcement. All the subjects were considered mentally retarded (degree not noted) and each had at least two additional handicaps. Both procedures proved efficacious in stimulating the production of those subjects exposed to them.

A final approach that has been investigated for its effects on work productivity is the use of self-monitoring. In a recent study, Zohn and Bornstein (1980) trained four moderately retarded sheltered workshop employees (two male, two female) to self-monitor their work output in assembling seven-piece hospital kits. The self-monitoring procedure, evaluated for efficacy by means of a multiple baseline across subjects and ABAB reversal design, resulted in significant production increases with two of the four subjects. Additionally, positive effects appeared to generalize to both work quality and on-task behavior. No follow-up data were obtained, and the authors note that previous research suggests the need for adjunctive measures (e.g., charting, reinforcement) to help ensure the maintenance of gains effected by self-monitoring procedures.

As noted previously, behavioral interventions have also been utilized to facilitate the acquisition of new work skills in retarded populations. Crosson (1969) describes a technique based on the principles of operant behavior to train mentally retarded workers to perform new tasks. The procedure he outlines involves the following steps: (1) specifying the functionally integrated units of behavior (operants) composing the response sequences required in the task, (2) analyzing the task in terms of stimuli or cues which can be associated with each operant, (3) removing from the original task sequence those segments of the task requiring more intensive programming to be dealt with in pretraining procedures, (4) demonstrating each component behavior in its proper sequence and prompting the trainee to model the behavior immediately, (5) reinforcing correct responses or acceptable approximations of responses to be shaped, (6) fading prompts once the target responses are reliably produced in the presence of a cue, (7) terminating reinforcement for a response once it is reliably emitted in the presence of the task stimulus only (i.e., without prompts), (8) establishing a chained schedule so that reinforcement is eventually made contingent upon the completion of the entire response sequence, and (9) gradually phasing reinforcement to higher order schedules (so as to match the work environment's natural incentive program) once the response sequence is reliably emitted.

Crosson (1969) presents data on seven severely retarded males which attest to the efficacy of these procedures. The subjects were trained to operate a drill press machine in the manufacturing of wooden pencil holders, a task requiring approximately 100 operants. All the subjects attained the criterion level (two errorless trials) for this sequence in less than three hours of training and were able to quickly regain criterion level performance at 2-month and 12-month follow-ups.

Using similar procedures, Cuvo, Leaf, and Borakove (1978) developed and evaluated a systematic program to train mentally retarded workers in janitorial service—an occupation which they point out is both practical and potentially available for the moderately retarded. Six trainable mentally retarded adolescents (three male, three female) participated in the program. The cleaning of a boys' restroom was subjected to a task analysis, which identified six subtasks involving 181 component responses. Of these 181 component responses, 20 were identified as difficult to train, and the subjects were required for these responses to progress through a series of four prompt levels, ordered from more to less assistance: (1) verbal instructions plus modeling, (2) verbal instructions plus graduated physical guidance, (3) verbal instructions, and (4) no help. For the remaining 161 responses, a four-prompt series was again used, but in the opposite order of presentation (i.e., from less to more assistance). More direct assistance prompts were administered only when subjects failed to respond appropriately to prompts of less assistance. Correct responses during training were reinforced with one M&M and praise, administered on a variable-ratio schedule and thinned over sessions. Program effectiveness was assessed by means of a multiple-baseline design across both subjects and responses (subtasks). Training resulted in rapid response acquisition specific to the subtask; that is, generalization to untrained responses did not occur. However, skill generalization did occur to a new environment (i.e., girls' restroom), and maintenance of skills was demonstrated over a two-week period.

These studies are typical of the rather sparse literature on the training of work skills with mentally retarded populations. As noted by Cuvo et al. (1978), the few studies in this area which delineate training procedures have typically utilized task analysis, prompting responses, or both (Brown, Bellamy, Perlmutter, Sackowitz, & Sontag, 1972; Brown & Pearce, 1970; DeMars, 1975; Gold, 1972). Autoinstructional techniques have also been used. For an overview of this approach, the reader is referred to Gold's (1973) review of the literature on such devices.

• CONCLUSIONS AND FUTURE DIRECTIONS •

As is often the case in emergent fields of inquiry, methodological sophistication sometimes takes a back seat to the exigencies of the clinical situation. Although one cannot be assured that such has occurred in the treatment of psychopathological disorders among mentally retarded persons, certainly design considerations have been less than optimal. In fact, a large number of studies have simply utilized inadequate designs, thereby limiting confidence in the establishment of causality (Matson, DiLorenzo, & Andrasik, in press). Future researchers thus need to place greater emphasis on experimental designs that will allow firm conclusions to be drawn regarding the relationship between treatment and the behavioral changes that ensue.

A second factor of some significance relates to the descriptive information provided by investigators. Too often, as in the studies reviewed in this chapter, it has been difficult to discover the details of the clinical context. The patient is usually classified (e.g., "profoundly retarded"), but IQ variance intervals (e.g., WAIS FSIQ = 43–51), Adaptive Behavior Scale test results, relevant developmental and institutional histories, and chronicity of target behaviors are often omitted. Such descriptive information is absolutely essential for replication purposes and of considerable assistance to consumers of empirical research. Similar detailed information should also be provided regarding environmental settings, intervention methods, and therapist characteristics. Related to this, investigators should also provide cost-effective analyses and data regarding subject compliance and cooperation. All of these factors provide future investigators with the kind of data base necessary to estimate the potential clinical utility.

Perhaps the most central problem for behavior therapists, however, is the extent to which demonstrated treatment effects generalize beyond the constraints of the particular investigation. The first sort of intrasubject generalization of import is generalization across environments. Will the subject trained to act in a socially skilled manner in a clinic also do so while in a department store? It is now clearly recognized that treatment does *not* automatically generalize from one environment to another (Foxx & Martin, 1975). What is required is a "technology of generalization" (Stokes & Baer, 1977) which incorporates into the treatment program those factors that make it most likely for behavior change to generalize to other settings (see Coleman et al., 1979). Only when such a technology is broadly implemented and empirically demonstrated as generalizable across settings, can a clinically robust treatment be assumed.

A second form of generalization of equal importance involves generalizability across behaviors. In this vein, we must begin to uncover the parameters of response class effects. That is, what behaviors, when treated, readily demonstrate generalization effects to other untreated behaviors? As such questions are pursued over programmatic and interrelated investigations, a response class taxonomy can be developed. Such a taxonomy might suggest behavioral clusters which covary prior to, during, and following treatment.

A final form of generalization involves generalizability over time or stability of treatment effects. All to often, an elaborate, lengthy treatment is verified as stable with one or two follow-up probes conducted three or six months after termination of treatment. In point of fact, more representative and demanding follow-ups are required (see Achenbach, 1978) to establish the durability of current treatment strategies.

This discussion of generalization can be summarized in the following major point: it is high time that behavior therapists admit to the complexity of the problems and begin to identify the complex solutions required (Hersen, 1981). Although it may be important to demonstrate that treatment A with subject B in setting C will result in a change of behavior D, it is of even greater importance to substantiate the socially meaningful quality of change as well. At the close of the treatment, are the subjects judged to be less impaired (i.e., psychotic, mentally retarded) or was the change clinically cosmetic (see Rychtarik & Bornstein, 1979)? The research in this field should demonstrate not only that change occurs, or even that the change is generalizable, but that the change is clinically meaningful as well.

• REFERENCES •

Achenbach, T. M. Psychopathology of childhood: Research problems and issues. *Journal of Consulting and Clinical Psychology*, 1978, *46*, 759–776.

Azrin, N. H., Kaplan, S. J., & Foxx, R. M. Autism reversal: Eliminating stereotyped self-stimulation of retarded individuals. *American Journal of Mental Deficiency*, 1973, *78*, 241–248.

Azrin, N. H., & Wesolowski, M. D. Eliminating habitual vomiting in a retarded adult by positive practice and self-correction. *Journal of Behavior Therapy and Experimental Psychiatry*, 1975a, *6*, 145–148.

Azrin, N. H., & Wesolowski, M. D. The use of positive practice to eliminate persistent floor sprawling by profoundly retarded persons. *Behavior Therapy*, 1975b, *6*, 627–631.

Barmann, B. C. Use of contingent vibration in the treatment of self-stimulatory hand-mouthing and ruminative vomiting behavior. *Journal of Behavior Therapy and Experimental Psychiatry*, 1980, *11*, 307–311.

Barmann, B. C., Croyle-Barmann, C., & McLain, B. The use of contingent-interrupted music in the treatment of disruptive bus-riding behavior. *Journal of Applied Behavior Analysis*, 1980, *13*, 693–698.

Barrett, B. H. Communitization and the measured message of normal behavior. In R. York & E. Edgar (Eds.), *Teaching the severely handicapped* (Vol. 4). Bixley, Ohio: Special Press, in press.

Barton, E. S. Behavior modification in the hospital school for the severely subnormal. In C. C. Kiernan & F. P. Woodford (Eds.), *Behavior modification with the severely retarded*. Amsterdam: Associated Science Publication, 1975.

Barton, E. S. Operant conditioning of appropriate and inappropriate social speech in the profoundly retarded. *Journal of Mental Deficiency Research*, 1973, *17*, 183–191.

Bauman, K. E., & Iwata, B. A. Maintenance of independent housekeeping skills using scheduling plus self-recording procedures. *Behavior Therapy*, 1977, *8*, 554–560.

Baumeister, A. A., & Forehand, R. Effects of contingent shock and verbal command on body rocking of retardates. *Journal of Clinical Psychology*, 1972, *28*, 586–590.

Baumeister, A. A., & Forehand, R. Stereotyped acts. In N. R. Ellis (Ed.), *International review of research in mental retardation* (Vol. 6). New York: Academic Press, 1973.

Becker, J. V., Turner, S. M., & Sajwaj, T. E. Multiple behavioral effects of the use of lemon juice with a ruminating toddler-age child. *Behavior Modification*, 1978, *2*, 267–278.

Berkson, G. Abnormal stereotyped motor acts. In J. Zubin & H. F. Hunt (Eds.), *Comparative psychopathology—Animal and human*. New York: Grune & Stratton, 1967.

Bornstein, P. H., Bach, P. J., McFall, M. E., Friman, P. C., & Lyons, P. D. Application of a social skills training program in the modification of interpersonal deficits among retarded adults: A clinical replication. *Journal of Applied Behavior Analysis*, 1980, *12*, 171–176.

Bostow, D. E., & Bailey, J. S. Modification of severe disruptive and aggressive behavior using brief timeout and reinforcement procedures. *Journal of Applied Behavior Analysis*, 1969, *2*, 31–37.

Brofenbrenner, V. Toward an experimental ecology of human development. *American Psychologist*, 1977, *32*, 513–531.

Brown, L., Bellamy, T., Perlmutter, L., Sackowitz, P., & Sontag, E. The development of quality, quantity, and durability in the work performance of retarded students in a public school prevocational workshop. *Training School Bulletin*, 1972, *68*, 58–69.

Brown, O., & Pearce, E. Increasing the production rates of trainable retarded students in public school simulated workshop. *Education and Training of the Mentally Retarded*, 1970, *5*, 15–22.

Bucher, B., & King, L. Generalization of punishment effects in the deviant behavior of a psychotic child. *Behavior Therapy*, 1971, *2*, 68–77.

Burchard, J. R., & Barrera, F. An analysis of time-out and response cost in a programmed environment. *Journal of Applied Behavior Analysis*, 1972, *5*, 271–282.

Calhoun, K. S., & Matherne, P. M. The effects of varying schedules of time out on aggressive behavior of a retarded girl. *Journal of Behavior Therapy and Experimental Psychiatry*, 1975, *6*, 139–141.

Charles, D. C., & McGrath, K. The relationship of peer and staff ratings to release from institutionalization. *American Journal of Mental Deficiency*, 1962, *67*, 414–417.

Chomshy, N. *Aspects of the theory of syntax*. Cambridge: MIT Press, 1965.

Clark, H. B. Use of modeling and reinforcement to train generative sentence usage. *Dissertation Abstracts International*, 1972, *33*, 5535–1.

Clark, H. B., Boyd, S. B., & Macrae, J. W. A classroom program teaching disadvantaged youths to write biographic information. *Journal of Applied Behavior Analysis*, 1975, *8*, 301–309.

Clark, H. B., Rowbury, T., Baer, A. M., & Baer, D. M. Timeout as a punishing stimulus in continuous and intermittent schedules. *Journal of Applied Behavior Analysis*, 1973, *6*, 443–455.

Cohen, M. E., & Close, D. W., Retarded adults' discrete work performance in a sheltered workshop as a function of overall productivity and motivation. *American Journal of Mental Deficiency*, 1975, *79*, 526–529.

Coleman, R. S., Whitman, T. L., & Johnson, M. R. Suppression of self-stimulatory behavior of a profoundly retarded boy across staff and settings: An assessment of situational generalization. *Behavior Therapy*, 1979, *10*, 266–280.

Cook, J. W., Altman, K., Shaw, J., & Blaylock, M. Use of contingent lemon juice to eliminate public masturbation by a severely retarded boy. *Behavior Research and Therapy*, 1978, *16*, 131–134.

Corbett, J. Aversion for the treatment of self-injurious behavior. *Journal of Mental Deficiency Research*, 1975, *19*, 79–95.

Crosson, J. E. A technique for programming sheltered workshop environments for training severely retarded workers. *American Journal of Mental Deficiency*, 1969, *73*, 814–818.

Cuvo, A. J. Decreasing repetitive behavior in an institutionalized mentally retarded resident. *Mental Retardation*, 1976, *14*, 22–25.

Cuvo, A. J., Leaf, R. B., & Borakove, L. S. Teaching janitorial skills to the mentally retarded: Acquisition, generalization, and maintenance. *Journal of Applied Behavior Analysis*, 1978, *11*, 345–355.

Davis, W. B., Wieseler, N. A., & Hunzel, T. E. Contingent music in management of rumination and out-of-seat behavior in a profoundly mentally retarded institutionalized male. *Mental Retardation*, 1980, *18*, 43–47.

Dayan, M. Behavior incidents in a state residential institution for the mentally retarded. *Mental Retardation*, 1970, *8*, 29–31.

DeMars, P. K. Training adult retardates for private enterprise. *The American Journal of Occupational Therapy*, 1975, *29*, 39–42.

Deutsch, M., & Parks, L. A. The use of contingent music to increase appropriate conversational speech. *Mental Retardation*, 1978, *16*, 33–36.

Doll, E. A. The essential of an inclusive concept of mental deficiency. *American Journal of Mental Deficiency*, 1941, *46*, 214–219.

Dorsey, M. F., Iwata, B. A., Ong, P., & McSween, T. E. Treatment of self-injurious behavior using a water mist: Initial response suppression and generalization. *Journal of Applied Behavior Analysis*, 1980, *13*, 343–354.

Drabman, R. S., Cordua Y Cruz, G., Ross, J., & Lynd, S. Suppression of chronic drooling in mentally retarded children and adolescents: Effectiveness of a behavioral treatment package. *Behavior Therapy*, 1979, *10*, 46–56.

Epstein, L. H., Doke, L. A., Sajwaj, T. E., Sorrell, S., & Rimmer, B. Generality and side effects of overcorrection. *Journal of Applied Behavior Analysis*, 1974, *7*, 385–390.

Evans, G. W., & Spradlin, J. E. Incentives and instructions as controlling variables of productivity. *American Journal of Mental Deficiency*, 1966, *71*, 129–132.

Favell, J. E., McGimsey, J. F., & Jones, M. L. Rapid eating in the retarded: Reduction by non-aversive procedures. *Behavior Modification*, 1980, *4*, 481–492.

Ford, J. E., & Veltri-Ford, A. Effects of time-out from auditory reinforcement on two problem behaviors. *Mental Retardation*. 1980 *18*, 299–303.

Forehand, R., & Baumeister, A. A. Deceleration of aberrant behavior among retarded individuals. In M. Hersen, R. M. Eisler, & P. M. Miller (Eds.), *Progress in behavior modification* (Vol. 2). New York: Academic Press, 1976.

Foxx, R. M. The use of overcorrection to eliminate the public disrobing (stripping) of retarded women. *Behaviour Research and Therapy*, 1976, *14*, 53–61.

Foxx, R. M., & Azrin, N. H. The elimination of autistic self-stimulatory behavior by overcorrection. *Journal of Applied Behavior Analysis*, 1973, *6*, 1–14.

Foxx, R.M., & Azrin, N. H. Restitution: A method of eliminating aggressive-disruptive behavior of retarded and brain-damaged patients. *Behaviour Research and Therapy*, 1972, *10*, 15–27.

Foxx, R. M., & Martin, E. D. Treatment of scavenging behavior (cophrophagy and pica) by overcorrection. *Behaviour Research and Therapy*, 1975, *13*, 153–162.

Frank, J. *Persuasion and healing: A comparative study of psychotherapy.* Baltimore: John Hopkins University Press, 1973.

Garcia, E. E. The training and generalization of conversational speech form in nonverbal retardates. *Dissertation Abstracts International*, 1972, *33*, 2833–B.

Gibson, F. W., Lawrence, P. S., & Nelson, R. O. Comparison of three training procedures for teaching social responses to developmentally disabled adults. *American Journal of Mental Deficiency*, 1976, *81*, 379–387.

Gold, M. W. Research on the vocational habilitation of the retarded: The present, the future. In N. R. Ellis (Ed.), *International review of research in mental retardation* (Vol. 6). New York: Adademic Press, 1973.

Gold, M. W. Stimulus factors in skill training of the retarded on a complex assembly task: Acquisition, transfer, and retention. *American Journal of Mental Deficiency*, 1972, *76*, 517–526.

Greene, R. J., Hoats, P. L., & Hornick, A. J. Music distortion: A new technique for behavior modification. *Psychological Record*, 1970, *20*, 107–109.

Griswell, R. M., & Lieberman, A. Teaching the mentally retarded job interviewing skills. *Journal of Counseling Psychology*, 1977, *24*, 332–337.

Grossman, H. J. *Manual on terminology and classification in mental retardation*. Washington, D.C.: American Association on Mental Deficiency—Special Publication Series, No. 2, 1973.

Hall, C., Sheldon-Wildgen, J., & Sherman, J. A. Teaching job interview skills to retarded clients. *Journal of Applied Behavior Analysis*, 1980, *13*, 433–442.

Hamilton, J. W., & Standhal, J. Suppression of stereotyped screaming behavior in a profoundly retarded institutionalized female. *Journal of Experimental Child Psychology*, 1969, *7*, 114–121.

Hamilton, J. W., Stephens, L., & Allen, P. Controlling aggressive and destructive behavior in severely retarded institutionalized residents. *American Journal of Mental Deficiency*, 1967, *71*, 852–856.

Harris, S. L., & Wolchik, S. A. Suppression of self-stimulation: Three alternative strategies. *Journal of Applied Behavior Analysis*, 1979, *12*, 185–198.

Harvey, J. R., Karan, O. C., Bhargava, D., & Morehouse, N. Relaxation training and cognitive behavioral procedures to reduce violent temper outbursting in a moderately retarded women. *Journal of Behavior Therapy and Experimental Psychiatry*, 1978, *9*, 347–351.

Heal, L. W., Sigelman, C. K., & Switzky, H. N. Research on community residential alternatives for the mentally retarded. In N. R. Ellis (Ed.), *International review of research in mental retardation* (Vol. 9). New York: Academic Press, 1978.

Heber, R. A manual on terminology and classification in mental retardation. *American Journal of Mental Deficiency Monograph*, 1959, *64*, 1–17.

Henricksen, K., & Doughty, R. Decelerating undesired mealtime behavior in a group of profoundly retarded boys. *American Journal of Mental Deficiency*, 1967, *72*, 40–44.

Hersen, M. Complex problems require complex solutions. *Behavior Therapy*, 1981, *12*, 15–29.

Hollis, J. H. Analysis of rocking behavior. In C. E. Meyers (Ed.), *Quality of life in severely and profoundly retarded people: Research foundations for improvement*. Washington, D.C.: American Association on Mental Deficiency, 1978.

Huddle, D. D. Work performance of trainable adults as influenced by competition, cooperation, and monetary reward. *American Journal of Mental Deficiency*, 1967, *72*, 198–211.

Hunt, J. G., & Zimmerman, J. Stimulating productivity in a simulated sheltered workshop setting. *American Journal of Mental Deficiency*, 1969, *74*, 43–49.

Jackson, D. A., & Wallace, R. The modification and generalization of voice loudness in a fifteen-year-old retarded girl. *Journal of Applied Behavior Analysis*, 1974, *7*, 461–471.

Johnson, W. L., & Baumeister, A. A. Self-injurious behavior: A review and analysis of methodological details of published studies. *Behavior Modification*, 1978, *2*, 465–487.

Kaufman, M. E., & Levitt, H. A study of three stereotyped behaviors in institutionalized mental defectives. *American Journal of Mental Deficiency*, 1965, *69*, 467–473.

Kazdin, A. E. The effect of response cost in suppressing behavior in a pre-psychotic retardate. *Journal of Behavior Therapy and Experimental Psychiatry*, 1971, *2*, 137–140.

Kazdin, A. E., & Polster, R. Intermittent token reinforcement and response maintenance in extinction. *Behavior Therapy*, 1973, *4*, 386–391.

Keilitz, I., Tucker, D. J., & Horner, R. D. Increasing mentally retarded adolescents' verbalizations about current events. *Journal of Applied Behavior Analysis* 1973, *6*, 621–630.

Kelly, J. A., Wildman,B. G., Urey, J. J. R., & Thurman, C. *Group skills training to increase the conversational repertoire of retarded adolescents.* Paper presented at the meeting of the Southeastern Psychological Association, New Orleans, March 1979.

Knapdzyk, D. R., & Yoppi, J. O. Development of cooperative and comparative play responses in developmentally disabled children. *American Journal of Mental Deficiency*, 1975, *80*, 245–255.

Kohlenberg, R. J. The punishment of persistent vomiting: A case study. *Journal of Applied Behavior Analysis*, 1970, *3*, 241–245.

Krisheft, C. H., Reynolds, M. C., & Stunkard, C. L. A study of factors related to rating post-institutional adjustment. *Minnesota Welfare*, 1959, *11*, 5–15.

Lovaas, O. I., & Simmons, J. Q. Manipulation of self-destruction in three retarded children. *Journal of Applied Behavior Analysis*, 1969, *2*, 143–157.

Luce, S. C., Delguardi, J., & Hall, R. V. Contingent exercise: A mild but powerful procedure for suppressing inappropriate verbal and agresssive behavior. *Journal of Applied Behavior Analysis*, 1980, *13*, 583–594.

Lucero, W. J., Frieman, J., Spoering, K., & Fehrenbacher, J. Comparison of three procedures in reducing self-injurious behavior. *American Journal of Mental Deficiency*, 1976, *5*, 548–554.

Luckey, R. E., Wilson, C. M., & Musick, J. K. Aversive conditioning as a means of inhibiting vomiting and rumination. *American Journal of Mental Deficiency*, 1968, *73*, 139–142.

Luiselli, J. K., Colozzi, G., Donellon, S., Helfen, C. S., & Pemberton, B. W. Training and generalization of a greeting exchange with a mentally retarded language-deficient child. *Education and Treatment of Children*, 1978, *1*, 23–30.

Luiselli, J. K., Helfen, C. S., Pemberton, B. W., & Reisman, J. The elimination of a child's in-class masturbation by overcorrection and reinforcement. *Journal of Behavior Therapy and Experimental Psychiatry*, 1977, *8*, 201–204.

Lutzker, J. R. Social reinforcement control of exhibitionism in a profoundly retarded adult. *Mental Retardation*, 1974, *12*, 46–47.

MacDonough, T. S., & Forehand, R. Response-contingent time-out: Important parameters in behavior modification with children. *Journal of Behavior Therapy and Experimental Psychiatry*, 1973, *4*, 231–236.

Marholin, D. S., Luiselli, J. K., Robinson, M., & Lott, I. T. Response-contingent taste-aversion in treating chronic ruminative vomiting of institutionalized profoundly retarded children. *Journal of Mental Deficiency Research*, 1980, *24*, 47–56.

Marholin, D. J., O'Toole, K. M., Touchette, P. E., Berger, P. L., & Doyle, D. A. "I'll have a Big Mac, large fries, large coke, and apple pie," . . . or teaching adaptive community skills. *Behavior Therapy*, 1979, *10*, 236–248.

Marholin, D. J. & Townsend, N. M. An experimental analysis of side effects and response maintenance of a modified overcorrection. *Behavior Therapy*, 1978, *9*, 383–390.

Martin, A. S., & Morris J. L. Training a work ethic in severely mentally retarded workers—Providing a context for the maintenance of skill performance. *Mental Retardation*, 1980, *18*, 67–71.

Martin, G. L., MacDonald, S., & Omichinski, M. An operant analysis of response interactions during meals with severely retarded girls. *American Journal of Mental Deficiency*, 1971, *76*, 68–75.

Martin, J. A., & Iagolli, D. M. Elimination of middle-of-the-night tantrums in a blind, retarded child. *Behavior Therapy*, 1974, *5*, 420–422.

Martin, P. L., & Foxx, R. M. Victim control of the aggression of an institutionalized retardate. *Journal of Behavior Therapy and Experimental Psychiatry*, 1973, *4*, 161–165.

Matson, J. L. Decreasing inappropriate verbalizations of a moderately retarded adult by a staff-assisted self-control program. *Australian Journal of Mental Retardation*, 1979, *5*, 242–245.

Matson, J. L., & Andrasik, F. (Eds.). *Treatment issues and innovations in mental retardation*. New York: Plenum Press, in press.

Matson, J. L., DiLorenzo, T. M., & Andrasik, F. A review of behavior modification procedures for treating social skill deficits and psychiatric disorders of the mentally retarded. In J. L. Matson & F. Andrasik (Eds.), *Treatment issues and innovations in mental retardation*. New York: Plenum Press, in press.

Matson, J. L., Horne, A. M., Ollendick, D. G., & Ollendick T. H. Overcorrection: A further evaluation of restitution and positive practice. *Journal of Behavior Therapy and Experimental Psychiatry*, 1979, *10*, 295–298.

Matson, J. L., Kazdin, A. E., & Esveldt-Dawson, K. Training interpersonal skills among mentally retarded and socially dysfunctional children. *Behavior Research and Therapy*, 1980, *18*, 419–427.

Matson, J. L., Ollendick, T. H., & Martin, J. E. Overcorrection revisited: A long term follow-up. *Journal of Behavior Therapy and Experimental Psychiatry*, 1979, *10*, 11–13.

Matson, J. L., & Senatore, V. *A comparison of traditional psychotherapy and social skills training for improving interpersonal functioning of mentally retarded adults.* Manuscript submitted for publication, 1981.

Matson, J. L., & Stephens, R. M. Increasing appropriate behavior of explosive chronic psychiatric patients with a social skills training package. *Behavior Modification*, 1978, *2*, 61–75.

Matson, J. L., & Zeiss, R. A. Group training of social skills in chronically explosive, severely disturbed psychiatric patients. *Behavior Engineering*, 1978, *5*, 41–50.

Matson, J. L., Zeiss, R. A., & Bowman, W. A comparison of social skills training and contingent attention to improve behavioral deficits of chronic psychiatric patients. *British Journal of Social and Clinical Psychology*, 1980, *19*, 57–64.

McDaniel, J. Group action in the rehabilitation of the mentally retarded. *Group Psychotherapy*, 1960, *13*, 5–13.

Mulhern, T., & Baumeister, A. A. An experimental attempt to reduce stereotypy by reinforcement procedures. *American Journal of Mental Deficiency*, 1969, *74*, 69–74.

Murphy, G. M. Overcorrection: A critique. *Journal of Mental Deficiency Research*, 1978, *22*, 161–173.

Muttan, A. K., Peck, D., Whitlow, D., & Fraser, W. Reversal of a severe case of self-mutilation. *Journal of Mental Deficiency Research*, 1975, *19*, 3–9.

Myers, D. V. Extinction, DRO, and response-cost procedures for eliminating self-injurious behavior: A case study. *Behavior Research and Therapy*, 1975, *13*, 189–191.

Ollendick, T. H., & Matson, J. L. Overcorrection: An overview. *Behavior Therapy*, 1978, *9*, 830–842.

Ollendick, T. H., Matson, J. L., & Martin, J. E. Effectiveness of hand overcorrection for topographically similar and dissimilar self-stimulatory behavior. *Journal of Experimental Child Psychology*, 1978, *25*, 296–403.

Page, T. J., Iwata, B. A., & Neef, N. A. Teaching pedestrian skills to retarded persons: Generalization from the classroom to the natural environment. *Journal of Applied Behavior Analysis*, 1976, *9*, 433–444.

Paloutzian, R. F., Hasazi, J., Streifel, J., & Edgar, C. L. Promotion of positive social interaction in severely retarded young children. *American Journal of Mental Deficiency*, 1971, *75*, 519–524.

Parlour, R. R., & Goldsmith, V. M. Legal hazards and protections for the mentally retarded: A review. *Journal of Psychiatry and Law*, 1979, *7*, 359–375.

Pendergrass, V. E. Timeout from positive reinforcement following persistent, high-rate behavior in retardates. *Journal of Applied Behavior Analysis*, 1972, *5*, 85–91.

Peniston, E. Reducing problem behaviors in the severely and profoundly retarded. *Journal of Behavior Therapy and Experimental Psychiatry,* 1975, *6*, 295–299.

Perry, M. A., & Cerreto, M. C. Structured learning training of social skills for the retarded. *Mental Retardation*, 1977, *15*, 31–34.

Phillips, E. L. *The social skills basis of psychopatholgoy: Alternatives to abnormal psychology.* New York: Grune & Stratton, 1978.

Phillips, E. L., & Zigler, E. Social competence: The action-thought parameter and vicariousness in normal and pathological behaviors. *Journal of Abnormal and Social Psychology*, 1961, *63*, 137–146.

Repp, A. C., & Deitz, D. E. Ethical issues in reducing responding of institutionalized mentally retarded persons. *Mental Retardation*, 1978a, *16*, 45–46.

Repp, A. C., & Deitz, D. E. The selective use of punishment: Suggested guidelines for administrators. *Mental Retardation*, 1978, *16*, 250–254.

Repp, A. C., Deitz, S. M., & Speir, N. C. Reducing stereotypic responding of retarded persons by the differential reinforcement of other behaviors. *American Journal of Mental Deficiency*, 1974, *79*, 279–284.

Risley, T. R. The effects and side effects of punishing the autistic behaviors of a deviant child. *Journal of Applied Behavior Analysis*, 1968, *1*, 21–34.

Rollings, J. P., Baumeister, A. A., & Baumeister, A. A. The use of overcorrection procedures to eliminate the stereotyped behaviors of retarded individuals: An analysis of collateral behaviors and generalization of suppressive effects. *Behavior Modification*, 1977, *1*, 29–46.

Ross, R. T. Behavioral correlates of levels of intelligence. *American Journal of Mental Deficiency*, 1972, *76*, 515–519.

Rychtarik, R. G., & Bornstein, P. H. Training conversational skills in mentally retarded adults: A multiple baseline analysis. *Mental Retardation*, 1979, *17*, 289–293.

Saposnek, D. T., & Watson, L. S. The elimination of the self-destructive behavior of a psychotic child: A case study. *Behavior Therapy*, 1974, *5*, 79–89.

Schalock, R. L., & Harper, R. S. Placement from community-based mental retardation programs: How well do clients do? *American Journal of Mental Deficiency*, 1978, *83*, 240–247.

Schipp, S. L., Baker, R. J., & Cuvo, A. J. The relationship between attention to work task and production rate of a mentally retarded client. *Mental Retardation*, 1980, *18*, 241–243.

Shapiro, E. S. Restitution and positive practice in reducing aggressive-disruptive behavior—A long term follow-up. *Journal of Behavior Therapy and Experimental Psychiatry*, 1979, *10*, 131–134.

Shapiro, E. S., Barrett, R. P., & Ollendick, T. H. A comparison of physical restraint and positive practice overcorrection in treating stereotypic behavior. *Behavior Therapy*, 1980, *11*, 227–233.

Skaarbrevik, K. J. A follow-up study of educable mentally retarded in Norway. *American Journal of Mental Deficiency*, 1971, *75*, 560–565.

Skinner, B. F. *Verbal behavior*. New York: Appleton Century Crofts, 1957.

Smolev, S. R. Use of operant techniques for the modification of self-injurious behavior. *American Journal of Mental Deficiency*, 1971, *76*, 295–305.

Steinman, W. M. *The effects of reinforcement on a vocational rehabilitation task*. Unpublished report, Children's Research Center, University of Illinois, Urbana, 1971.

Stephens, R. M., Matson, J. L., Westmoreland, T., & Kulpal, J. *Modification of psychotic speech with mentally retarded patients*. Manuscript submitted for publication, 1981.

Stephens, W. B. *Success of young male retardates*. Austin: University of Texas, 1964.

Stokes, T. F., & Baer, D. M. An implicit technology of generalization. *Journal of Applied Behavior Analysis*, 1977, *10*, 349 – 367.

Stokes, T. F., Baer, D. M., & Jackson, R. L. Programming the generalization of a greeting response in four retarded children. *Journal of Applied Behavior Analysis*, 1974, *7*, 599 – 610.

Stolz, S. B., & Wolf, M. M. Visually discriminated behavior in a "blind" adolescent retardate. *Journal of Applied Behavior Analysis*, 1969, *2*, 65 – 77.

Tate, B. G., & Baroff, G. S. Aversive control of self-injurious behavior in a psychotic boy. *Behaviour Research and Therapy*, 1966, *4*, 281 – 287.

Trace, M. W., Cuvo, A. J., & Criswell, J. L. Teaching coin equivalence to the mentally retarded. *Journal of Applied Behavior Analysis*, 1977, *10*, 85 – 92.

Tredgold, A. F. *A textbook on mental deficiency.* London: Bailiere, Lindal, and Cox, 1952.

Turner, S. M., Hersen, M., & Bellack, A. S. Social skills training to teach prosocial behaviors in an organically impaired and retarded patient. *Journal of Behavior Therapy and Experimental Psychiatry*, 1978, *9*, 253 – 258.

Twardosz, S., & Baer, D. M. Training two severely retarded adolescents to ask questions. *Journal of Applied Behavior Analysis*, 1973, *6*, 555 – 561.

Vukelich, R., & Hake, D. F. Reduction of dangerously aggressive behavior in a severely retarded resident through a combination of positive reinforcement procedures. *Journal of Applied Behavior Analysis*, 1971, *4*, 215 – 225.

Webster, D. R., & Azrin, N. H. Required relaxation: A method of inhibiting agitative-disruptive behavior of retardates. *Behavior Research and Therapy*, 1973, *11*, 67 – 78.

Wehman, P., Karan, O., & Rettie, C. Developing independent play in three severely retarded women. *Psychological Reports*, 1976, *39*, 995 – 998.

Weisberg, P., Passman, R. H., & Russell, J. E. Development of verbal control over bizarre gestures of retardates through imitative and nonimitative reinforcement procedures. *Journal of Applied Behavior Analysis*, 1973, *6*, 487 – 495.

Wells, K. C., Forehand, R., Hickey, K., & Green, K. D. Effects of a procedure derived from the overcorrection principle on manipulated and nonmanipulated behaviors. *Journal of Applied Behavior Analysis,* 1977, *10*, 679–687.

Wheeler, A. J., & Sulzer, B. Operant training and generalization of a verbal response form in a speech deficient child. *Journal of Applied Behavior Analysis*, 1970, *3*, 139 – 147.

White, J. C., & Taylor, D. J. Noxious conditioning as a treatment for rumination. *Mental Retardation*, 1967, *5*, 30 – 33.

Wiesen, A. E., & Watson, E. Elimination of attention seeking behavior in a retarded child. *American Journal of Mental Deficiency*, 1967, *72*, 50 – 52.

Wolf, M. M., Birnbrauer, J. S., Williams, T., & Lawler, J. A note on apparent extinction of the vomiting behavior of a retarded child. In L. P. Ullman & L. Krasner (Eds.), *Case studies in behavior modification*. New York: Holt, 1965.

Wolf, M. M., Risley, T. R., Johnston, M., Harris, F., & Allen, E. Application of operant conditioning procedures to the behavior problems of an autistic child: Follow-up and extension. *Behaviour Research and Therapy*, 1967, *5*, 103–111.

Wolf, M. M., Risley, T. R., & Mees, H. Application of operant conditioning procedures to the behavior problems of an autistic child. *Behaviour Research and Therapy*, 1964, *1*, 305–312.

Wolfensberger, W. *The principle of normalization in human services.* Toronto: National Institute on Mental Retardation, 1972.

Wortmann, H., & Paluck, R. J. Assertive training with institutionalized severely retarded women. *Behavior Therapist*, 1979, *2*, 24–25.

Wyatt v. *Stickney*, 344 F. Supp., 373, 344 F. Supp. 387 (M. D. Ala. 1972).

Zimmerman, J., Overpeck, C., Eisenberg, G., & Garlick, B. Operant conditioning in sheltered workshops. *Rehabilitation Literature*, 1969, *30*, 326–334.

Zisfein, L., & Rosen, M. Effects of a personal adjustment training group counseling program. *Mental Retardation*, 1974, *12*, 51–53.

Zohn, C. M., & Bornstein, P. H. Self-monitoring of work performance with mentally retarded adults: Effects upon work productivity, work quality, and on-task behavior. *Mental Retardation*, 1980, *18*, 19–25.

Index

a
2 b
3 c
4 d
5 e
6 f
7 g
8 h
9 i
8 0 j